The Paul Goodman Reader

Edited by Taylor Stoehr

The Paul Goodman Reader
The Paul Goodman Reader © 2011 by Sally Goodman
Introduction © 2011 by Taylor Stoehr
This edition © 2011 by PM Press

Acknowledgements
The editor thanks Sally Goodman and previous publishers (especially Black Sparrow Press) for permission to reprint these selections; Sally Goodman, Joel Goodman, Rachel Goodman, and Columbia University Press for permission to reprint the selection from Communitas.

ISBN: 978-1-60486-058-0
Library of Congress Control Number: 2009912462

Cover: John Yates
Interior design by briandesign

10 9 8 7 6 5 4 3 2 1

PM Press
PO Box 23912
Oakland, CA 94623
www.pmpress.org

Printed in the USA on recycled paper.

Contents

Introduction

When I met Paul Goodman in February 1950, he was almost exactly in the middle of his career as a writer, having begun with high school poems and stories in 1927, and having finished his last essays and poems in 1972. At our first meeting, he inscribed a copy of his latest novel for me, self-published and hot off Dave Dellinger's Libertarian Press—*The Dead of Spring,* a book he still regarded as his best single work the year he died. I am holding that very copy, printed on the cheapest paper with a plastic spring binder, its yellow and black cardboard cover illustrated by his artist/architect brother Percy, though later adorned with scribbles by my own young children, now in their mid-fifties. I remember how puzzled and fascinated I was back then, reading the story of a youth so close to my own age, in love for the first time, and facing trial for treason against what Goodman called the Sociolatry. I understood the first predicament, not the second. As I turn these pages now, all brown and brittle, I find myself thinking once again that he was right, this book was his greatest literary achievement.

How ironic that the following year, on the occasion of his fortieth birthday, Goodman wrote an essay "On Being a Writer" in which he seemed to be throwing in the towel, saying that his career had been a failure, he had not won the audience he longed for, and so no matter how much he loved his art, it was time to turn to something else. Soon he began to take patients as a Gestalt therapist, the blend of psychoanalysis and existentialism which he had helped Fritz and Lore Perls to theorize. Charging a dollar or two for a session, he earned a thousand dollars that year to supplement his wife's salary as a secretary—still close to poverty level, but in 1951 it was possible to live in the Empire City in decent poverty, as it no longer is today.

Of course Goodman did not stop writing. Though his books did not sell and only one new volume (his 1940 dissertation) appeared between 1951 and 1959, his stories and poems and essays could be read in dozens of magazines, prominent or obscure, paid and unpaid. What he could not sell or give away piled up in his drawer, a stack that would later allow him to publish two, three, even five books during some years of his fame in the '60s. This *Paul Goodman Reader,* compiled for those not yet born when I met him, includes a generous sample from the book he gave me back in 1950, and from the hundreds of other works written before and after that poignant midpoint, at once zenith and nadir of his career. Although weighted toward the social criticism that made him famous, this collection attempts to do justice to his full literary and philosophic range in order to bring his unique message before a new generation.

In the four decades of his maturity as an author, Goodman averaged a book a year, most of them published in his lifetime and a number still in print after half a century. Few of his contemporaries left such a bountiful legacy, but what distinguished his work was not so much quantity as its extraordinary range, variety of forms, and unfailing ring of authenticity. Goodman was best known for his ten books on American culture and public policy, but he had prepared himself by more deeply philosophical studies of the disciplines in which his social criticism was grounded—language and esthetics (*The Structure of Literature*), community planning (*Communitas*), anarchist politics (*The May Pamphlet*), religion (*Kafka's Prayer*), and psychotherapy (*Gestalt Therapy*). During this same dozen years, roughly 1940 to 1952, he also completed four novels, including *The Empire City,* a four-volume comic epic in the tradition of *Don Quixote* and *Candide,* as well as dozens of short stories and poems. His plays were produced by companies like The Living Theatre that gave "off-Broadway" its first hits. Despite his self-described "failure," by 1951 Goodman had already enjoyed a rich and various career as a man of letters.

His writings were the product of much study, life experience, collaboration with others, and soul work. He had the best education available in his day, all of it free: first in PS 22, a tiny "model school" conducted by the Manhattan's teachers' college; then in the first of the experimental "fast track" junior high schools, newly opened on the grounds of an old orphanage; next in the city's elite "public prep school," Townsend Harris Hall, with free admission by competitive exams; and finally the City College of New York, in its heyday of talented undergraduates from the cream of the new immigrant community. After graduation came five years of joyous self-education, enhanced by unofficial mentoring from Richard McKeon, a brilliant young professor of philosophy who not only allowed him to sit in on his courses at Columbia, but later invited Goodman along with him to the University of Chicago to earn his doctorate while teaching in the newly established Great Books program. During these years, 1931 to 1940, he was also turning out scores of stories and poems, a number of which were published and even won prizes.

Always restive in discipleship, both with McKeon and earlier with the legendary Morris Raphael Cohen at City College, Goodman gravitated toward very different kinds of mentors in his thirties and collaborated as an equal with practitioners of disciplines he wanted to master himself: his architect brother

Percival Goodman; comrades in the lively anarchist groups that published *Politics, Resistance,* and *Liberation*; and his colleagues Fritz and Lore Perls, co-founders of the Gestalt therapy movement. His life experience and soul work included two marriages, fatherhood, and a period of single-parenting; a grueling year of self-analysis using the exercises of Wilhelm Reich; life as an active and open bisexual with several job losses as a result; and resistance to military conscription in wartime, which cost him in reputation and livelihood though he managed to stay out of both jail and the army.

As it happened, Goodman's broad interests, prodigious learning, and creative imagination were exactly what was needed to meet the temper of his times. Most of all, his choices at age twenty to live outside conventional society, and to take charge of his own fate as an artist and free-lance thinker, laid the intellectual and experiential foundations of the book that established his legitimacy as a public figure and brought him instant fame when it appeared early in 1960. *Growing Up Absurd* went beyond its immediate occasion—the beatniks and the teenaged gangs that were making news that year—to launch a wide-ranging critique of American Society and its failure to make a world worthy of earnest and idealistic young people. It was a prescient vision not only of the decade to come, but of our present moment of crisis half a century later. Because he published this compelling analysis of the need for social change when he did, his prophetic ideas were in the air from the beginning, and became the very breath animating the youth movement. Even his denigrators, the vanguardists who walked the more desperate path of armed struggle in the later '60s, were themselves launched on his ideas, whether they knew it or not.

Goodman always maintained that these prophetic ideas were nothing new, familiar enough in the international anarchist tradition, and implicit in the Jeffersonian radical democracy upon which the United States was founded. He saw himself as neither an expert nor even a political person, but as a "man of letters" who had something to say because he approached matters not from the distance of the specialist or the generalist, but concretely and holistically—up close, fully engaged, his own world at stake. He rarely did "research" on any subject—he paid attention. In the *Reader*'s opening selection, his 1962 preface to *Utopian Essays and Practical Proposals*, Goodman responded to reviewers who were calling him "an ignorant man who spread himself thin on a wide variety of subjects, on sociology and psychology, urbanism and technology, education, literature, esthetics, and ethics"—that is, the topics of these "utopian essays" and of the four other books he published that same year:

> It is true that I don't know much, but it is false that I write about many
> subjects. I have only one, the human beings I know in their man-made

scene. I do not observe that people are in fact subdivided in ways to be conveniently treated by the "wide variety" of separate disciplines. If you talk separately about their group behavior or their individual behavior, their environment or their characters, their practicality or their sensibility, you lose what you are talking about. . . . I prefer to preserve the wholeness of my subject, the people I know, at the cost of being everywhere ignorant or amateurish. I make the choice of what used to be called a Man of Letters, one who relies on the peculiar activity of authorship—a blending of memory, observation, criticism, reasoning, imagination, and reconstruction—in order to treat the objects in the world concretely and centrally.

Ten years later, looking back on his career in his last book, *Little Prayers and Finite Experience,* he hadn't changed his views. "A man of letters knows only a little about some major human concerns, but insists on relating what he knows to his concrete experience. So he explores reality. A generalist is interdisciplinary. A man of letters finds that the nature of things is not easily divided into disciplines." And the task of such a man, focused on the "finite" and "concrete" as he described himself on the dust-jacket of his book, was "to restore the matrix of primary experience in a society bedeviled, in his opinion, by political, social, and moral abstractions."

Goodman's allegiance to "the matrix of primary experience" was grounded in the fact that he was an artist first, a political thinker only because the times demanded it of him. Long before his career as a social critic, he was writing his masterwork of prophetic fiction, a multi-volume "human comedy"—Balzac and Zola in the dress of twentieth-century modernism, a cross between Kafka, Cocteau, and *The Good Soldier Švejk,* the classic on every anarchist's bookshelf. Goodman's comic epic *The Empire City* begins in 1940, the brink of American entry into the Second World War, and ends in the era of Eisenhower, with its resolve to safeguard postwar affluence by retaining the total mobilization that had yanked the country out of the Depression. At the end of his administration Eisenhower himself named it "the military-industrial complex." In the high style of grand opera *The Empire City* tells the story of how Goodman and his friends experienced the war and its aftermath: "This book is the annals of our open conspiracy. How we lived through the war. How we died in their war. How the duration lasted longer than the war."

It was the "aftermath" that disturbed Goodman most, the monstrous "political, social, and moral abstraction" that was called the Permanent War Economy in the late Forties, the Cold War in the Fifties, and the Organized System in the Sixties—but which his novel dubbed "the Duration," referring to frequent wartime announcements that gas, or meat, or free speech, or labor union agitation, would be rationed or restricted "for the duration." As the war ended, one of his characters prophesied bitterly, *This time the Duration will last longer than the war.* From this point on—a time of official "peace"—we would no longer be living in the dead of winter, but the dead of spring. In the original edition of his novel that word was printed upside down.

Goodman's prophetic conception of the Duration appealed to both the imagination and the conscience of his readers, as academic sociology and fact-finding journalism rarely do. And although his vision of our future was far from jolly, it was deeply comic, full of "the laughter of the gods" that rings in Homer and Cervantes and Voltaire. According to Kenneth Rexroth, Goodman's West Coast counterpart who shared both his classicist and his anarchist perspectives, such a mixture was precisely what American readers needed:

> Things being the way they are, you would think that America would produce a great flowering of the picaresque, comic, satirical novel, that *Don Quixotes* and *Satyricons* would be on every bush. Alas, not so. We have very few and perhaps none as thorough and, beneath its comedy, as profound as *The Empire City.*

The Empire City received many enthusiastic reviews like Rexroth's, but its readers were few, unlike *Growing Up Absurd* which followed in a few months. People were bemused by a novel in the form of comic epic, and the war and its aftermath had left them too dazed and shell-shocked to recognize their own condition portrayed with such pointblank existential absurdity. On the other hand, *Growing Up Absurd* struck a chord, especially among the young, because it examined "the Sociolatry" in more conventional form—straight-forward analysis of how the lack of a meaningful adult world for the young to grow up into resulted in their widespread and justifiable disaffection. The Organized System that causes even greater anxiety and dismay among young people today could be characterized in the same terms that Goodman used in 1960:

> Slums of engineering—boondoggling production—chaotic congestion—tribes of middlemen—basic city functions squeezed out—garden cities for children—indifferent workmen—underprivileged on a dole—empty "belonging" without nature or culture—front politicians—no patriotism—an empty nationalism bound for a cataclysmically disastrous finish—wise opinion swamped—enterprise sabotaged by monopoly—prejudice rising—religion otiose—the popular culture debased—science specialized—science secret—the

average man inept—youth idle and truant—youth sexually suffering
and sexually obsessed—youth without goals—poor schools.

He closed his book with a broad consideration of American culture at mid-century, outlining twenty-odd "uncompleted revolutions" of modern times—fundamental social changes that, had they been accomplished, would have fostered the healthier society he now asked his readers to imagine:

> Where the community is planned as a whole, with an organic
> integration of work, living, and play . . . . Where a lot of money is
> spent on public goods. Where workers are technically educated and
> have a say in management. Where no one drops out of society and
> there is an easy mobility of classes . . . . Where democracy begins
> in the town meeting, and a man seeks office only because he has a
> program. Where . . . young men are free of conscription . . . . Where
> races are factually equal . . . . Where the popular culture is a daring
> and passionate culture . . . . And where education is concerned with
> fostering human powers as they develop in the growing child.

This telling comparison of what *might be* with what actually *was* the state of American society rang true to their own experience and became much of the inspiration for Goodman's "crazy young allies," as he called them affectionately in 1960. Primarily composed of radical youth from the urban North, the Free Speech Movement at Berkeley (FSM) and the nationwide Students for a Democratic Society (SDS) owed almost as much to his inspiration as the simultaneous coming to life of the Student Nonviolent Coordinating Committee (SNCC) owed to Martin Luther King, Jr. It was probably not mere coincidence that "The Port Huron Statement" was written the same year (1962) that Goodman published five new books and three dozen shorter pieces, while also speaking on scores of college campuses. At the very moment when SDS was drafting its manifesto in Port Huron, *Liberation* magazine, virtual switchboard of the incipient movement, devoted much of its June issue to "The World of Paul Goodman," with commentary and reviews by seasoned radicals alongside selections from Goodman's *May Pamphlet*, now titled "A Revolutionary Program." His ideas were already shaping what was to be the New Left.

But things changed rapidly during the '60s. The crises of the ensuing decade were soon to undermine and eventually destroy all rapport between new cohorts of activists and the man whose writings had inspired much of what the young rebels were attempting to put into practice. In 1964 campus revolts made headlines, first in Berkeley, then spreading to every major college in the country. Goodman praised the anarchist leadership structure and early initiatives of the FSM, but as the results played out in "free universities" such as he had recommended in *Community of Scholars*, he was disappointed at what seemed to him their frivolous content. He found too much *Sensitivity Training* and *Psychedelic Experience* on the one hand, *Castro's Cuba* and *Mao's Little Red Book* on the other hand—and not enough of the self-education for social reconstruction he promoted at every campus he visited. Goodman considered both the new counter-culture and the more politically-minded radicals as increasingly anti-intellectual, uninterested in ideas outside their own narrowing trajectories, while they in turn perceived him as just another academic liberal hung up on the past. And the issues themselves were also shifting. By the late '60s "taking it to the streets" in a series of mass demonstrations had given young activists both a taste of power and a dose of frustration at their failure to change public policy. North and South, angry young idealists of SDS and SNCC began to resort to guerilla rhetoric and tactics.

Goodman saw much to admire and much to deplore in these developments, and he did not bite his tongue. He thought of himself as a Dutch Uncle, well-disposed but necessarily harsh with his young "allies." When the Vietnam War superseded nuclear testing as the major international crisis, there was a period when the young and their Uncle Paul seemed to be on the same page again. In 1967 Goodman joined Grace Paley and Karl Bissinger in forming a NYC organization of adults championing the young draft resisters, an initiative that later became RESIST, a national push by persons not themselves eligible for conscription to defy the government and take risks comparable to those who refused to register or be inducted, like Goodman's own twenty-year-old son Mathew.

But the government response to protest—lies and escalation of the conflict—made the young furious, and confrontations with police in riot gear turned increasingly violent, a mirror image of the war itself. Goodman was a pacifist, an advocate of nonviolence in the tradition of Gandhi and Martin Luther King. He was disappointed when desperate protesters facing naked state power began to fight back with eggs and stones, barricades and football helmets, while a handful went underground to construct bombs and manifestoes. Even worse, some Leninist leaders in SDS sought to "radicalize" the older generation now joining demonstrations by provoking police brutality, not difficult to do. Goodman was outraged by such manipulation of earnest citizens out on a limb.

The mainstream media was eager to publish Goodman's criticism of violence in the movement, along with his advocacy of peaceful, deep-going social change. But Goodman's "reformism" and its warm welcome in the *New York Times* and other powerful opinion-mongers made him suspect to his younger compatriots. He had been more acceptable when only *Liberation* and *Dissent* would publish him, in the days before *Growing Up Absurd.* The common goals that had once brought them together—educational reform, autonomy and a future for the young, an end to social injustice, nonviolent direct action against militarism in all its forms—now seemed to be blotted out by their all-consuming desire to "Smash the State."

Goodman's social criticism charted these shifting positions as the '60s unfolded, and so it has considerable historical interest, but the aim of the present selection is to gather for new readers the elements in his thought that first inspired the radical youth, especially those ideas and attitudes that speak most tellingly to our own condition today—still in wartime, still in thrall to commodities and media, still disgraced by poverty and racism, still governed by venal and self-serving politicians, and ever farther on the road to irreversible ecological deterioration. Starting with *Growing Up Absurd* and reiterated in all his major works, Goodman challenged readers to face such calamities by paying attention to opportunities for social transformation that have remained unrecognized or ignored by American society—what we might call the unclaimed legacy of modernism. These opportunities were set forth in his list of incomplete social "revolutions," many of them initiated with great promise in the years just before the First World War, but then stalled, watered down, or undermined. In their stead arose the all-pervasive Organized System that primarily serves to maintain the power structure and shore up institutions that only pretend to meet the needs of citizens.

Little has changed in the last fifty years so far as these matters are concerned—only the vastly greater amount of shoring up necessary to keep the powers-that-be in place. Our failure to accept the challenge of initiating ongoing social transformation, and instead relying on the state to solve everything for us, has resulted in the universal sentiment that "Nothing Can Be Done." Afraid to risk ourselves, our comforts, and our crib of security, we have lost what Goodman called the "habit of freedom," and pay the price in endemic cynicism and despair, buffered by the grossest hedonism. All this was in the offing when Goodman was alive, and he warned us against it, taking care to focus on the creative potential in our rich tradition, abundant means, and capable citizens—albeit under unprecedented attack from our own leaders and institutions. His message was primarily positive, not negative, though his lips were "touched by coals of fire," as he liked to say of the Old Testament prophets.

First and foremost, he assessed private and public wellbeing in the light of how the people he knew face-to-face, his friends and neighbors, actually exercised their autonomy. It disturbed him to see so many perfectly adequate human beings trading their ordinary powers of initiative and self-discovery for the illusory security of state control, and the paltry riches of the market-place. At every level, but especially in the areas of livelihood and civic responsibility, Goodman saw people taking "orders from authorities who do not know the actual problem and the available means . . . at a cost to vitality. Behavior is more graceful, forceful, and discriminating without the intervention of the state, wardens, corporation executives, central planners, and university presidents. These tend to create a chronic emergency that makes them necessary."

Goodman's ideas about initiative and autonomy were grounded in both his psychology and his anarchist politics. He believed with Wilhelm Reich that human nature was self-regulating—left to their own devices people by and large know what is good for them. Face-to-face group activity—Peter Kropotkin's "mutual aid"—is the best way of utilizing individual creativity for the benefit of the larger community. But when social structures and institutions grow too large, out of touch with the concrete objects of concern, the fundamental self-reliance of ordinary people is subverted. The "aim of politics," then, is very simple—"to increase autonomy"—and therefore it should be "mostly undoing" the work of politicians. In his opinion, anarchism was the only safe polity, because its decentralist criteria protect citizens from the bad choices of central authorities who tend to bring their disasters down on whole communities.

Closely related to his understanding of the importance of autonomy and volition as sources of human creativity was Goodman's view of the nature of power itself. His definitive assessment of the delusion of "Getting into Power" was written for Liberation in 1962, during the dog days of the Kennedy administration. In his analysis, the power of the state is ultimately lodged in its massive institutions and not their officials. No matter who is "in power," large institutions have a life of their own, and those who think they control them are mere personnel, temporarily filling roles that inevitably tend to perpetuate themselves. Getting into power means giving up your own powers in order to do the bidding of official machinery—and usually being well paid for it. Whether labeled the New Frontier, the Organized System, the Permanent War Economy, the Cold War, or the Global War on Terror, the U.S. power structure has remained the same for decades—self-aggrandizing and self-perpetuating, while undermining the creative abilities of leaders and citizens alike: "the very exercise of abstract power, managing and coercing, itself tends to stand in the way and alienate, to thwart function and diminish energy."

For Goodman, genuine power resided in the creativity of individuals banding together to solve their mutual problems and to experiment with new ways of fostering health and happiness for everyone, not just the rich and powerful. His utopian ideals, spelled out in *Communitas,* called for many confederated neighborhoods organized around work-places where workers themselves were in charge of production and all its conditions, and where public good—residing in product, means of production, or ultimate use—outweighed efficiency or the profit motive. Not least important to him were opportunities for the young to find their way to meaningful work through training and apprenticeship in local enterprises, where authority and citizenly responsibility were transparent and continuously open to new ideas and participation. For him, the models were William Morris's guild socialism, Dewey's education for democracy, and the syndicalism of French and Spanish anarchists.

Goodman respected the ability of those who practice trades and professions to determine the requisite skills and knowledge of their callings, and he distrusted state motives in monitoring and licensing vocations, whether through mandated schooling or bureaucratic credentialing by agencies primarily concerned with their own authority. Therefore, in his vocabulary (contrary to that of the young radicals) "professionalism" was not a term of opprobrium but an ideal to live up to. Both in times of relative stability and in personal or public crisis, doing one's proper work, following one's own bent, was the crucial act of belonging and justification in community, the foundation of citizenship as well as livelihood and practical life. This was neither hunkering down in rugged individualism nor accepting collectivist imperatives of mass society, but relying instead on face-to-face encounters with equals as the building blocks of solidarity and legitimacy in the public realm.

A corollary to these views was his concern that professionals live up to their trust, and refuse to remain passive and silent when government or business abused scientific technology, human talent, or material resources without thought for anything but power and profit. It was the responsibility of scientists and intellectuals, as well as workers at every level, to demand that the products of their labor serve the public good, and not the greed or dominion of power brokers and politicians.

One reason why it was so necessary to remind his readers of their responsibilities had to do with the increasing presence and deadening effect of official speech on public consciousness—what Goodman called "format." With the development of media as a means of social control, official announcements, press conferences, news, and other varieties of "communication" from on high had become the domain of experts in mystification, buzz words flashing in a cloud of empty abstractions, repeated so often that people go into trance-state when the verbalizing begins.

Goodman regarded formatted speech as fundamentally opposed to colloquial speech, the language of ordinary people talking to each other. Although similar to the Newspeak Orwell predicted in *1984*, in Goodman's more optimistic view the gobbledygook we all know so well is not likely to take over our minds and tongues. The vigor of lively conversation predominates in most human interactions, and format can spread its pall only in conditions of chronic anxiety, the universal alarms sounded by politicians and media. Colloquial speech—and the impulses of life transmitted through it—is impossible to squelch or effectively control. But in so-called "emergencies," whether contrived or real, the sound bytes and slogans drown out the unrehearsed exchanges that contain genuine thoughts and feelings, and thus suppress the very sources of new ideas when they are most needed.

Goodman's faith in the everyday vitality of spontaneous speech was typical of his attitude toward human nature and its satisfactions. Our common possession of such simple and free gifts is what makes life interesting and worth living. His demands of any polity were for these same vital signs—"only that the children have bright eyes, the river be clean, food and sex be available, and nobody be pushed around." Of course, it has become increasingly difficult to inhabit such a world.

One of the great losses of our times, a disaster that can seem to plague affluent cultures like ours even more than those where material wealth is hard to come by, is the vanishing of what Goodman called "decent poverty." He himself lived most of his life below the poverty line, so far as annual income can measure such things. When I first met him in 1950, his family income was under $1000 but his rent only $26 a month, for four or five rooms above a paint store on Ninth Avenue in downtown Manhattan. His bookshelves were old orange-crates and until 1947 he had no phone, but the pictures on the wall were originals, presented by friends, who also got together to paint his apartment when he moved to new quarters in 1953. In those days, it was possible for poets and painters and ordinary working-class people to live well in the city on very little money. Thus from his perspective it did not seem disastrous "if some people are rich and others poor, so long as they are *pauvres*, decently poor, and not *misérables* (Peguy's distinction). I myself never found that much difference between being very poor and modestly rich." Goodman would no doubt have felt the loss in our time of what he considered essential goods of life—not marketable things, but leisure, public space not given over to automobiles or advertising, fresh air and sweet silence—ever more scarce in the tide of increasing technological dependencies.

Regardless of his earnest critiques, Goodman never despaired of his fellow human beings. His writings are filled with praise as well as nostalgia for marvelous human powers and collective achievements both past and present, despite our self-delusion and folly. Almost every page will give you hope, and it was a principle with him not to carp or criticize unless he could think of a better alternative that could stand for the possibility of a third way—"a ray of light instead of the gloom of metaphysical necessity."

In Goodman's opinion, the despair and cynicism of people in his time, especially the intellectuals, were traceable to a flawed conception of human nature—or, to put it more bluntly, a belief that there is no such thing as human nature. They seemed convinced that culture and behavior were almost entirely constructed by conditions and forces irrevocably determined by the inertia of history:

> This is like saying that tragic poetry or mathematics was "rooted" in the Greek way of life and is not "inherently" human. This kind of thinking is the final result of the recent social-scientific attitude that culture is added onto a featureless animal, rather than being the invention-and-discovery of human powers. This is effectually to give up the modern enterprise altogether. But we will not give it up.

To Goodman the materialism of Marxists, the retreat to the self of French existentialists, and the fantasy world of "progress" beloved by Americans were facets of a single mistaken view of the species and its potential which went against what seemed to him the plain truth, as echoed in his own heroes of philosophy and spiritual life—Plato and Kant, Lao-tzu and Chuang-tzu, Goethe and Kierkegaard. Each in his own way they were champions of love and faith, who believed with him that that free choice is not an illusion of the marketplace, that something real exists beyond the horizon as well as underfoot, and unconditioned possibility is not incompatible with being grounded in practical, social, and creative experience of a world.

In accord with such notions, Goodman was able to affirm human virtues as persistent and renewable as sun and rain and the grass in springtime—but there was no doctrine or dogma, no recipe for the good society. He liked the Taoist concept of "the way," an orientation that might be strengthened through practice but would be stifled by codification and prescription. In his mid-twenties he had spoken of this orientation as "the habit of freedom," something one might encourage in the young, but ought not spell out as a program or discipline. In his mature years he called it the anarchist "attitude," an openness to experience and attentiveness to opportunity, with plenty of patience and fortitude in the welter of modern life, amid master plans, curricula, and foreign policy agendas. He also believed that living in present society as if it were *already* the natural society we desire would help to create that millenarian community, though it might get you arrested. Contrariwise, we all recognize in our own hearts the moments when we betray our best impulses, conforming against our nature to the pressures of expedience, temporary satisfaction, public opinion, or spiritual lethargy. These signals, positive or negative, can certainly be dimmed and blinkered, all the more so in today's harried and distracted society, but it takes unremitting fear or deep trauma to blot them out entirely.

I doubt that Goodman would have judged the situation today as hopeless, though it is more intractable than it was in his time. The chronic emergency that he could smell in the air at mid-century has reached new toxic levels. People are afraid of anything that threatens their sense of security, and steep themselves in the anodynes of popular culture that temporarily allay anxiety at the cost of vitality and consciousness. Very few are willing to enter the realm of possibility, "the fertile void" of Goodman's Lao-tzu, where the guard-rails are down and one can no longer rely on the authorities to maintain public security and private prerogatives. Hardly anyone still believes that there are lives not worth living, or things worth dying for. People barely remember the heady feeling in the '60s of taking one's life into one's own hands for better or worse, or the then-pervasive spirit of belonging to something larger than oneself. That decade offered us yet another installment in the "social revolutions" we have not had the courage to complete, but whose untapped promise remains available—not as some enormous power shift, but in small, local increments, wherever we find ourselves truly engaged. As Goodman repeatedly said, what we need are "piecemeal reforms," not vast restructuring but "creative solutions that diminish tension by changing two percent of this and four percent of that." It was the direction and spirit of change that would make a difference, and in this regard we all have power and responsibility.

At his own crossroads in 1951, when he doubted his own powers and entered a decade of purgatory he called "a useless time," Goodman did not despair. Challenging himself "to have an extra ounce of strength," he finished the fourth volume of *The Empire City*—even though he had no hope of finding a publisher for it. He had published *The Dead of Spring* by subscription, sending out 200 postcards to friends asking for $5 for two copies of the book, if enough of them responded. Now, in the novel's final installment, Goodman's hero suddenly loses courage, temporarily gives up his faith that he is sane, that there is a world for him. He goes mad, crossing the border into conformity with the belief-system that everyone else seemed to accept. But a few encounters with "normal" absurdity soon bring the young man out of his delusions, and Goodman carries him through more inspiriting adventures to the end of the book, where he leaves his hero "spoiling for a fight." He "doesn't know what fight and doesn't know how to get into it," but it is clear enough in hindsight that Goodman's own duel was to be fought with the incarnate Organized

System, and therefore could not take place in fiction, where abstractions have no dramatic plausibility and cannot be called to account "for real."

A timely invitation to write a book on juvenile delinquency resulted in *Growing Up Absurd* and gave Goodman the challenge he was seeking. Here he was able to confront the System and its apologists directly, with observations and arguments drawn from his own experience, writing neither as a novelist nor a social scientist, but as a man of letters who could pay attention to concrete actuality as well as the larger pattern. Soon he was being invited by his "crazy young allies" to visit dozens of colleges to tell them personally how to stay sane in a demented world—while somehow managing to remain centered and productive himself, despite his peripatetic life as a campus celebrity. He was grounded in his ideas, and his ideas grew from who he was. Most people he met recognized this immediately, and whether cause or effect, a powerful sense of solidarity and hope seemed to spring up around him wherever he went. He was able to establish instant personal rapport with young activists, famous intellectuals, regents of universities, dropouts and street people. That same vital energy could be experienced each time new writing appeared from him. His direct, practical approach, his impatience with obfuscating abstractions, his good humor and often sheer glee, his forthright challenges to entrenched authority—all these were as present in his books as in his person. And that, I think, is a crucial aspect of his legacy. When one reads his words, the voice is unmistakable, still a living presence. *The Paul Goodman Reader* brings that living presence before a new generation, those now entrusted with the survival of the collective human enterprise and of the planet itself. If we are willing to heed his challenge and take responsibility for the creative initiative and solidarity with all humanity that is our birthright, however much in perilous abeyance, then as he said valiantly at the end of *Growing Up Absurd,* "perhaps the future may make more sense than we dared hope."

Taylor Stoehr

Preface to *Utopian Essays and Practical Proposals*

Frequently in the following essays I return to the characteristic moral dilemma of the Americans today: "It is only by the usual technological and organizational procedures that anything can be accomplished. But with these procedures, and the motives and personalities that belong to them, fresh initiative is discouraged and fundamental change is prevented." There is a style in which problems are stated, there are established techniques, there are channels of influence; often all these are pretty irrelevant. If there's an increase of delinquency or addiction, our only recourse is more repressive legislation, although experience and theory prove that this does not work and creates worse problems. If there are urban problems of congestion, poor transportation, and slums, our recourse is to new and bigger technological wonders, although experience and theory prove that these soon create worse problems. When economic expansion begins to produce a glut of goods more and more dubious in value and threatening unemployment, our recourse is to increase the rate of expansion and to step up the advertising, though the goods become even more useless and the jobs that provide these goods even more meaningless. A psychologist would say that our people suffer from a compulsion neurosis; they are warding off panic by repeating themselves; inevitably, they are very busy and very conformist. There is no effort radically to remedy the causes and improve the center, and there is little effort to think up new directions that would offer opportunities for more normal growth, and to educate to more prudent motives and methods. Indeed, given our usual agencies and offices, and the kind of technicians and even the kind of social scientists that we have, it is hard to see who could make the effort. Therefore the logical conclusion of the American moral dilemma is the conclusion that dilemmas generally have: "Really, we cannot do anything. We are trapped by modern times."

Naturally, as a live animal and the heir of a great culture, I cannot accept this unsatisfactory syllogism, although, like everybody else, I have had occasion to experience its validity. I do not grant the premises. By analyzing the usual procedures and motivations, it can be shown, I think, that they are not always necessary and that they are rarely the best. And indeed, one can make bold to suggest better things that can be done by better means. So this is a book of Utopian Essays and Practical Proposals. Partly I have a spiteful motive in writing such a book in the present climate of our society. It is to establish that if you do not do better, it is not because there are no alternatives, but because you do not choose to. Modern science and modern cities need not work out as they do with us. Our problems are not technological and sociological; they are moral and political. The question is, is it worthwhile to bring this home to people? Does it not merely arouse guilt and anxiety? For, if we conclude that our problems are moral and political, a more glaring problem at once presents itself: Why do people not choose better? What are they afraid of? They are afraid of losing their jobs; each one is afraid to be embarrassed by thinking and acting differently from his fellows; nobody really knows enough to risk a radical change, and so forth. But such surface explanations accept, and buttress, the very system of procedures and motivations that is at issue. Why isn't everybody eager to make his job worthwhile? Why is there not a premium on originality? How, in social and also technical matters, have people become so distrustful of the evidence of their senses and feelings? Frankly, I find these questions puzzling. I do not know the answers, but I think I know where to look.

2.

As my books and essays have appeared, I have been severely criticized as an ignorant man who spreads himself thin on a wide variety of subjects, on sociology and psychology, urbanism and technology, education, literature, esthetics, and ethics. It is true that I don't know much, but it is false that I write about many subjects. I have only one, the human beings I know in their man-made scene. I do not observe that people are in fact subdivided in ways to be conveniently treated by the "wide variety" of separate disciplines. If you talk separately about their group behavior or their individual behavior, their environment or their characters, their practicality or their sensibility, you lose what you are talking about. We are often forced, for analytic purposes, to study a problem under various departments—since everybody can't discuss everything at once, but woe if one then plans for people in these various departments! One will never create a community, and will destroy such community as exists.

The separate disciplines are the best wisdom we have; I wish I knew them better. But there is a real difficulty with them that we might put as follows: In my opinion, it is impossible to be a good lawyer, teacher, statesman, physician, minister of religion, architect, historian, social worker, or psychologist, without being a good deal of all of them at once; yet obviously—especially today when there is such a wealth of indispensable specialist knowledge—it is impossible to be expert in more than one or two "fields." Again, I do not have an answer; but I prefer to preserve the wholeness of my subject, the people I know, at the cost of being everywhere ignorant or amateurish. I make the choice of what used to be called a Man of Letters, one who relies on the peculiar activity of authorship—a blending of memory, observation, criticism, reasoning, imagination, and reconstruction—in order to treat the objects in the world concretely and centrally. And may I say this?—if to many people my thinking seems always to have a kind of surprising optimism, a foolish optimism, my hunch is that it is because I keep trying to see people whole and beginning—still growing—and then they seem less limited than they do to sociologists or psychologists, politicians or journalists. But it doesn't much matter whether one has an "optimistic" or a "pessimistic" outlook, for the question still remains, Now what?

I seem to be able to write only practically, inventing expedients. (When I write as a poet, my poems are my expedients.) My way of writing a book of social theory has been to invent community plans. My psychology is a manual of therapeutic exercises. A literary study is a manual of practical criticism. A discussion of human nature is a program of pedagogical and political reforms. This present book is no exception. It is social criticism, but almost invariably (except in moments of indignation) I find that I know what I don't like only by contrast with some concrete proposal that makes more sense.

I have arranged these essays under the usual "wide variety" of headings—social-psychology, architecture, youth problems, literature, etc. As I have explained, I do not take these divisions very seriously. But there is, instead, in all these essays a certain unity of method, and I should like to spell it out.

(1) Whatever the subject, I try to keep it *imbedded in its social-psychological causes*, relying heavily on the familiar authors in psychoanalysis, functionalist anthropology, and social history. (I here regret the lack of a medical training, for I am sure that physiological causes are relevant, but I do not know them.)

(2) I try to find in the subject *a structural idea that I can show actually operating*. When I have this, I have something to say. For instance, when I see that there is an intrinsic relation among a certain stage of life, a certain kind of work, and a certain kind of community, I have an essay on Youth Work Camps. Or I understand Advance-Guard art when I see that it is an "inner" response to an indigestible "introjected" social norm. Sometimes I use the same device negatively, pointing to an evident incoherence or failure of structure in order to define the nature of a situation—for example, the contradiction in the University between its tradition and its practice; or the incoherence in recent painting between the framing and the thing that is being framed.

(3) But finally, I tend to see the subject as *ongoing into the immediate future, requiring to be coped with.* That is, characteristically I choose subjects that are political, personal, or literary problems of practice, and this is why my essays come so often to suggesting expedients, "just to live on a little," as Goethe said. And the problems are my problems. As a writer I am hampered by the present law on pornography, and as a man and a father by the sexual climate of that law; so it is a problem for *me.* It is as a New Yorker that I propose to ban the cars from the streets and create a city of neighborhoods. As an intellectual man thwarted, I write on the inhibition of grief and anger and look for a therapy to unblock them. And it is because I am hungry for the beauty of a practical and scientific environment that I am dismayed by our "applied science" and would like to explain it away.

Apart from history or fiction, a human subject matter is not "explained" unless we cope with its immediate future; what it is is what it is about to be, and this means what we can try to make it. This has an existentialist ring, but I trust that my thinking is less merely willed than French existentialism, less cut off from body, culture, and spirit. The reader will see that by and large I prefer the language of pragmatism and, best, an organism/environment psychology of novelty, excitement, and growth. The existing is prior to hopes and plans; and the "Right Method" is to find in the existing the occasion that has future, freedom to act.

3.

The present crisis in which an American writes is a peculiar one. He confronts in his audience the attitude that things are well enough, there is nothing to be grievous or angry about, and anyway our situation is inevitable. This attitude is the audience's technological and organizational helplessness mollified by the famously high standard of living. It puts a writer in the position of, as we Jews say, banging a teakettle, when his readers couldn't care less. At the same time, these same people are evidently in the grip of anxiety in the face of changes and threatening changes that they don't begin to prepare for. Instead, they eat up books that glumly expose our plight; and they turn to the daily headlines for new shocking surprises. So a writer, instead of being able to devote himself to the truth and use of his subject matter, finds himself delivering sermons to rebuild morale and to prove that common reason is, in spite of all, practical. But worst of all, if he can successfully achieve these two marvels, of noisily affirming obvious goods and of proving that where there's life there's hope, the writer is wondered at and praised as a refreshing idealist of the olden times. A hundred years ago, Ruskin said bitterly, "I show men their plain duty and they reply that my style is charming." My own experience is that when I suggest a practical proposal plain as the nose on your face, people weep with pleasure for the reminder of paradise lost.

What idea do these people have? The idea of Jeffersonian democracy is to educate its people to govern by giving them initiative to run things, by multiplying sources of responsibility, by encouraging dissent. This has the beautiful moral advantage that a man can be excellent in his own way without feeling special, can rule without ambition and follow without inferiority. Through the decades, it should have been the effort of our institutions to adapt this idea to ever changing technical and social conditions. Instead, as if by a dark design, our present institutions conspire to make people inexpert, mystified, and slavish.

One is astounded at the general slavishness. The journalists at the President's press conference never ask a probing question; they have agreed, it seems, not to "rock the boat." Correspondingly, the *New York Times* does not print the news, because it is a "responsible newspaper." Recently, the Commissioner of Education of the State of New York spoke of the need for young people to learn to "handle constructively their problems of adjustment to authority"—a remarkable expression for doing what you're told. Then I have heard young people in a philosophy class express their resentment against Socrates as a moral aristocrat who had principles to decide his behavior, whereas "most people are not up to that." To them there are apparently different grades of humanity. Griping sailors sit on a fence and slavishly snicker at the ensigns who walk by with girls; and in the corporations, the junior executives talk about the Rat Race, yet kowtow to rank. This is slavish. It is a short step to the mentality of the operators and hipsters who take it for granted that the legitimate world belongs to the Others, and who then spitefully try to prove that earnest people are frauds or suckers.

So we drift into fascism. But people do not recognize it as such, because it is the fascism of the majority.

Politics

The Anarchist Principle

A narchism is grounded in a rather definite proposition: that valuable behavior occurs only by the free and direct response of individuals or voluntary groups to the conditions presented by the historical environment. It claims that in most human affairs, whether political, economic, military, religious, moral, pedagogic, or cultural, more harm than good results from coercion, top-down direction, central authority, bureaucracy, jails, conscription, States, preordained standardization, excessive planning, etc. Anarchists want to increase intrinsic functioning and diminish extrinsic power. This is a social-psychological hypothesis with obvious political implications.

Depending on varying historical conditions that present various threats to the anarchist principle, anarchists have laid their emphasis in varying places: sometimes agrarian, sometimes free-city and guild-oriented; sometimes technological, sometimes anti-technological; sometimes communist, sometimes affirming property; sometimes individualist, sometimes collective; sometimes speaking of Liberty as almost an absolute good, sometimes relying on custom and "nature." Nevertheless, despite these differences, anarchists seldom fail to recognize one another, and they do not consider the differences to be incompatibilities. Consider a crucial modern problem, violence. Guerilla fighting has been a classical anarchist technique; yet where, especially in modern conditions, any violent means tends to reinforce centralism and authoritarianism, anarchists have tended to see the beauty of non-violence.

Now the anarchist principle is by and large true. And far from being "Utopian" or a "glorious failure," it has proved itself and won out in many spectacular historical crises. In the period of mercantilism and patents royal, free enterprise by joint stock companies was anarchist. The Jeffersonian bill of rights and independent judiciary were anarchist. Congregational churches were anarchist. Progressive education was anarchist. The free cities and corporate law in the feudal system were anarchist. At present, the civil rights movement in the United States has been almost classically decentralist and anarchist. And so forth, down to details like free access in public libraries. Of course, to later historians, these things do not seem to be anarchist, but in their own time they were all regarded as such and often literally called such, with the usual dire threats of chaos. But this relativity of the anarchist principle to the actual situation is of the essence of anarchism. There *cannot* be a history of anarchism in the sense of establishing a permanent state of things called "anarchist." It is always a continual coping with the next situation, and a vigilance to make sure that past freedoms are not lost and do not turn into the opposite, as free enterprise turned into wage-slavery and monopoly capitalism, or the independent judiciary turned into a monopoly of courts, cops, and lawyers, or free education turned into School Systems.

Freedom and Autonomy

Many anarchist philosophers start from a lust for freedom. Where freedom is a metaphysical concept or a moral imperative, it leaves me cold—I cannot think in abstractions. But most often the freedom of anarchists is a deep animal cry or a religious plea like the hymn of the prisoners in *Fidelio*. They feel themselves imprisoned, existentially by the nature of things or by God; or because they have seen or suffered too much economic slavery; or they have been deprived of their liberties; or internally colonized by imperialists. To become human they must shake off restraint.

Since, by and large, my experience is roomy enough for me, I do not lust for freedom, any more than I want to "expand consciousness." I might feel differently, however, if I were subjected to literary censorship, like Solzhenitzen. My usual gripe has been not that I am imprisoned but that I am in exile or was born on the wrong planet; recently that I am bedridden. My real trouble is that the world is impractical for me, and I understand that my stupidity and cowardice make it even less practical than it could be.

To be sure, there are outrages that take me by the throat, like anybody else, and I lust to be free of them. Insults to humanity and the beauty of the world that keep me indignant. An atmosphere of lies, triviality, and vulgarity that suddenly makes me sick. The powers-that-be do not know the meaning of magnanimity, and often they are simply officious and spiteful; as Malatesta used to say, you just try to do your thing and they prevent you, and then you are to blame for the fight that ensues. Worst of all, the earth-destroying actions of power are demented; and as in ancient tragedies and histories we read how arrogant men committed sacrilege and brought down doom on themselves and those associated with them, so I sometimes am superstitiously afraid to belong to the same tribe and walk the same ground as our statesmen.

But no. Men have a right to be crazy, stupid, and arrogant. It's our special thing. Our mistake is to arm anybody with collective power. Anarchy is the only *safe* polity. It is a common misconception that anarchists believe that "human nature is good" and so men can be trusted to rule themselves. In fact we tend to take the pessimistic view; people are not be trusted, so prevent the concentration of power. Men in authority are especially likely to be stupid because they are out of touch with concrete finite experience and instead keep interfering with other people's initiative and making them stupid and anxious. And imagine being deified like Mao Tse-tung or Kim Il Sung, what that must do to a man's character. Or habitually thinking about the unthinkable, like the masters of the Pentagon.

To me, the chief principle of anarchism is not freedom but autonomy. Since to initiate, and do it my way, and be an artist with concrete matter, is the kind of experience I like, I am restive about being given orders by external authorities, who don't concretely know the problem or the available means. Mostly, behavior is more graceful, forceful, and discriminating without the intervention of top-down authorities, whether State, collective, democracy, corporate bureaucracy, prison wardens, deans, pre-arranged curricula, or central planning. These may be necessary in certain emergencies, but it is at a cost to vitality. This is an empirical proposition in social psychology and I think the evidence is heavily in its favor. By and large, the use of power to do a job is inefficient in the fairly short run. Extrinsic power inhibits intrinsic function. As Aristotle said, "Soul is self-moving."

In his recent book *Beyond Freedom and Dignity*, B.F. Skinner holds that these are defensive prejudices that interfere with the operant conditioning of people toward their desired goals of happiness and harmony. (It is odd these days to read a cracker-barrel restatement of Bentham's utilitarianism.) He misses the point.

What is objectionable about operant conditioning is not that it violates freedom but that the consequent behavior is graceless and low-grade as well as labile—it is not assimilated as second nature. He is so impressed by the fact that an animal's behavior can be shaped at all to perform according to the trainer's goal, that he does not compare the performance with the inventive, flexible and maturing behavior of the animal initiating and responding in its natural field. And incidentally, dignity is not a specifically human prejudice, as he thinks, but the ordinary bearing of any animal, angrily defended when organic integrity or own space is insulted.

To lust for freedom is certainly a motive of political change stronger than autonomy. (I doubt that it is as stubborn, however. People who do their job their own way can usually find other means than revolt to keep doing it, including plenty of passive resistance to interference.) To make an anarchist revolution, Bakunin wanted, in his early period, to rely precisely on the outcast, delinquents, prostitutes, convicts, displaced peasants, lumpen proletarians, those who had nothing to lose, not even their chains, but who felt oppressed. There were enough troops of this kind in the grim heyday of industrialism and urbanization. But naturally, people who have nothing are hard to organize and consolidate for a long effort, and they are easily seduced by a fascist who can offer guns, revenge, and a moment's flush of power.

The pathos of oppressed people lusting for freedom is that, if they break free, they don't know what to do. Not having been autonomous, they do not know how to go about it, and before they learn it is usually too late. New managers have taken over, who may or may not be benevolent and imbued with the revolution, but who have never been in a hurry to abdicate.

The oppressed hope for too much from the New Society, instead of being stubbornly vigilant to do their own things. The only achieved liberation movement that I can think of was the American revolution, made largely by artisans, farmers, merchants, and professionals who had going concerns to begin with, wanted to get rid of interference, and afterwards enjoyed a prosperous quasi-anarchy for nearly thirty years—nobody cared much about the new government. They were protected by three thousand miles of ocean. The Catalonian revolution during the Spanish Civil War could have gone well, for the same reasons, but the fascists and communists did them in.

Anarchy requires competence and self-confidence, the sentiment that the world is *for* one. It does not thrive among the exploited, oppressed, and colonized. Thus, unfortunately, it lacks a powerful drive toward revolutionary change. Yet in the affluent liberal societies of Europe and America there is a hopeful possibility of the following kind: Fairly autonomous people, among the middle class, the young, craftsmen, and professionals, cannot help but see that they cannot continue so in the present institutions. They cannot do honest and useful work or practice a profession nobly; arts and sciences are corrupted; modest enterprise must be blown out of all proportion to survive; the young cannot find vocations; it is hard to raise children; talent is strangled by credentials; the natural environment is being destroyed; health is imperiled; community life is inane; neighborhoods are ugly and unsafe; public services do not work; taxes are squandered on war, schoolteachers, and politicians.

Then they may make changes, to extend the areas of freedom from encroachment. Such changes might be piecemeal and not dramatic, but they must be fundamental; for many of the present institutions cannot be recast and the tendency of the system as a whole is disastrous. I like the Marxist term "withering away of the State," but it must begin now, not afterwards; and the goal is not a New Society, but a tolerable society in which life can go on.

Reflections on Drawing the Line

1.

A free society cannot be the substitution of a "new order" for the old order; it is the extension of spheres of free action until they make up most of the social life. (That such liberation is step by step does not mean that it can occur without revolutionary disruption, for in many spheres—e.g., war, economics, sexual education—any genuine liberation whatsoever involves a total change.)

In any present society, though much and even an increasing amount is coercive, nevertheless, much is also free. If it were not so, it would be impossible for a conscientious libertarian to cooperate or live there at all; but in fact we are constantly drawing the line beyond which we refuse to cooperate. In creative work, in passion and sentiment, in spontaneous recreation, there are healthy spheres of nature and freedom: it is the spirit of these that we most often extrapolate to all acts of utopian free society, to making a living, to civil life and law. But indeed, even the most corrupt and coercive functions of the present society draw on good natural power—the pity of it—otherwise the society could not survive for one moment; for free natural power is the only source of existence. Thus, people are fed, though the means, the cost, and the productive relations are coercive, and the total war would be the end of us all were it not for the bravery and endurance of mankind.

Free action is to live in present society as though it were a natural society. This maxim has three consequences, three moments:

(1) In the spheres which are in fact free and natural, we exercise personal excellence and give mutual aid.

(2) In many spheres which seem to be uncoerced, we have nevertheless been trapped into unnatural ways by the coercion that has formed us; for example, we have become habituated to the American timetable and the standard of living, though these are unnatural and coercive through and through. Here the maxim demands that we first correct ourselves.

(3) Finally, there are those natural acts or abstentions which clash openly with the coercive laws: these are the "crimes" which are beholden on a free

man to commit, as his reasonable desire demands and as the occasion arises. (See below, "A Touchstone . . .")

The free spirit is rather millenarian than utopian. A man does not look forward to a future state of things which he tries to bring about by suspect means; he draws now, so far as he can, on the natural force in him that is no different in kind from what it will be in a free society, except that there it will have more scope and be persistently reinforced by mutual aid and fraternal conflict. *Merely by continuing to exist and act in nature and freedom, a free man wins the victory, establishes the society;* it is not necessary for him to be the victor *over* any one. When he creates, he wins; when he corrects his prejudices and habits he wins; when he resists and suffers, he wins. I say it this way in order to tell honest persons not to despond when it seems that their earnest and honest work is without "influence." The free man does not seek to influence groups, but to act in the natural groups essential to him—for most human action is the action of groups. Consider if a million persons, quite apart from any "political" intention, did only natural work and did the best they could. The system of exploitation would disperse like fog in a hot wind. But of what use is the action, born of resentment, that is bent on correcting abuses yet never does a stroke of nature?

The action drawing on the most natural force will in fact establish itself. Might is right: but do not let the violent and the cowed imagine for a moment that their brutality is "might." What great things have *they* accomplished, in practice, art, or theory? Their violence is fear hidden from themselves by conceit, and nothing comes from it.

2.

Now I have been liberally using the terms "nature," "natural," and their contraries to attribute value and disvalue, as "natural and unnatural institutions." Do not these terms in this use lead to self-contradiction? For obviously the bad institutions as well as the good have come to be by natural process. A bad convention exists by natural causes; how are we to call it unnatural?

Let us consider the example of a language like English, and I want to distinguish three notions: physical and social nature, natural convention, and unnatural convention. It is physically and socially natural for people to speak: they have speech organs; they communicate with these; children express their feelings with determinate cries and imitate their parents' speech behavior. But any speech is some language or other. Speech organs, need to communicate, the expression of feelings, the desire to imitate and identify: these give the potentiality of speaking some language or other; historical circumstances make the language, in fact, English. It is usual to call the historical language conventional, but it is a "natural convention," in that the convention of English is a means of making the power of speech into a living act. Here we have the clue to how we can speak of an "unnatural convention": *an unnatural convention is one that prevents a human power from becoming a living act.* Thus, English is becoming unnatural because of its use in advertising. The technique of advertising is to establish an automatic reflex response, an immediate connection between certain words and the behavior of paying out money: thus it debauches the words so that they no longer express felt need, nor communicate a likeness of affection between persons, continuous with the imitation of parents and peers, nor correspond to the desire for objects really experienced. These functions of honest speech are shunted over by a successful advertisement. But these functions are the strongest and the creative power in speech. Therefore we can say that the abuse of English prevents the power of speech from becoming a living act; it is unnatural.

But it is objected that automatic response is also natural: it is physically and socially necessary for life, as consider the words "Look out!" or "Fire!" But let us patiently consider the order and ratio of such alarm words to the rest of speech. If they are too numerous, their emergency is blunted, just as indiscriminate profanity has no expletive force. What is the natural order of emergency and non-emergency situations, so that the strongest powers of health, safety, and pleasure may not be prevented from becoming living acts? The sense of emergency, natural in itself, still inhibits vegetation, memory, reflection. (It likewise inhibits, by the way, the religious, eschatological sense of emergency.) Taken at face value, the techniques of advertising and automatic political slogans express a state of chronic alarm!

Yet to be sure, as we consider it deeper, this *is* the historical situation; there is nothing conventional about such techniques, and our poor English, like a faithful servant, is sacrificed to urgent need. The society that needs to buy up the products of its industry *is* in a state of chronic alarm: what time has it for vegetation, memory, reflection? And the "high" standard of living thus purchased exists in emergency conditions that are preventive of any natural standard of living whatever, for there is no vegetative pleasure and reflection, and no emptiness in which inventions can flower. In haste and alarm, hearing and buying, a man cannot get his bearings, he is swept along, falls into debt and is open to still further coercion. No one can even quit a job. But we do not need to go thus roundabout through the analysis of linguistic usage to know that our way of life is compulsive. We can see it by direct observation on the street.

People are both frightened and deadened. It is a poor kind of democracy in which nobody stands out instead of everybody standing out. (Instead there are, pathetically, "celebrities.") Those who constrain strong natural power are always themselves under constraint. The prison guard is himself in jail, yes even the Warden.

But in any great collaboration, in art or theory or practice, the signature of each collaborator is apparent in the outcome. The plaid has the bright color of its threads.

3.

What is natural coercion and what is unnatural coercion? I doubt that I can answer this hard question to my own satisfaction, but sufficiently for the gross facts that we are concerned with. Education has always elements of natural coercion, but government by state or society is unnatural.

Natural coercion seems to go with natural dependency. An infant is dependent, he is part of his mother's field. A growing child is more voluntarily dependent; he is secure in the grownups' care and attention, and he grows in independence partly by imitation and partly by withdrawal from those in whom he is secure. A child grows teeth as he ceases to suckle, and he begins to walk when he is big enough to begin to walk away—*into* independence, for it is something positive. Yet coercion and violence inevitably occur, for the child grows in the predetermined culture of the adults and among the anger of the adults being themselves. To a child this must seem like any other reality—the part that doesn't make sense—but intensely interesting. At least he learns to keep out of the way. (In my opinion this is all he learns, for beautiful new truths are not communicated by a clout on the head.)

A pupil depends on a teacher who exercises authority and sets up the lessons. There is probably more of this than is necessary, but again the progress of the pupil and the aim of the teacher is the independence of the pupil from the teacher. If a person has maintained his trust through the previous storms of life, he can learn from teachers. A person who cannot surrender to archaic attitudes of dependency is probably not truly docile. But if previous childish dependency has been too frightened or cowed, a young person both will not trust his teachers and cannot grow to become their peer. He is prevented from drawing on the knowledge and power embodied in them. By this sign, therefore, we can say that the parental coercion was violent and unnatural.

The discouragement of childish sexuality leads to later anxiety; toilet training leads to "ruliness"; etc. So these must be called unnatural coercion. In general, when strong drives are frustrated and punished and a child begins to inhibit himself, to fill the vacuum of his life he identifies with precisely those who frustrate him: they are wise, they are authorities. The child has now lost both his desires and his power of initiation.

What is unique about human nature, however, is its *long* dependency. This is a great opportunity, for education, but it has also proved to be a great disaster. To the child, it seems to me, the danger is not generally that his ego will fail to crystallize, a case of psychosis, but that it will crystallize too rapidly, in too closed a system, against the inner and outer world from which in the end we must draw the forces of life. This has been especially noted with regard to the sexual drives, against which the ego sets itself, becoming erotized in turn—for when you can't love anything else you have to love yourself. But not enough has been said about the uncanny ignorance, stupidity, incuriosity, lack of perception and observation that characterize us, and which must also be attributed to inhibition by the too narrow, shut-in, and conceited ego. And so we fall into the opposite disaster, that the grownups have never learned to cope with the environment. They are dependent on governments.

Education is the furnishing by adults of imitable patterns of interpretation and attitude, *not* to train the child, but on the contrary so that the child, by relying on them and trying them, can take his time and not have to stand too quickly alone as sole authority. Adults provide and decide where children cannot yet provide and decide. This is coercion, always partly corporal, putting the child in the way of experience and out of the way of automobiles and poison. We can define natural coercion as a knowledgeable decision that preserves for the child his greatest inner and outer power to work up into experience and art.

But I do not think there is any use of docility to government, for it has not much to teach. Of the simple goods, food, shelter, safety, over which great constituted bodies like governments and economic systems claim authority, there is not a single one that the average adult person ought not to be competent to decide about. Every one knows he is hungry and wants food, or knows enough to come in out of the rain. If he has not developed to this point, it is that he has been maimed by unnatural coercion. But it is the way of authority to maim initiative and then prove that people have no initiative, and to pre-empt the means of livelihood and then show that people do not have the means to cope. There is plenty of rhetoric, and the use of force, to persuade people to continue as we do; but there is absolutely no public discussion and reasoning to consider whether the way we do *anything*—produce goods, run the schools, communicate ideas, elect officers—is the most efficient and sensible. Yet this is supposed to be an experimenting animal.

At present, of course, almost every man considers himself incompetent to provide the simplest goods. The state and other established institutions do decide for him. People are stupefied largely because they have so few interesting problems to work on; and finally they cannot decide whether they are cold, hurt, lonely, or even bored. They are not sure of anything. They are in a chronic state of alarm. Under these circumstances, orators easily pose as fathers and leaders. And this is called progressive, it is a New Deal. The "conservatives," on the other hand, want to stay with the oppressions of 1910 or perhaps Prince Metternich. It is only the anarchists who are really conservative, for they want to conserve sun and space, animal nature, primary community, experimenting inquiry.

4.

A man is dependent on his mother Earth. We are forever dependent in the universe, but not on princes.

It is false that social relationships are primarily interpersonal. The strongest bonds in natural groups are continuous with passions and impulses previous to the organization of the egos of the members. These are love and fraternity. How different is the juridical equality of the social psychologists of "interpersonal relationships" from the creative unanimity and rivalry of revolutionary fraternity! Brothers vie to excel individually, but catching fire from each other they achieve what none of them had it in him to do alone.

It is not our social nature to go it alone. It does not follow that one must conform to Society. It is enough to find-and-make a band, two hundred, of the like-minded, to know that oneself is sane though the rest of the city is batty.

The free man manifests the nature in him much more vehemently than we who have been trained to uniformity. His voice, gestures, and countenance express the great range of experience from child to sage. When he hears the hypocrite orator use words that arouse disgust, he vomits in the crowd.

We can conceive of a man whose ego takes far longer to crystallize than ours; whose ego still is forming out of vast systems of inner and outer experience, and works with forces beyond those that we have settled for. Such a vast ego belongs to Christ or Buddha; we may confidently predict that it will perform miracles. To him they are matter-of-fact.

In the mixed society of coercion and nature, our characteristic act is Drawing the Line, beyond which we cannot co-operate. All the heart-searching and purgatorial anxiety concerns this question, *Where to draw the line?* I'll say it bluntly: the anxiety goes far beyond reason. Since the extreme positions are clear black and white, and they exist plain to suffer and enjoy, and since it can be shown that one step leads to another in either direction: in the in-between murk *any* apparently arbitrary line is good enough. And one's potential friends among the people, to whom one wants to set an example, are moved by the challenging action, not the little details of consistency.

No particular drawn line will ever be defensible logically. But the right way from any line will prove itself more clearly step by step and blow by blow.

Yet to each person it seems to make all the difference where he draws the line! This is because just these details are the symbolic key to his repressed powers—and with each repression, guilt for the acceptance of it. Thus one man will speak in their court but will not pay a tax; another will write a letter but will not move his feet; another is nauseated by innocent bread and fasts. Why are the drawn lines so odd and logically inconsistent? Why are they maintained with such irrational stubbornness—precisely by free people who are usually so amiable and easy-smiling? The actions of nature are by no means inconsistent; they are sequences of even rather simple causes; following the probabilities does not lead one astray but to see one's way more clearly. But the fact is that each of us has been unconsciously coerced by our training and acceptance; the inner conflicts now begin to appear, in the inconsistency of drawing the line, and all the fear, guilt, and rage. Let us draw our lines and have this out!

A free man would have no such problems; he would not have finally to draw a line in their absurd conditions which he has disdained from the very beginning. The truth is that he would regard coercive sanctions as no different from the other destructive forces of brute nature, to be prudently avoided.

A free man, so long as he creates and goes by his clear and distinct ideas, can easily maintain in his soul many apparent contradictions; he is sure they will iron out; a loose system is the best system. But woe if at the same time he is persuaded into prejudices and coerced into conforming: then one day he will have the agony of drawing the line.

Well! there is a boyish joke I like to tell. Tom says to Jerry:

"Do you want to fight? Cross that line!" and Jerry does. "Now," cries Tom, "you're on my side!"

We draw the line in their conditions; we proceed on our conditions.

What Must Be the Revolutionary Program?

S till barring from consideration the threat of war, we must now ask: what is a revolutionary program in the sociolatry? (By "revolutionary" I here refer to the heirs of Rousseau and the French Revolution: the conviction that man is born free and is in institutional chains; that fraternity is the deepest political force and the fountain of social invention; and that socialism implies the *absence* of state or other coercive power.)

For if indeed, with the steady expansion of technical productivity, the attitude of the masses has for a century moved toward sociolatry and the attitude of the bourgeoisie toward accepting a low but stable rate of profit, then the Marxian program is not only bankrupt but reactionary. The Marxian economic demands (for wages and conditions) cement the sociolatry; the Marxian political demands (for expropriation of the expropriators by seizing power) lead to state socialism.

It is with diffidence that I dissent from the social psychology of Karl Marx. When I was young, being possessed of an independent spirit I refused to embrace the social science of Marx, but proceeded, as an artist and a human being, to make my own judgments of the social behavior I saw about. And then I found, again and again, that the conclusions I slowly and imperfectly arrived at were already fully and demonstrably (and I may say, beautifully) expressed by Karl Marx. So I too was a Marxist! I decided with pleasure, for it is excellent to belong to a tradition and have wise friends. This was Marx as a social psychologist. But as regards political action, on the other hand, I did not see, it never seemed to me, that the slogans of the Marxians, nor even of Marx, lead toward fraternal socialism; rather they lead away from it. Bakunin was better. Kropotkin I agree with.

Now *(still* barring the war!) there is a great advantage for the revolutionist in the existence of sociolatry and of even a tyrannical welfare state. The standard of living and the present use of the machinery of production may rouse our disgust, but it is an ethical disgust; it is not the fierce need to act roused by general biological misery. We may therefore act in a more piecemeal, educational, and thoroughgoing way. The results of such action will also be lasting and worthwhile if we have grown into our freedom rather than driven each other into it. Our attack on the industrial system can be many sided and often indirect, to make it crash of its own weight rather than by frontal attack.

Nor is it the case that the absence of tension and despair makes it impossible to awaken revolutionary feeling. For we know that the society we want is universally present in the heart, though now generally submerged: it can be brought into existence piecemeal, power by power, everywhere: and as soon as it appears in act, the sociolatry becomes worthless, ridiculous, disgusting by comparison. There is no doubt that, once awakened, the natural powers of men are immeasurably stronger than these alien institutions (which are indeed only the pale sublimations of natural powers).

On the one hand, the kind of critique that my friends and I express: a selective attitude toward the technology, not without peasant features, is itself a product of our surplus technology; on the other hand, we touch precisely the vulnerable point of the system, its failure to win human allegiance.

Then, as opposed to the radical programs that already presuppose the great state and corporative structure, and the present social institutions in the perfected form of the Sociolatry, we must—in small groups—draw the line and try action more directly satisfactory to our deep nature. (a) It is essential that our program can, with courage and mutual encouragement and mutual aid, be put into effect by our own effort, to a degree at once and progressively more and more, without recourse to distant party or union decisions. (b) The groups must be small, because mutual aid is our common human nature mainly with respect to those with whom we deal face to face. (c) Our action must be aimed not, as utopians, at a future establishment; but (as millenarians, so to speak) at fraternal arrangements today, progressively incorporating more and more of the social functions into our free society.

(1) It is treasonable to free society not to work at a job that realizes our human powers and transcends an unthinking and unchoosing subdivision of labor. It is a matter of guilt—this is a harsh saying—to exhaust our time of day in the usual work in office and factories, merely for wages. The aim of economy is not the efficient production of commodities, but cooperative jobs themselves worth doing, with the workers, full understanding of the machines and processes, releasing the industrial inventiveness that very many have. (Nor is it the case, *if we have regard to the whole output of social labor,* that modern technical efficiency requires, or is indeed compatible with, the huge present concentrations of machinery beyond the understanding and control of small groups of workers.)

(2) We must reassess our standard of living and see what parts are really useful for subsistence and humane well-being, and which are slavery to the

emulation, emotional security, and inferiority roused by exploitative institutions and coercive advertising. The question is not one of the quantity of goods (the fact that we swamp ourselves with household furnishings is likely due to psychic causes too deep for us willfully to alter), but that the goods that make up the "standard of living" are stamped with alien values.

(3) We must allow, and encourage, the sexual satisfaction of the young, both adolescents and small children, in order to free them from anxious submissiveness to authority. It is probably impossible to prevent our own neurotic prejudices from influencing children, but we can at least make opportunity for the sexual gratification of adolescents. This is essential in order to prevent the patterns of coercion and authority from re-emerging no matter what the political change has been.

(4) In small groups we must exercise direct initiative in community problems of personal concern to ourselves (housing, community plan, schooling, etc.). The constructive decisions of intimate concern to us cannot be delegated to representative government and bureaucracy. Further, even if the Government really represented the interests of the constituents, it is still the case that political initiative is itself the noble and integrating act of every man. In government, as in economic production, what is superficially efficient is not efficient in the long run.

(5) Living in the midst of an alienated way of life, we must mutually analyze and purge our souls until we no longer regard as guilty or conspiratorial such illegal acts as spring from common human nature. (Group psychotherapy is identical with contactful neighbor-love that pays attention and comes across.) With regard to committing such "crimes" we must exercise prudence not of inhibitions but such prudence as a sane man exercises in a madhouse. On the other hand, we must see that many acts commonly regarded as legal and even meritorious are treason against our natural society, *if they involve us in situations where we cease to have personal responsibility and concern for the consequences.*

(6) We must progressively abstain from whatever is connected with the war.

I am sensible that this program seems to demand very great initiative, courage, effort, and social invention; yet if once, looking about at our situation whatever it is, we *draw a line* (wherever we draw it!), can we not at once proceed? Those of us who have already been living in a more reasonable way do not find these minimal points too difficult; can those who have all their lives taken on the habits (if not the ideas) of the alienated society, expect not to make drastic changes? If we are to have peace, it is necessary to *wage* the peace. Otherwise, when their war comes, we also must hold ourselves responsible for it.

The Missing Community

1.

The use of history, Benjamin Nelson used to say, is to rescue from oblivion the lost causes of the past. History is especially important when those lost causes haunt us in the present as unfinished business.

I have often spoken in this essay of the "missed revolutions that we have inherited." My idea is that it is not with impunity that fundamental social changes fail to take place at the appropriate time; the following generations are embarrassed and confused by their lack. This subject warrants a special study. Some revolutions fail to occur; most half-occur or are compromised, attaining some of their objectives and resulting in significant social changes, but giving up on others, resulting in ambiguous values in the social whole that would not have occurred if the change had been more thoroughgoing. For in general, a profound revolutionary program in any field projects a new workable kind of behavior, a new nature of man, a new whole society; just as the traditional society it tries to replace is a whole society that the revolutionists think is out of date. But a compromised revolution tends to disrupt the tradition without achieving a new social balance.

It is the argument of this book that *the accumulation of the missed and compromised revolutions of modern times, with their consequent ambiguities and social imbalances, has fallen, and must fall, most heavily on the young, making it hard to grow up.*

A man who has attained maturity and independence can pick and choose among the immense modern advances and somewhat wield them as his way of life. If he has a poor society, an adult cannot be very happy, he will not have simple goals nor achieve classical products, but he can fight and work anyway. But for children and adolescents it is indispensable to have a coherent, fairly simple and viable society to grow up into; otherwise they are confused, and some are squeezed out. Tradition has been broken, yet there is no new standard to affirm. Culture becomes eclectic, sensational, or phony. (Our present culture is all three.) A successful revolution establishes a new community. A missed revolution makes irrelevant the community that persists. And a compromised revolution tends to shatter the community that was, without an adequate substitute. But as we argued in a previous chapter, it is precisely for the young that the geographical and historical community and its patriotism are the important environment, as they draw away from their parents and until they can act on their own with fully developed powers.

In this chapter, let us collect the missed or compromised fundamental social changes that we have had occasion to mention; calling attention to what *was* achieved and what *failed* to be achieved, and the consequent confused situation which then actually confronts the youth growing up.

2.

Let us start with the physical environment.

Technocracy. In our own century, philosophers of the new technology, like Veblen, Geddes, or Fuller, succeeded in making efficiency and know-how the chief ethical values of the folk, creating a mystique of "production," and a kind of streamlined esthetics. But they did not succeed in wresting management from the businessmen and creating their own world of a neat and transparent physical plant and a practical economics of production and distribution. The actual results have been slums of works of engineering, confused and useless overproduction, gadgetry, and new tribes of middlemen, promoters, and advertisers.

Urbanism. As Le Corbusier and Gropius urged, we have increasingly the plan and style of functional architecture; biological standards of housing; scientific study of traffic and city services; some zoning; and the construction of large-scale projects. But nowhere is realized the ideal of over-all community planning, the open green city, or the organic relation of work, living, and play. The actual results have been increasing commutation and traffic, segregated ghettos, a "functional" style little different from packaging, and the tendency to squeeze out some basic urban functions, such as recreation or schooling, to be squeezed out altogether.

Garden City. The opposite numbers, the Garden City planners after Ebenezer Howard, have achieved some planned communities protected by greenbelts. But they did not get their integrated towns, planned for industry, local commerce, and living. The result is that actual suburbs and garden cities are dormitories with a culture centering around small children, and absence of the wage earner; and such "plans" as the so-called shopping centers disrupt such village communities as there were. The movement to conserve the wilds cannot withstand the cars, so that all areas are invaded and regulated.

3.

Let us proceed to economic and social changes.

New Deal. The Keynesian economics of the New Deal has cushioned the business cycle and maintained nearly full employment. It has not achieved its ideal of social balance between public and private works. The result is an expanding production increasingly consisting of corporation boondoggling.

Syndicalism. Industrial workers have won their unions, obtained better wages and working conditions, and affirmed the dignity of labor. But they gave up their ideal of workers' management, technical education, and concern for the utility of their labor. The result is that a vast majority couldn't care less about what they make, and the "labor movement" is losing force.

Class Struggle. The working class has achieved a striking repeal of the iron law of wages; it has won a minimum wage and social security. But the goal of an equalitarian or freely mobile society has been given up, as has the solidarity of the underprivileged. The actual result is an increasing rigidity of statuses; some of the underprivileged tending to drop out of society altogether. On the other hand, the cultural equality that has been achieved has been the degradation of the one popular culture to the lowest common denominator.

Production for Use. This socialist goal has been missed, resulting in many of the other failures here listed.

Sociology. During the past century, the sociologists have achieved their aim of dealing with mankind in its natural groups or groups with common problems, rather than as isolated individuals or a faceless mass. Social science has replaced many prejudices and ideologies of vested interests. But on the whole, social scientists have given up their aim of fundamental social change and an open-experimental method determining its goals as it went along: the pragmatist ideal of society as a laboratory for freedom and self-correcting humanity. The actual result is an emphasis on "socializing" and "belonging," with the loss of nature, culture, group solidarity and group variety, and individual excellence.

4.

Next, political and constitutional reforms.

Democracy. The democratic revolution succeeded in extending formal self-government and opportunity to nearly everybody, regardless of birth, property, or education. But it gave up the ideal of the town meeting, with the initiative and personal involvement that alone could train people in self-government and give them practical knowledge of political issues. The actual result has been the formation of a class of politicians who govern, and who are themselves symbolic front figures.

The Republic. Correspondingly, the self-determination won by the American Revolution for the regional states, that should have made possible real political experimentation, soon gave way to a national conformity; nor has the nation as a whole conserved its resources and maintained its ideals. The result is a deadening centralism, with neither local patriotism nor national patriotism. The best people do not offer themselves for public office, and no one has the aim of serving the Republic.

Freedom of Speech. Typical is the fate of the hard-won Constitutional freedoms, such as freedom of speech. Editors and publishers have given up trying to give an effective voice to important but unpopular opinions. Anything can be printed, but the powerful interests have the big presses. Only the safe opinion is proclaimed and other opinion is swamped.

Liberalism. The liberal revolution succeeded in shaking off onerous government controls on enterprise, but it did not persist to its goal of real public wealth as the result of free enterprise and honestly informed choice on the market. The actual result is an economy dominated by monopolies, in which the earnest individual entrepreneur or inventor, who could perform a public service, is actively discouraged; and consumer demand is increasingly synthetic.

Agrarianism. Conversely, the Jeffersonian ideal of a proud and independent productive yeomanry, with natural family morals and a co-operative community spirit, did in fact energize settling the West and providing the basis for our abundance. But because it has failed to cope with technological changes and to withstand speculation, "farming as a way of life" has succumbed to cash-cropping dependent on distant markets, and is ridden with mortgages, tenancy, and hired labor. Yet it maintains a narrow rural morality and isolationist politics, is a sucker for the mass culture of Madison Avenue and Hollywood, and in the new cities (e.g., in California, where farmers have migrated) is a bulwark against genuine city culture.

Liberty. Constitutional safeguards of person were won. But despite the increasing concentration of state power and mass pressures, no effort was made to give to individuals and small groups new means easily to avail themselves of the safeguards. The result is that there is no longer the striking individuality of free men; even quiet nonconformity is hounded; and there is no asylum from coast to coast.

Fraternity. This short-lived ideal of the French Revolution, animating a whole people and uniting all classes as a community, soon gave way to a dangerous nationalism. The ideal somewhat revived as the solidarity of the working class, but this too has faded into either philanthropy or "belonging."

Brotherhood of Races. The Civil War won formal rights for Negroes, but failed to win social justice and factual democracy. The actual result has been segregation, and fear and ignorance for both whites and blacks.

Pacifism. This revolution has been entirely missed.

5.

Let us proceed to some more general moral premises of modern times.

Reformation. The Protestant Reformation won the possibility of living religiously in the world, freed individuals from the domination of the priest, and led, indirectly, to the toleration of private conscience. But it failed to withstand the secular power; it did not cultivate the meaning of vocation as a community function; and in most sects the spirit of the churches did not spring from their living congregations but was handed down as dogma and ascetic discipline. The final result has been secularism, individualism, the subordination of human beings to a rational economic system, and churches irrelevant to practical community life. Meantime, acting merely as a negative force, the jealous sectarian conscience has driven religion out of social thought.

Modern Science. The scientific revolution associated with the name of Galileo freed thinking of superstition and academic tradition and won attention to the observation of nature. But it failed to modify and extend its method to social and moral matters, and indeed science has gotten further and further from ordinary experience. With the dominance of science and applied science in our times, the result has been a specialist class of scientists and technicians, the increasing ineptitude of the average person, a disastrous dichotomy of "neutral" facts versus "arbitrary" values, and a superstition of scientism that has put people out of touch with nature, and also has aroused a growing hostility to science.

Enlightenment. The Enlightenment unseated age-old tyrannies of state and church and won a triumph of reason over authority. But its universalism failed to survive the rising nationalisms except in special sciences and learning, and its ideal of encyclopedic reason as the passionate guide to life degenerated to the nineteenth-century hope for progress through science and learning. And we now have an internationalism without brotherhood or peace, even concealing science as a strategic weapon; and a general sentiment that the rule of reason is infinitely impractical.

Honesty. The rebellion for honest speech that we associate with Ibsen, Flaubert, etc., and also with the muckrakers broke down the hypocrisy of Victorian prudishness and of exploiting pillars of society; it reopened discussion and renovated language; and it weakened official censorship. But it failed to insist on the close relation between honest speech and corresponding action. The result has been a weakening of the obligation to act according to speech, so that, ironically, the real motives of public and private behavior are more in the dark than ever.

Popular Culture. This ideal, that we may associate in literature with the name of Sam Johnson and the Fleet Street journalists, in the plastic arts with William Morris and Ruskin, freed culture from aristocratic and snobbish patrons. It made thought and design relevant to everyday manners. But it did not succeed in establishing an immediate relation between the writer or artist and his audience. The result is that the popular culture is controlled by hucksters and promoters as though it were a saleable commodity, and our society, inundated by cultural commodities, remains uncultivated.

6.

Finally, some reforms directly connected with children and adolescents.

No Child Labor. Children have been rescued from the exploitation and training of factories and sweat shops. But, relying on the public schools and the apprentice-training in an expanding and open economy, the reformers did not develop a philosophy of capacity and vocation. Nor, since there were many small jobs, did they face the problems of a growing boy needing to earn some money. In our days, the result is that growing youths are idle and vocationally useless, and often economically desperate; and the schools, on the contrary, become apprentice-training paid for by public money.

Compulsory Education. This gave to all children a certain equality of opportunity in an open expanding industrial society. Formal elementary discipline was sufficient when the environment was educative and provided opportunities for advancement. In our circumstances, formal literacy is less relevant, and overcrowding and official interference make individual attention and real teaching impossible; so that it could be said that the schools are as stupefying as they are educative, and compulsory education is often like jail.

Sexual Revolution. This has accomplished a freeing of animal functioning in general, has pierced repression, importantly relaxed inhibition, weakened legal and social sanctions, and diminished the strict animal-training of small children. The movement has not so much failed as that it is still in process, strongly resisted by inherited prejudices, fears, and jealousies. By and large it has not won practical freedom for older children and adolescents. The actual present result is that they are trapped by inconsistent rules, suffer because of excessive stimulation and inadequate discharge, and become preoccupied with sexual thoughts as if these were the whole of life.

49

Permissiveness. Children have more freedom of spontaneous behavior, and their dignity and spirit are not crushed by humiliating punishments in school and in very many homes. But this permissiveness has not extended to provide also means and conditions: Young folk might be sexually free but have no privacy; they are free to be angry, but have no asylum to escape from home, and no way to get their own money. Besides, where upbringing is permissive, it is necessary to have strong values and esteemed behavior at home and in the community, so that the child can have worth-while goals to structure his experience; and of course it is just these that are lacking. So permissiveness often leads to anxiety and weakness instead of confidence and strength.

Progressive Education. This radical proposal, aimed at solving the dilemmas of education in the modern circumstances of industrialism and democracy, was never given a chance. It succeeded in destroying the faculty psychology in the interests of educating the whole person, and in emphasizing group experience, but failed to introduce learning-by-doing with real problems. The actual result of the gains has been to weaken the academic curriculum and foster adjustment to society as it is.

7.

Let us consider the beginning, the ending, and the middle of these little paragraphs.

The headings printed in bold type are, in their summation, a kind of program of modern man. It is evident that every one of these twenty-odd positions was invented-and-discovered as a response to specific historical conditions. The political positions were developed to oppose the absolutism of the kings who had unified the warring feudal states; the program for children and adolescents has been a response to modern industrialism and urbanism; and so forth. But it does *not* follow, as some sociologists think, that they can therefore be superseded and forgotten as conditions change.

Consider the following of C. Wright Mills: "The ideals that we Westerners associate with the classic, liberal, bourgeois period of modern culture may well be rooted in this one historical stage of this one type of society. Such ideals as personal freedom and cultural autonomy may not be inherent, necessary features of cultural life as such." This is like saying that tragic poetry or mathematics was "rooted" in the Greek way of life and is not "inherently" human. This kind of thinking is the final result of the recent social-scientific attitude that culture is added onto a featureless animal, rather than being the invention-and-discovery of human powers. This is effectually to give up the modern enterprise altogether. But we will not give it up. New conditions will be the conditions of, now, this kind of man, stubbornly insisting on the ideals that he has learned he has in him to meet.

Yet the modern positions are not even easily consistent with one another, to form a coherent program. There have been bitter conflicts between Liberty and Equality, Science and Faith, Technology and Syndicalism, and so forth. Nevertheless, we will not give up one or the other, but will arduously try to achieve them all and *make* a coherent program. And indeed, experience has taught that the failure in one of these ideals at once entails failure in others.

For instance, failure in social justice weakens political freedom, and this compromises scientific and religious autonomy. "If we continue to be without a socialist movement," says Frank Marquart, "we may end up without a labor movement." The setback of progressive education makes the compulsory school system more hopeless, and this now threatens permissiveness and sexual freedom; and so forth. So we struggle to perfect all these positions, one buttressing another, if we are to fulfill our unique modern destiny.

There is no doubt, too, that in our plight new modern positions will be added to these, and these too will be compromised, aborted, their prophetic urgency bureaucratized and ironically transformed into the opposite. But there it is.

8.

If we now collect the actual, often ironical, results of so much noble struggle, we get a clear *but exaggerated* picture of our American society. It has: slums of engineering—boondoggling production—chaotic congestion—tribes of middlemen—basic city functions squeezed out—garden cities for children—indifferent workmen—underprivileged on a dole—empty "belonging" without nature or culture—front politicians—no patriotism—an empty nationalism bound for a cataclysmically disastrous finish—wise opinion swamped—enterprise sabotaged by monopoly—prejudice rising—religion otiose—the popular culture debased—science specialized—science secret—the average man inept—youth idle and truant—youth sexually suffering and sexually obsessed—youth without goals—poor schools.

This picture is not unjust, but it is, again, exaggerated. For it omits, of course, all the positive factors and the ongoing successes. We have a persisting grand culture. There is a steady advance of science, scholarship, and the fine arts. A steady improvement in health and medicine. An economy of abundance and, in many ways, a genuine civil peace and a stubborn affirming of democracy. And most of all there are the remarkable resilience and courage that belong to human beings. Also, the Americans, for all their folly and conformity, are often thrillingly sophisticated and impatient of hypocrisy.

Yet there is one grim actuality that even this exaggerated picture does not reveal, the creeping defeatism and surrender by default to the organized system of the state and semimonopolies. International Business Machines and organized psychologists, we have seen, effectually determine the method of school examinations and personnel selection. As landlords, Webb and Knapp and Metropolitan Life decide what our domestic habits should be; and, as "civic developers" they plan communities, even though their motive is simply a "long-term modest profit" on investment while millions are ill housed. The good of General Motors and the nation are inseparable, says Secretary Wilson—even though the cars are demonstrably ruinous for the cities, ruinous for the young, etc. Madison Avenue and Hollywood not only debauch their audiences, but they pre-empt the means of communication, so nothing else can exist. With only occasional flagrant breaches of legality, the increasingly interlocking police forces and the FBI make people cowed and speechless. That Americans can allow this kind of thing instead of demolishing it with a blow of the paw like a strong lion, is the psychology of missed revolutions.

9.

For our positive purposes in this book, it is the middle parts of our paragraphs that warrant study: the failures, the fallings-short, the compromises. Imagine that these modern radical positions had been more fully achieved: we should have a society where: A premium is placed on technical improvement and on the engineering style of functional simplicity and clarity. Where the community is planned as a whole, with an organic integration of work, living, and play. Where buildings have the variety of their real functions with the uniformity of the prevailing technology. Where a lot of money is spent on public goods. Where workers are technically educated and have a say in management. Where no one drops out of society and there is an easy mobility of classes. Where production is primarily for use. Where social groups are laboratories for solving their own problems experimentally. Where democracy begins in the town meeting, and a man seeks office only because he has a program. Where regional variety is encouraged and there is pride in the Republic. And young men are free of conscription. Where all feel themselves citizens of the universal Republic of Reason. Where it is the policy to give an adequate voice to the unusual and unpopular opinion, and to give a trial and a market to new enterprise. Where people are not afraid to make friends. Where races are factually equal. Where vocation is sought out and cultivated as God-given capacity, to be conserved and embellished, and where the church is the spirit of its congregation. Where ordinary experience is habitually scientifically assayed by the average man. Where it is felt that the suggestion of reason is practical.

And speech leads to the corresponding action. Where the popular culture is a daring and passionate culture. Where children can make themselves useful and earn their own money. Where their sexuality is taken for granted. Where the community carries on its important adult business and the children fall in at their own pace. And where education is concerned with fostering human powers as they develop in the growing child.

In such an utopian society, as was aimed at by modern radicals but has not eventuated, it would be very easy to grow up. There would be plenty of objective, worth-while activities for a child to observe, fall in with, do, learn, improvise on his own. That is to say, it is not the spirit of modern times that makes our society difficult for the young; it is that that spirit has not sufficiently realized itself.

In this light, the present plight of the young is not surprising. In the rapid changes, people have not kept enough in mind that the growing young also exist and the world must fit their needs. So instead, we have the present phenomena of excessive attention to the children as such, in psychology and suburbs, and coping with "juvenile delinquency" as if it were an entity. Adults fighting for some profoundly conceived fundamental change naturally give up, exhausted, when they have achieved some gain that makes life tolerable again and seems to be the substance of their demand. But to grow up, the young need a world of finished situations and society made whole again.

Civil Disobedience

Law and Legitimacy

During the early Thirties, students got a thorough extracurricular education in the political economy. They experienced the Depression, the labor movement, the New Deal, the subtle in-fighting of Left sects; and Marxian, Keynesian, managerial and technocratic theories provided adequate terms for discussion. Present-day students are hopelessly ill-informed, and uninterested, in these matters. But they have had other experiences. Sitting-in and being jailed, demonstrating, resisting the draft, defying authority in the schools and on the streets have confronted them with the fundamental problems of political science, the premises of allegiance and legitimacy by which political societies operate at all. For a teacher it is thrilling, if poignant, to see how real these abstractions have become.

But the theoretical framework for discussion has been astonishingly meager. Learning by doing, the young have rediscovered a kind of populism and "participatory democracy"; they have been seduced by theories of mountain guerrilla warfare and putschism, and some of them like to quote Chairman Mao that political power comes from the barrel of a gun. But I have heard little analysis of what Sovereignty and Law really are in modern industrial and urban societies, though it is about these that there is evidently a profound conflict in this period. In the vacuum of historical knowledge and philosophical criticism, the dissenters are too ready to concede (or boast) that they are lawless and civilly disobedient. And the powers that be, police, school administrators, and the Texan President, are able to sound off, and practice, clichés about Law and Order that are certainly not American political science. So it is useful to make some academic remarks about elementary topics. Alas, it is even necessary, to rehearse our case—I am writing in the spring of 1968, and some of us are under indictment.

Administrators talk about Law and Order and Respect for Authority as if these things had an absolute sanction: without them there can be no negotiation, whether the situation is a riot, a strike of municipal employees, a student protest against Dow Chemical, or burning draft cards. The tone is curiously theocratic, as if the government existed by divine right. Law and Order sounds like the doctrine of the authoritarian personality, where the Sovereign has been internalized from childhood and has a nonrational charisma. But although this psychology does exist, by and large the Americans are not conformist in this way. Indeed, they have become increasingly skeptical, or cynical, of their moral rigidity, at the same time as they resort more readily to violent suppression of deviation or infringement.

The "reasons," given in editorials, are that we must have safe streets; in a democracy, there is a due process for changing the laws; violation is contagious and we are tending toward "anarchy." But do safe streets depend on strictly enforcing the law? Every editorial *also* points out that sociologically the means of keeping the peace is to diminish tension, and economically and politically it is to give the disaffected a stake and a say. And in the history of American cities, of course, peace has often been best preserved by bribery, deals under the table, patronage of local bosses, blinking or negligent enforcement. In the complex circumstances of civil disorder, the extralegal is likely to give rough justice, whereas strict enforcement, for instance when the reform-minded *Daily News* makes the police close Eighth Avenue bars, is sure to cause unnecessary suffering.

Even when it is not substantively unjust, Law and Order is a cultural style of those who know the ropes, have access to lawyers, and are not habitually on the verge of animal despair; such a high style, however convenient for society, cannot be taught by tanks and mace. But what is most dismaying is that a well-intentioned group like the Commission on Civil Disorders regards Order and Due Process as a neutral platform to discuss substantive remedies; it cannot see that to an oppressed group just these things are the usual intolerable hangup of White Power: theft, repression and run-around.

I do not think there is empirical evidence that all violation is contagious. The sociological probability, and what little evidence there is, is the other way: those who break the law for political reasons, articulate or inarticulate, are less likely to commit delinquencies or crimes, since there is less *anomie*; they have a stake and a say if only by being able to act at all. And Jefferson, of course, argued just the opposite of punctilious law: since laws are bound to be defied, he said, it is better to have as few as possible, rather than to try for stricter enforcement.

When a disaffected group indeed has power, nobody takes absolutism seriously. The organized teachers and garbage collectors of New York disregarded the Condon-Wadlin and Taylor laws against strikes by municipal employees, and got their way—nor did the Republic fall in ruins. Only the New York *Times*, not even governor Rockefeller or Mayor Lindsay, bothered to mention the threat to Law and Order.

I suppose the climax of divine-right theory in American history has been the law making draft-card burning a felony, punishable by five years in prison or $10,000 fine or both. Since draft-card burning does not help a youth avoid the draft, what is this felony? It is *lèse majesté*, injury to the sacred sovereignty of Law embodied in a piece of paper. Yet congress enacted this law almost unanimously.

Certainly the disobedient do not *feel* that the law is sacred. If it were, any deliberate infringement—whether by Dr. Spock, a Black Power agitator, a garbage collector or a driver risking a parking ticket—would involve a tragic conflict genre of Corneille: Love vs. Duty. Among infringers, I see a good deal of calculation of consequences, and on the part of Dr. Spock, Dr. King, etc., an admirable courage and patriotism, but I do not see the signs of inner tragic conflict.

The Authority of Law is Limited

If we turn, now, to the more tonic American conception that the sanction of law is the social compact of the sovereign people, we see that it is rarely necessary, in the kinds of cases we are concerned with, to speak of "civil disobedience" or "lawlessness." What social promises do people actually consider binding? There are drastic limitations. Let me list half a dozen that are relevant to present problems.

(Of course, few believe in the mythical hypothesis of compact, or in any other single explanation, to account for the real force of law. We must include custom, inertia, prerational community ties, good-natured mutual regard, fear of the police, a residue of infantile awe of the overwhelming, and the energy bound up in belonging to any institution whatever. Yet compact is not a mere fiction. Communities do come to such agreements. Immigrants sometimes choose one system of laws over another; and, negatively, there are times when men consciously ask themselves, "What have I bargained for? Do I want to live with these people in this arrangement?")

Since an underlying purpose of the compact is security of life and liberty, it is broken if the sovereign jails you or threatens your life; you have a (natural) duty to try to escape. In our society, this point of Hobbes' is important. There is a formidable number of persons in jail, or certified as insane, or in juvenile reformatories; and there is an increasing number of middle-class youth who have been "radicalized," returned to a state of nature, by incarceration. Likewise, the more brutal the police, the less the allegiance of the citizens.

In large areas of personal and animal life, as in the case of vices harmless to others, high-spirited persons have a definite understanding that law is irrelevant and should be simply disregarded. Almost all "moral" legislation—on gambling, sex, alcohol, drugs, obscenity—is increasingly likely to be nullified by massive non-publicized disobedience. Not that these areas are "private" or trivial, but one does not make a social contract about them. The medievals more realistically declared that they were subject to canon law, not to the king. For better or worse, we do not have courts of conscience, but it is a human disaster for their functions to be taken over by policemen and night magistrates.

The sovereign cannot intervene in professional prerogatives, as by a law against teaching evolution. Every teacher is duty-bound to defy it. A physician will not inform against a patient, a lawyer a client, a teacher a student, a journalist an informant. At present, there is bound to be a case where a scientist publishes his government-classified or company-owned research, because scientists have an obligation to publish. (By and large, however, for narrow economic reasons, professionals have been playing the dangerous game of giving more and more prerogative in licensing to the State. By deciding who practices, the State will finally determine what is practiced.)

By the Bill of Rights, speech, religion, and political acts like an assembly and petition are beyond the reach of the law. As I have argued elsewhere, it is a mistake to interpret these "rights" as a compact; rather they state areas of anarchy in which people cannot make contracts in a free society, any more than to sell themselves into slavery.

Obviously the compact is broken if the law goes berserk, for example if the government prepares for nuclear war. Therefore we refused the nuclear shelter drills.

The law cannot command what is immoral or dehumanizing, whether co-operation with the Vietnam War or paying rent where conditions are unlivable. In such cases, it is unnecessary to talk about allegiance to a "higher law" or about conflict with the judgments of Nuremberg (though these might be legally convenient in a court), for a man cannot be responsible for what demoralizes and degrades him from being a responsible agent altogether. And note that all these classes of cases have nothing to do with the usual question: "Is every individual supposed to decide what laws he will obey?"—for it is the social contract itself that is irrelevant or self-contradictory.

Finally the bindingness of promises is subject to essential change of circumstances. Due process, electing new representatives to make new laws, is supposed to meet this need and roughly does; but due process is itself part of the social agreement and in times of crises, of course, it is always a live question as to whether it is adequate or whether sovereignty reverts closer to the people, seeking the General Will by other means. The vague concept that sovereignty resides in the People is usually meaningless, but precisely at critical moments it begins to have a vague meaning. American political history consists spectacularly of illegal actions that become legal, belatedly confirmed by the lawmakers. Civil rights trespassers, unions defying injunctions, suffragettes and agrarians being violent, abolitionists aiding runaway slaves, and back to the Boston Tea Party—were these people practicing "civil disobedience" or were they "insurrectionary"? I think neither. Rather, in urgent haste they were exercising their sovereignty, practicing direct democracy, disregarding the apparent law and sure of the emerging law. And by the time many cases went through a long, often deliberately protracted, course of appeals, the lawbreakers were no longer guilty, for their acts were no longer crimes. Hopefully, the current Vietnam protest is following the same schedule. To be sure, this direct political process is not always benign; the Ku Klux Klan also created law by populist means.

Thus, if we stick to a literal social contract, asking what is it that men really mean to promise, the authority of law is limited indeed. It is often justifiable to break a law as unwarranted, and reasonable to test it as unconstitutional or outdated. By this analysis it is almost never necessary, except for cases of individual conscience, to invoke a fancy concept like "civil disobedience," which concedes the warrant of the law but must for extraordinary reasons defy it.

The Function of Law and Order

Clearly, law has more authority than this among the Americans. We are not nearly so rational and libertarian. We do not believe in divine right but we do not have a social contract either. What would be a more realistic theory, more approximate to the gross present facts? I am afraid that it is something like the following:

There is an immense social advantage in having any regular code that everybody abides by without question, even if it is quite unreasonable and sometimes outrageous. This confirms people's expectations and permits them to act out their social roles. If the code is violated, people become so anxious about their roles that they want government to exert brute force to maintain Law and Order—this is part of government's role in the division of labor. Law and Order in this sense does not need moral authority; it is equivalent to saying, "Shape up; don't bother us; we're busy."

The sanction is avoidance of anxiety. This explains the tone of absolutism, without the tradition, religion or moral and ritual imperatives that humanized ancient theocracies. Gripped by anxiety, people can commit enormities of injustice and stupidity just in order to keep things under control. For instance, we enact draconian penalties for drugs, though our reasoned opinion is increasingly permissive. Minority groups that do not or cannot shape up must be squelched and kept out of sight, though everybody now concedes that they have just grievances and that suppression doesn't work anyway. The polls vote for stepping up the Vietnam war just when information, in the press and on television, is that the war is more and more evil and also militarily dubious. Squeamishness and stubbornness can go as far as using nuclear weapons, a massacre on the streets, and concentration camps for dissenters.

Conversely, the strategy of those who protest—the "civil disobedients," the "guerrilla fighters," the "rioters"—ceases to be justice and reconstruction and becomes simply to prevent business as usual. Lively young people, distinguished scholars, and the most talented leaders of the poor spend their time thinking up ways to make trouble. Our ideal aim is certainly to get the politically degenerate Americans back to liberty, law and the business of the commonwealth, but sometimes the purpose gets lost in the shuffle.

The Regime Itself is Illegitimate

The rising tide of "civil disobedience" and "lawlessness" is not defiance of law and order; it is a challenge that the regime itself is illegitimate. Maybe it asks a question: Can the modern society we have described be a political society at all? In my opinion, even the rising rate of crime is due mainly to *anomie*, confusion about norms and therefore lack of allegiance, rather than to any increase in criminal types (though that probably also exists under modern urban conditions).

"Civil disobedience" especially is a misnomer. According to this concept the law expresses the social sovereignty that we have ourselves conceded, and therefore we logically accept the penalties if we disobey, though we may have to disobey nevertheless. But in the interesting and massive cases, the warrant of the law is *not* conceded and its penalties are not agreed to. Indeed, I doubt that people *en masse* ever disobey what they agree to be roughly fair and just, even if it violates conscience.

Thus, Gandhi's major campaigns were carried on under the slogan Swaraj, self-rule for the Indians; the British Raj who was disobeyed had no legitimate sovereignty at all. It was a war of national liberation. The reasons for the nonviolence, which was what the "civil disobedience" amounted to, were twofold: Materially, Gandhi thought, probably correctly, that such a tactic would be ultimately less destructive of the country and people. (The Vietcong have judged otherwise, probably incorrectly.) Spiritually, Gandhi knew that such a means—of disciplined personal confrontation—would elevate people rather than brutalize them, and ease the transition to a necessary future community with the British.

The campaigns led by Dr. King in the South illustrate the drive against illegitimacy even more clearly. Segregation and denial of civil rights are illegitimate on the face of them; no human being would freely enter into such a degrading contract. Besides, King was able to rely on the contradiction between the illegitimate laws and a larger legitimate tradition of Christianity, the Declaration of Independence and the federal Constitution. Once the blacks made the challenge, the white Southerners could not maintain their inner confusion, and the federal government, though late and gracelessly, has had to confirm the protest.

Now, in resistance to the draft, Dr. Spock and Dr. Coffin declare that they are committing "civil disobedience" and are "willing and ready" to go to jail if convicted. No doubt they have a theory of what they are doing. Most of the co-conspirators, however, including myself, regard the present regime as frighteningly illegitimate, especially in military and imperial affairs; and we are not "willing" to accept the penalties for our actions, though we may have to pay them willy-nilly. The regime is illegitimate because it is dominated by a subsidized military-industrial group that cannot be democratically changed. There is a "hidden government" of CIA and FBI. The regime has continually lied and withheld information to deceive the American people; and with a federal budget of $425 millions for public relations, democratic choice becomes almost impossible. Even so, the President deliberately violated the overwhelming electoral mandate of 1964; it transpires that he planned to violate it even while he was running. The regime presents us with *faits accomplis*; the Senate balks with talk but in fact rubber-stamps the *faits accomplis*; it has become an image like the Roman senate in the first century. Many have resigned from the government, but they then do not "come clean" but continue to behave as members of the oligarchy. Disregarding the protests of millions and defying the opinion of mankind, the regime escalates an unjust war, uses horrible means, is destroying a culture and a people. Pursuing this berserk adventure, it neglects our own national welfare. Etc., etc. Then we judge that the government is a usurper and the Republic is in danger. On our present course, we will soon end up like the Romans, or 1984, or not survive at all.

Naturally, if the government is illegitimate, then at a public trial we ought to win. If the Americans are still a political community, we will—but of course, that is the question.

Let me make another point. The methods of protest we are using are positively good in themselves, as well as for trying to stop the Vietnam war. They characterize the kind of America I want, one with much more direct democracy, decentralized decision-making, a system of checks and balances that works, less streamlined elections. Our system should condone civil disobedience vigilant of authority, crowds on the street and riot when the provocation is grave. I am a Jeffersonian because it seems to me that only a libertarian, populist and pluralist political structure can make citizens at all in the modern world. This brings me back to the main subject of this essay, the social, technological and psychological conditions that underlie the present crisis of sovereignty and law.

The Sense of Sovereignty Lost

In highly organized countries, each in its own way, most of the major social functions, the economy, technology, education, communications, welfare, warfare and government, form a centrally organized system directed by an oligarchy. I do not think this structure is necessary for industrialization or high technology; it is not even especially efficient, certainly not for many functions. But is has been inevitable because of the present drives to power, reinvestment, armament and national aggrandizement.

The effects on citizenship have been variously compelling. Where the tradition was authoritarian to begin with and the national ideology is centralizing, as in Fascist Germany or Communist Russia, citizens have given allegiance to the industrial sovereign not much differently than to older despotisms, but with less leeway for private life, local custom or religion. In Communist China, where the new ideology is centralizing but the tradition was radically decentralist, there is a turbulence and struggle of allegiances. But in the United States, where both ideology and tradition have been decentralist and democratic, in the new dispensation citizenship and allegiance have simply tended to lapse. Since they can no longer effectually make important decisions about their destiny, Americans lose the sense of sovereignty altogether and retreat to privatism. Politics becomes just another profession, unusually phony, with its own professional personnel.

Our situation is a peculiar one. The Americans do not identify with the ruling oligarchy, which is foreign to their tradition; a major part of it—the military-industrial and the CIA and the FBI—is even a "hidden government." The politicians carefully cajole the people's sensibilities and respect their freedom, so long as these remain private. And we have hit on the following accommodation: in high matters of State, War and Empire, the oligarchy presents *faits accomplis*; in more local matters, people resent being pushed around. Budgets in the billions are not debated; small sums are debated.

The Constitution is what I described above: the social compact is acquiescence to the social machine, and citizenship consists in playing appropriate roles as producers, functionaries and consumers. The machine is productive; the roles, to such as have them, are rewarding. And human nature being what it is, there develops a new kind of allegiance, to the rich and streamlined style. This provides the norm of correct behavior for workmen, inspires the supermarkets, and emboldens soldiers at the front.

A typical and very important class is the new professionals. Being essential to tend the engine and steer, they are well paid in salary and prestige. An expensive system of education has been devised to prepare the young for these roles. At the same time, the professionals become mere personnel. There is no place for the autonomy, ethics, and guild spirit that used to characterize them as people and citizens. *Mutatis mutandis*, the same can be said of the working class.

On the other hand, large groups of the population are allowed to drop out as socially useless, for instance, farmers, racial minorities, the incompetent, the old, many of the young. These are then treated as objects of social engineering and are also lost as citizens.

In an unpolitical situation like this, it is hard for good observers to distinguish between riot and riotous protest, or between a juvenile delinquent, a rebel without a cause and an inarticulate guerrilla. On a poll, to say "I don't know," might mean one is judicious, a moron, or a cynic about the question or the options. Student protest may be political or adolescent crisis or alienation. Conversely, there is evidence that good behavior may be dangerous apathy or obsessional neurosis. According to a recent study, a selection by schoolteachers of well-rounded "all-American boys" proves to consist heavily of pre-psychotics.

With this background, we can understand "civil disobedience" and "lawlessness." What happens politically in the United States when the system steers a disastrous course? There is free speech and assembly and a strong tradition of democracy, but the traditional structures of remedy have fallen into desuetude or become phony. Bourgeois reformers, critical professionals, organizations of farmers and workmen, political machines of the poor have mainly been co-opted. Inevitably protest reappears at a more primitive or inchoate level.

The "civil disobedients" are nostalgic patriots without available political means. The new "lawless" are the oppressed without political means. Instead of having a program or a party, the protesters try, as Mario Savio said, to "throw themselves on the gears and the levers to stop the machine." Students think up ways to stop traffic; professionals form groups simply to nullify the law; citizens mount continual demonstrations and jump up and down with signs; the physically oppressed burn down their own neighborhoods. I think few of these people regard themselves as subversive. They know, with varying degrees of consciousness, that they are legitimate, the regime is not.

A promising aspect of it is the revival of populism, sovereignty reverting to the people. One can sense it infallibly during the big rallies, the March on Washington in '63 or the peace rallies in New York and at the Pentagon in

April and October '67. Except among a few Leninists, the mood is euphoric, the heady feeling of the sovereign people invincible—for a couple of hours. The draft-card burners are proud. The elders who abet them feel like Americans. The young who invest the Pentagon sing "The Star-Spangled Banner." The children of Birmingham attacked by dogs look like Christians. Physicians who support Dr. Levy feel Hippocratic, and professors who protest classified research feel academic. On the other hand, the government with the mightiest military power in the history of the world does not alter its course because of so much sweetness and light. The police of the cities are preparing an arsenal of anti-riot weapons. Organized workmen beat up peace picketers. We look forward apprehensively to August in Chicago.

But I am oversimplifying. In this romantic picture of the American people rising to confront the usurper, we must notice that Lyndon Johnson, the Pentagon and the majority of Americans are also Americans. And they and the new populists are equally trapped in modern times. Even if we survive our present troubles with safety and honor, can anything like the social contract exist again in contemporary managerial and technological conditions? Perhaps "sovereignty" and "law," in any American sense, are outmoded concepts.

This is the furthest I can take these reflections until we see more history.

The Crisis of Belief

Among the young especially, the crisis is a religious one, deeper than politics. The young have ceased to "believe" in something, and the disbelief occurs at progressively earlier years. What is at stake is not the legitimacy of American authority but of any authority. The professions, the disciplines, reasoning about the nature of things—and even if there is a nature of things—these are all distrusted.

Thus, for instance, the dissenting scientists and professors of MIT and Harvard, who want to change the direction of research and alter the priorities of technology, do not seem to me to understand the profound change in popular feeling. (They often seem just to be griping that the budget for basic Research has been reduced). Put it this way: modern societies have been operating as if religion were a minor and moribund part of the scheme of things. But this is unlikely. Men do not do without a system of meanings that everybody puts his hope in even if, or especially if, he doesn't know anything about it—what Freud called a "shared psychosis," meaningful simply because shared, and with the power that resides in dream. In advanced countries it is science and technology themselves that have gradually and finally triumphantly become the system of mass faith, not disputed by various political ideologies and nationalisms that have been religious. Marxism called itself "scientific socialism," as against moral and Utopian socialisms, and this has helped it succeed.

For three hundred years, science and scientific technology had an unblemished and justified reputation as a wonderful adventure, pouring out practical benefits and liberating the spirit from the errors of superstition and traditional faith. During the twentieth century, science and technology have been the only generally credited system of explanation and problem-solving. Yet in our generation they have come to seem to many, and to very many of the best of the young, as essentially inhuman, abstract, regimenting, hand in glove with Power, and even diabolical. Young people say that science is anti-life, it is a Calvinist obsession, it has been a weapon of white Europe to subjugate colored races, and manifestly—in view of recent scientific technology—people who think scientifically become insane.

The immediate reasons for this shattering reversals of values are fairly obvious—Hitler's ovens and his other experiments in eugenics, the first atom bombs and their frenzied subsequent developments, the deterioration of the physical environment and the destruction of the biosphere, the catastrophes impending over the cities because of technological failures and psychological stress, the prospect of a brainwashed and drugged 1984. Innovations yield diminishing returns in enhancing life. And instead of rejoicing, there is now widespread conviction that beautiful advances in genetics, surgery, computers, rocketry, or atomic energy will surely only increase human woe.

In such a crisis it is not sufficient to ban the military from the universities, and it will not even be sufficient, as liberal statesmen and many of the big corporations envisage, to beat the swords into ploughshares and turn to solving problems of transportation, desalinization, urban renewal, garbage disposal, cleaning up the air and water, and perfecting a contraceptive. If the present difficulty is religious and historical, it will be necessary to alter the entire relationship of science, technology, and human needs, both in fact and in men's minds.

I do not myself think that we will turn away from science. In spite of the fantasies of hippies, we are going to continue to live in a technological world; the question is, is that viable?

The closest analogy I can think of is the Protestant Reformation, a change of moral allegiance: not giving up the faith, but liberation from the Whore of Babylon and a return to the faith purified.

Science, the chief orthodoxy of modern times, has certainly been badly corrupted, but the deepest flaw of the affluent societies that has alienated the young is not, finally, imperialism, economic injustice, or racism, bad as these are, but the nauseating phoniness, triviality, and wastefulness, the cultural and moral scandal that Luther found when he went to Rome in 1510. And precisely science, which should have been the wind of truth to clear the air, has polluted the air, helped to brainwash, and provided weapons for war. I doubt that most young people today have even heard of the ideal of the dedicated researcher, truculent and incorruptible, and not getting any grants—the "German scientist" that Sinclair Lewis described in *Arrowsmith*. Such a figure is no longer believable. I don't mean, of course, that he doesn't exist; there must be thousands of him, just as there were good priests in 1510.

The analogy to the Reformation is even more exact if we consider the school system, from educational toys and Head Start up through the universities. This system is manned by the biggest horde of monks since the time of Henry VIII. It is the biggest industry in the country. It is mostly hocus-pocus. And the Abbots of this system are the chiefs of Science—e.g., the National

Science Foundation—who talk about reform but work to expand the school budgets, step up the curriculum, inspire the endless catechism of tests, and increase the requirements for mandarin credentials.

These abuses are international, as the faith is. For instance, there is no essential difference between the military-industrial systems, or the school systems, of the Soviet Union and the United States. There are important differences in way of life and standard of living, but the abuses of technology are very similar—pollution, excessive urbanization, destruction of the biosphere, weaponry, disastrous foreign aid. Our protesters naturally single out our own country, and the United States is the most powerful country, but the corruption we are speaking of is not specifically American nor capitalist; it a disease of modern times.

But the analogy is to the Reformation; it is not to primitive Christianity or some other primitivism, the abandonment of technological civilization. There is indeed much talk about the doom of Western civilization, young people cast horoscopes, and a few Adamites actually do retire into the hills, but for the great mass of mankind, that's not where it's at. Despite all the movements for National Liberation, there is not the slightest interruption to the universalizing of Western civilization, including most of its delusions, into the so-called Third World.

Needless to say, the prospect of a new Reformation is a terrifying one. Given the intransigence and duplicity of established Power on the one hand, and the fanaticism of the protesters on the other, we may be headed for a Thirty Years' War.

"Getting Into Power"
The ambiguities of
pacifist politics

"War is the health of the State"—modern history teaches no other lesson, whether we think of the weird personal, fanatic, and dynastic wars of the sixteenth and seventeenth centuries or the economic and geopolitical wars of recent generations. The sovereign national States have lived and grown by preparing for war and waging war; and as the Powers have aggrandized themselves, they have become more crashingly destructive. I do not mean that men have not used also simpler social organizations, feudal, tribal, free city, in order to kill one another *en masse*, but centralized sovereign power, radiating from baroque capitals, has proved to be the ideal executive of murderous will. In our own nation at present, it would be impossible to describe the economy without regarding war-making as a crucial factor; the foreign relations of the United States are carried on entirely in terms of bellicose power-blocs, and either to expand "influence" or to hang onto it; and to mention my own field where I can speak at first hand, our primary education and heavily State-subsidized higher education have become regimented to apprentice-training for war, more directly if less sickeningly than the psychological national regimentation endemic in French and German schooling. (The Russians go in for both the technological and psychological aspects.)

This solidifying of national sovereign bellicosity is at present all the more irrational, and of course all the more necessary, if the sovereigns are to maintain themselves, since the cultural, technological, economic, and communications relations of the world are now overwhelmingly supra-national. (What a pity that, partly to combat colonialism and partly out of the emulative stupidity and cupidity of their Western-trained leaders, peoples of Africa and Asia are adopting the same fatal and outmoded style.)

The only possible pacifist conclusion from these facts is the anarchist one, to get rid of the sovereignties and to diminish, among people, the motivations of power and grandiosity. This means, regionally, to decentralize or centralize directly in terms of life-functions, empirically examined. My own bias is to decentralize and localize wherever it is feasible, because this makes for alternatives and more vivid and intimate life. It multiplies initiative. And it is safer. On the basis of this weakening of the powers, and of the substitution of function for power, it would be possible also to organize the world community, as by the functional agencies of the United Nations, UNICEF, WHO, somewhat UNESCO); and to provide *ad hoc* cooperation like the Geo-physical Year, exploring space, or feeding the Chinese.

Rigidly applied, this logic would seem to make pacifist State politics absurd. It is not in the nature of sovereign power to decree itself out of existence. (Thus, it is absurd for picketers of the White House to petition Mr. Kennedy as the President, rather than to sermonize him as a man or lecture him as a boy.) Also, such politics confuses the basic issue, that *pacifism is necessarily revolutionary.* A moment's recollection of the defection of the French and German socialist deputies from their pacifism in 1914 will show that this confusion is not trivial. Nevertheless, the attitude of the General Strike for Peace is as follows: in November we shall urge people actively and explicitly to refuse to vote, to strike against voting, except for candidates who are unambiguously committed to immediate action to relax the Cold War, for instance Stuart Hughes or Robert Kastenmeier. Our reasoning is that, in our increasingly monolithic society and economy, any anti-war activity is likely to exert a revolutionary influence willy-nilly. And secondly, as Professor Hughes himself has said, the machinery of an electoral campaign *can* be a powerful means of education, especially by compelling mention of what the mass media ordinarily refuse to mention. We wish to cooperate with pacifist activity of *every* kind, whether SANE, Quaker, Third Party politics, or Committee for Nonviolent Action, because although "objectively" we are in a revolutionary situation in that the Powers-that-be are certainly bent on destroying themselves and everything else, nevertheless people do not take this seriously and there is an almost total lack of practical will to make the necessary reorganization of society. To say it grimly, unlike 1914, people do not even have political representatives to betray them.

The spirited candidacy of Stuart Hughes for Senator—like an actualization of Leo Szilard's courageous plan to finance and organize a national party for peace—makes it useful to review the ambiguities involved in this kind of politics.

Personally, what I enjoy about Professor Hughes' campaign is that often, when the students were out getting signatures to put him on the ballot, people would say, "Do you mean he is *neither* a Democrat *nor* a Republican? Then give me the pen!" (It is said, by people from Massachusetts, that this response is peculiarly appropriate to the ordinary local politics of Massachusetts; but I take this as local boasting.) In the deadly routine that the Americans have sunk into, the mere possibility of an *alternative* is a glorious thing, *especially* if there is the framework of a permanent organization. Also such a campaign must be a remarkable experience for Hughes himself, to confront many people who do not at all have the same assumptions. And it gives some concrete activity to his phalanx, the New England professors of the Council of Correspondence. The students of Brandeis, Harvard, etc., are also busy with it: but for them this kind of political involvement might be, in my opinion, more ambiguous, and that is why I am writing this essay.

For let me turn to an issue much deeper and more fateful for pacifism than these questions of strategy and tactics. This is the assumption, now appallingly unanimous among the ordinary electorate, professional politicians, most radicals, and even political scientists who should know better, that politics is essentially a matter of "getting into power," and then "deciding," directing, controlling, and coercing, the activities of society. The model seems to be taken from corporations with top-management, and there is something prestigious about being a "decision-maker." (Even C. Wright Mills was mesmerized by this image; but, as I tried to show recently in *Commentary*, in such a set-up less and less of human value is really decided by any responsible person, though plenty of disvalue is ground out by the set-up itself.) It is taken for granted that a man wants "power" of this kind, and it is quite acceptable for people like Joseph Kennedy and his sons to work toward it, even though this is directly contrary to the political ideal that the office and its duties seek the man rather than the man the office. It is axiomatic that a Party's primary purpose is to get into power, although this was not the original idea of "factions," in Madison's sense, which were functional but divisive interest groups. More dangerously still, it is taken for granted that a nation wants to be a Great Power, and maintain itself so at any cost, even though this may be disadvantageous to its culture and most of its citizens.

And following the popular Leviathan like a jolly-boat, the political-sociologists devote their researches to the analysis and simulation of power struggles, as if this were their only possible subject; and as advisers, they take part in the power struggles, rather than helping to solve problems. Unfortunately, the thinking of Hughes and Szilard seems to share some of this assumption about the paramountcy of "getting into power"—just as Dave Riesman is always hounding people who are in "power." And frankly, when I question such a universal consensus, I wonder if I am on the right planet. Nevertheless, these persons are deluded. They are taking a base and impractical, and indeed neurotic, state of affairs as if it were right and inevitable. The state of affairs is impractical because, finally, no good can come of it; though of course, since it *is* the state of affairs, it must be transiently coped with and changed. Unless we remember much more clearly than we seem to, what this "power" is, our behavior in the madhouse cannot be prudent and therapeutic. So with chagrin I find myself forced to review elementary political theory and history.

Living functions, biological, psycho-sociological, or social, have very little to do with abstract, preconceived "power" that manages and coerces from outside the specific functions themselves. Indeed, it is a commonplace that abstract power—in the form of "will power," "training," "discipline," "bureaucracy," "reform-schooling," "scientific management," etc.—uniformly *thwarts* normal functioning and debases the persons involved. (It has a natural use, in emergencies, when not high-grade but minimal low-grade behavior is required.) Normal activities do not need extrinsic motivations, they have their own intrinsic energies and ends-in-view; and decisions are continually made by the on-going functions themselves, adjusting to the environment and one another.

We may then define the subject of normal politics. It is the constitutional relations of functional interests and interest groups in the community in which they transact. This is the bread-and-butter of ancient political theory and obviously has nothing to do with sovereignty or even power—for the ancients the existence of Power implies unconstitutionality, tyranny. But even modern authors who move in a theory of "sovereignty," like Spinoza, Locke, Adam Smith, Jefferson, or Madison, understand that the commonwealth is strongest when the functional interests can seek their own level and there is the weakest exercise of "power." E.g. Spinoza tries to play power like a fish, Jefferson to de-energize it, Madison to balance it out.

Let us now quickly sketch the meaning of the recent transcendent importance of "power" and "getting into power," as if otherwise communities could not function.

First, and least important, there is the innocuous, nonviolent, and rather natural development of a kind of abstract power in an indigenous (non-invaded) society.

The functions of civilization include production, trade and travel, the bringing up of the young in the mores; also subtle but essential polarities like experimentation and stability; also irrational and superstitious fantasies like exacting revenge for crime and protecting the taboos. Different interests in the whole will continually conflict, as individuals or as interest groups; yet, since all require the commonwealth, there is also a strong functional interest in adjudication and peace, in harmonizing social invention or at least compromise. It is plausible that, in the interests of armistice and adjudication, there should arise a kind of abstract institution above the conflict, to settle them or to obviate them by plans and laws; this would certainly be Power. (This derivation is plausible but I doubt that it is historical, for in fact it is just this kind of thing that lively primitive communities accomplish by quick intuition tone of voice, exchange of a glance. and suddenly there is unanimity, to the anthropologist's astonishment.) Much more likely, and we know historically, abstract power is invented in simple societies in emergencies of danger, of enemy attack or divine wrath. But such "dictatorship" is *ad hoc* and surprisingly lapses. Surprisingly, considering that power corrupts; yet it makes psychological sense, for emergency is a negative function, to meet a threat to the pre-conditions of the interesting functions of life; once the danger is past, the "power" has no energy of function, no foreground interest, to maintain it. To give a very late example: it seemed remarkable to the Europeans, but not to the Americans, that Washington, like Cincinnatus, went home to his farm; and even the Continental Congress languished. There were no conditions for "power."

(Indeed—and this is why I have chosen the example—in the last decades of the eighteenth century, in many respects the Americans lived in a kind of peaceful community anarchy, spiced by mutinies that were hardly punished. The Constitution, as Richard Lee pointed out, was foisted on them by trickery, the work of very special interest groups; it would have been quite sufficient simply to amend the Articles.)

Altogether different from this idyll is the universal history of most of the world, civilized or barbarian. Everywhere is invasion, conquest, and domination, involving for the victors the necessity to keep and exercise power, and for the others the necessity to strive for power, in order to escape suffering and exploitation. This too is entirely functional. The conqueror is originally a pirate; he and his band do not share in the commonwealth, they have interests apart from the community preyed on. Subsequently, however, piracy becomes government, the process of getting people to perform by extrinsic motivations, of penalty and blackmail, and later bribery and training. But it is only the semblance of a commonwealth, for activity is directed. Necessarily, such directed and extrinsically motivated performance is not so strong, efficient, spontaneous, inventive, well structured, or lovely as the normal functioning of a free community of interests. Very soon society becomes lifeless. The means of community action, initiative, decision, have been preempted by the powerful. But the slaveholder, exploiters, and governors share in that same society and are themselves vitiated. Yet they never learn to get down off the people's back and relinquish their power. So some are holding on to an increasingly empty power; others are striving to achieve it; and most are sunk in resignation. Inevitably, as people become stupider and more careless, administration increases in size and power; and conversely. By and large, the cultures that we study in the melancholy pages of history are pathetic mixtures, with the ingredients often still discernible: there is a certain amount of normal function surviving or reviving—bread is baked, arts and sciences are pursued by a few, etc.; mostly we see the abortions of lively social functioning saddled, exploited, prevented, perverted, drained dry, paternalized by an imposed system of power and management that preempts the means and makes decisions *ab extra*. And the damnable thing is that, of course, everybody believes that except in this pattern, nothing could possibly be accomplished: if there were no marriage-license and no tax, none could properly mate and no children be born and raised; if there were no tolls there would be no bridges; if there were no university charters, there would be no higher learning; if there were no usury and no Iron Law of Wages, there would be no capital; if there were no mark-up of drug prices, there would be no scientific research. Once a society has this style of thought, that every activity requires licensing, underwriting, deciding by abstract power, it becomes inevitably desirable for an ambitious man to seek power and for a vigorous nation to try to be a Great Power. The more that have the power-drive, the more it seems to be necessary to the others to compete, or submit, just in order to survive. (And importantly they are right.) Many are ruthless and most live in fear.

Even so, this is not the final development of the belief in "power." For that occurs when to get into power, to be prestigious and in a position to make decisions, is taken to be the social good itself, apart from any functions that it is thought to make possible. The pattern of dominance-and-submission has then been internalized and, by its clinch, fills up the whole of experience. If a man is not continually proving his potency, his mastery of others and of himself, he becomes prey to a panic of being defeated and victimized. Every vital function must therefore be used as a means of proving or it is felt as a symptom of weakness. Simply to enjoy, produce, learn, give or take, love or be angry (rather than cool), is to be vulnerable. This is different, and has different consequences, from the previous merely external domination and submission. A people that has life but thwarted functions will rebel when it can, against feudal dues, clogs to trade, suppression of thought and speech, taxation without representation, insulting privilege, the iron law of wages, colonialism. But our people do not rebel against poisoning, genetic deformation, and imminent total destruction.

Rather, people aspire to be top-managers no matter what the goods or services produced. One is a promoter, period; or a celebrity, period. The Gross National Product must increase without consideration of the standard of life. There is no natural limit, so the only security is in deterrence. The environment is rife with projected enemies. There is a huddling together and conforming to avoid the vulnerability of any idiosyncrasy, at the same time as each one has to be one-up among his identical similars. Next, there is excitement in identifying with the "really" powerful, the leaders, the Great Nations, the decision-makers, dramatized on the front page. But these leaders, of course, feel equally powerless in the face of the Great Events. For it is characteristic of the syndrome that as soon as there is occasion for any practical activity, toward happiness, value, spirit, or even simple safety, everyone suffers from the feeling of utter powerlessness; the internalized submissiveness now has its innings. Modern technology is too complex; there is a population explosion; the computer will work out the proper war-game for us; they've got your number, don't stick your neck out; "fall-out is a physical fact of our nuclear age, it can be faced like any other fact" (*Manual of Civil Defense*); "I'm strong, I can take sex or leave it" (eighteen-year-old third-offender for felonious assault). In brief, the under-side of the psychology of power is that Nothing Can Be Done; and the resolution of the stalemate is to explode. This is the Cold War.

I have frequently explored this psychology of proving, resignation, and catastrophic explosion (Wilhelm Reich's "primary masochism"), and I shall not pursue it again. It is filling the void of vital function by identifying with the agent that has frustrated it; with, subsequently, a strongly defended conceit, but panic when any occasion calls for initiative, originality, or even animal response. Here I have simply tried to relate this psychology to the uncritical unanimous acceptance of the idea of "getting into power in order to . . ." or just "getting into power" as an end in itself. There is a vicious circle, for (except in emergencies) the very exercise of abstract power, managing and coercing, itself tends to stand in the way and alienate, to thwart function and diminish energy, and so to increase the psychology of power. But of course the consequence of the process is to put us in fact in a continual emergency, so power creates its own need. I have tried to show how, historically, the psychology has been exacerbated by the miserable system of extrinsic motivation by incentives and punishments (including profits, wages, unemployment), reducing people to low-grade organisms no different than Professor Skinner's pigeons; whereas normal function is intrinsically motivated toward specific ends-in-view, and leads to growth in inventiveness and freedom. Where people are not directly in feeling contact with what is to be done, nothing is done well and on time; they are always behind and the emergency becomes chronic. Even with good intentions, a few managers do not have enough *mind* for the needs of society—not even if their computers gallop through the calculations like lightning. I conclude that the consensus of recent political scientists that political theory is essentially the study of power-maneuvers, is itself a neurotic ideology. Normal politics has to do with the relations of specific functions in a community; and *such a study would often result in practical political inven-*

tions that would solve problems—it would not merely predict elections and solve nothing, or play war-games and destroy mankind.

Let me sum up these remarks in one homely and not newsy proposition: throughout the world, it is bad domestic politics that creates the deadly international politics. Conversely, pacifism is revolutionary: we will not have peace unless there is a profound change in social structure, including getting rid of national sovereign power.

Concretely, our system of government at present comprises the military-industrial complex, the secret paramilitary agencies, the scientific war-corporations, the blimps, the horse's asses, the police, the administrative bureaucracy, the career diplomats, the lobbies, the corporations that contribute Party funds, the underwriters and real-estate promoters that batten on Urban Renewal, the official press and the official opposition press, the sounding-off and jockeying for the next election, the National Unity, etc., etc. All this machine is grinding along by the momentum of the power and profit motives and style long since built into it; it *cannot* make decisions of a kind radically different than it does. Even if an excellent man happens to be elected to office, he will find that it is no longer a possible instrument for social change on any major issues of war and peace or the way of life of the Americans. Indeed, as the members of the Liberal Project have complained, office does not give even a good public forum, for the press does not report inconvenient speeches.

So we must look, finally, not to this kind of politics, but to direct functioning in what concerns us closely, in order to dispel the mesmerism of abstract power altogether. This has, of course, been the thinking of radical pacifism. The civil disobedience of the Committee for Nonviolent Action is the direct expression of each person's conscience of what it is impossible for him to live with. The studied withdrawal and boycotting advocated by the General Strike for Peace is a direct countering of the social drift toward catastrophe that occurs just because we cooperate with it. (The same holds for refusal in what is one's "private" important business, like the Women's Strike against poisoned milk or young men's refusing the draft.) Best of all, in principle, is the policy that Dave Dellinger espouses and tries to live by, to live communally and without authority, to work usefully and feel friendly, and so *positively to replace an area of power with peaceful functioning.* Interestingly, even a critical and purgative group like *The Realist* is coming around to this point of view—with a hard row to hoe among urban poor people. Similar is to work in foreign lands as a citizen of humanity, trying to avoid the Power blocs and their aims; e.g. the Friends Service. The merit of all these activities is that they produce a different kind of human relations and look to a different quality of life. This is a global and perhaps impossibly difficult task. But think. There is no history of mankind without these wars, which now have come to the maximum: can we have any hope except in a different kind of human relations?

It will be said that there is no time. Yes, probably. But let me cite a remark of Tocqueville. In his last work, *L'Ancien Régime*, he notes "with terror," as he says, how throughout the eighteenth century writer after writer and expert after expert pointed out that this and that detail of the Old Régime was unviable and could not possibly survive; added up, they proved that the entire Old Régime was doomed and must soon collapse; and yet *there was not a single man who foretold that there would be a mighty revolution.*

Social Criticism

In the past decade, there has accumulated a whole literature of sweeping critique of American institutions that has come to be called Social Criticism, and I shall try to locate some specific properties of this genre. I think it has peculiarities, different from other literature of protest, polemic, and satire. Much of it has been excellent and acute as sociology and moral philosophy; much of it has been immensely popular, including some pretty meretricious performances. There is no doubt that it has had an important influence on the cultural tone of the present, yet very little influence on apparent social and political behavior. This certainly merits examination. In this essay, I shall avoid mentioning particular works and authors, but just think of the ground covered, the multiplicity of targets!—the lonely crowd, the manufactured taste, the wasteful production, the tailfin cars, the pseudo-news, suburban emptiness, career anxiety, the paper-economy, the disillusionment of youth, the administered colleges, the conformist executive, the bureaucratic labor-union, the inhuman housing, the perverted use of sociology and psychology, the garrison state, the power-elite, the damaging motherhood, the poisoned land, the insidious advertising, the devolution of democracy. I stop at twenty.

In some of the authors, the peculiar "social criticism" quality, desperate sweeping attack on the general cultural tone, is part of a more specialist scientific analysis, including constructive suggestions, in economics and technology, sexology and pedagogy, ecology and city-planning, etc. And the criticism naturally aims at traditional objects of political and moral reform, at race-prejudice, poverty, political graft, bureaucratic stupidity, the arms race. Nevertheless we must explore how Social Criticism is different from scientific analysis and reform politics.

Conversely, there is nothing new about Social Criticism itself. Especially since the First World War, in such diverse writers as Benda and Ortega, or Mumford and Borsodi, or Freud, the tone is often very like our contemporary critique. In the preceding century, since the Industrial Revolution, much moral philosophy and even most of sociology, sounds somewhat like Social Criticism, in Coleridge, Ruskin, Proudhon, Marx, Veblen. Earlier, the tone is, if anything, more unmistakable, among the satirists and *philosophes*, Voltaire, Swift, Rousseau, Mandeville, and so back to Erasmus and the Reformation, Rabelais and Cervantes, and the Millenarians and proto-reformers of the Middle Ages. The sentiment that it is not this-or-that that is wrong, but all of the way men go about living. But it is just in this historical perspective that we can notice how the present literature is unique.

2.

Let's make a quick survey of other literatures of social protest. First there is the satire and invective of a Loyal Opposition. It is loyal in the sense that it accepts the existing social structure or State, but attacks the government or party in power. In muck-raking, however, this opposition is more outraged and desperate, for it is felt that the abuse includes all the available parties, not merely the one ostensibly in power. Muck-raking therefore verges easily into frankly revolutionary propaganda; it wants to subvert the State and change the social institutions. The question is, which institutions? How profound a change is necessary? Economy and politics? Law? Technology? Family and Morals? Science and Religion? Education and Child-Care?

In theory, frank revolutionists like Marx and Proudhon wanted rather total change, and they reasoned that changes in productive and legal relations would encompass all the other necessary changes. In fact, however, they assumed that enlightened men—enlightened according to the contemporary standard—industrialized or craftsmanlike, were solid stuff to make a revolution with. They really did not question the education, science, esthetics, family morals, or technology of the times. The problem was, as Engels said, to replace the government over people by an administration of things.

But if we go back to the French Revolutionary writers, Voltaire, Rousseau, de Sade, we meet a more thoroughgoing dismay and a tone in some ways more like our own. For they felt that not only was the regime corrupt but it had corrupted the entire nature of man. But the *nature* of man was not corrupt; mankind was not inhuman but vicious; and the cure was Enlightenment itself, to make men rational, wholesome, and free. Accordingly, there was, until 1787, almost no overtly "revolutionary" writing (perhaps Paine); rather, the writers are busy with primitive anthropology, permissive pedagogy, the religion of reason, politics as a science, natural economics. The revolution was bound to occur; they were looking to a post-revolutionary reconstruction. It was as if, on the one hand, the thorough-going critique of regime and of mankind corrupted by it made any attempt at political power seem irrelevant, if not wicked; but, on the other hand, the power of the regime itself was largely illusory, because it was grounded in superstition and was morally bankrupt, whereas men were potentially reasonable and good and would simply be stronger. We can see exactly this strain persisting through the nineteenth and twentieth centuries in the radical anarchist writers, who look to total revolution and reconstruction by pedagogy, civil liberty, and decentralization in industry and administration.

But there was finally, in the eighteenth century and earlier, back through the Reformation, a rather different strain of critique that also interestingly resembles our own. Men—so Swift or Erasmus felt—are really impossible by nature, and nothing can be done. The tone is dismayed but detached and often humorous (except when it becomes pious, as in Bunyan). Our humanity is, has been, and will be a disaster. Luckily, God keeps things going. In this vein, Social Criticism merges on one side with general moral satire and on the other side with eschatological religion.

3.

How does our Social Criticism resemble and differ from these older strains? Our writers too are variously politically and morally outraged, revolution-ist, Utopian, apocalyptic, or humorously complacent. What constitutes their writing as a genre is a peculiar combination of these attitudes that, naturally, closely answers our contemporary social plight.

(1) They express a fairly global dismay. Each critic tends to choose a par-ticular target for his informed protest, but it is clear that he considers it as part of a pervasive evil. As we have seen, urbanism, economy, work-attitudes, administration, education, etc. are each singled out as being in intolerably bad shape. Taken together, they make up pretty much the whole of social life. But significantly, unlike in former times, there is not much complaint about basic subsistence, health, exploitation of labor, cruelty to children; though of course there are angry books on poverty, poisoning, and nuclear war. This is signifi-cant because the great revolutionary motivation of physical pain and immedi-ate distress is, in America, diminished; the biological dangers that are cried up require imagination to understand.

(2) The criticism is not only global but irrefutable. The writers polemically exaggerate, but by and large the readers feel that their books make articulate what everybody has dumbly known anyway.

And there is almost no rebuttal, except snide insults in *Time* or peevish reviews that point out inaccuracies but concede that there is much in the main burden. One has the impression that the authors of the Establishment dare not rebut or are morally bankrupt; and indeed, that the powers-that-be are so strong, or think they are, that they do not need moral justification, but will continue just as they please no matter what is said. There is no doubt that the overbearing centralization, war-budgeting, commercialism are continually both more ruthless and blander.

(3) Nevertheless, similar to the lull before the French Revolution, there is little expression of revolutionary spirit, certainly not in the form of an organized counter-program, nor even—except in the apocalyptic poets—of an emotional plea for withdrawal or rebellion commensurate with the evil. It is as if there were no "total" alternative. Partly, I think, this is because of the conviction that under contemporary conditions any sweeping revolution, whether brought about by violent or political means, would end up with the very same evils and maybe worse. Partly, it is that there is a lack of social imagination of alternatives to the way of life. As I have frequently argued, this lack of imagination, the sentiment that "Nothing Can Be Done," is self-causing and self-proving in the very conditions that the critics attack.

(4) Rather, eerily, in the face of admitted general evils and continuing debasement that men do not strive to change, it is not a common feeling among the critics that *Man* is to be despaired of. This kind of issue is hardly raised, except among professional theologians who, in the manner of Niebuhr, are smug about it and condone even the Cold War. Among the critical, even nuclear annihilation is not regarded religiously but as a kind of objective apocalypse that does not spring from human corruption or divine wrath. (Among ordinary people there is a kind of disgusting panic at crises like the Cuban crisis of last fall, including frantic inquiries about tickets to New Zealand; but a week later business goes on as usual. So also the Jews went to the gas-chambers.) In brief, although social life is criticized as quite generally intolerably unworthy and possibly suicidal—and though the criticism is not refuted—yet men are not moved, nor urged, to change their ways. Even more strange, this human callousness or apathy is not itself challenged as the evil. Not much is said about either despairing of, or changing, "human nature." Indeed, "changes in human nature," for example, by drugs or conditioning, are correctly taken as the province of the Establishment itself, at its worst.

4.

Such is the paradoxical combination of attitudes of Social Criticism. It is not hard to see the underlying conditions of modern life that call for such a combination. Simply, that industrialization, urbanization, political growth, and the technological applications of accumulating physical science have occurred under the auspices of centralizing power, for the purposes of profits and aggrandizement, and in a logistic and bureaucratic style that suited the discipline of national armies, the collection of taxes, and the production of standard commodities in an economy of scarcity. But diminishing initiative and creating fundamental stupidity. To revert to Engel's formula, we have an administration of things of such a sort that men have become things. In advanced countries immediate physical hardship has diminished, and people are by and large allowed, or even encouraged, to cower into private life for human comfort; but meanwhile top-down public administration controls functions of daily behavior, common sense, taste, education, communication, and science that were formerly either spontaneous or traditional.

In recent decades, the abuse has galloped. Advanced countries have become over-capitalized, over-organized and wrongly organized, over-educated and wrongly educated to a degree that the capitalization and organization, and their thought and style, seem to run like an automatic machine, by its own motivation and for its own sake. The running is valueless and dangerous, but the critics of it, while registering their dismay, do not blame the persons who "run" it or are run by it, and they do not rally people against it, for people have become brainwashed. They cannot act otherwise than as parts of the machine. There is no thinkable alternative, and any suggestion of one rouses anxiety. Any revolutionary action, it is deeply believed, must use the same methods and must come out with the same results as being parts of a very similar machine.

In my opinion, the brainwashing and the timid conformity are not technological or moral, but are caused by confusion, stupidity, and anxiety. People would not be so much influenced by mass-communications, bureaucratic routines, and the pressures of garrison states, if they were in a more normal mental state to begin with. Normally it does not take long reflection to make a little sense, and the mutual encouragement of a few people leads to the beginning of action. But under the best circumstances, the industrial, urban, and technological revolutions involve immense new learning and adjustment; they should have taken place in moderate doses to meet real needs, with plenty of reasoning and voluntary choice, instead of pellmell and compelled by irrelevant power and profit considerations. Just as industrially backward people are cast into tribal and cultural chaos by the beginnings of industrialism, which they have not developed in their own style, so more slowly industrialized societies have been unready for the later stages. Surplus productivity and the plethora of goods and leisure become themselves problematic. Add the fairly sudden diminishing of religious and other traditions without replacement by any comparable interpretations of human experience; and the rapid development of the world community hampered, distorted, and disordered by Nation-States and Great Powers, imperialism and neo-imperialism. These sources of confusion would themselves create enormous public anxiety. But again add to them brute fear, of vast wars and civil policing, and the anxiety has deepened to actual paralysis of initiative and blacking out of social invention. Certainly at present we cannot hope for any generally useful thought or social experiment till we get rid of the Cold War; yet how to do that under the present auspices? People feel that they cannot afford to risk any change, at the same time that they know they are doomed if they continue as at present.

It is this contemporary plight that Social Criticism is about. Though the different critics pursue different quarries, there is one global cluster of complaints. Our society is out of human scale, mechanical, stupid, venal, base, biologically dangerous, massified and socialized without community, regimenting and brainwashing, dedicated to procedure and format rather than function and meaning. Its moral justification is really a self-proving superstition; it "solves" in its own style problems that it has created itself; its research is incestuously staffed from its own bureaucrats who work for their own aggrandizement and cannot see anything else.

5.

Given the underlying reality, such criticism is inevitable. As I have said, it is rarely rebutted, but the critics themselves are called Luddite, snobbish, bucolic, eighteenth-century, sixteenth-century, Utopian. These charges simply mean that people are so brainwashed that they cannot, or do not want to, conceive of technology, city-planning, and politics, or even advertising and the TV managed otherwise than at present. Another charge is that the critics are oblivious to the realities of power, *Realpolitik*, the profit-system, the power elite; one cannot change the system by decrying it, one must get power. Since the very machinery of getting into power and wielding power is at present a chief cause of the trouble, it is pointless to ask us to affirm "realities" that defeat our purposes. (In his last period, by the way, C. Wright Mills was entranced by the need to get into power. In *The Causes of World War Three* he has a paean to the great *advantage* of unified top-down decision-making, since the boss can then solve all at one stroke!—Max Weber's bureaucracy and charisma gone mad.) People are trapped in a system admittedly absurd, but the critics do not offer any alternatives.

A more serious charge is that the criticism is merely destructive. Literally, this is rarely true. Many of the critics sketch out alternatives to what they are criticizing, sometimes knowledgeably, sometimes amateurishly. Intellectual men do not oppose something without some vague concrete image of what would replace it; the thought of how things should be done is what makes one dissatisfied with how they are done. (Needless to say, nothing comes of these positive suggestions, which are "Utopian.") Furthermore, many things in our society hardly need to be replaced. What may be called for is not doing, or fulfilling the function in a simpler or more direct way. If a society suffers from glut, ritual, and greed, destructive ridicule is positive.

But this is the real weakness of Social Criticism, as of all moral satire. It disregards the fact that people *cannot* do otherwise than they do, and especially if the message is simply to stop, survey the scene, and make easier sense. This rouses intense anxiety, for people would have to fill the void with their own initiative, which is just what they are afraid of. It is easier to sell other complicated expedients or the "posture of sacrifice," as the President has called it. Social Criticism is ineffectual not because it does not explain how to get power and administer its ideals, but because it does not awaken initiative, the source of power. Despite the prevalent superstition to the contrary, there could be alternative ways of modern life, and some of the critics propose them, but the point is for people to feel themselves differently than they do. I suppose that, for this, we require not critics but prophets. Or, as Wilhelm Reich kept telling us, psychiatrists.

6.

Paying attention to the products of the social machine and the inane workings of the machine itself, Social Critics have mostly ignored the underlying social psychology, obvious as it is. Their cultural dismay is genuine, but they take much too lightly the absence of initiative, morale, or commitment; their tone has neither indignation nor Utopian aspiration; they seem to be reconciled to people having no souls, in Aristotle's simple sense that the soul is self-moving and initiating and goes toward its good. Perhaps they are misled by the absence of immediate physical suffering (the authors who deal with insanity, police brutality, juvenile delinquency are far more passionate and political); certainly they misread the psychology of the middle-class. They take the conformity as unpleasant complacency rather than resignation; they do not understand that the smiling and togetherness cover anxiety; in the apathy about nuclear war, they do not recognize paralysis caused by the repression of explosive masochism, ready for panic.

In this misunderstanding, our critics are inferior to their predecessors. The social-revolutionaries, for example, Marx or Bakunin, correctly relied on physical deprivation to rouse action (they did not foresee that in the advanced economy the standard of living would rise). The *philosophes*, even when they were mechanists, were sure that people had initiating souls and would resist indignity if once they were disenchanted of their superstitions. Among the older moralists, those who were more good-natured, like Erasmus, Montaigne, and Mandeville, were not cynical about the impossible animal Man, because they knew that man's inevitable vices and follies were natural and gave real satisfaction; and those who were bitter or fiery, like Swift or Luther, took vice and hypocrisy as belonging to men fallen, something to despise or contest with the Devil. By contrast, what does the tone of our contemporary critics mean, whether witty, sensational, cynical, or "objective"?

Evidently, the Social Criticism is part of the system that it criticizes. As one who writes it myself, let me mention several human feelings that it expresses. Most weakly, we are indulging in a kind of griping, not much different from dissatisfied soldiers in any regiment. So society lets off steam, while the real war rolls on. More important (in my own case) it is a kind of spite, the vitality of the powerless, the attempt to make the powerful feel bad, guilty, cheap, foolish, as they roll on.

An obvious virtue of some Social Criticism—part and parcel of the social mores—is to one-up one's fellows. For instance, everybody on Madison Avenue is doing a certain song and dance, but the social critic knows it and points it out, to their disgrace; he himself, to be sure, continues to perform on Madison Avenue, but he can pose, or perhaps feel himself, as a superior individual, a critic. A more desperate and honorable nuance of the same— which feels more like myself—is the defiant cry of lonely reason in a city of unreason, literarily bearing witness. I have seen a gentleman from one of the Foundations burst into tears because proposals of mine were so right and so useless. They were Paradise Lost.

Alas, it is this very witness-bearer who is most useful, perhaps indispensable, for the system he is attacking. He is their court jester, who keeps clear before them the true, the good, and the beautiful as they do otherwise. He helps articulate and work off whatever self-contempt they feel. He provides the excellent entertainment of conversation-pieces. Great national magazines print one such piece of trenchant honesty every fourth issue. It can be said, indeed, that it is precisely the excellent Social Criticism that has hastened the brazenness of the powers-that-be as they roll on, and has made them more ruthless. For now the more sensitive and intelligent know they are morally bankrupt and they proceed like pure hipsters. It is only the utter stuffed shirts and horse's asses who can make public speeches with a good conscience, as they roll on. (This is the chief difference between Democrats and Republicans.)

To be sure, these fools are rolling themselves, and perhaps the country, to destruction. As writers, we are only writers; and everybody knows, these days, that writing can be taken in stride. It has no relation to action, or even, sometimes, it contains suggestive ideas that can be misused out of context. Nevertheless, what we critics say is largely true; it has that property, though no influence.

7.

Arthur Schlesinger, the sage of the White House, has publicly urged us dissenters (especially me) to continue our indispensable role of dissent. And my own experience has, indeed, been the following: I am invited to be part of the left wing at national *conferences* and *panel-discussions,* too numerous to mention; I have not been invited to sit down on a decision-making board; and the decisions of the actual boards are *not* such as we critics could approve.

Even more interesting is the relation of Social Criticism to the social sciences. Some of us writers are almost universally praised, even in the learned journals, for the insight that we have as "generalists," disregarding disciplinary boundaries; the "fresh look" that we have by not wearing professional blinders; and the forthrightness of our propositions that are not written in Choctaw. All this means, usually, is that we point to something relevant that is obvious, but that professionals are carefully trained to overlook. I have not heard nor personally experienced, however, that we writers are called on to help in scientific work on practical problems. Thus, since there is no social science that is not pragmatic and experimental, our own knowledge remains dilettantish; while professional social science continues as it has been, with social engineering for the *status quo* or academic boondoggling.

Such experiences impress one neither with the honor or practicality of the established powers; nor with the practical relevance of Social Critics.

Politics Within Limits

If I undertake to say
the conscience of my country,
    I only do my duty.
    But, Lord, it was not I

who chose it, but the hungry heart
and level look that you allotted
    to me when you did burden
    with different gifts different men.

There is an odd abstraction "Society," that has exercised a superstitious compulsion on political scientists since the time of Bentham, Comte, Hegel, and Marx; instead of the loose matrix of face-to-face communities, private fantasies, and shifting subsocieties in which most people mostly live their lives. It is understandable that fatherly czars or divine-right monarchs would have the delusion that all the sparrows are constantly under their tutelage as Society; and that Manchester economists would sternly rule out of existence all family, local, and non-cash transactions that cannot be summed up on the Stock Exchange. The usual strategy of Enlightenment philosophers, however, was to cut such big fictions down to size and to have simple real abuses to reform. But after the French Revolution, it was as if, to substitute for the slogan L'Ancien Régime, it was necessary to have a concept equally grand, Society.

Comte and Bentham wanted to make the big fiction of Society for real—Comte knew that it started as a fiction—in order to use it to tidy up "everything" or at least "the greatest good for the greatest number." For metaphysical reasons, Hegel was satisfied that the more socialized a man, and the more self-conscious of it, the more real he was. But the pathetic case is Marx, who concentrated on Society and indeed wanted to empower Society, precisely to get rid of it and go back to simpler personal and community existence.

Certainly there are occasions when my existence as a mere member of Society is overwhelmingly important and not at all an abstraction, for example when they herd me onto a big airliner, with its backup of thousands of anony-mous operatives and their schedules and instruments. But even so, after the initial shock, I soon recover and become restive for a more attractive seat-mate, or look for a couple of empties so I can stretch out and go to sleep, or I press my nose to the window and watch the clouds and the receding earth.

Usually my need for Society is satisfied by a very loose criterion: "Lucky is the man who can band together with enough of those like-minded with himself—it needs only a couple of hundred—to reassure him that he is sane, even though eight million others are quite batty" (*Empire City*, iv, 19, i).

By a good intuition, the best of the young dissidents disown abstract Society and want to be "just human." But they still reify it too much as the hostile "System," which exists but less than they think. Since they do not know concretely enough what they mean by "just human," they need a tan-gible adversary to give themselves shape. (But how, at my age, would I know what they mean?)

Most words of ordinary speech, of course, are simple abstractions, for classes of persons, things, relations, and so forth. Except in poetry and socia-ble chatter, the feel of the usual words is not Here, Now, Next—these are reduced to adverbs. Instrumental speech is likely to be abstract.

Simple abstractions need not be problematic. I can say, "There are our friends coming" and soon the words are "You—Here—Now—We—Next." But when there are difficulties—for instance, what if they are not our friends, and do not even speak our language and do not want to share our experience?—then we must resort to psychotherapy, politics, and pastoral theology to unmake alienation.

The critical question for me is how to have, or make, those abstractions "Organism," "Environment," "History," so that they can possibly interact to reconstitute primary experience. I have written ten books on this question in various contexts. "To have an environment and not take it as an object, is Tao," said Chuang-tzu. Sometimes I state my program in the form, "How to take on Culture without losing Nature," but that is already too abstract.

A conclusion I have reached is this: Like Luther, but unlike Hegel or Marx, I think that the way to overcome alienation is to go home and not on a tour through history and the realms of being. It is also true, however, that a man who is on the Way deviates and does not err.

In *Gestalt Therapy*, I reason my way into the subject as follows: If we envisage an animal moving, continually seeing new scenes and meeting new problems to cope with, it will continually have to make a creative adjust-ment. Selecting, initiating, shaping, in order to appropriate the novelty of the environment to itself, and to screen out what would destroy homeostasis.

Adjusting, because the organism's every living power is actualized only in its environment. And the environment, for its part, must be amenable to appropriation and selection; it must be plastic to be changed and meaningful to be known. The precipice that you fall off is not your environment.

Aristotle says it succinctly, "Food is the unlike that can become like." Or, in a passage I have already quoted, "Perceiving is the identity of the object of sense and the activated sensory organ."—I like to quote Aristotle on these matters because he was the sophisticated climax of *prima facie* observations, and his formulations are dryly pithy lecture notes. But I do not think his doctrine was different from Kant's, who was critical of two thousand years of philosophizing and came to the same *prima facie* observations, "The percept is blind, the concept is empty," "the synthetic unity of apperception," "judgment is not a categorical proposition."

Then I conclude, abnormal psychology is the therapy of disturbances of creative adjustment, for example, rigid or archaic responses.

And we can speak similarly of abnormal sociology: it is politics, to remedy institutions that hinder experience from occurring, for example, roles rather than vocations, individuals or collectives rather than people in communities, whatever prevents citizens from initiating and deciding, or makes it complicated for craftsmen and professionals to practice.

There is no politics but remedial politics; often the first remedy is to take "Society" less seriously, and to notice what society one has.

As I review my books of social criticism and my occasional trips in therapy and politics, I am pleased at how they flow temperamentally from my biases about experience. My kind of anarchism, pacifism, and decentralism; opposition to mandarinism and schooling; emphasis on vocation and profession; ecology and neighborhood in physical planning; rural reconstruction; intermediate technology for underdeveloped regions; my "neolithic conservatism"—these are congenial to a bias for the concrete, finite, and artistic, *universale in re* and intrinsic end-in-view. Such as they are, my political ideas are authentic. In fact, I haven't changed them since I was a boy, though there has been a lot of history since then. This must be partly because I don't learn anything, but it is partly because political truth is so simple that a boy can see it with a frank look, namely: Society with a big S can do very little for people except to be tolerable, so they can go on about the more important business of life.

It's an impressive list of topics that I spread myself thin over. To me, naturally, my opinions confirm one another by being coherent with one another wherever I look. The proof of a literary style is that it is viable over a wide range of experience, to say it.

A generalist is a man who knows something about many special sciences, in order to coordinate their conclusions in a system that has little relation to reality. A man of letters knows only a little about some major human concerns, but insists on relating what he does know to his concrete experience. So he explores reality. A generalist is interdisciplinary. A man of letters finds that the nature of things is not easily divided into disciplines.

My social ideas are temperamentally mine, but they do not derive logically from my biases, as a doctrine. I would abhor a politics, pedagogy, or town-planning deduced from metaphysics or epistemology, or even scientifically deduced, rather than being pragmatic and not immoral. One must not manipulate real people because of an idea or a confirmed hypothesis. Indeed, I say "not immoral" rather than "moral" because positive morality, when used as a principle for action, can be more abstract and imperial than anything. There are far too many missionaries among my friends.

But instead of being abstract or moral, my corresponding defect is that I am an artist and fundamentally unpolitical. I don't (timidly) bestir myself to oppose anything or try to change it unless I first have imagined a simpler and more artistic way to do it, neater, making use of available materials, less senseless, less wasteful. If a bad situation is not amenable to my flash of inventiveness, I find it hard to identify with it as mine; I feel there's nothing that I can contribute. Meantime people are suffering. But a political person ploughs into the situation and makes a difference in it just by his action. Sometimes a good idea then turns up.

Artistic visions have their virtues. (Let me speak no evil of the Creator Spirit.) They are better than carping criticism. They give people a ray of light instead of the gloom of metaphysical necessity. Activism and ideology both do more harm than good. But art has the unpolitical self-sufficiency of art. I am not zealous to make my models real. And they have the timidity of being personal; I draw no strength from my fellows; I cannot lead and find it hard to follow.

One cannot rely on artists for a political message. Tolstoy makes war seem sublime and attractive. Homer makes it senseless and horrible.

But I mustn't overstate my diffidence. I, like anybody else, see outrages that take me by the throat, and no question of not identifying with them as mine. Insults to the beauty of the world that keep me indignant. Lies, triviality, and vulgarity that suddenly make me sick. The powers-that-be do not know what it is to be magnanimous; often they are simply officious and spiteful. As Malatesta used to say, you try to live better and they intervene, and then you are to blame for the fight that happens. Worst of all, it is clear from their earth-destroying actions that these people are demented, sacrilegious, and will bring down doom on themselves and those associated with them; so sometimes I am superstitiously afraid to belong to the same tribe and walk the same ground as they.

Yet men have a right to be crazy, stupid, or arrogant. It is our specialty. Our mistake is to arm anybody with collective power. Anarchy is the only safe polity.

It is a moral disaster to suppress indignation, nausea, and scorn; it is a political (and soon moral) disaster to make them into a program. Their right political use is negative, to band together to stop something.

It is a common misconception that anarchists hold that "human nature is good" and therefore men can rule themselves. But we tend rather to be pessimistic. We are phlegmatic because we do not have ideas. And men in power are especially liable to be stupid because they are out of touch with concrete finite experience and instead keep interfering with other people's initiative, so they make them stupid too. Imagine being deified like Mao Tse-tung or Kim Il Sung, what that must do to a man's character. Or habitually thinking the unthinkable, like our Pentagon.

Most anarchist philosophers start from a lust for freedom. Sometimes this is a metaphysico-moral imperative, with missionary zeal attached, but mostly it is a deep animal cry or religious yearning, like the hymn of the prisoners in Fidelio. They have seen or suffered too much restraint—serfdom, factory slavery, deprived of liberties, colonized by an imperialist, befuddled by the church.

My experience, however, has by and large been roomy enough. "They" have not managed to constrict it too much, though I have suffered a few of the usual baits, many of the punishments, and very many of the threats. I do not need to shake off restraint in order to be myself. My usual gripe has been not that I am imprisoned, but that I am in exile or was born on the wrong planet. My real trouble is that the world is impractical for me; by impatience and cowardice I make it even less practical than it could be.

For me, the chief principle of anarchism is not freedom but autonomy, the ability to initiate a task and do it one's own way. Without orders from authorities who do not know the actual problem and the available means. External direction may sometimes be inevitable, as in emergencies, but it is at a cost to vitality. Behavior is more graceful, forceful, and discriminating without the intervention of the state, wardens, corporation executives, central planners, and university presidents. These tend to create a chronic emergency that makes them necessary. In most cases, the use of power to do a job is inefficient in the fairly short run. Extrinsic power inhibits intrinsic function. "Soul is self-moving," says Aristotle.

The weakness of "my" anarchism is that the lust for freedom is a powerful motive for political change, whereas autonomy is not. Autonomous people protect themselves stubbornly but by less strenuous means, including plenty of passive resistance.

The pathos of oppressed people, however, is that, if they break free, they don't know what to do. Not having been autonomous, they don't know what it's like, and before they learn, they have new managers who are not in a hurry to abdicate. The oppressed hope for too much from New Society, instead of being vigilant to live their lives. They had to rely on one another in the battle, but their solidarity becomes an abstraction and to deviate is called counterrevolutionary.

The possibility of my weaker position is that autonomous people might see that the present situation is disastrous for them, and that their autonomy is whittled away. They cannot help but see it. There is not enough useful work and it is hard to do it honestly or to practice a profession nobly. Arts and sciences are corrupted. Modest enterprise must be blown out of all proportion to survive. The young cannot find their vocations. Talent is stifled by credentials. Taxes are squandered on war, schoolteachers, and overhead. And so forth, and so on. The remedies for all this might be piecemeal and undramatic, but they must be fundamental, for many of the institutions cannot be recast and the system itself is impossible. A good deal could be made tolerable by wiping a good deal off the slate.

The aim of politics is to increase autonomy, and so it is mostly undoing. I like the Marxist formula "the withering away of the State," but it is the method, not the result.

The central organization of administration, production, and distribution is sometimes unavoidable, but it mathematically guarantees stupidity. Information reported from the field must be abstracted, and it loses content at every level; by the time it reaches headquarters it may say nothing relevant. Or it may say what (it is guessed) headquarters wants to hear. To have something to report, the facts of the field are molded into standard form and are no longer plastic. Those in headquarters cannot use their wits because they are not in touch. Those in the field lose their wits because they have to speak a foreign tongue, and can't initiate anything anyway. On the basis of the misinformation it receives, headquarters decides, and a directive is sent down that may fit nobody in particular. At each level it is enforced on those below in order to satisfy those above, rather than to do the work. When it is applied in the field, it may be quite irrelevant, or it may destroy the village in order to save it.

The criteria for the success of such operations are abstractions like Gross National Product, Standard of Living, body count, passenger-miles, Ph.D.s awarded. These at best have no relation to the common wealth, satisfaction of life, peace, experience of travel, or knowing anything. But at worst they impede the common wealth, peace, experience of travel, and so forth.

Nevertheless, central organization, that mathematically guarantees stupidity, is sometimes unavoidable; and just by existing, it exerts disproportionate power. This is a puzzler. The Articles of Confederation and the acrimoniously debated Federalist Constitution gave an answer that worked pretty well, in quite simple conditions, for almost thirty years.

I suppose the most sickening aspect of modern highly organized societies is the prisons and insane asylums, vast enclaves of the indigestible, that the rest live vaguely aware of, with low-grade anxiety.

We have been getting rid of the stupid but at least human notions of punishment, revenge, "paying the debt," and so forth. But instead, there persists and grows the Godlike assumption of "correcting" and "rehabilitating" the deviant. There is no evidence that we know how; and in both prisons and asylums it comes to the same thing, trying to beat people into shape, treating the inmates like inferior animals, and finally just keeping the whole mess out of sight.

The only rational motive for confining any one is to protect ourselves from injury that is likely to be repeated. In insane asylums, more than 90 percent are harmless and need not be confined. And in prisons, what is the point of confining those—I don't know what percent, but it must be fairly large—who have committed one-time crimes, for example, most manslaughters and passional or family crimes, while they pay up or atone? People ought indeed to atone for the harm they have done, to get over their guilt and be "rehabilitated," but this is much more likely to occur by trying to accept them back into the community, rather than isolating and making them desperate. Certainly the old confession on the public square was a better idea.

It is doubtful that punishing some deters others. Varying the penalties has no statistical effect on occurrence, but only measures the degree of abstract social disapproval. And it is obvious that the great majority who do not steal, bribe, forge, and so forth, do not do so because of their life-style, more subtle influences than gross legal risks; other cultures, and some of our own subcultures, have other styles and other habits—for example, the youth counterculture has much increased shoplifting and forging of official documents.

The chief reason that so-called "moral legislation" has no influence in deterring vices is that temptation to the vices does not occur in the same psychological context as rational calculation of legal risks—unlike business fraud or risking a parking ticket. And it is likely that much authentic criminal behavior is compulsive in the same way.

There are inveterate lawbreakers and "psychopathic personalities" who cannot be trusted not to commit the same or worse crimes. (I think they will exist with any social institutions whatever.) It is unrealistic to expect other people not to panic because of them, and so we feel we have to confine them, instead of lynching them. But our present theory of "correction" in fact leads to 70 percent recidivism, usually for more serious felonies; to a state of war and terrorism between prisoners and guards; and to increasing prison riots. Why not say honestly, "We're locking you up simply because we're afraid of you. It is not necessarily a reflection on you and we're sorry for it. Therefore, in your terms, how can we make your confinement as painless and profitable to you as we can? We will give you as many creature satisfactions as you wish and we can afford, not lock you in cells, let you live in your own style, find and pursue your own work—so long as *we* are safe from you. A persisting, and perhaps insoluble, problem is how you will protect yourselves from one another."

It may be objected, of course, that many sober and hardworking citizens who aren't criminals are never given this much consideration by society. No, they aren't, and *that* is a pity.

Writing *Communitas,* my brother and I used only one methodical criterion: diminish intermediary services that are not directly productive or directly enjoyed, like commuting, packaging, sewer lines, blue books. These do not pay off as experience, but they clutter it up and rigidly predetermine it—you walk where the streets go. The social wealth and time of life that go into intermediaries cannot be used for something else. There are slums of engineering. Economists of the infrastructure do not think enough about this when they saddle underdeveloped regions with dead weight.

It is melancholy to consider the fate of John Dewey's instrumentalism, the idea that meaning and value are imbedded in means and operations, that the end-in-view is in practice. Instrumentalism was attacked as anti-intellectual, as base because it omitted ideals; but indeed it was an attempt to rescue intellect from being otiose and merely genteel. It was part of the same impulse as functionalism to rescue architecture, and industrial democracy and agrarian populism to rescue democracy. These meant to dignify the everyday and workaday from being servile means for Sunday goals. Now, however, we take it for granted that immense means are employed and operations carried on *instead* of meaning and value. No end-in-view, no experience, nothing practical. A university is administered to insure its smooth administration. The government makes work in order to diminish unemployment. A candidate runs for office in order to be elected. A war is fought to use new weapons. Only the last of these sounds harsh.

At best, survivals of the past, for example "Western culture," and the busy business of present society, must also be crushing weights on anybody's poor finite experience, unless he can somehow appropriate them as his own by education and vocation.

Most people in most ages pick up a good store of folkways and folk songs in the same way as they learn the language, however that is. They prudently manage to screen out most of the high thought and culture that is not for them, unless they are harassed by schoolteachers; yet they also get wonderful flashes of it: on solemn religious occasions; from works of high music, art, and architecture that have become like folkways; from important civic occasions that give food for profound thought, like constitutional crises, struggles for social justice, law suits; and most jobs and crafts, whether mechanics or farming or cooking or child-rearing, involve a good deal of fundamental science and high tradition that intelligent people pick up. Ordinary life can be culturally rich, and sometimes has been. It is a dubious society when the workdays, holidays, and election days do not provide enough spirit for most people, and we try to give a liberal education abstractly by lessons in school. It cannot he done.

In critical periods, alienated young people may choose on principle not to take on the traditions at all. At the end of the Middle Ages, the *moderni* declared they were throwing out the past and they deserted the Scholastic regent professors and set up their own colleges. The youth of Sturm und Drang threw out the courtly manners and morals. Today seems to be a similar time. Young people astoundingly may not know *Greensleeves* and *Annie Laurie*; they do not become thoughtful on days that commemorate events that happened thousands of years ago—like Huck Finn, they aren't interested in people who are dead; they take for granted what Harvey and Newton had to puzzle out; they don't care that Tyrannosaurus lorded it over the Cretaceous. The curriculum of a Free University might be, typically, Sensitivity Training, Psychedelic Experience, MultiMedia, Astrology, Castro's Cuba, History of Women, and Black Studies. These are not the major humanities, yet it is better to study what they can appropriate as experience than what they can't. (I am puzzled that they do not study nothing, a deeply philosophical subject. They seem to have to go to school.)

Some of us, finally, live in the high culture, its spirit reviving in us and being more or less relevant to 1972, not with an easy adjustment. Our contemporaries are as likely to be Seami and Calderón as people we can talk to. People like us have a use. It would be woeful if the great moments of spirit did not survive. And the present institutions are lifeless if their spirit is not revived. But I don't know any method to teach what we know, namely that Beethoven, the Reformers, the authors of *The Federalist,* were real people and meant what they did. The great difficulty is that, in order to know them in our terms, it is first necessary to make the abnegation of learning them in their terms. And the less culture one has to begin with, the harder this is to do.

Vocation is taking on the business of the community so it is not a drag. If I find what I am good at and good for, that my community can use and will support, securely doing this, I can find myself further; and the social work is humanized because a real person is really doing it.

Having a vocation is always somewhat of a miracle, like falling in love and it works out. I can understand why Luther said that a man is justified by his vocation, for it is already a proof of God's favor. Naturally, it is psychologically easier if the family or community has provided intimate models to a child, and if it encourages him as he follows his own bent. It is harder if a child is poor or is restricted by his status, high or low, and has to take what offers or what he must. Faraday's career is a good example of both advantage and deprivation, and of the miracle. His father was a journeyman blacksmith. When he was adolescent, they apprenticed him to a bookbinder for seven years. Although he could hardly read, he used to take home the books of natural philosophy that came into the shop for rebinding, and copy out the diagrams. The clients talked to him—he must have been likeable as well as smart. They invited him to lectures. Because of his ability to fashion apparatus, at twenty he became the laboratory assistant of Humphry Davy. So he had the right background, he had the right hardships to make him make an effort, and he had the genius of Faraday.

Our present practice is poor. Big Society has slots to fill; the young are tested for their aptitudes and schooled to fill the slots. There are no intimate models. The actual jobs are distant and unknown. Talent is co-opted; it does not develop at the youth's choice and time. A strong talent may well balk and deny his very talent. This is abstract.

But there may be an even more lifeless future, now widely proposed. The young must be trained to be adaptable to "play various roles." This will "free" people from being "tied down." Young people I have talked to like this idea; being "just human" means not limited to a vocation or profession. They want to be "into" various activities. As presumably Shakespeare was heavily into writing plays and Niels Bohr was into atomic physics. It is a curious view of personality and commitment.

To be a citizen is the common vocation. It is onerous unless one has an authentic talent for it, which I don't have, but we have to take over society as our (hopefully finite) experience or it takes us over infinitely. Even when I can only gripe, I write letters to the editor. I gave a collection of them the explanatory title *The Society I Live In Is Mine*.

A child or adolescent has the right to naïve patriotism, loyal pride in the place where he is thrown—he didn't choose to be born here. Without a sneaking nostalgia that there is some sense, honorable history, and good intentions in these people, we are in a harsh exile indeed.

For a child, even the idiot patriotism of nationalism is better than none. My little daughter, now nine, is going to an Hawaiian public school where they inundate the kids with

"Columbia the Gem of the Ocean" and the Pledge of Allegiance, plus some pathetic Hawaiiana—the school is 95 percent quarter-Polynesian. But in New York she had been attending a "progressive" private school where instead of "America the Beautiful" they were likely to sing,

> O ugly for polluted skies,
> grain grown with pesticides . . .

and I am just as pleased that (for a few months) she is reading about the shot heard round the world and Thomas Jefferson without mention of his being a slaveholder. I see that it makes her happier to believe the noble rather than the base. It is touching.

"I have no idea what is the secret mission of the Navy vessels lying off my lanai in Waimanalo, but I wish they would get it over with and stop obstructing the horizon."—letter to the *Honolulu Star-Bulletin*. In fact they were practicing living in an underwater habitat built by the Oceanic Institute, nothing objectionable. But my resentment was that the Navy just sat there day after day, as if they owned the place.

I like Hegel's idea that property is an extension of personality; it is obviously so if we consider my tools, my clothes, my room, and my view of the horizon. And I would prefer to consider big capital property in the same light rather than that it is made purely by statute, state power. But it is largely our common inheritance that has been sequestered by a few. Property has come to mean not facilitating use, but excluding others from use.

Socialists object to any theory of natural property. They would in fact usually allow private use in clothes, tools, and so forth, but not as a natural right, rather as a right given by the collective. I think this is dispiriting; in order to assert my right and do my business, I would first have to take myself abstractly, as a member of all society. And of course prove my orthodoxy.

The issue of property has been wrongly put. The question is not whether personality extends into the environment—of course it does—but what kind of personality a man has. If he is exclusive and squeamish and rides roughshod over people, then his property will also be like that and will be objectionable. If he imagines that huge holdings do not enclose the commons, exploit the common wealth, and deprive other people, he is a fool. If the Navy would explain to me how it is temporarily appropriating that stretch of water for an interesting experiment, I might feel that *my* property in that stretch of water is being improved. I would willingly cooperate. My horizon would no longer be obstructed.—To be sure, I distrust *any* experiments of the Navy, but that is another story.

Nor is the issue between "private property" and "social property." Who would want to be private? We exist mainly, though not altogether, in community relations. To be a private individual is largely pathological. For a society to act as a collective is largely pathological.

The error of those who are mistakenly called "conservative" is not their laissez-faire economics. It is probable that competitive free enterprise is a more productive system than mercantilism, monopoly capitalism, or socialist collectivism. But as in the past, free enterprises still parcel out the commons as if it were on the market. They treat moral, cultural, and esthetic affairs that belong to the community as if they were economic affairs, for example, giving access to the young, conserving the environment, helping the needy. But these are necessary for society to be tolerable at all. The tolerable background for any economic activity cannot be an object of economic activity.

And they make a corresponding mistake in their economics. In most of our present production, the chief value comes from the genius of Watt, Faraday, Rutherford, and so on; from the industry of our fathers who cleared the woods and laid out the roads; and from natural resources. We all happen to have inherited these gold mines. It is unreasonable for a few who control capital and thereby can make use of the inheritance, not to pay everybody royalties, for example, at least the guaranteed income.

Finally, in developed economies, both socialists and capitalists make a disastrous ethical mistake, mortgaging the present to the future. They put too much effort into profit, accumulating surpluses for new productivity and infrastructure, rather than first assuring a small profit for stability and livelihood. Growth Rate and Gross National Product become abstract fetishes, for which they sacrifice the present by skimping it, and take the life out of the future by overdetermining it.

Needless to say, the more the abstract Growth Rate flourishes, the more millions of people are likely to be left out and reduced to misery, for nobody pays attention to their petty concrete needs, which have nothing to do with Growth Rate and Gross National Product. There is a bigger pie to divide, but it can't be divided into inefficient items like food for a technologically displaced farmer or miner. In the long run he will surely be better off; in the fairly short run he will surely be quite dead.

Let me again quote the anecdote: "What," asked Coleridge, "about the little village that is rather self-sufficient and does not take part in the National Economy?" "Why, such a place is of no importance," said the Manchester economist.

"Sir? are 500 Christian souls of no importance ?"

In *Communitas* (Scheme III), we make the dumb-bunny suggestion of a dual economy with dual money: Let the big economy expand as madly as it wants, but see to it that there is also a small independent subsistence economy, producing subsistence goods at small-economy prices. (Recently, however, we have come to see that for ecological reasons the big economy can't expand like mad either.)

Equalitarians object to special privilege; for instance, they don't like it that my sheepskin promises to me "all the rights, privileges, and immunities" of a doctor of philosophy. But my ancestor Abelard and his students fought and suffered for those rights and immunities; we (maybe) need them to do our thing; I am not at all willing to renounce them—indeed, I am a stickler for them.

Again the issue is put wrongly. It would be better if every person and his community of interest had far more rights, privileges, and immunities. Children have special rights, privileges, and immunities. Those who have worn themselves out bringing up children have special rights, privileges, and immunities—I guiltlessly say "Young man, tote my bag." As a writer I need liberties and immunities that do not belong to a man who will never write a line; he does not care about freedom of the press, and in fact he won't defend it. The real issue is that many rights, privileges, and immunities that once had an historical warrant and enhanced experience and activity, have now become a racket. For example, professionals do need a peer group and to be professionally responsible only to their peer group, their oath, and the nature of things; but the economic blackmail of the medical associations is a racket. Lily whites may have a claim to club and eat with the like-minded, but not to deprive blacks of a share in the common wealth by segregating a restaurant on the main street, a neighborhood of a thousand houses, a national industry.

Professionals are bound to develop a ritual and secret language and mystify the laity, but this is acceptable (within limits)—their thing is a mystery and they have to do it their own way. What is unacceptable is for them to get the State to certify them as the only legal practitioners and exempt themselves from competition and criticism. The pretext is to protect the public from quacks; the effect is to increase the number of quacks, including those who are certified.

I am suspicious of equal law for everybody, like the *jus gentium* of the Romans that emerged with an Empire from which no one could escape. It is safer to have a bewildering tangle of unique prerogatives, and lots of borders to cross.

The main reason that Jefferson was a champion of freehold farming as a way of life was that it was independent of political pressures. It kept open the possibility of anarchy that he hankered for—"Let Shays' men go. If you discourage mutiny, what check is there on government?" If a farmer doesn't like the trend, he can withdraw from the market, eat his own crops, and prudently stay out of debt. If he has a freehold, they can't throw him off his land. (In Jefferson's day, he couldn't be drafted.) Other kinds of tenure have a similar privilege, academic tenure or seniority on the job, but of course the whole enterprise can shut down.

My own admiration for farming is its competence. The wonderfully direct connection between causes and effects, whether the seeds, the soil, the weather, the breeding, the plumbing in the barn, or the engine of the tractor; and of course growing it and then eating it. Needless to say, a farmer understands most of this only empirically, practically, not scientifically. He is not altogether in control. That too is very good; there are gods.

And Wordsworth had a good insight of the beauty and morality of rural life. The ecology of a country scene is so exquisitely complicated that we finally have to take it as just given. This simplifies it morally, we can relax a little. But I can't take the traffic or housing in Manhattan as given; it is an artifact and I have to do something about it. Also, the country scene has been so worked over for millions of years that it is bound to have unity and style, heroic in scale, minute in detail. But for various well-known reasons, the man-made scene is bound to be ugly. If people change their ways, it could become at least modest.

Sciences are sacred because they devote themselves—indeed, in a priestly way—to the natures not made by us, so they enable us to make sense and not live wishes, hopes, and nightmares. Being observant, humble, and austerely self-denying, dedicated scientists accumulate the reward of their Calvinist virtues. Great powers flow through them—which they can use to our disadvantage. Therefore they ought to bind themselves by oath to benefit and not harm the community, and it is better if this oath is public and explicit, like the Hippocratic oath.

When, instead, they come on like petty clerks of the powers-that-be and as petty bankers of their own economic interests, the forces of nature are unleashed without human beings to interpret and exorcise them.

We others, artists and literary men, are easygoing toward nature and mix into our service a good deal of ourselves. So we accumulate little force, but it is domesticated. We do not need to bind ourselves with an oath, except not to censor.

Futurologists take current trends that may or may not be good, and by extrapolating them for twenty years perform the sleight of hand of making them into norms that we must learn to conform to and prepare ourselves for. As a group they are extraordinarily slavish to the *status quo*—science fiction writers are often far more critical and daring. They seem to want to delete from primary experience its risky property of passing into the Next, beyond a horizon that very swiftly becomes dim and dark. Aristotle: "The past and present are necessary, the future is possible."

Luckily, human beings have enormous resources of anxiety, common sense, boredom, virtue, and perversity, to distort or reverse almost any trend you want.

The mania of planning for the future springs, of course, from the fact that current technology, urbanization, population, and communications are intractable—or at least the managers have lost their pragmatic inventiveness—so that it seems to be less desperate to grin and codify them. As Kafka advised, "Leopards break into the temple; make it part of the ritual."

My own prediction, however, is that there will be increasing disorder for twenty years, and that might be very well. Some things—some times—break up into fragments of just the right size and shape. People en masse learn only by being frightened anyway—ten thousand dead one morning of the smog, a city wiped out by an accidental bomb. It's not that we are stupid, but it takes a big fact, not a syllogism, to warrant a big response. If only the process of disorder is not aggravated by reactionary Law and Order, liberal Futurology, and radical Idealism.

I am bemused, as I spell out this politics of mine, at the consistent package of conservative biases, the ideology of a peasant or a small entrepreneur who carries his office and capital under his hat. Localism, ruralism, face-to-face organization, distrust of planning, clinging to property, natural rights, historical privileges and immunities, letters to the editor that view with alarm, carrying on the family craft, piecemeal reforms, make do, and let me alone.

No. It is not a possessive peasant nor a threatened small entrepreneur, but a small child who needs the security of routine. There is no father. Mother is away all day at work. He is self-reliant because he has to be. It is lonely, but nobody bugs him, and the sun is pouring through the window.

Where the emphasis in a philosophy of experience is on the foreground empirical facts, as in Dewey, we come out with a bias toward experiment and a politics of progressivism. Where the emphasis is on the phenomenology, the horizons and backgrounds of experience, we come out with conservation and conservatism. The difference is the old principle of acculturation from tribe to tribe: if the new item is a plough or a technique for baking pottery, it diffuses rapidly; if it is a change of taboo, child-rearing, or esthetics, it is resisted, it diffuses slowly or not at all.

Since as experience I want the concrete and finite, with structure and tendency, a Next so I can live on a little, and a dark surrounding, politically I want only that the children have bright eyes, the river be clean, food and sex be available, and nobody be pushed around. There must not be horrors that take me by the throat, so I can experience nothing; but it is indifferent to me what the Growth Rate is, or if some people are rich and others poor, so long as they are *pauvres*, decently poor, and not *misérables* (Péguy's distinction). I myself never found that much difference between being very poor and modestly rich.

Idolatry makes me uneasy. I don't like my country to be a Great Power. I am squeamish about masses of people enthusiastically building a New Society.

The great conservative solutions are those that diminish tension by changing 2 percent of this and 4 percent of that. When they work, you don't notice them. Liberals like to solve a problem by adding on a new agency and throwing money at it, a ringing statement that the problem has been solved. Radicals like to go to the root, which is a terrible way of gardening, though it is sometimes sadly necessary in dentistry.

> Schultz, the neighbor's big black dog,
> used to shit on our scraggly lawn,
> but we feed him marrow bones
> and he treats our lawn like his own home.

> The kids of Fulton Houses in New York
> smashed windows on our pretty block for spite;
> we gave them hockey sticks to play with
> and they smashed more windows.

> The dog is an anarchist like me,
> he has a careless dignity
> that is, we never think about it,
> which comes to the same thing.

> The kids are political like you,
> they want to win their dignity. They won't.
> But maybe their children will be friendly dogs
> and wag their tails with my grandchildren.

Technology and Planning

Introduction to *Communitas*

Background and Foreground

Of the man-made things, the works of engineering and architecture and town plan are the heaviest and biggest part of what we experience. They lie underneath, they loom around, as the prepared place of our activity. Economically, they have the greatest amount of past human labor frozen into them, as streets and highways, houses and bridges, and physical plant. Against this background we do our work and strive toward our ideals, or just live out our habits; yet because it is background, it tends to become taken for granted and to be unnoticed. A child accepts the man-made background itself as the inevitable nature of things; he does not realize that somebody once drew some lines on a piece of paper who might have drawn otherwise. But now, as engineer and architect once drew, people have to walk and live.

The background of the physical plant and the foreground of human activity are profoundly and intimately dependent on one another. Laymen do not realize how deep and subtle this connection is. Let us immediately give a strong architectural example to illustrate it. In Christian history, there is a relation between the theology and the architecture of churches. The dimly-lit vast auditorium of a Gothic Catholic cathedral, bathed in colors and symbols, faces a bright candle-lit stage and its richly costumed celebrant: this is the necessary background for the mysterious sacrament of the mass for the newly growing Medieval town and its representative actor. But the daylit, small, and unadorned meeting hall of the Congregationalist, facing its central pulpit, fits the belief that the chief mystery is preaching the Word to a group that religiously governs itself. And the little square seating arrangement of the Quakers confronting one another is an environment where it is hoped that, when people are gathered in meditation, the Spirit itself will descend anew. In this sequence of three plans, there is a whole history of dogma and society. Men have fought wars and shed their blood for these details of plan and decoration.

Just so, if we look at the town plan of New Delhi we can immediately read off much of the history and social values of a late date of British imperialism. And if we look at the Garden City plan of Greenbelt, Md., we can understand something very important about our present American era of the "organiza-tion man."

We can read immediately from the industrial map of the United States in 1850 that there were sectional political interests. Given a certain kind of agri-cultural or mining plan, we know that, whatever the formal schooling of the society may be, a large part of the environmental education of the children will be technological; whereas a child brought up in a modern suburb or city may not even know what work it is that papa does "at the office."

Contemporary Criticism of Our American Way of Life

For thirty years now, our American way of life as a whole has been subjected to sweeping condemnation by thoughtful social and cultural critics. From the great Depression to World War II, this criticism was aimed mostly at our eco-nomic and political institutions; since the war, it has been aimed, less trench-antly but more broadly, at the Standard of Living, the popular culture, the ways of work and leisure. The critics have shown with pretty plain evidence that we spend our money for follies, that our leisure does not revive us, that our condi-tions of work are unmanly and our beautiful American classlessness is degen-erating into a static bureaucracy; our mass arts are beneath contempt; our pros-perity breeds insecurity; our system of distribution has become huckstering and our system of production discourages enterprise and sabotages invention.

In this book we must add, alas, to the subjects of this cultural criticism the physical plant and the town and regional plans in which we have been living so unsatisfactorily. We will criticize not merely the foolish shape and power of the cars but the cars themselves, and not merely the cars but the factories where they are made, the highways on which they run, and the plan of live-lihood that makes those highways necessary. In appraising these things, we employ both the economic analysis that marked the books of the 30s and the socio-psychological approach prevalent since the war. This is indicated by our sub-title: "The Means of Livelihood and the Ways of Life." (In social theory, this kind of analysis provides one necessary middle term in the recent litera-ture of criticism, between the economic and the cultural analyses, which have usually run strangely parallel to one another without touching.)

Nevertheless, except for this introductory chapter, this present book is *not* an indictment of the American way of life, but rather an attempt to clarify it and find what its possibilities are. For it is confused, it is a mixture of con-flicting motives not ungenerous in themselves. Confronted with the spec-tacular folly of our people, one is struck not by their incurable stupidity but by their bafflement about what to do with themselves and their productivity. They seem to be trapped in their present pattern, with no recourse but to complicate present evils by more of the same. Especially in the field of big physical planning, there has been almost a total drying-up of invention, of new solutions. Most of the ideas discussed in this book come from the 20s or before, a few from the early 30s. Since World War II, with all the need for housing, with all the productive plant to be put to new work and capital to invest, the major innovation in community planning in the United States has been the out-of-town so-called "community center" whose chief structure is a supermarket where Sunday shoppers can avoid blue laws.

Typical American behavior is to solve a problem of transit congestion by creating a parallel system that builds up new neighborhoods and redoubles the transit congestion; but no effort is made to analyze the kinds and conditions of work so that people commute less. With generous intent, Americans clear a slum area and rebuild with large projects that re-create the slum more densely and, on the whole, sociologically worse, for now class stratification is built organically into the plan; but rarely is an effort made to get people to improve what they have, or to find out where they ought to move. (The exceptions—of the Hudson Guild in New York teaching six Puerto Rican families to make furniture and paint the premises, or of a block getting together to plant nine trees—are so exceptional that they warrant medals from the American Institute of Architects.) A classical example of our present genius in planning is solving the traffic jam on the streets of a great city in the West by making a system of freeways so fast and efficient with its cloverleaves as to occupy 40 percent of the real estate, whose previous occupants then move to distant places and drive back bumper-to-bumper on the freeways.

If, however, someone plans in a physicianly way to remedy the causes of an ill rather than concentrate on the symptoms, if he proposes a Master Plan to provide for orderly future development, if he suggests an inventive new solution altogether, then he is sure to be called impractical, irresponsible, and perhaps a subversive alien. Indeed, in the elegant phrase of the famous Park Commissioner of an Eastern metropolis, a guardian of the public welfare and morals in the field, such people are *Bei-unskis*, that is, Russian or German refugees who say, "*Bei uns* we did it this way."

Inherent Difficulties of Planning

Yet even apart from public foolishness and public officials, big physical planning is confusing and difficult. Every community plan is based on some:

Technology
Standard of Living
Political and Economic Decision
Geography and History of a Place.

Every part of this is thorny and the interrelation is thorny.

There may be historical miscalculation—wrong predictions in the most expensive matters. Consider, for instance, a most celebrated example of American planning, the laying-out of the District of Columbia and the city of Washington. When the site on the Potomac was chosen, as central in an era of slow transportation, the plan was at the same time to connect the Potomac waterway with the Ohio, and the new city was then to become the emporium of the West.

But the system of canals which would have realized this ambitious scheme did not materialize, and therefore, a hundred years later, Washington was still a small political center, pompously overplanned, without economic significance, while the commerce of the West flowed through the Erie Canal to New York. Yet now, ironically enough, the political change to a highly centralized bureaucracy has made Washington a great city far beyond its once exaggerated size.

Planners tend to put a misplaced faith in some one important factor in isolation, usually a technological innovation. In 1915, Patrick Geddes argued that, with the change from coal to electricity, the new engineering would, or could, bring into being Garden Cities everywhere to replace the slums; for the new power could be decentralized and was not in itself offensive. Yet the old slum towns have largely passed away to be replaced by endless conurbations of suburbs smothered in new feats of the new engineering—and the automobile exhaust is more of a menace than the coal smoke. Our guess is that these days nucleonics as such will not accomplish miracles for us, nor even automation.

The Garden City idea itself, as we shall see in the next chapter, has had a pathetic history. When Ebenezer Howard thought it up to remedy the coal slums, he did not contemplate Garden Cities without industry; he wanted to make it possible for people to live decently *with* the industry. Yet, just when the conditions of manufacture have become less noisome, it has worked out that the Green Belt and Garden Cities have become mere dormitories for commuters, who are also generally not the factory workers whom Howard had in mind.

Political Difficulties

The big, heavy, and expensive physical environment has always been the chief locus of vested rights stubbornly opposing planning innovations that are merely for the general quick profits. A small zoning ordinance is difficult to enact, not to speak of a master plan for progressive realization over twenty or thirty years, for zoning nullifies speculation in real estate. Every advertiser in *American City* and *Architectural Forum* has costly wares to peddle, and it is hard to see through their smokescreen what services and gadgets are really useful, and whether or not some simpler, more inexpensive arrangement is feasible. Since streets and subways are too bulky for the profits of capricious fads, the tendency of business in these lines is to repeat the tried and true, in a bigger way. And it happens to be just the real estate interests and great financiers like insurance companies who have influence on city councils and park commissioners.

But also, apart from business interests and vested rights, common people are rightly very conservative about changes in the land, for they are very powerfully affected by such changes in very many habits and sentiments. Any community plan involves a formidable choice and fixing of living standards and attitudes, of schedule, of personal and cultural tone. Generally people move in the existing plan unconsciously, as if it were nature (and they will continue to do so, until suddenly the automobiles don't move at all). But let a new proposal be made and it is astonishing how people rally to the old arrangement. Even a powerful park commissioner found the housewives and their perambulators blocking his way when he tried to rent out a bit of the green as a parking lot for a private restaurant he favored; and wild painters and cat-keeping spinsters united to keep him from forcing a driveway through lovely Washington Square. These many years now since 1945, the citizens of New York City have refused to say "Avenue of the Americas" when they plainly mean Sixth Avenue.

The trouble with this good instinct—not to be regimented in one's intimate affairs by architects, engineers, and international public-relations experts—is that "no plan" always means in fact some inherited and frequently bad plan. For our cities are far from nature, that has a most excellent plan, and the "unplanned" tends to mean a gridiron laid out for speculation a century ago, or a dilapidated downtown when the actual downtown has moved uptown. People are right to be conservative, but what *is* conservative? In planning, as elsewhere in our society, we can observe the paradox that the wildest anarchists are generally affirming the most ancient values, of space, sun, and trees, and beauty, human dignity, and forthright means, as if they lived in neolithic times or the Middle Ages, whereas the so-called conservatives are generally arguing for policies and prejudices that date back only four administrations.

The best defense against planning—and people do need a defense against planners—is to become informed about the plan that is indeed existent and operating in our lives; and to learn to take the initiative in proposing or supporting reasoned changes. Such action is not only a defense but good in itself, for to make positive decisions for one's community, rather than being regimented by others' decisions, is one of the noble acts of man.

Technology of Choice and Economy of Abundance

The most curious anomaly, however, is that modern technology baffles people and makes them timid of innovations in community planning. It is an anomaly because for the first time in history we have, spectacularly in the United States, a surplus technology, a technology of free choice that allows for the most widely various community-arrangements and ways of life. Later in this book we will suggest some of the extreme varieties that are technically feasible. And with this technology of choice, we have an economy of abundance, a standard of living that is in many ways *too* high—goods and money that are literally thrown away or given away—that could underwrite sweeping reforms and pilot experiments. Yet our cultural climate and the state of ideas are such that our surplus, of means and wealth, leads only to extravagant repetitions of the "air-conditioned nightmare," as Henry Miller called it, a pattern of life that used to be unsatisfactory and now, by the extravagance, becomes absurd.

Think about a scarcity economy and a technology of necessity. A cursory glance at the big map will show what we have inherited from history. Of the seven urban areas of the United Kingdom, six coincide with the coal beds; the seventh, London, was the port open to the Lowlands and Europe. When as children we used to learn the capitals and chief cities of the United States, we learned the rivers and lakes that they were located on, and then, if we knew which rivers were navigable and which furnished waterpower, we had in a nutshell the history of American economy. Not long ago in this country many manufacturers moved south to get cheaper labor, until the labor unions followed them. In general, if we look at the big historical map, we see that the location of towns has depended on bringing together the raw material and the power, on minimizing transportation, on having a reserve of part-time and seasonal labor and a concentration of skills, and sometimes (depending on the bulk or perishability of the finished product) on the location of the market. These are the kinds of technical and economic factors that have historically determined, with an iron necessity, the big physical plan of industrial nations and continents.

They will continue to determine them, but the iron necessity is relaxed. For almost every item that men have invented or nature has bestowed, there are alternative choices.

What used to be made of steel (iron ore and coal) may now often be made of aluminum (bauxite and waterpower) or even of plastic (soybeans and sunlight). Raw materials have proliferated, sources of power have become more ubiquitous, and there are more means of transportation and lighter loads to carry. With the machine-analysis of manufacture, the tasks of labor become simpler, and as the machines have become automatic our problem has become, astoundingly, not where to get labor but how to use leisure. Skill is no longer the arduously learned craftsmanship of hundreds of trades and crafts—for its chief habits (styling, accuracy, speed) are built into the machine; skill has come to mean skill in a few operations, like turning, grinding, stamping, welding, spraying and half a dozen others, that intelligent people can learn in a short time. Even inspection is progressively mechanized. The old craft-operations of building could be revolutionized overnight if there were worthwhile enterprises to warrant the change, that is, if there were a social impetus and enthusiasm to build what everybody agrees is useful and necessary.

Consider what this means for community planning on any scale. We could centralize or decentralize, concentrate population or scatter it. If we want to continue the trend away from the country, we can do that; but if we want to combine town and county values in an agri-industrial way of life, we can do that. In large areas of our operation, we could go back to old-fashioned domestic industry with perhaps even a gain in efficiency, for small power is everywhere available, small machines are cheap and ingenious, and there are easy means to collect machined parts and centrally assemble them. If we want to lay our emphasis on providing still more mass-produced goods, and raising the standard of living still higher, we can do that; or if we want to increase leisure and the artistic culture of the individual, we can do that. We can have solar machines for hermits in the desert like Aldous Huxley or central heating provided for millions by New York Steam. All this is commonplace; everybody knows it.

It is *just* this relaxing of necessity, this extraordinary flexibility and freedom of choice of our techniques, that is baffling and frightening to people. We say, "If we want, we can," but offered such wildly possible alternatives, how the devil would people know what they want? And if you ask them—as it was customary after the war to take polls and ask, "What kind of town do you want to live in? What do you want in your post-war home?"—the answers reveal a banality of ideas that is hair-raising, with neither rational thought nor real sentiment, the conceptions of routine and inertia rather than local patriotism or personal desire, of prejudice and advertising rather than practical experience and dream.

Technology is a sacred cow left strictly to (unknown) experts, as if the form of the industrial machine did not profoundly affect every person; and people are remarkably superstitious about it. They think that it is more efficient to centralize, whereas it is usually more inefficient. (When this same technological superstition invades such a sphere as the school system, it is no joke.) They imagine, as an article of faith, that big factories must be more efficient than small ones; it does not occur to them, for instance, that it is cheaper to haul machined parts than to transport workmen.

Indeed, they are outraged by the good-humored demonstrations of Borsodi that, in hours and minutes of labor, it is probably cheaper to grow and can your own tomatoes than to buy them at the supermarket, not to speak of the quality. Here once again we have the inevitable irony of history: industry, invention, scientific method have opened new opportunities, but just at the moment of opportunity, people have become ignorant by specialization and superstitious of science and technology, so that they no longer know what they want, nor do they dare to command it. The facts are exactly like the world of Kafka: a person has every kind of electrical appliance in his home, but he is balked, cold-fed, and even plunged into darkness because he no longer knows how to fix a faulty connection.

Certainly this abdication of practical competence is one important reason for the absurdity of the American Standard of Living. Where the user understands nothing and cannot evaluate his tools, you can sell him anything. It is the user, said Plato, who ought to be the judge of the chariot. Since he is not, he must abdicate to the values of engineers, who are craft-idiots, or—God save us !—to the values of salesmen. Insecure as to use and value, the buyer clings to the autistic security of conformity and emulation, and he can no longer dare to ask whether there is a relation between his Standard of Living and the satisfactoriness of life. Yet in a reasonable mood, nobody, but nobody, in America takes the American standard seriously. (This, by the way, is what Europeans don't understand; we are not such fools as they imagine—we are far more at a loss than they think.)

Still Another Obstacle

We must mention still another obstacle to community planning in our times and a cause of the dull and unadventurous thinking about it: the threat of war, especially atomic war. People feel—and they are bang right—that there is not much point in initiating large-scale and long-range improvements in the physical environment, when we are uncertain about the existence of a physical environment the day after tomorrow. A sensible policy for highways must be sacrificed to the needs of moving defense. Nor is this defeated attitude toward planning relieved when military experts come forth with spine-tingling plans that propose the total disruption of our present arrangements solely in the interest of minimizing the damage of the bombs. Such schemes do not awaken enthusiasm for a new way of life.

But even worse than this actual doubt, grounded in objective danger, is the world-wide anxiety that everywhere produces conformity and brain washed citizens. For it takes a certain basic confidence and hope to be able to be rebellious and hanker after radical innovations. As the historians point out, it is not when the affairs of society are at low ebb. but on the upturn and in the burst of revival that great revolutions occur. Now compare our decade since World War II with the decade after World War I. In both there was unheard of productivity and prosperity, a vast expansion in science and technique, a flood of international exchange. But the decade of the 20s had also one supreme confidence, that there was never going to be another war; the victors sank their warships in the sea and every nation signed the Kellogg-Briand pact; and it was in that confidence that there flowered the Golden Age of avant-garde art, amid many of the elegant and audacious community plans that we shall discuss in the following pages. Our decade, alas, has had the contrary confidence—God grant that we are equally deluded—and our avant-garde art and thought have been pretty desperate.

The future is gloomy, and we offer you a book about the bright face of the future! It is because we have a stubborn faith in the following proposition: the chief, the underlying reason that people wage war is that they do not wage peace. How to wage peace?

The Importance of Planning in Modern Thinking

There is an important sense in which physical community planning as a major branch of thought belongs to modern times, to the past hundred years. In every age there have been moral and cultural crises—and social plans like the *Republic*—and also physical plans to meet economic, ecological, or strategic needs. But formerly the physical plans were simply technical solutions: the physical motions and tangible objects of people were ready means to express whatever values they had; moral and cultural integration did not importantly depend on physical integration. In our times, however, every student of the subject complains, one way or another, that the existing physical plant is not expressive of people's real values: it is "out of human scale," it is existentially "absurd," it is "paleo-technological." Put philosophically, there is a wrong relation between and ends. The means are too unwieldy for us, so our ends are confused, for impracticable ends are confused dreams. Whatever the causes, from the earliest plans of the modern kind, seeking to remedy the evils of nuisance factories and urban congestion, and up to the most recent plans for regional development and physical science fiction, we find always the insistence that reintegration of the physical plan is an essential part of political, cultural, and moral reintegration. Most physical planners vastly overrate the importance of their subject; in social change it is not a primary motive. When people are personally happy it is astonishing how they make do with improbable means—and when they are miserable the shiniest plant does not work for them. Nevertheless, the plans discussed in this book will show, we think, that the subject is more important than urban renewal, or even than solving traffic jams.

Neo-Functionalism

Finally, let us say something about the esthetic standpoint of this book. The authors are both artists and, in the end, beauty is our criterion, even for community planning, which is pretty close to the art of life itself. Our standpoint is given by the historical situation we have just discussed: the problem for modern planners has been the disproportion of means and ends, and the beauty of community plan is the proportion of means and ends.

Most of modern architecture and engineering has advanced under the banner of functionalism, "form follows function." This formula of Louis Sullivan has been subject to two rather contrary interpretations. In Sullivan's original statement he seemed to mean not that the form grows from the function, but that it is appropriate to it, it is an interpretation of it; he says, "a store must look like a store, a bank must look like a bank." The formula aims at removing the ugliness of cultural dishonesty, snobbery, the shame of physical function. It is directly in the line of Ibsen, Zola, Dreiser. But it also affirms ideal forms, given by the sensibility of the culture or the imagination of the artist; and this is certainly how it was spectacularly applied by Sullivan's disciple, Frank Lloyd Wright, who found his shapes in America, in the prairie, and in his personal poetry.

In a more radical interpretation—e.g., of the Bauhaus—the formula means that the form is given by the function: there is to be no addition to the arrangement of the utility, the thing is presented just as it works. In a sense, this is not an esthetic principle at all, for a machine simply working perfectly would not be noticed at all and therefore would not have beauty nor any other sensible satisfaction. But these theorists were convinced that the natural handling of materials and the rationalization of design for mass production must necessarily result in strong elementary and intellectual satisfactions: simplicity, cleanliness, good sense, richness of texture. The bread-and-butter values of poor people who have been deprived, but know now what they want.

Along this path of interpretation, the final step seemed to be constructivism, the theory that since the greatest and most striking impression of any structure is made by its basic materials and the way they are put together, so the greatest formal effect is in the construction itself, in its clarity, ingenuity, rationality, and proportion. This is a doctrine of pure esthetics, directly in the line of post-impressionism, cubism, and abstract art. In architecture and engineering it developed from functionalism, but in theory and sometimes in practice it leaped to the opposite extreme of having no concern with utility whatever. Much constructivist architecture is best regarded primarily as vast abstract sculpture; the search of the artist is for new structural forms, arbitrarily, whatever the function. Often it wonderfully expresses the intoxication with new technology, how we can freely cantilever anything, span any space. On the other hand, losing the use, it loses the intimate sensibility of daily life, it loses the human scale.

We therefore, going back to Greek antiquity, propose a different line of interpretation altogether: form follows function, but let us subject the function itself to a formal critique. Is the *function* good? Bona fide? Is it worthwhile? Is it worthy of a man to do that? What are the consequences? Is it compatible with other, basic, human functions? Is it a forthright or at least ingenious part of life? Does it make sense? Is it a beautiful function of a beautiful power? We have grown unused to asking such ethical questions of our machines, our streets, our cars, our towns. But nothing less will give us an esthetics for community planning, the proportioning of means and ends. For a community is not a construction, a bold Utopian model; its chief part is always people, busy or idle, en masse or a few at a time. And the problem of community planning is not like arranging people for a play or a ballet, for there are no outside spectators, there are only actors; nor are they actors of a scenario but agents of their own needs— though it's a grand thing for us to be not altogether unconscious of forming a beautiful and elaborate city, by how we look and move. That's a proud feeling.

What we want is style. Style, power and grace. These come only, burning, from need and flowing feeling; and that fire brought to focus by viable character and habits.

This, then, is a book about the issues important in community planning and the ideas suggested by the planners. Our aim is to clarify a confused subject, to heighten the present low level of thinking; it is *not* to propose concrete plans for construction in particular places. We are going to discuss many big schemes, including a few of our own invention; but our purpose is a philosophical one: to ask what is socially implied in any such scheme as a way of life, and how each plan expresses some tendency of modern mankind. Naturally we too have an idea as to how *we* should like to live, but we are not going to try to sell it here. On the contrary! At present *any* plan will win our praise so long as it is really functional according to the criterion we have proposed: so long as it is aware of means and ends and is not, as a way of life, absurd.

A great plan maintains an independent attitude toward both the means of production and the standard of living. It is selective of current technology because how men work and make things is crucial to how they live. And it is selective of the available goods and services, in quantity and quality, and in deciding which ones are plain foolishness.

From the vast and curious literature of this subject during the past century, we have chosen a manual of great modern plans, and arranged them according to the following principle: What is the relationship between the arrangements for working and the arrangements for "living" (animal, domestic, avocational, and recreational)? What is the relation in the plan between production and consumption? This gives us a division into three classes:

A. *The Green Belt*—Garden Cities and Satellite Towns; City neighborhoods and the Ville Radieuse;

B. *Industrial Plans*—the Plan for Moscow; the Lineal City; Dymaxion;

C. *Integrated Plans*—Broadacres and the Homestead; the Marxist regional plan and collective farming; the T.V.A.

The first class, controlling the technology, concentrates on amenity of living; the second starts from arrangements for production and the use of technology; the third looks for some principle of symbiosis. It does not much matter whether we have chosen the most exciting or influential examples—though we have chosen good ones—for our aim is to bring out the principle of interrelation. Certainly we do not treat the plans in a way adequate to their merit, for they were put forth as practical or ideally practical schemes—some of them were put into effect—whereas we are using them as examples for analysis.

The questions we shall be asking are: What do these plans envisage about:

Kind of technology?

Attitude toward the technology?

Relation of work and leisure?

Domestic life?

Education of children and adults?

Esthetics?

Political initiative?

Economic institutions?

Practical realization?

By asking these questions of these modern plans, we can collect a large body of important issues and ideas for the inductions that we then draw in the second part of this book.

Two Points of Philosophy and an Example

In principle, technology, the use of instruments, is a branch of moral philosophy, subject to the criteria of prudence, efficiency, decency, and so forth. I need not demonstrate, in 1967, that those who abuse our technology at present are not interested in moral philosophy, are certainly not being prudent and decent, and are only in a narrow sense careful of efficiency and costs—they altogether neglect social costs. But even if we are interested in moral philosophy and want to use our technology prudently and decently, there are modern dilemmas that are hard to solve. So here let me make two small points of philosophical analysis that are usually overlooked.

In the first place, as technology increases, as there is a proliferation of goods and as civilization becomes more complex, there is a change of the scale on which things happen. Then, if we continue to use the concepts that apply to a smaller scale, we begin to think in deceptive abstractions. There are certain functions of life that we think we are carrying on, and that were carried on, on a smaller scale, but which now on a larger scale are only seemingly being carried on. Sometimes, indeed, because of the error in our thinking, we get an effect opposite from that which was intended.

Consider penology, a poignant example. When some fellows sat in stocks in the town square and people passed by and jeered at them or clucked their tongues, it is possible, though the psychology is dubious, that the effect might have been reform or penitence. (In my opinion, public confession on the square was more likely to lead to penitence and social integration.) But the Tombs in New York, a jail for many thousands locked up in cages, obviously has no relation whatever to penitence, reform, or social integration. In fact it is a school for crime, as is shown by the rate of repeaters who come back on more serious charges. This kind of penology on this scale has the opposite effect from that intended: it produces crime. Yet we have come by small steps from the fellow in stocks on the town square up to the Tombs or San Quentin. It seems to be "penology" all along the line, but there has been a point at which it has ceased to be penology and has become torture and foolishness, a waste of money and a cause of crime. And even the social drive for vindictiveness, which is probably the chief motive for punishment, is not satisfied; instead, there is blotting out of sight and *heightening* of social anxiety.

The change of scale has produced the same contrary effect in schooling. When there was academic instruction for many for a short time, or for a few for a longer time, it is possible that some academic education occurred. To be sure, most education for most people happened by means other than schools. Society functioned very well and many people became very expert and learned without going to school—in 1900, 6 percent graduated from high school and less than half of 1 percent went to college. Now, however, 100 percent are forced to go to high school and last year 75 percent graduated. Nearly 40 percent now go to college and by 1970 we are planning for 50 percent. On this scale, it is my observation as a reporter, very little education is occurring. For academic purposes, we might do just as well if we closed all the schools, though of course they serve for baby sitting, policing, and so forth. We could surely provide all the academic instruction that is achieved by far simpler and cheaper methods. Yet by small steps we have come to the present, using the same framework of administration and the same language, although the reality has entirely changed with the change of scale.

Take communications, as it is called. Newspapers, public speaking, and vaudeville meant one thing when they occurred in a simpler context, with the means of communication generally available to all. They mean another thing when we have mass media, semimonopolist broadcasting, licensed channels. The effect, by and large, has been homogenization and brainwashing—that is, precisely to prevent communication. We speak of our mass media as communications, yet they are importantly the preventing of communication. There is certainly very little talk back. Indeed, since television time is so expensive and by law the networks must give equal time on "controversial issues," the inevitable effect has been to avoid controversy altogether.

Grimly, the same damaging abstraction has been occurring in medicine. Since the doctors are swamped, there is a tendency in urban medicine to deal in vital statistics rather than health. I was recently at a conference in San Francisco concerned with the contraceptive pill. The doctors agreed that the pill was a heroic means of contraception and in private conversation they were dubious about its use because of the different effects on different women. Most of them felt, however, that since the pill's contraceptive effects were sure and since there was population pressure and economic pressure among the poor, it was a good policy publicly to promote its use. Classically, though, medicine was primarily concerned with the health of each individual. I am sure each of us is very much concerned about his own health. Vital statistics and the welfare of society 10 years from now are other kinds of questions, also very important, but because of the change in scale of operation, medicine has begun to lose its classical function and practice begins to have only an approximate relation to that function. This process can go very far, as it has already done in schooling. For instance, hospitals that are very large because of technological advantages may come to be run for administrative convenience even to the disadvantage of patients.

To conclude with a global example that includes the previous ones, we now see that city planning has turned into something called "urbanism," planning for urban areas. In this planning there is no such word as "home," but only dwelling units and housing. Yet it is a real question whether it is possible to have good housing, to provide people with homes, if we slip into thinking of dwelling units. It is a question whether urban areas are governable as cities, or whether just this way of thinking does not worsen anomie. Historically, when the city's functions occurred on a smaller scale and with smaller bureaucracies, an average citizen could understand their integration, even when he did not control it. There was shape and style, something to belong to and be loyal to. Vandalism and neglect were not indifferent. It was not possible for large segments of the population just to drop "out of society." And the sense of citizenship is indispensable for the high culture that is one of the most interesting functions of cities. Florence in its heyday had a hundred thousand inhabitants, Athens about the same; Goethe's Weimar had twenty-five thousand. In New York, a metropolitan region of fifteen million, I doubt that there are more than one hundred thousand who take part in the city with the feeling that in some sense it is theirs, that they understand its integration and control it or try to control it. The others just live there.

But of course there *are* changes in scale, brought about by new technologies and increased populations. How to cope with these? One suggestion has been that instead of pretending to education, communication, health, and so forth in a mass context that makes these things impossible, it would be better if we began to provide two entirely distinct sets of services: the old (and indispensable) professions with a personal responsibility to clients, and the disciplines of social engineering (a term I here use uninvidiously) working mainly on background conditions and treating persons in respects where individual differences are unimportant and personal response is not called for. Our present procedure, however, both destroys the old professions and embarrasses forthright social engineering. Thus, the ancient academic ritual of text, examination, and commencement, that made sense with academic types in a community of scholars, makes no sense in mass universities; yet we also cannot forthrightly use teaching machines and television for brute instruction and provide other means of usefully occupying the time of the nonacademic.

Physicians are not trained for home visits, family medicine, and preventive psychiatry, and the conditions of medical practice become more and more routine; yet we cannot forthrightly provide mass routine checkups, and it is only a few specialists in Public Health who show any medical concern for the background conditions of physical and mental disease.

Architecture and neighborhood planning are determined by bureaucrats according to abstract standards rather than the preferences of inhabitants, and all planning is subordinated to highway planning: yet we do not use our technology to clean the air and the rivers or rationalize transportation.

Local and competing newspapers have lapsed, town meetings and ward politics have lapsed, political oratory is ghost-written and not subject to cross examination, there is no vaudeville or local live theater except in a few metropolitan centers. Instead, we have packaged opinion and bland controversy on the mass media. Yet with these, there is no effort either to raise the cultural level by high-standard fare or to open the media to searching extremes that question the usual premises. The mass media can be used only to discuss mass-acceptable options, and then no new wisdom can enter the arena. For instance, instead of the usual spectrum from doves to hawks in a television panel on Vietnam, we ought to consider the views of those who think we have entered the phase of a universal American empire that should regulate the world and, on the other hand, of those who hold that the entire structure of sovereignty and power is long outmoded and unworkable.

I have spoken of the "disciplines of social engineering working mainly on background conditions." This brings me to the second philosophical issue I want to raise. In fact, at present we do not really have these disciplines. The social-psychological, anthropological, and ecological studies that are necessary for good social engineering and the right use of new technology are not sufficiently developed. We do not know the remote effects of what we institute in education, medicine, or urbanism; I have given a few examples to show how the remote effects might be the opposite of our intentions. We may use computers to estimate requirements, costs, and benefits, but in the fields we are discussing the theories on which the programs are based are puerile.

Let us suppose, however, that we do have better studies and better programs. There then arises the philosophical question: can we directly apply our best theories to human and social situations? I think not, for to preplan too thoroughly is to kill life; and the more subtle the theory, the more dangerous the attack. This is the invidious sense of "social engineering." Prudence and science are one thing, determining how people are to live and breathe is quite another. It is probably best just to open a space in which they can live and breathe in their own way. That is, we should aim at decency, not excellence.

We cannot draw the lines a priori, but in every case there is something to plan for and much to refrain from planning for. This often means when to technologize, to achieve a decent background, and when not to technologize, to achieve freedom.

Contrast an ideal forest preserve with a real State park. The forest preserve would be a kind of museum. We would put a hedge around a piece of the past, the antiquity of the globe untouched, saying that this place is not to change. You would come there by car but enter on foot. You may camp where you choose but there are no campsites and you don't need a permit—only be prudent and don't set the trees on fire. The forest preserve would be a kind of wilderness area with no rules whatever. But the State park is part of the urban complex; it is an extension into the green places of the rules of the city. You need a permit to camp and must camp at the specified places. This has advantages; you have a platform, and wood and water are provided. The fee *is* nominal, but there is a fee.

When I was young, we could freely pitch a tent on Fire Island Beach and freely build our fires or build a shack and squat. Because of the pressure of real estate developers, this has been forbidden and you now cannot squat in the sun and wind; many more cops patrol the beach and it is part of their duties to see that you do not. One feels trapped. One must make social arrangements and pay rent. But it is not the money that is onerous, it is that one has to obey their rules. They have planned for us, no matter how benevolent the plan.

The possibility of an escape into freedom from social rules is, of course, the pastoral ideal, as well described by Leo Marx. But the pastoral ideal can apply also in urban places. (Some of my novels have been called urban pastorals, and so they are.) One of the objections to much recent architecture and public housing is that it presents an impenetrable glass front; there are no holes and basements to creep into for games and sex. The waterfront has been improved into a concrete wall or a lovely promenade; there are no railroad yards or abandoned piers where one could hide from truant officers or fish. It is interesting that Jane Jacobs, who is a zealot against the new architecture because she wants to preserve neighborly sociability, nevertheless balks at the pastoral ideal of dark places and nooks. She wants everything bright and public, for safety. And to be sure, urban life has become more dangerous than the jungle. But I doubt that safety can be assured by architectural design or doormen. People who feel trapped and powerless will follow you home or finally assault you in public.

The philosophical point I wish to make is that there must be a kind of constitutional limit to planning, even at the expense of efficiency and the "best" solution. An analogy is the protection of freedom of speech in the Bill of Rights.

In the interpretation of the "absolutists," Justices Black and Douglas, freedom of speech is not to be balanced in terms of its social aspects, it is anarchic, prior to law—you can say what you damned please, up to the limits of actual emergency, however troublesome, violent, or conflictful your speech may be. And as a writer, let me say that unless I have this freedom of speech, I do not have freedom at all. I cannot know beforehand what words will come to me, and if I feel that there is a limit to what I can say, then nothing new will ever come to me.

A realistic method of guaranteeing freedom from excessive physical planning and social engineering is to condone or even encourage people's resistance to them. I say "realistic" because there is in effect a rising wave of popular protest in the country. The courts can encourage resistance by a tolerant attitude toward sit-ins, certain kinds of trespass, and civil disobedience. Bureaucratic control can be largely delegated away to "black power," "student power," etc. And it would be advantageous to replace many bureaucratically-run social services with a guaranteed income, which would enable powerless people to form their own cooperatives and suit themselves. These countervailing factors would then have to be taken into account in the programs of the social engineers. At present, needless to say, politicians who have to cadge votes are acutely conscious of inarticulate popular resistance and do draw the line. But planners disregard it because it is inarticulate, and since they—organized, rational, and well-financed—have more staying power than the populace, there is steady encroachment on freedom.

Another method of guaranteeing freedom from excessive planning brings me back to my first point, the revival of old-fashioned professionals responsible to clients and the immediate community rather than to society and social trends. Unless people become things, they will always live in the small scale as well as the big scale, and more intensely in the small scale than in the big scale. It is the role of their professionals, whom they ought to be able to hire and fire, to articulate, interpret, and design for them their small-scale needs in education, medicine, law, and housing. These will inevitably include spontaneity, individual differences, personal response, local options, and the need for freedom. Big-scale planners and social engineers will then have something articulate to cope with.

With this much introduction, let me launch into some remarks on rural reconstruction as interpreted in modern conditions. I want to propose a new look at rural-urban symbiosis.

It is important to understand that the present urbanization throughout the world is not a result of technological advance. Indeed, the thrust of modern technology has been against urbanization; consider electrification, power tools, telephone, radio and television, the automobile. And automation implies, if anything, the concentration of a great plant in a small space with a few workers, and the freedom of location of the programmers and the managers. Patrick Geddes assumed that with electrification the cities, amassed around steam power, would cease to grow. Ralph Borsodi thought that power tools would lead to dispersal, and Frank Lloyd Wright thought that the automobile would do it. Marx and Engels and Kropotkin blamed excessive urbanization on the power structure and looked to a better rural-urban symbiosis.

As has always been the case, our present urbanization is the consequence of a policy of enclosure. Poor people and farmers never leave home willingly. The young leave the land for adventure and bright lights; the especially gifted have to seek out the centers of culture and opportunity. But the mass of country people stay as long as they can make a living. Enclosure takes place in various ways. In the 18th century they shut off the commons to raise sheep; at the same time the city factories were developing and needed cheap labor, so there was a place for desperate farmers to find work, beginning at age nine. This combination of the "squirearchy" and the new capitalists is described in *The Deserted Village* and by Wordsworth. In our own century, during the 70 years that we have had control in Puerto Rico, we have destroyed this beautiful and fertile land by another classical method; old-fashioned mercantilism of the genre of George III. We have forbidden the Puerto Ricans to ship and travel directly without touching at United States ports, we have imposed severe quota restrictions on the processing of Puerto Rican sugar, we have ruled out coffee, and we have sequestered the more fertile plain for industrial use. Thus we have destroyed the agricultural base. But in the past two decades we have imposed on the top a thin crust of high technology and now the country is ravaged. Thirty-five percent of the population is on relief. People flee a thousand a week to New York, and flee back a thousand a week to the slums of San Juan. In other parts of the world, for example the Virgin Islands or Latin America, enclosure occurs by the importation of some industry, e.g. oil or hotels, with a wildly inflationary standard. A few natives are paid $70 a week where the average cash income was $70 a year. Then the *campesinos*, in sheer self-respect must flock to the city where there is no provision for them; they settle in thousands in tin shacks and die of cholera. Meantime, there is no effort to subdivide the land and get rid of feudal landowners; when there is such an effort, we dispatch the Marines.

Our American enclosure—the rural population is now 6 percent actually farming—has come about through cooperation in the American cash style amounting virtually to a conspiracy among chain-grocers, big plantations, suburban developers, and highway bureaucrats, steadily abetted by public policy. It is said to be efficient, and, indeed, one farmer can now feed thirty. Nevertheless, the price of food has *not* fallen (during the war in Vietnam, of course, it has risen), although the farmers' take has declined by about 8 percent a decade. Nor indeed do the retailers make much—at A&P wages are low and still the profit on store sales is 1 percent; 11 percent of A&P's 12 percent profit goes to their own middlemen, packagers, processors, transporters, jobbers. Thus it seems clear that the new "agrindustry" is not all that efficient. At present, 70 cents of the food dollar is spent in national chains and, naturally, food technology has been developed according to this pattern. If the technologists had put their wits to intensive agriculture by small growers, as in Holland, no doubt that method too would have become much more efficient.

The result has been depopulation of vast areas of the country at the same time that there are evident signs of overpopulation in the urban areas. As John Calhoun puts it, there are too many social signals in the urban centers, so that the circuits are clogged and normal development is impossible; there is not enough social space for trying out, there is too much noise, there is no solitude to develop personality, all experience is preprocessed, there is no relief from chronic anxiety. Of the million Negroes in New York, more than half came during the last 20 years as a result of the failure of southern sharecropping. Seven hundred thousand Puerto Ricans have come to New York City in the past 30 years. Of course, since New York has a housing shortage, it is necessary to provide public housing. This costs $20,000 a unit—which money could have been spent to keep the immigrants in the country. Clearly if the Negroes had wanted to come north, they would have done so 40 years ago, for they were not well treated in Mississippi and Alabama.

At present, however, or certainly during this generation, there is no chance of rural reconstruction on an agricultural base; indeed, the skills are rapidly vanishing. Possibly there may be a revival of specialized intensive farming, selling fresh food to nearby cities, if people can begin to demand a quality standard of living. This cannot occur in the ring surrounding the cities, for that has been suburbanized, but conceivably it might happen in the next ring.

But there is a chance of rural revival on a different principle: to help solve urban problems that are not easily or cheaply soluble in urban conditions. Such a principle would bring the country into the mainstream of modern problems, which are urban, and it would channel urban cash into rural areas now depopulating. Consider some possibilities.

It is advantageous for city children to spend a year or two at a country school and live on a family farm. Something similar is not uncommon for the upper middle class, but it would be profoundly awakening for slum children who have not, by age 13, been half a mile from home. Cost per child in a New York School is $850 a year; for little more than this sum one could help support the failing rural school and provide worthwhile cash for a farmer (perhaps three children to a farmer, who need merely feed them well and not beat them). The Farmers' Union and the 4-H clubs have offered to administer such a program.

It is advantageous to allow urban welfare money to be used for living in a rural neighborhood. Twenty-five hundred dollars buys destitution in a big city, but in a depopulating area, where one can also farm for part of subsistence, it provides a very decent life, including running an old car. Indeed, if we had a rational world, it would be possible for welfare recipients to use urban welfare money in foreign regions which have noninflationary prices, e.g., parts of Mexico, Crete, Sicily.

In our present system of enclosure, country vacations in motels and resorts have become part of the urban system. It would be advantageous to try to revive something more like the old visiting of country cousins at the farm.

The majority of patients in big mental institutions are harmless but cannot cope, or would hurt themselves and stop traffic, in urban environments. Very many are really getting no treatment and are just rotting away, though at great social expense. For the same money they could be boarded with rural families, and there is evidence that in such conditions there would be more remissions.

In functions like these, I am drawing on the classical pattern of regionalism, the capital and its country in symbiosis, each with a contrasting but complementary set of conditions and functions. This is, of course, the opposite of our homogenizing "conurbation" and regional planning. And the meaning of contemporary endless suburbanization is that one is never really in the city or in the country. The center becomes blighted and decays; the country is depopulated and returns to swamp. In the conurbation, regional planning means highway planning, smog planning, or efforts to equalize taxation; these are necessary, of course, but hardly sufficient for human needs.

The symbiotic conception of an urban-rural region requires administrative changes, e.g., to use New York City school money or welfare money in Vermont, central Pennsylvania, or the northern counties of New York. Or to use urban public housing money for improving farms in Mississippi or Alabama.

Rural reconstruction on this basis could well be culturally administered by revived Land Grants colleges, whose functions have now entirely been perverted to teaching urban know-how (usually in a second-rate fashion). Likewise there ought to be a renaissance of local newspapers, which are now nothing but advertising and gossip sheets. And there ought to be established numerous local radio and TV stations—each region can have 17 television channels, of which usually only two are in use. There cannot be rural reconstruction unless one's home place stands for something and is worth remaining in; but there are ways to strive for this.

In conclusion, let me repeat that I do not think there can be a significant cutback in urbanization in this generation. Nevertheless, the kind of rural reconstruction proposed can alleviate urban problems in terms of 2 percent of this and 5 percent of that. More important, it recreates options in an increasingly monolithic society. And finally, the pattern of rural subsistence with sources of cash from providing useful social services is tranquil and beautiful in itself.

The Human Uses of Science

Some Criteria for Selecting Technology

Start with the criterion of *Utility*. And consider the limiting case of Afro-Asian regions of dire poverty and drudgery, populous and industrially backward. What capital and technicians are useful?

The demand of the Western-trained leaders in these regions (it is hard to know what the people would choose) is to industrialize totally on advanced Western models as quickly as possible, and attain something like the American standard of living. The policy to accomplish this may be to concentrate at once on heavy industry, steel mills, machine tools; or, less radically, to devote part of the production to native goods for export, to build up a balance of trade. Either way, the policy means hard work without immediate rewards, curtailment of consumption, a stringent and likely totalitarian dictatorship both for work-discipline and for very long-range planning, a corresponding increase of the bureaucracy, the enforcing of new work habits, the disruption of the age-old community forms, occasional famines, sometimes the need to repress tribal revolts. Further, there are bound to be immense mistakes; nor is it surprising if, at the end of the process, much has been created that is already outmoded, and even more that does not, after all, suit the native conditions, materials, and uses. Such things could be documented again and again from the history of the industrialization of Russia, India, Israel, China, the Congo, etc., etc.

This policy is understandable as a reaction of despair to economic and political colonialism, leading people to produce bombers and bombs before anything else. Importantly, however, it is an illusion sprung from a superstitious notion of what it means to be modern and scientific. As such, it is abetted by foreign promoters who are interested in exporting pipe lines, mining machinery, and paved roads. But also governments and international agencies, claiming to have only benevolent aims, willingly go along with it. Yet if there were no wish to make profits or wield political influence, it would certainly be more useful to restrict the import of technology, specifically to give each region as soon as possible a self-supporting livelihood: the industries and techniques directly necessary for the maximum mass production of basic subsistence, food, shelter, medicine, and clothing where it is essential. And otherwise hands off! (It is dismaying to see photographs proving American benevolence by showing Africans in a school learning business methods and typing, and dressed in collars and ties. Is any of this package useful? Is even literacy according to our methods so indispensable for these people?)

To make people quickly self-supporting would be a far cheaper gift and in the long run a safer investment. People would be better off almost at once and could then think up the advantages that come marginally next in order. They could make their own community adjustments to the new conditions. In the production of subsistence goods there cannot be great mistakes, for people know the values involved. Less prior training is required. Less is wasted on politicians and policemen; it is more difficult for grafters to take their toll. People come to a higher standard according to their own style and choice, and therefore can develop a living culture out of what they have, instead of suffering a profound alienation. And the relation of means and ends is fairly direct, so that people are not mystified.

For such a policy, the primary technicians required are geographers and physicians, to ascertain the health and resources of each region; then engineers and anthropologically trained craftsmen teachers and agronomists. There is not so much need for geologists, metallurgists, etc., nor for economists and urbanists. And no need at all for geopoliticians, promoters, and commissars.

If we turn, next, to our own, the most advanced country, the need for selection is equally obvious, though less drastic. It is now generally conceded that much of our production for consumption is humanly useless, of poor quality, wasteful and demoralizing. (Meantime, economically, 30 percent of our people live in hardship, there is a critical shortage of housing, and so forth.) But in discussing the Affluent Society, let us by-pass utility as a familiar topic, and develop other criteria.

Efficiency, among us, tends to be measured solely in terms of a particular machine—e.g., gasoline per mile—or in terms of a particular complex of industrial operations—e.g., using the by-products. But if we look at our production more philosophically, in larger wholes and more remote effects, we see that some of our most cherished technical assumptions lead to inefficiency. We centralize as if the prime mover were still a huge steam engine that had to keep hot. For instance, it can be demonstrated that, except in highly automated factories where labor cost is small compared to fixed capital, or in heavy mining attached to its site, for the most part large industrial plants and concentrations of industry are less efficient than smaller ones that assemble parts machined in small shops; it is cheaper to transport the parts than the workers, a worker wastes more than an hour a day going to work and parking, etc. (No doubt an important reason for the concentration of big plants has nothing to do with technical efficiency, but with managerial control. I would strongly urge the unions to ask for some of that travel time to be paid, as the mine workers asked for portal-to-portal pay. Maybe that would lead to more efficient planning. As it is, however—for a reason that quite escapes me—a workman cannot count his carfare or fuel as a business expense against his income tax!) Certainly in the layout of cities, almost any kind of neighborhood plan and community-centered production would be far more efficient than our suburbs.

Similarly, by the evident principle that as the unit cost of production falls, the unit cost of distribution rises, it is likely that much of the vast technology of food processing and transportation is inefficient. Back in the thirties, when times were harder, Ralph Borsodi showed experimentally that, using domestic electrical apparatus, it was cheaper in hours and minutes of effort to grow and can one's own tomatoes than to buy the national brands—not to speak of the quality; other items, e.g., wheat and bread, were cheaper not on an individual but on a small co-operative basis; and still other items were cheaper maximum-mass-produced and nationally distributed. (I don't think anybody has ever tried or proved that our actual system of price-controlling semimonopolies is good for anything at all.) My conclusion is not that we ought to produce every item in the most efficient way—we have a surplus and it is not necessary to be all that efficient—but rather that, since our economists do not habitually survey alternate possibilities and make an accounting, our national housekeeping has become slovenly. Because of our slovenliness, we fall in bondage to the supermarket, we cannot get going a co-operative movement, our goods are poor in quality.

A more human-scaled production has obvious political and cultural advantages; it allows for more flexible planning, it is more conducive to scientific education and invention. We complain of the deadening centralism and conformity, and we put up with them because they are "efficient." But they are inefficient.

We hear rhetoric on the theme of learning to master the machine lest the machine master us. Let us consider a couple of criteria for the selection of technology and the users of technology that directly address this problem. If possible, the operation of a machine should be Transparent and *Comprehensible* to its users. This can be aided by the design and casing of the machine, and by the education of the users. An important corollary is that a machine ought to be *repairable* by its *user*. Our present plight is that, in the use of cars, telephones, electricity and gas systems, radio equipment, refrigeration, etc., etc., the mass of people are in bondage to a system of service men for even trivial repairs. The service men notoriously take advantage, but much worse is the tendency of the manufacturers to build obsolescence and nonrepairability *into* the machinery. (This is a negative criterion indeed! But it is inevitable that a caste possessing mysterious knowledge will shear the sheep.) What is the consequence? Psychologically, we have developed an anxious climate in which we don't know how to buy because we can't judge quality. It would be very different if we began to introduce the convention that a consumer must learn to take apart a machine and know how it works before he is encouraged to buy it—much as some of us still frown on an adolescent who cannot fix his broken bicycle. To make an analogy: considering the quantity of cars and mileage, there are remarkably few automobile accidents, but this is because the Americans have been tested and know how to drive.

Fifty years ago, the twin ideas of Progressive Education (learning by doing) and Functionalism in planning and design were matured to meet just this problem of making people more adequate to their new technological means, and of molding the new means into a shape and style more able to be grasped. Both movements, and also the related pragmatic philosophy, were criticized as antihumanistic, as abandoning classical education and traditional canons of beauty. But their principle was precisely humanistic, to reintegrate the new scientific specialism with the common intellectual and moral life. We can see that this is an American hope, to have the industrial revolution and a broad fundamental democracy; it still haunts us in our philosophizing about the high schools. (In Europe, similar ideas were almost always far more social-revolutionary, whether we think of Rousseau or Fourier, Kropotkin or the original Bauhaus.)

The British biologist Patrick Geddes, when he championed these ideas fifty years ago, however, saw that we must also select among the technologies. He was in the moral tradition of Ruskin, Morris, and the Garden City planners; they had experienced the profound dehumanization of the coal towns. But Geddes imagined that history was on his side, for the "neotechnology" of electricity had come to replace the "paleo technology" of coal and steam. Electricity satisfied the criterion of cleanliness (*Amenity*); and its easy transmission allowed ubiquitous sources of power, therefore we could plan more freely, e.g., for the culture of cities (the phrase is Lewis Mumford's, a disciple of Geddes). Some of what Geddes hoped for has come about; but on the whole the "forces of history" have not helped us much, in the absence of positive political and moral selection. And by a melancholy irony—history is good at creating melancholy irony—most of us followers of Geddes wryly praise the hideous old slums over the neotechnological slums, for they had more human scale and pullulation of life!

Finally, let us turn to some uncritical applications of science in biology and psychology. The most obvious illustration is the craze for antibiotic drugs.

These have been mass produced and promoted—with a simply fascinating lack of corresponding reduction in price—with a now conceded disregard of the organism as a whole. A powerful therapy, indicated for emergencies (e.g., for a dangerous mastoiditis), is used for a quick cure of minor or really systemic infections. Similarly, central-system sedatives and tranquilizers are administered with disregard to malnutrition, bad living habits, and bad environment. Meantime, the scientific "untechnological" tradition of medicine, from Hippocrates on—diet, exercise, natural living, airs, and places—is neglected; and the crucial factor of resistance to disease, the profoundest secret in medicine (just as prevention is its glory), is not studied. Mass immunity to a host of particular symptoms seems to be the sought-for goal, rather than the optimum possible health of each particular organism. But the aim of medicine is not, as such, to increase the average life span of a population—a person can be kept alive as a vegetable for years—but to foster the quality of life. If we want a single word for the criterion of selection that is here being abused, it is perhaps *Relevance* to the thing being treated.

The irrelevant application of technology to psychology is too rich to cope with; it would carry us away. Let us just mention the usual typical items. Dr. Skinner of Harvard has invented a machine that is useful for reinforcing appropriate responses, so it is now to be mass produced as a teaching machine, though it is irrelevant to the chief factors in either teaching or learning. (The purpose is to save money on teachers and have even bigger classes.) A new computer is installed in Iowa that can score millions of standard tests in very little time, so my boy's class is interrupted to take these tests, and the curriculum will surely be modified for the convenience of a mechanical scorer. In a town in Maine a well-financed research project, involving seventeen variables and plenty of work for the rented computer, discovers that boys tend to elect shop and girls tend to elect cooking; the author of the report comments "We used to think that this was so, now we know." What criterion is being violated here?

Perhaps it is *Modesty*: to have as few machines, methods, products (and research projects, as possible. Space is limited; people are multiplying; but the machines have multiplied most, with overpowering effect. The bridges and roads are more impressive than the rivers they span and the places they connect. Most immodest of all are the techniques of communication that have cluttered up the void and silence with images and words. It is now the rule that books are written to keep presses running, and the more radio channels we tap, the more drivel will be invented to broadcast.

Thus I have touched on half a dozen criteria for the humane selection of technologies: utility, efficiency, comprehensibility, repairability, ease and flexibility of use, amenity, and modesty. These values are esteemed by scientists and engineers; they are common ground between science and the humanities; they do not entail any conflict. Why are they not generally evident in our "scientific" society? I have purposely chosen only large and economically, rather than culturally, important examples: the type of foreign aid, the planning and distribution of cities, the organization of production, the American standard of living and public health, the methods of education.

2.

Return now to the thread of our argument, the confusion of science and technology and the rhetoric of lumping them together.

Let a group that is pushing a particular technology be opposed, and this rhetoric is immediately called on. Thus the big drug companies, being investigated for their outrageous pricing and monopolistic stifling of small competitors, have righteously exclaimed that without their methods of mass production, promotion, and pricing, scientific research comes to an end—there will be no more Listers and Pasteurs. Equally far-fetched is the uncriticized assumption of all the large suppliers of scientific technology that they alone are the right sponsors and entrepreneurs of scientific thought and research: this gives them the license to raid the universities for talent, to fill the public schools with their brochures, to influence the appropriation of school funds, to get tax exemptions for "scientific" foundations that are really parts of the firm, and even to dictate the lines of further research and sometimes actively to discourage "unprofitable" lines of research. In foreign aid and the export of capital, firms that have equipment to sell, and materials and fuels to buy, are wonderfully persuasive about helping backward societies to become modern scientific societies. The Pentagon also is an enthusiastic advocate and underwriter of pure research—though not especially on the genetic effects of radioactive fall-out.

For a couple of hundred years, our proliferating technologies have been selected on the criteria of marketability and profitability, and by and large the market has furthered usefulness and efficiency. (But not invariably. Moral economists like Ned Ludd and Coleridge, Ruskin and Ebenezer Howard have been critical for the same two centuries.) In the past fifty years, however, new conditions have developed that are unambiguously baneful. There has been systematic corruption of the public notion of what is useful. (An early typical example was the campaign that put across bleached flour as tastier and more "refined," since it spoiled less in the grain elevators.) The growing public ineptitude and ignorance, and a growing mystique of technical experts, have made rational restraint difficult. And finally, by an inevitable reflex, the stream of science itself is channeled and hampered by the too abundant technology that it has created.

This, I submit, is the context of the current debate about what should be taught and how it should be taught. Then it is dismaying to read arguments, like Sir Charles Snow's, from the "scientific point of view," that completely disregard it. Sir Charles is so puffed up with the importance of science in its technical applications that he fails to ask any scientific questions, or to have any qualms of scientific conscience. Apparently some scientists feel so grand about being on the governing board that they are stone-blind to the evident fact that they are not the makers of policy. Do they choose as scientists to have scientific knowledge kept secret? Are they satisfied as scientists that space exploration has so speedily become a means of spying that Russians and Americans cannot co-operate? (It is said that at present our instruments for gathering information are superior, but the Russian rockets can carry more payload: now, what would be logical? who is proposing it?) "The sciences," wrote Jenner—to Paris in 1803!—"are never at war." This follows from the essence of science as a consensus of observers.

But perhaps this is the kind of wisdom to be got from the humanities.

The fact that just now scientific technology is controlling, abusing, and threatening to devastate mankind is neither here nor there as an argument for how we should educate our youth to make a better world. There were long periods when priests had power, other periods when soldiers had it, and even periods when literary mandarins had it. All of them did useful things and all of them made a mess. So I would propose that scientists think twice about what kind of power they have, what they are co-operating with, and with whom, and try a little harder to know themselves. There is a well-known humanistic technique for this chastening enterprise, the method of Socrates. (Psychotherapy is one of its modern branches.) A little history, too, should be a required course.

Education

The Present Moment in Education

1.

In every society, the education of the children is of the first importance. But in all societies, both primitive and highly civilized, until quite recently most education occurred incidentally. Adults did their work and other social tasks. The children were not excluded. The children were paid attention to and learned to be included; they were not "taught."

In most institutions and in most societies *incidental education* has been taken for granted. Incidental education takes place in community labor, master-apprentice arrangements, games, plays, sexual initiations, and religious rites.

Generally speaking, this incidental process suits the nature of learning better than direct teaching. The young experience cause and effect rather than pedagogic exercise. Reality is often complex, but every young person can take that reality in his own way, at his own time, according to his own interests and own initiative. Most importantly, he can imitate, identify, be approved, be disapproved, cooperate, or compete without suffering anxiety through being the center of attention.

The archetype of successful incidental education is that of an infant learning to speak, a formidable intellectual achievement that is universally accomplished. We do not know how it is done, but the main condition seems to be what we have been describing: Activity is going on involving speaking. The infant participates; he is attended to and spoken to; he plays freely with his speech sounds; it is advantageous to him to make himself understood.

Along with incidental education, most societies also maintain institutions specifically devoted to teaching the young, such as identity rites, catechisms, nurses, pedagogues, youth houses, and formal schooling. I think there is a peculiar aspect to what is learned through such means, rather than what is picked up incidentally.

Let me emphasize that it is only in the last century that a majority of the children in industrialized countries have gotten much direct teaching. Only in the past few decades has formal schooling been generally extended into adolescence and further. For example, in the United States in 1900, only 6 percent of the youngsters went through high school, and only one quarter of 1 percent went through college. Yet now, formal schooling has taken over, well or badly, very much of the more natural incidental education of most other institutions.

This state of affairs may or may not be necessary, but it has had consequences. These institutions, and the adults who run them, have correspondingly lost touch with the young; and on the other hand, the young do not know the adults who are involved in their chief activities.

Like jails and insane asylums, schools isolate society from its problems, whether in preventing crime, or in curing mental disease, or in bringing up the young. To a remarkable degree, the vital functions of growing up have become hermetically redefined in school terms. Community service means doing homework. Apprenticeship means passing tests for a job in the distant future. Sexual initiation is high school dating. Rites of passage consist in getting a diploma. Crime is breaking the school windows. Rebellion is sitting in on the Dean. In the absence of adult culture, the youth develop a subculture.

Usually, there has been a rough distinction between the content of what is learned in incidental education and what is learned in direct pedagogy. Teaching, whether directed by elders, priests, or academics, deals with what is not evident in ordinary affairs; pedagogy aims to teach what is abstract, intangible, or mysterious. As the center of attention, the learner is under pressure. All education socializes, but pedagogy socializes deliberately, instilling the morals and habits which are the social bonds.

There are two opposite interpretations of why pedagogy seeks to indoctrinate. In my opinion, both interpretations are correct. On the one hand, elders instill an ideology which will support their system of exploitation and the domination of the old over the young, and they, the elders, make a special effort to confuse and mystify because their system does not recommend itself to common sense.

On the other hand, there is a vague but important wisdom that must be passed on, a wisdom which does not appear on the surface and which requires special pointing out and cloistered reflection. The champions of the liberal arts colleges maintain that, one way or another, the young will pick up contemporary know-how and mores, but that the greatness of Mankind—Hippocrates, Beethoven, Enlightenment, Civil Liberties, the Sense of the Tragic—all will lapse without a trace unless scholars work at perpetuating these values. I sympathize with the problem as they state it; but, in fact, I have not heard of any method whatever, scholastic or otherwise, of teaching the humanities without killing them. I remember how at age twelve, browsing in the library, I read

Macbeth with excitement; yet in class I could not understand a word of *Julius Caesar*, and I hated it. I'm pretty sure this is a common pattern. The survival of the humanities would seem to depend on random miracles which are becoming less frequent.

Unlike incidental learning which is natural and inevitable, formal schooling is deliberate intervention and must justify itself. We must ask not only whether such schooling is well done, but is it *worth* doing? *Can* it be done? Is teaching possible at all?

There is a line of critics from Lao-tzu and Socrates to Carl Rogers who assert that there is no such thing as teaching either science or virtue; and there is strong evidence that schooling has little effect on either vocational ability or on citizenship. Donald Hoyt, in *American College Testing Reports* (1965), found that in any profession, college grades have had no correlation with life achievement.

At the other extreme, Dr. Skinner and the operant-conditioners claim that they can "instruct" for every kind of performance, and that they can control and shape human behavior much as they can the behavior of animals who have been sealed off from their ordinary environment. But it is disputable whether children are good subjects for such instruction in any society we might envisage.

The main line of educators from Confucius and Aristotle to John Dewey hold that one can teach the child good habits in morals, arts, and sciences through practice. The art is to provide the right tacks at the right moments; and Froebel, Herbert, Steiner, Piaget, etc., have different theories about this. But sociologists like Comte and Marx hold that social institutions overwhelmingly determine what is learned—so much so, that it is not worthwhile to be concerned with pedagogy. My bias is that "teaching" is largely a delusion.

In every advanced country, the school system has taken over a vast part of the educational functions of society. The educationists design toys for age two, train for every occupation, train for citizenship, train for sexuality, and explain and promote the humanities.

With trivial exceptions, what we mean by *school*—curriculum, texts, lessons, scheduled periods marked by bells, teachers, examinations, and graded promotion to the next step—was the invention of some Irish monks of the seventh century who thought to bring a bit of Rome to wild shepherds. It has been an amazing success story, probably more important than the Industrial Revolution.

No doubt it was a good thing, at first, for wild shepherds to have to sit still for a couple of hours and pay strict attention to penmanship and spelling.

The imposed curriculum was entirely exotic and could only be learned by rote anyway. Mostly, of course, it was only aspiring clerics who were schooled.

By an historical accident, the same academic method later became the way of teaching the bookish part of some of the learned professions. There is no essential reason why law and medicine are not better learned through apprenticeship, but the bookish method was clerical, and therefore scholastic. Perhaps any special education based on abstract principles was part of a system of mysteries, and therefore clerical, and therefore scholastic.

The monkish rule of scheduled hours, texts, and lessons is also not an implausible method for giving a quick briefing to large numbers of students, who then embark on their real business. Jefferson insisted on universal compulsory schooling for short terms in predominantly rural communities, in order that children might be able to read the newspapers and catechized in libertarian political history. During the following century, in compulsory urban schools, the children of immigrants were socialized and taught standard English. The curriculum was the penmanship, the spelling, and the arithmetic needed for the business world.

At present, however, the context of schooling is quite different. The old monkish invention of formal schooling is now used as universal social engineering. Society is conceived as a controlled system of personnel and transactions, with various national goals depending on the particular nation. And the schools are the teaching machines for all personnel.

There is no other way of entry for the young. Teaching aims at psychological preparation in depth. Schooling for one's role, in graded steps, takes up to 20 years and more; it is the chief activity of growing up; any other interest may be interrupted—but not schooling. The motivation for a five-year-old's behavior is thus geared 15 years in the future.

In highly productive technologies like ours which do not need manpower, the function of long schooling is to keep the useless and obstreperous young *away* from the delicate social machine. The function of the school is to babysit the young and police them.

Yet the schools are not good playgrounds or reservations either. The texture of school experience is similar to adult experience. There is little break between playing with educational toys and watching educational TV, or between being in high school and dating, or between being in college and being drafted, or between being personnel of a corporation and watching NBC.

Since the trend has been to eliminate incidental education and deliberately to prepare the young for every aspect of ordinary life through schooling, we would expect pedagogy to have become functional. Yet radical students complain that today's schooling is ideological through and through. The simplest, and not altogether superficial, explanation of this paradox is that scholastic mystery has transformed adult business. It is society that has become mandarin.

None of this works. Contemporary schooling does not prepare for jobs and professions. For example, evidence compiled by Ivan Berg of Columbia shows that on the job dropouts do as well as high school graduates.

Nor has today's education made for peaceful baby-sitting and policing. Instead of an efficient gearing between the teaching machine and the rest of the social machine, the schools seem to run for their own sake. There IS a generation gap. Many youngsters fail; many drop out; others picket.

Predictably, the response of school administrators has been to refine the process; to make the curriculum more relevant, to start schooling earlier, to employ new technologies in teaching, to eliminate friction by admitting students to administrative functions.

But the chief objection to engineering in education is that it is inefficient. It tries to program too much, to pre-structure syllabi and lesson-plans. But human behavior is strong, graceful, and discriminating only to the extent that, in concrete situations, it creates its own structures as it goes along. Things can be learned securely, quickly, and naturally only through coping. As John Holt has pointed out, the teacher wants the child to learn the lesson according to the teaching plan; but the child quickly learns how to con the teacher, for getting a passing grade is the child's real problem of the moment.

It has frequently been said that human beings use only a small part—"just 2 percent"—of their abilities. Some educators therefore propose that much more demanding and intellectual tasks be set at a much earlier age. There is no doubt that most children can think and learn far more than they are challenged to. Yet it is likely that by far the greatest waste of ability occurs because a playful, hunting, sexy, dreamy, combative, passionate, artistic, manipulative, destructive, jealous, magnanimous, selfish and disinterested animal is continually thwarted by social organization—and perhaps especially by schooling.

If so, the main purpose of pedagogy should be to counteract and delay socialization as long as possible. For our situation is the opposite of the situation in the seventh century. Since the world has become overly scholastic, we must protect the wild shepherds.

Current high thought among schoolmen, for instance those of the National Science Foundation and those of the Harvard School of Education, is that the contemporary syllabus is indeed wasteful and depressing. But they would expand the schools and render the programming more psychological. Since the frontiers of knowledge are changing so rapidly, there is no use in burdening children with data that will be outdated in ten years, or with skills that will soon be better performed by machines; rather children must learn *to learn:* their cognitive faculties must be developed; they must be taught the big Ideas, concepts like the conservation of energy. This is exactly what Robert Hutchins was saying forty years ago.

Or more daringly, the children must not be *taught,* but be allowed to *discover.* They must be encouraged to guess and to brainstorm rather than be tested on the right answers.

In my opinion, in an academic setting, these proposals are never bona fide. As Gregory Bateson has noted with dolphins and trainers, and as John Holt has noticed in middle class schools, learning to learn means picking up the structure of behavior of the teachers, becoming expert in the academic process. In actual practice, the young discoverers are bound to discover what will get them past the College Board examinations. Guessers and dreamers are not free to balk and drop out for a semester to brood and let their theories germinate in the dark, as proper geniuses do.

It is a crucial question whether "cognitive faculties" does not mean the syntax of school performance. There is an eccentric passage in an early work of Piaget where he says that children in the playground seem to be using intellectual concepts, e.g. causality, a couple of years earlier than they are "developed" in the classroom, but he sticks to the classroom situation because it allows for his "scientific" observation. Yet this might mean that the formal routine of the classroom has hindered the spontaneous use of the intellect, and that the "concept" which is developed in the classroom is not an act of intellect grasping the world at all, but is a method of adjustment to the classroom, the constricted seats, the schedule, the teacher's expectation, the boring subject-matter to which one must pay attention.

2.

Progressive education is best defined as a series of reactions to a school system that has become rigid. Progressive education aims to include what has been repressed; it aims to right the balance.

Moreover progressive education is a political movement; progressive education emerges when the social problem is breaking out. To put it more positively, an old regime is not adequate to cope with new conditions; new energy is needed. The form that progressive education takes in each era is prophetic of the next social revolution.

Rousseau reacted to the artificiality and insincerity of the royal court, and the parasitism, the callous formalism, and the pervasive superstition of the courtiers. The establishment of his day had simply become incompetent to govern. A generation later, it abdicated.

John Dewey reacted to a genteel culture that was irrelevant in an industrialized society. Dewey reacted to rococo decoration, to puritanism that denied animal nature, to censorship, and to rote performance imposed on children. Again, after a generation (by the end of the New Deal) Dewey's moral vision had largely come to be. In his lifetime, most of the program of the Populists and the Labor Movement had become law; education and culture (among whites) had become utilitarian and fairly classless; the revolution of Freud and Spock was well advanced; censorship was on its way out; and there was no more appliqué decoration.

A.S. Neill's Summerhill School, a recent form of progressive education, was likewise a reaction against social-engineering. Neill reacted against the trend to 1984 as Orwell came to call it, against obedience, authoritarian rules, organizational role-playing instead of being, the destruction wrought by competition and grade-getting. Since going to class is for children in the immutable nature of things, Neill's making of attendance a matter of choice was a transformation of reality; and to the extent that there was authentic self-government at Summerhill and to the extent that small children were indeed given power, the charisma of all institutions was challenged.

Progressive education has been criticized as a middle-class gimmick. The black community, especially, resents being used for "experiments." Poor children, it is claimed, need to learn the conventional wisdom so they can compete for power in the established system. Black parents demand "equality education" and expect their children to wear ties. In my opinion, this criticism is wrongheaded. The scholastic evidence shows that the more experimental the high school, the more successfully its graduates compete in conventional colleges.

Black communities should run their own schools, and they should run them on the model of Summerhill. This has indeed been the case with the sporadic Freedom schools which have been influenced, directly or indirectly, by Neill.

I don't agree with the theory of *Head Start* that disadvantaged children require special training to prepare them for learning. I find nothing wrong with the development of their intellectual faculties; they have learned to speak, and they can make practical syllogisms very nicely, if they need to. If they have not learned the patterns by which they can succeed in school, the plausible move is to change the school. But, as Elliott Shapiro has suggested, the trouble might be that these children have been pushed too early to take responsibility for themselves and for their little brothers and sisters as well. The trouble is that their real problems have been all too insoluble. It's not that these children can't reason; the fact is that pure reason is of no use to them in their coping with their all too real difficulties.

What these kids need is freedom from pressure to perform. And, of course, they need better food, more quiet, and a less impoverished environment to grow up in—AT THEIR OWN PACE. These things are what the First Street School on the Lower East Side in New York, which was somewhat modeled on Summerhill, tried to provide.

Nevertheless, we must say that progressive education has been almost a total failure. The societies that have emerged after fulfilling their programs, were not what the visionaries had hoped for. French or American democracy was not what Rousseau had in mind. Dewey's social conceptions have ended up as technocracy, labor bureaucracy, and suburban conformity. The likelihood is that A.S. Neill's hope, too, will be badly realized. It is not hard to envisage a society in the near future in which self-reliant and happy people will be attendants of a technological infrastructure over which they have no control whatever, and whose purposes do not seem to them to be any of their business. Indeed, Neill describes with near satisfaction such success-stories among his own graduates. Alternately, it is conceivable that an affluent society will support its hippies like Indians on a reservation.

How to prevent these outcomes? Perhaps Neill protects his community a few years too long, both from the oppressive mechanistic world and from adolescent solitude—it is hard to be alone in Summerhill. Moreover, it seems to me that there is something inauthentic in Neill's latitudinarian lack of standards. For example, Beethoven and Rock 'n' Roll are considered equivalent (though Neill himself prefers Beethoven). We are not only free organisms but parts of a mankind that historically has made strides with great inspirations and through terrible conflicts. We cannot slough off that accumulation of cultures, however burdensome, without becoming trivial. It seems to me that the noisy youth subculture of today is not grownup—which is to the good—but also that it can *never* become grown-up.

Generally, the young of today have strong feelings for honesty, frankness, loyalty, fairness, affection, freedom and the other virtues of generous natures. They quickly resent the hypocrisy of politicians and administrators, and parents who mouth big abstractions, but who act badly. But the young themselves—like most politicians and administrators and many parents— seem to have forgotten the concrete reality of ideals like magnanimity, compassion, honor, consistency, civil liberty, integrity and justice—ideals which maintain and which re-create Mankind. Naturally, without these ideals and the conflicts they engender, there is no tragedy. Most young persons seem to disbelieve that tragedy exists, they always interpret impasse as timidity, and casuistry as finking out. I may be harsh, but though I am often astonished by their physical courage, I am not often impressed by their moral courage.

3.

My own thinking is that:

(1) Incidental education (taking part in the ongoing activities of society) should be the chief means of learning.

(2) Most high schools should be eliminated. Other kinds of youth communities should take over the social functions of the high school.

(3) College training, generally, should follow—not precede—entry into the professions.

(4) The chief task of educators should be to see that the activities of society provide incidental education. If necessary, government and Society should invent new useful activities offering new educational opportunities.

(5) The purpose of elementary pedagogy through age twelve should be to protect and nourish a child's free growth, since both the community and family pressure are too much for a child to withstand.

4.

Let me review the arguments for this program:

We must drastically cut back schooling because our extended tutelage is against nature and actually arrests growth.

The effort to channel growing up according to a preconceived curriculum discourages the young and wastes many of the best of our powers to learn and cope.

Schooling does not prepare for real performance; it is largely carried on for its own sake. Only the academically talented, only 10 to 15 percent according to Conant, thrive in this useless activity without being bored, and without being harmed.

Our system of education, isolating as it does the young from the older generation, alienates the young.

Yet it makes no sense for many of the brightest and most sensitive of our young to simply drop out or to confront society with hostility. This state of affairs does not lead to social reconstruction. The complicated and confusing conditions of our times require fresh thinking, and therefore, what we need is participation, particularly by the young.

Young radicals seem to believe that political change will solve our chief problem. Or that our problems will solve themselves after political change. This is a delusion. Our novel problems of urbanization, technology, and ecology have not heretofore been faced by any political faith. The fact is that the educational systems of other advanced countries are no better than ours.

It has been my Calvinistic and Aristotelian experience that most people cannot organize their lives without productive activity. Of course, this does not necessarily mean paid activity. The professions, the services, industries, arts and sciences are the arenas. Radical politics and doing one's thing are careers for only a very few.

As things are, American society either excludes the young, or corrupts the young, or exploits the young. I believe we must make the rules of licensing and hiring more realistic, and we must get rid of mandarin requirements. We must design apprenticeships that are not exploitative.

Society desperately needs much work, both intellectual and manual, in urban renewal, in ecology, in communications, and in the arts. All these spheres could make use of young people. Many such enterprises are best organized by young people themselves, like the community development and the community action of "Vocations for Social Change." There are also excellent apprenticeships open for the brainy at the think-tanks like the Oceanic Institute at Makapuu Point, or in the Institute for Policy Studies in Washington, both of which are careless about checking diplomas. Our aim should be to multiply the paths of growing up. There should be ample opportunity for a young boy or girl to begin his career again, to cross over from one career to another, to take a moratorium, to travel, or to work on his own. To insure freedom of option, and to insure that the young can maintain and express their critical attitude, adolescents should be guaranteed a living. Giving a young person the present cost of a high school education would provide enough money for a young person to live on.

The advantage of making education less academic has, of course, occurred to many people. There are a myriad of programs to open the school to the world by: (1) recruiting professionals, artists, gurus, mothers, and dropouts as teachers' aides; and (2) granting academic credit for work-study, for community action, for the writing of novels, for service in mental hospitals, for spending one's junior year abroad, and for other kinds of released time.

Naturally, I am enthusiastic for this development, and I only want it to go the small further step of abolishing the present school establishment, instead of aggrandizing it.

There is also a movement in the United States, as there is in Cuba and China, for adolescent years to be devoted to public service. This is fine if the service is not compulsory nor regimenting.

It is possible for everyone's education to be tailor-made according to his own particular developing interest. Choices along the way will often be ill-conceived and wasteful, but such choices will nevertheless express desire, and will therefore immediately coincide with reality. Such choices will, therefore, converge to find the right vocation for a young person more quickly than through any other method. One's vocation is what one is good at and can do. Vocation is what employs a reasonable amount of one's powers. The use of the full power of a majority of the people would make for a stable society which would be far more efficient than our own. In such a set-up, those who have peculiar excellences are more likely to find their way when they have entry by doing something they can do well, and then proceeding to their more particular interests, and by being accepted for *what* they can do.

Academic schooling, of course, could be chosen by those with academic talents. Obviously, schools would be better off if unencumbered by sullen uninterested bodies. But the main use of academic teaching should be for those already busy in the sciences and the professions, who need academic courses along the way to acquire further knowledge. Cooper Union in New York City used to fulfill this function very well.

Of course, in such a set-up, employers would themselves provide ancillary academic training. In my opinion, this ancillary schooling would do more than any other single thing to give blacks, rurals, and other culturally deprived youth a fairer entry and a chance for advancement. As we have seen, there is no correlation *on the job* between competence and prior schooling.

This leads to another problem. Educationally, schooling on the job is usually superior to academic schooling, but the political and moral consequences of such a system are ambiguous. At present, a youth is hired because of his *credentials,* rather than for his actual skill. This system allows a measure of free-market democracy. However, if he is to be schooled on the job, he must be hired essentially for his promise. Such a system can lead to company paternalism like Japanese capitalism. On the other hand, if the young have options and they are allowed to organize and criticize, on-the-job education is the quickest way to workers' management which, in my opinion, is the only effective democracy.

University education—liberal arts and the principles of the professions—should be reserved only for adults who already know something, and who have something about which to philosophize. Otherwise, as Plato pointed out, such "education" is just mere verbalizing.

To provide a protective and life-nourishing environment for children through age twelve, Summerhill is an adequate model. I think Summerhill can be easily adapted to urban conditions. Probably, an even better model would be the Athenian pedagogue touring the city with his charges; but for this to work out, the streets and the working-places of the city will have to be made safe and more available than it is likely they will be. The prerequisite of city-planning is that children be able to use the city; for no city is governable if it does not grow citizens who feel that the city is theirs.

The goal of elementary pedagogy is a very modest one: a small child should be able, under his own steam, to poke interestedly into whatever goes on; and he should be able, through observation, through questions, and through practical imitation, to get something out of such poking around. In our society this is what happens at home pretty well up to age four; but after that, such random poking around becomes forbiddingly difficult.

I have often spelled out this program of incidental education, and I have found no takers. Curiously, I get the most respectful if wistful attention at teachers' colleges, even though what I propose is quite impossible under present administration. Teachers know how much they are wasting the children's time, and teachers understand that my proposals are fairly conservative.

However, in a general audience the response is incredulity. Against all evidence, people are convinced that what we are now doing must make sense or we wouldn't be doing it. It does not help if I point out that in dollars and cents it might be cheaper—and it would certainly be more productive—to eliminate most schools and have the community itself provide more of the education. Yet the majority in a general audience are willing to admit that they themselves got very little out of their school years. Occasionally, an old reactionary businessman agrees with me enthusiastically that book- learning isn't worth a penny. Among radical students, my proposals are met by a sullen silence. They want Student Power, and for the most part, they are unwilling to answer whether they are authentically students at all. I think they're brainwashed. Naturally, it makes no difference to them if they demand "University Reform," or if the University is shut down altogether.

Instead of Student Power, what they should be demanding is (a) a more open entry into society, and (b) that education money should be spent more usefully, and (c) that licensing and hiring should be handled without consideration of irrelevant diplomas; and so forth. Youth Power can make the authentic demand for the right to take part in initiating and deciding the functions of society that concern them, as well as the right to govern their own lives— which are nobody else's business. Bear in mind that I am speaking of youths between age 17 and 25. At all other times in man's history, these individuals would already have found their places in the real world.

The Universe of Discourse
in Which They Grow Up

1. Interlocking Mass Media

In the institutional speech, a child hears only one world view. Every mass-medium caters to, and confirms, a big common-denominator of opinion and taste, but even more influential is that all of them interlock. "News" is what is selected as newsworthy by a few news-services; three almost identical broad-casting networks abstract from the same; and the same is abridged for the *Junior Scholastic*. Even for this news, only sixty towns in America have competing newspapers. (In 1900 there were 600.) The "standard of living," the way to live decently, is what is shown in the ads in a few mass-circulation magazines and identically in the TV commercials. Movie sets of respectable life come from the same factories. Political thought is the platforms of two major parties that agree on all crucial issues, like the Cold War and the Expanding Economy.

Much of this public speech is quite meaningless. The ads compete with high rhetoric but the commodities are nearly the same. Politicians are polemical but avoid any concrete issues that might differentiate the candidates, for that would lose votes. The real meaning of the speeches, the goal of profits and power, is *not* stated. By age eleven or twelve, bright children, perhaps readers of *Mad* magazine, recognize that the speech is mere word-play.

The school system is a universal trap that teaches the same. Sixty percent graduate from high school, the others being rural or underprivileged Latin-Americans and Negroes. (In 1900, six percent graduated from high school.) But the entire school system is increasingly geared to the graduate-universities and the same national purpose of expanding the economy and training for the Cold War and the corporations. Even the primary schools are flooded with cor-poration brochures.

Apart from family, children have little speech with any adults except in school. The crowding and regimentation in the schools allow little contact. The public speech cannot be tested against direct observation or experience. Urban and suburban children do not see actual crafts and industries. Playthings are pre-fabricated toys, not pickups; and instead of practical carpentry, plumbing, and mechanics, there are do-it-yourself kits. The very purpose of progressive education, to learn the world by doing in it, in order to change it, is inevitably perverted to adjustment and socialization. The endless conurbation destroys the contrast of city and country. Few children know anything about animals. Even basic foods are packaged and distributed, and increasingly precooked, in the official style.

Conversely, a child hears less of any rival style or thought. The rival world-view of (even hypocritical) religion is no longer influential, and children do not know the Bible. Eccentric and imaginative classical children's literature is discouraged by librarians because it does not fit educators' word-lists and is probably unhygienic; but concocted approved books state the official world-view. The residual, more exciting, reading, the comic books, does not contrast to life but withdraws from it; it lets off steam rather than develops feeling. The movies are the same more insidiously, because they are apparently adult. Finally, the ideal models of careers with their philosophies—scientist, explorer, nurse, actor, writer—have been normalized to Madison Avenue stereotypes: Organization Men with varying costumes.

2. Brainwashing

But this one system of meaning, although homogenous and bland, is not sparse or quiet. On the contrary, the quantity of public speech, plays, information, is swamping; and the tone is jumpy and distracting. In the schools, which are increasingly tightly scheduled and graded, exposure occurs with intense pressure of tests for retention and punishment for failure.

No one can critically appreciate so many ideas and images. At the same time as the concrete relation of the public words to experience or personal need is at best confused, there is less solitude or moratorium to figure it all out. And add to this confusion the anxiety that, if the information is not correctly parroted, one will fall off the ladder and be a dropout.

We thus have a uniform world-view, the absence of any viable alternative, confusion about the relevance of one's own experience and feelings, and a chronic anxiety leading one to cling to the one world-view as the only security: such a combination is brainwashing. In all societies and periods of history small children are subjected to brainwashing, for they are weak, ignorant, economically dependent, and subject to be bullied. Since our own society has less corporal punishment, less extreme poverty, less fear of death, and less brutal toilet and sexual disciplining, I doubt that the early brainwashing goes as deep as it sometimes has. But the ideological exposure is unusually thorough. Profit-societies, like garrison-states, invade every sphere of life. The perspective of personal and practical experience is impossible for a child to maintain; but his parents are equally baffled, for with centralized top-down decision-making, few of the adults exercise initiative or know what goes on. There is continual positive reinforcement and very little negative reinforcement.

Thus, despite our technology of surplus, our civil peace, and so much educational and cultural opportunity, it is hard for an American child to grow toward independence and individual identity; to retain his curiosity and initiative, and to acquire a scientific attitude, scholarly habits, productive enterprise, poetic speech.

Unfortunately, the pervasive philosophy to which children are exposed as they grow up is the orthodoxy of a social machinery which, in its economy, politics and administration, is quite uninterested in persons, except to man and aggrandize itself. Especially young persons.

3. Adolescent Embarrassment

What happens when, with this background of language and learning, the child becomes adolescent: awkward and self-conscious, sexually hungry and falling in love, searching for identity, metaphysical, shaken in religious faith or undergoing religious conversion, his Oedipus complex reviving, making a bid for freedom from home, grandiosely ambitious and day-dreaming, looking for a vocation and human service? At best, in organic communities, rational communication breaks down at such an age and the community has recourse to rites of passage.

The American world-view is worse than inadequate; it is irrelevant and uninterested. Adolescents are abandoned. They are insulted by not being taken seriously. Our social machine does not require or desire its youth to find identity; it does not want new initiative, but hands and brains to keep itself running. Our orthodoxy does not bear metaphysics. Religious troubles are treated as merely psychotic; they are certainly disruptive of urban order and scholastic scheduling. Vocational guidance has little to do with vocation. Many, maybe most, of the careers that are open are not *prima facie* services to humanity; that is not why businesses are run, nor why bombs are stockpiled. Idealism is astonishingly without prestige.

The adolescent sexual situation is peculiarly ambiguous. In our transitional phase of the sexual revolution, there is a breakdown of repression (keeping out of mind) and also less inhibition of behavior; yet neither in the economy, nor in the housing, nor in the family pattern is there any provision for changed mores. On the contrary, the years of tutelage even tend to lengthen—especially for middle-class youth in colleges whose administrations regard themselves as *in loco parentis*. The official mental-hygienic ideology bears little relation to the stormy images and imperative demands of adolescent love. In the elementary and junior high schools sexual facts do not officially exist. But an adolescent is expected to be sexual or there is alarm.

Embarrassment—the inability to express or reveal one's needs and feelings to the others—is universal among adolescents; but in our society it is especially problematic. There are unusually many areas of embarrassment; yet there is also a strong tendency to brazen it out and act without feeling or meaning. The embarrassment contains hostility to those who will not pay attention or will put one down; and despair at the futility of trying to make oneself clear. There is not even a public language relevant to one's burning private facts. (How pathetic it is to hear adolescents using the language of TV marriage-counselors, or of movies!) Inevitably, the hostility is retroflected as self-denigration; the adolescent ceases to believe in the rightness or even the existence of his own wants, so that his rebellious claims seem even to himself to be groundless, immature, ridiculous.

Broadly speaking, the difficulties of adolescent communication are kinds of embarrassment. Let us discuss adolescent speechlessness, in-group language and subculture, and how adolescents finally cope with the official adult philosophy, for the most part swallowing it hook, line and sinker.

4. Speechlessness

Paling and blushing embarrassment in expressing lust or admiration is largely due to confusion caused by powerful feelings that have been untried, or vague new ideas that seem presumptuous. It is akin to ingenuous shame, which is exhibition suddenly inhibited because it is (or might be) unacceptable. With courage and encouragement, such embarrassment can falter into sweet or ringing poetic speech, by which the youth explains himself to himself and finds his identity. More common in our society, however, is for the youth to inhibit his stammering and to brazen out the situation with a line imitated from the mass-media or salesmanship. For example, the strategy is to "snow" the girl rather than talk to her, proving that one is grown-up, has an erection, and so forth, but sacrificing feeling, originality, and growth. And preventing love.

Speechless embarrassment grounded in hostility occurs when a boy or girl is reprimanded, advised, or perhaps merely accosted by an authoritarian adult, for instance a guidance counselor. The youth maintains a sullen silence and will not give the adult the time of day. His presumption is that the adult is setting a trap, could not understand his point of view, does not care anyway. He cannot adopt a line, or try to explain or demur, for the adult has more words. He will be taken as fresh, hostile, or in bad taste. Therefore it is best to say nothing, expressing unconsciously a blazing contempt. The youth's thoughts are not too erroneous, except that the authority is usually not malevolent but busy and perhaps insensitive.

More pathetic in high schools and colleges is the following: The adult, a good teacher, does care for the young persons and would like to reach them in meaningful terms, not in terms of the orthodoxy. Then, as Frank Pinner has pointed out, the teacher's "dissensual" ideas will be met by a wall of silence that makes communication impossible. The young are so unsure, and their distrust is such, that in the crisis of possible contact they prefer to cling to safe conformity; even though among themselves they may bitterly attack these same conformist ideas.

Worse, there is an hermetic silence about anything deeply threatening or disturbing, unspeakable even to one's peers, no less adults. One may boast to a friend about a sexual conquest or fret about grades in school, but one may not reveal that one is in love or has a lofty aspiration. Or to give a tragic example: Puerto Rican boys will chatter endless small talk and one-up one another, but no one will mention that one of their number has just been sent to jail or that one just died from an overdose of heroin. If I mention such things, they do not hear. They cannot psychologically afford to relate themselves (their verbal personalities) to the terrible realities of life. Inevitably their thoughts and talk are boring; they never know anything to do; they feel no affection. Conversely, their behavior—even shocking deeds like murder—often happens as if unconsciously. It does not belong to *them*.

Suppose, on the other hand, that a compassionate and skillful adult will not let the adolescent avoid his concern and does begin to communicate with him. For instance, the adult might follow what is not said or the unexpressed meaning of what is said; he may firmly dismiss the usual line, cliché, and autobiography as boring; and bring hostility and dodging into the foreground. Then the youth begins to say "I mean . . . I mean . . ." as he loses his conviction that he means what he is saying. Next, more sincerely, he says, "You know . . . You know what I mean . . . you know" hoping that the attentive adult will know *for* him. Next he begins to stammer and becomes speechless.

5. Subculture

To diminish embarrassment, there is developed an exaggerated "adolescent subculture," with its jargon, models, ideology, and authors.

An intense youth sub-society is to be expected everywhere. In our culture, the interesting sexual exploration, dancing, simple exciting music, athletics, cars and races, clubs and jackets, one-upping conversation, seem natural to youth; just as many adult interests and occupations are naturally irrelevant and boring to them. The sharing of secrets, mysterious even to themselves, is a powerful bond of union among youth, and is certainly nobody else's business. The Youth Houses of some primitive communities institutionalize all this rather better than our boarding-schools and colleges which are ridden by adult regulations.

The development of the sub-society into a full-blown subculture, however, is not normal but reactive. It signifies that the adult culture is hostile to the adolescent interests, or at least not to be trusted; that parents are not people and do not regard youth as people; that one is excluded from adult activities; that the chief adult occupations are *not* worth growing up into as one becomes ready for them; but that, on the contrary, youth is pressured to prepare for these intrinsically boring jobs, regardless of proper time or inward urges.

Normally there is not a youth culture and an adult culture, but youth is a period of growing up, practicing autonomy, in the one culture. With us, youth is and feels itself to be, an exploited and manipulated class. It therefore has secrets, language, a lore of sabotage, grievance, and defense, *against* the adult culture.

Secondarily, since the intellectual life of callow boys and girls in isolation from the grown-up economy and culture is thin gruel, youth interests are vastly puffed up into fads, disk-jockeys, politically organized gangs and wars, literature, drugs and liquor, all frantically energized by youthful animal spirits. Economically, the teen-age market is more than $10 billion a year, in jackets, portable radios, sporting goods, and so forth. Needless to say, this secondary institution is a drag on the youthful mind. It is desperately conservative and exerts a tremendous pressure of blackmail against non-conformers or those ignorant of the latest; they will be unpopular. It makes it hard to talk sense, whether grown-up or adolescent; or indeed to dissent intelligently from the official philosophy and standard of life. (Contrast a rebellious movement like Romanticism, that made a good deal of sense, adult and adolescent, against the Old Regime, neo-classicism, and the Congress of Vienna.)

A certain number gang up and commit defiant delinquencies. These are partly the revolt of nature, partly reactive against whatever constitutes correct behavior, and partly a pathetic bid for attention—"We're so bad they give us a Youth Worker."

An appropriate, but pathetic, characteristic of recent adolescent subculture is taking on some of the language and culture of marginal groups, poor Negroes and Latin-Americans, addicts, Beat drop-outs from the colleges and the Organized System. These too are abused and disregarded, and youth sides with them. But the culture is fragmentary, hardly articulate, without future. (Also there is something exploiting about imitating out-caste people who live as they do not by choice but by necessity.)

For many of the woefully embarrassed, this speech—saying "man" and "cat"—and the rest of adolescent culture make conversation possible. Something to talk about and a style to say it in. The words of one syllable of jive, the thoughts of one syllable of Beat, the content of kicks, movies, and high school dances, are not a wide discourse, but they foster being together and everybody can participate.

But the small talk drives out real talk. It is incredibly snobbish and exclusive of sincerity and originality. Embattled against the adult world that must inexorably triumph, adolescent society jealously protects itself; but its language and thought, ironically, prevent each youth from learning anything or gaining moral courage to stand him in stead.

6. Cut Off from Childhood

A defect of adolescent subculture is that it rules out childhood. To be naive, to express weakness or dependency, or any feeling at all, is forbidden. The natural tendency of adolescents to regard the little brothers and sisters as a nuisance and somewhat shameful is reinforced to the point of not talking to them, as if they were not human.

Among the poor, of course, the elder children must help out with the younger, but this, in the absence of the working mother, has the effect of forcing a too early responsibility on the older children and increasing their resentment. It is said that such kids are especially hard to teach because, having to be a grown-up too soon, they cannot afford not to know it all.

As we saw, child language and thought are not themselves very authentic, influenced by suburban hygienic reading-matter and TV. At the *Mad* magazine age of puberty, the adolescents rebel against both this phony good behavior and the oppressive adult world. By the same token, there does not remain any bridge of communication to childhood, to real childhood fantasy, wickedness, and truth. Without this bridge, adolescents forget their own past and cannot understand the inner feelings of little brother and sister.

When, in moments of crisis, they regress, they again glue themselves to the TV. There is no other meaningful world.

7. Introjection

To adolescents of sixteen the adult world must seem like a closing cage containing a treadmill. Some must get jobs which are unlikely to fit them and in which they will have no initiative. Others must engage in the factitious competition for college-entrance. Either process is formidable with forms and tests. There is a crisis of ignorance of the ropes and ignorance of themselves. Disregarded by the adults, they have in turn excluded adult guidance or ideas looking toward the future. But their adolescent bravado is now seen to be unrealistic and even ridiculous. Having learned nothing, nor fought any battles, they are without morale.

Their weakness can be observed vividly on college campuses. The students gripe about the moral rules by which, at eighteen and nineteen years of age, they are still absurdly harassed (whereas young assembly-line workers are free to come and go, have sex, drink); but they can only gripe because they have never had this issue, or any issue, out with their parents. Similarly, they are unhappy about the overcrowded classes, the credits, the grading; they know they do not want the education they are getting; yet they are so confused about what they do want that they are speechless.

Ironically, just in the colleges, supposed to be communities of scholars, face-to-face communication is diminished. The adolescent subculture that persists is increasingly irrelevant to the business going on, except to sabotage it; yet as our colleges operate, the adolescent community is not replaced by close acquaintance with learned adults. The teachers hold the students off and, as I argued in *The Community of Scholars*, it is a chief function of administrators to keep the students out of contact with the teachers and the teachers out of contact with one another.

The dialogue with the subject-matter, with Nature or History, is as skimpy as with the teacher. The student is told the current doctrine and trained to give it back accurately. And still proving his masculinity and doing a snow-job, the student thinks that the purpose is to master the subject rather than love it and explore it.

Necessarily, in the conflict with the adult world the young suffer a crushing defeat. The result is that most of them give up on themselves and conform completely. They swallow the orthodoxy whole, making various rationalizations. For instance, they will return to the fray later when they are better prepared; the most important thing is to get married and raise a normal family; $50,000 a year is the goal of life; better dead than red. Some hold onto meaning and feeling for their family life or their "individual" or "personal" behavior; others allow the public doctrine full sway.

The psychology of this introjection is that, defeated and empty of meaning, they identify with what has conquered them, and so they feel strong and secure.

Seeing the abjectness with which these youth capitulate, one has the impression that the very ease of their childhood—the absence of corporal punishment and poverty—has now betrayed them; they have not become hardened and hateful enough. (I do not mean by this that it is better to punish and deprive.)

An alternative philosophy that has recommended itself to some older adolescents is hipsterism. A hipster cushions the crushing defeat by society by playing convenient roles in the dominant system, including its underworld, to manipulate it for his own power or at least safety. The bother with this idea (it is the argument of Thrasymachus in Plato's *Republic*) is that he then cannot grow by loving or believing anything worthwhile; he must be ahead of every game; and he exhausts himself in business with what he holds in contempt, increasing his own cynicism and self-contempt. But it provides the satisfaction of mastery and victory which ward off his panic of powerlessness, passivity, and emasculation. Hipsterism is the philosophy of chronic emergency, during which, of course, communication consists of camouflage and secrecy, "playing it cool," or of gambits of attack, to get the upper hand.

8. What Is "Communication"?

The conditions I have been describing, and the youthful responses to them, sadly limit communication and even the concept of it. Mostly, "communication" is the transfer of a processed meaning from one head to another, which will privately put it in a niche in its own system of meanings shared, or presumably shared, with the others. In the consensus, the exchanged information adds a detail or a specification, without disturbing personality or altering behavior, though it may serve as a signal for an action from the usual consensual repertory. The sentiment of consensus, "understanding," is so important that much speech and reading does not even give new information but is a ritual touching of familiar bases. But the case is not much different with active speech that is supposed to effect choice, for instance, in politics, for no disturbing issues are broached; the underlying consensus is assumed; no important alternative is offered.

The consensus is, I say, "presumably shared"; but any dialectic to test this assumption would be in bad form. In theory, the exchange of information is supposed to alter the organisms conversing, since they make internal readjustments to it; but my observation is that no such alteration occurs. The chief meaning of the conversation is its own smooth going on.

The active speech of salesmanship is more lively, because it is meant importantly to change behavior, toward buying, rather than to soothe it. Thus, strikingly, the TV commercials are the only part of TV that manipulates the medium itself, the film and the screen, esthetically, musically, inventively, playing with words, images, and ideas: The pitch of a salesman is likely to be *ad hominem*, in bad form, both flattering and threatening. (Needless to say, there is no dialogue; the hearer is passive or dumbly resistant.) Apart from the one pre-thought transaction, however, the consensus is powerfully protected;

the TV ad and the program that it pays for avoid anything that might surprise, provoke, or offend any single person in an audience of millions—except those who are offended by the cajoling and bullying of the ad itself.

Consider what is omitted from this narrow concept of communication as the exchange of highly processed information with which each communicant copes internally. (1) The function of speech as the shaping expression of preverbal needs and experiences by which a speaker first discovers what he is thinking. Such speech cannot be entirely pre-thought and controlled; it is spontaneous. (2) The function of speech as personally initiating something by launching into an environment that is *unlike* oneself. Initiating, one presumes there is no consensus; otherwise why bother speaking? (3) Most important of all, the function of speech as dialogue between persons committed to the conversation, or between a person and a subject-matter in which he is absorbed, that results in change of the persons because of the very act of speaking. Speaking is a way of making one's identity, of breaking into the human environment, of getting out of oneself and losing oneself in order to grow. It depends not on prior consensus with the others, but on trust of them.

In my opinion, the speech defined in most contemporary communication theory is very like the speech of these defeated adolescents. It is not poetic, pragmatic, communal, or heuristic. Its function is largely to report in a processed *lingua franca*. And indeed, movements of speech reform like General Semantics, Logical Positivism, Basic English, restrict themselves to enhancing the efficient performance of this one narrow function.

Speech cannot be personal and poetic when there is embarrassment of self-revelation, including revelation to one-self, and when there is animal and communal diffidence and suspicion, shame of exhibition and eccentricity, clinging to social norms. Speech cannot be initiating when the chief social institutions are centralized and bureaucratized, with decisions made top-down, so that in fact there is little opportunity for initiation by individuals or face-to-face groups where individuals can make themselves heard. It cannot be exploratory, heuristic, creative when pervasive chronic anxiety keeps people from risking losing themselves in temporary confusion and from relying for help on communicating, even if the communication is Babel. As it is, people have to "think" before they speak, rather than risking speaking and finding out what they mean by trying to make sense to the others and themselves.

By and large, at present—omitting the poets—only the speech of natural science is pragmatic, heuristic, and communal. It is pragmatic because scientists have first-hand knowledge of their laboratory operations and simple sensory observations. It is heuristic because they are encouraged, within the field, to adventure, guess, be way out, and to rely on esthetic or even playful formulation as an heuristic to further experiment. And scientists form a tight, mutually respectful but combative, community of discourse. But of course, their field of discourse is a small one; their personalities are restricted; and the style of their speech is both too special and too thin to serve for general human communication.

The Unteachables

This is a hard generation to teach what I think ought to be taught in colleges. This is not because the students are disrespectful or especially lazy; in my experience, they respect us more than we usually deserve and they work earnestly on much too heavy schedules. Of course, many of the students, probably the majority, ought not to be in academic settings at all (they ought to be getting their education in a variety of other ways) causing overcrowding, dilution, and standardization. But there are some other difficulties within the very essence of higher education which I want to discuss in what follows: (1) the culture we want to pass on is no longer a culture for these young; (2) the young are not serious with themselves; (3) and the auspices, methods, and aims of many of the colleges are irrelevant to the actual unprecedented present or the foreseeable future.

The culture I want to teach (I am myself trapped in it and cannot think or strive apart from it) is our Western tradition: the values which come from Greece, the Bible, Christianity, chivalry, the Free City of the twelfth century, the Renaissance, the heroic age of science, early nineteenth-century utilitarianism and late nineteenth-century naturalism. To indicate what I mean, here is a single typical proposition about each of these: The Greeks aspired to a civic excellence in which mere individual success would be shameful. The Bible teaches a created world and history in which we move as creatures. Christians have a spirit of crazy hope because we are always in the last times. Chivalry demands, in love and war, a personal loyalty, upon which honor depends. The Free Cities invented for us the juridical rights of social corporations. The Renaissance affirmed the imperious right of gifted individuals to seek immortality. Scientists carry on their disinterested dialogue with Nature, regardless of dogma or consequences. The Enlightenment decided once and for all that there is a common sensibility of all mankind. The Revolution showed that equality and fraternity are necessary for liberty. The economists assert that labor and enterprise must yield tangible satisfactions, not merely busy-work, profits, and power. The naturalists urge us to an honest ethic, intrinsic in our human condition.

Of course, these familiar crashing ideals are often in practical, and even theoretical, contradiction with one another, but that conflict itself is part of the Western tradition. And certainly they are only ideals—they never existed on land or sea—of the holy spirit and the human spirit that constitute the University, which is also an ideal.

As a teacher, naturally, I rarely mention such things. I take them for granted as assumed by everybody. But I am rudely disillusioned, for both the students and my younger colleagues take quite different things for granted. For instance, I have heard that the excellence of Socrates was a snobbish luxury that students nowadays cannot afford; that we know the created world only through "communications" like TV; that personal loyalty is appropriate only to juvenile gangs; that law is power; that fame is prestige and sales; that science is mastering Nature; that there is no such thing as humanity, only different patterns of culture; that education and ethics are programs for conditioning reflexes; and that the purpose of political economy is to increase the Gross National Product.

I do not mean to belittle these views, though I describe them somewhat bitterly. They make a lot of theoretical sense and they are realistic. It is better to believe them than hypocritically to assert ideals for which you do not strive. The bother with these views, however, is that they do not structure either enough life or a worthwhile life; that is, *as ideals* they are false. I think this is felt by most of the students and it is explicitly said by many young teachers. They regard me, nostalgically, as not really out of my mind but just "out of joint"— indeed, as a little enviable, because, although my values are delusions, one is justified by them if one believes and tries to act upon them. The current views do not seem to offer justification, and it is grim to live on without justification.

There is no mystery about how the thread of relevance snapped. Our history has been too disillusioning. Consider just the recent decades, overlooking the hundreds of years of hypocrisy. During the first World War, Western culture disgraced itself irremediably (read Freud's profound expression of dismay). The Russian revolution soon lost its Utopian élan, and the Moscow Trials of the 1930s were a terrible blow to many of the best youth. The Spanish Civil War was perhaps the watershed—one can almost say that 1938 was the year in which Western culture became irrelevant. The gas chambers and the atom bomb exposed what we were capable of doing. Since the second war, our American standard of living has sunk into affluence and nobody praises the "American Way of Life." Throughout the world, initiative and citizenship have vanished into personnel in the Organization. Rural life has suddenly crowded into urban sprawl, without forethought for community or the culture of cities. And the Cold War—deterrence of mutual overkill—is normal politics.

In this context, it is hard to talk with a straight face about identity, creation, Jeffersonian democracy, or the humanities.

But, of course, since young people cannot be merely regimented, they find their own pathetic, amiable, and desperate ideals. The sense of creatureliness reappears in their efforts, to make a "normal" adjustment and a "normal" marriage. The spirit of apocalypse is sought for in hallucinogenic drugs. Pride is physical toughness and self-aggrandizement. Social justice recurs as helping marginal groups. Science recurs as superstitious scruples about "method." Art regains a certain purity by restricting itself to art-action. Pragmatic utility somehow gets confused with engineering. Personal integrity is reaffirmed by "existential commitment," even though without rhyme or reason. None of this, nor all of it together, adds up to much; nobody's heart leaps up.

Perhaps my difficulty in teaching students now comes down to one hard nugget; I cannot get them to realize that the classical work was *about* something; it is not just part of the history of literature; it does not merely have an interesting symbolic structure. When Milton or Keats wrote, he was *for real*—he meant what he said and expected it to make a difference. The students do not grasp that any of that past excellence was for real and still is—for some of us. Their present goes back to about 1950. Naturally they do not have very impressive model heroes.

Since there are few self-justifying ideas or impressive models for them to grow up on, young people do not have much confidence nor take themselves very earnestly—except for private conceits, which many of them take very seriously indeed.

In fact, adults actively discourage earnestness. As James Coleman of Johns Hopkins has pointed out, the "serious" activity of youth is going to school and getting at least passing grades; all the rest—music, driving, teenage commodities (more than $10 billion annually), dating, friendships, reading, hobbies, need for one's own money—all this is treated by the adults as frivolous. The quality of meaning of it makes little difference. Of course, many of these "frivolous" activities are those in which a child would normally find his identity and his vocation, explore his feelings, and learn to be responsible. It is a desperately superficial society if the art and music that form tastes are considered unimportant. Nevertheless, if any of these—whether a "hobby" that interferes with homework or "dating" that makes a youth want to be independent and to work through his feelings responsibly—threatens to interfere with the serious business of school, it is unhesitatingly interrupted, sometimes with threats and sanctions. And astoundingly, for the majority of the middle class, this kind of tutelage now continues for sixteen years, during which the young sit facing front and doing pre-assigned lessons. At twenty-one however, the young are responsibly supposed to get jobs, marry, vote for Presidents and bring up their own children.

The schedule and the tutelage are resisted; teenagers counter with their own subculture; there are all kinds of youth problems. But by and large the process succeeds, by *force majeure*. But it is not a generation notable for self-confidence, determination, initiative, pure taste or ingenuous idealism.

The favored literature expresses, as it should, the true situation. (It is really the last straw when the adults, who have created the situation for the young, try to censor their literature out of existence.) There are various moments of the hang-up. There are the stories that "make the scene"—where making the scene means visiting a social region where the experiences do not add up to become one's own, with friends who do not make any difference. These stories, naturally, do not dwell on the tragic part, what is missed by making the scene. As an alternative, there are picaresque, hipster, adventure-stories, whose heroes exploit the institutions of society, which are not their institutions, and win triumphs for themselves alone. Then there are novels of sensibility, of very early disillusionment with a powerful world that does not suit and to which one cannot belong, and the subsequent suffering or wry and plaintive adjustment. Finally, there is the more independent Beat poetry of willed withdrawal from the unsatisfactory institutions and the making of a world—often apocalyptic—out of one's own guts, with the help of Japanese sages, hallucinations, and introspective physiology; this genre, when genuine, does create a threadbare community; but of course it suits very few.

In order to have something of their own, in a situation where they are rendered powerless and irresponsible, many of the young maintain a fixed self-concept through thick and thin, as if living out autobiographies of a predetermined life. And it is this they nourish in the heroes of their literature. They defend the conceit with pride or self-reproach; it comes to the same thing, whether one says "I'm the greatest" or "I'm the greatest goof-off." They absorbingly meditate on this fiction and, if vocal, boringly retell it. In this action of affirming their self-concepts, they are, as I have said, very earnest, but it is an action that prevents awareness of anything or anybody else.

Such tutelage and conceit are not a climate in which to learn any objective subject matter. They are also a poor climate for love or any satisfactory sexual behavior. In my opinion, the violence of the sexual problems of teenagers is largely caused by the adult structure of control itself, and the consequent irresponsibility and conceit. (Of course this is hardly a new thing.) If students could regulate themselves according to their own institutions and impulses, there would soon be far more realism, responsibility, and seriousness, resulting in consideration for the other, responsibility for social consequences, and sincerity and courage regarding one's own feelings. For example, a major part of attractiveness between two people normally is fitness of character—sweetness, strength, candor, attentiveness—and this tends to produce security and realism. Instead, we find that they choose in conformity to movie-images, or to rouse the envy of peers, or because of fantastic ideas of brutality or sexuality. In courting, they lie to one another, instead of expressing their need; they conceal embarrassment instead of displaying it; and so they prevent any deepening of feeling. Normally, mutual enjoyment leads to mutual liking, closer knowledge, caring for. Instead, sexual activity is used as a means of conquest and epic boasting, or of being popular. Soon, if only in sheer self-protection, it is an axiom not to care for or become emotionally involved. Even worse, they do not follow actual desire, which has in it a lot of fine discrimination and organic prudence; but instead they do what they think they ought to desire, or they act for kicks or for experiment. There is fantastic, excessive expectation, and inevitable disappointment or disgust. Much of the sexual behavior is not sexual at all, but is conformity to gang behavior because one has no identity, or proving because one has no other proofs, or looking for apocalyptic experience to pierce the dullness.

In brief, adults do not take adolescents seriously, as if they really *had* those needs and feeling; and so, finally, the adolescents cannot make sense of their own needs and feelings.

The chief obstacle to college teaching however resides neither in the break with tradition nor in the lack of confidence and seriousness of the students, but in the methods and aims of the colleges themselves. My book, *The Community of Scholars*, is a modern retelling of Veblen's account in *The Higher Learning in America* of the cash-accounting mentality prevalent in administrators, professors, and the students themselves, the mania for credits and grades, the tight scheduling, the excessive load, the false economy of huge classes, the lack of contact between teacher and teacher, teacher and student; the lust for rank, buildings and grounds, grants, and endowments; the mobility for advancement and salary hikes; and the overestimation of the "tangible evidence" of publication. All this adds up to no educational community at all.

It is impossible to look candidly at the present vast expansion and tight interlocking of the entire school system—from the graduate schools to the grade schools—without judging that it has three main functions: apprentice-training for the government and a few giant corporations, baby-sitting of the young during a period of rising unemployment in which most youth are economically superfluous, and the aggrandizement of the school system itself which is forming a monkish class greater than any since the sixteenth century. It is this unlucky combination of power-drive, commercial greed, public and parental guilt, and humanitarianism that explains the billions of federal, corporation, and foundation money financing the expansion. Inevitably, the functions are sometimes in contradiction: e.g. the apprentice-training of technicians requires speed-up, advanced placement, an emphasis on mathematics and sciences, and incredible amounts of testing and competition for weeding out. But the unemployment requires the campaign against drop-outs, and the Secretary of Labor has just asked that the compulsory schooling age be raised to eighteen—even though in some high schools they now station policemen to keep order.

These motives appear on the surface to be hard-headed and realistic but they are disastrously irrelevant to the education of our young for even the next four or five years. For example—with regard to the apprentice-training—Robert Theobald, the economist, quotes a Rand estimate that, with the maturity of automation only 2 percent of the population will be required to provide the present hardware and routine services and the college-trained, middle-management position especially will be unnecessary. At present, for the average semiskilled job in an automated plant, no prior education whatever is required. And my hunch is that throughout the economy, the majority of employees are "over-hired," that is, they have more schooling than they will ever use on the job. The employers ask for high school and college diplomas simply because these are to be had for the asking.

Nevertheless we live in a highly technical and scientific environment and there is a crucial need for scientific education for the majority. But this is necessary not in order to run or devise the machinery—which a tiny fraction of the highly talented will do anyway—but in order to know how to live in the scientific environment. Thus, the educational emphasis ought to be on the intrinsic interests of the sciences as humanities, and on the ethics of the scientific way of life, on practical acquaintance with machines (in order to repair and feel at home with them), and on the sociology, economics, and politics of science (in order that citizens may not be entirely ignorant in the major area of policy). These purposes are very like the program that progressive education set for itself at the beginning at this century. But these purposes are radically different from present scientific schooling, which is narrow and directed toward passing tests in order to select the few who will be technical scientists.

Unexpectedly, this pressure and narrow specialization are having another baneful effect: they put a premium on immaturity of emotional development and age. Students who have done nothing but lessons all their lives (and perhaps especially those who get good grades) are simply too childish to study social sciences, psychology, politics, or literature. It is possible to teach mathematics and physics to them, for the subjects suit their alert and schematizing minds, but it is difficult to teach them subjects that require life-experience and independence. (I have suggested elsewhere that prestigious liberal arts colleges should lead the way by requiring two years of post high school experience in some maturing activity such as making a living, community service or travel before college entrance.)

But undoubtedly the worst consequence of the subservience of the colleges and universities to the extramural aims of apprenticeship and babysitting is that the colleges become just the same as the world; the corporations, the colleges and the grade schools have become alike. Higher education loses its special place as critic, dissenter, stubborn guardian of standards, *sub specie aeternitatis*—which means, in effect, looking to the day *after* tomorrow. The students have no way of learning that the intellect has a function, that it swings a weight of its own. Professors rarely stand out crotchety against the consensus. The "important" men are more likely to be smooth articles and grant getters. The young seldom find impressive model heroes in the colleges.

What then? In spite of all this, we obviously cannot contemplate a future in which the bulk of our youth will be "useless." This very way of phrasing it is absurd, for the use and worth of society is measured by its human beings, not by its production of goods and services. It is this generation's great good fortune that it may see these goods and services produced with astonishing ease and abundance, but we must get rid of the notion that the automatic techniques appropriate for producing hardware, for logistics, or for chains of command have any relation whatever to education or to any other personal, humane, or creative action.

What ought education to be for, at present? The foreseeable future (I am not thinking of a distant Utopia) *must* provide us a world in which we will go on making an effort from inner necessity, with honor or shame depending on it, because these goals of the continuing human adventure are worthwhile—community culture, community service, high culture, citizenly initiative, serious leisure, and peace. Education toward such a world is the only kind that is realistic. When students and teachers break out of lock step and insist on such education, the colleges will become themselves again.

Youth Work Camps

The idea of work camps for unemployed teen-agers has always been attractive, it has somehow seemed "right." So it recurs whenever, as now, the competitive labor market begins to fail these youth. The camps are first set up as a facility for delinquent youth—the first such camps in California antedated by a few years the Civilian Conservation Corps of the Depression, and now in New York we have set up delinquent camps. Then they are proposed for "predelinquent" youth; and then for all who are not easily employed though otherwise unproblematic. Various reasons are given. The camp situation is therapeutic for the emotionally disturbed; it gets them out of their (and our) environment. Work is therapeutic. Youth are taught work habits and even particular skills that serve them on their "return to the community." And public projects like conservation are carried through. (Indeed, the actual productive work done proves—surprisingly, as in the case of the ccc—immensely valuable; it was an economic use of human resources otherwise wasted.)

These arguments are sound, but I do not think they hit the essential "rightness" of the idea of work camps, which is simply: that *there is an intrinsic relationship among middle adolescence, living in camps, and the need for work and a certain kind of work.* Camps and the right work are not, for that age, a device for an emergency but are a natural institution of society. One does not "return" from them to the community, they are part of the community, akin to the Youth House of primitive cultures. Under certain conditions, parts of the complex are informally provided in the active community itself, for instance, when the city itself has real vocations and there is a general institution of apprenticeships. But at present it is worth while to explore this philosophical idea of the youth work camp, because it is a standard to judge what is wrong with our own community and its work.

To begin with, a residential camp is a subcommunity away from the parental home. In America we are so committed to the psychological value, if not sanctity, of the family that we have insensibly slipped, in modern urban and technological conditions, into the error of a later and later "maturity." The mayoral prescription to curb youth by stricter home supervision is not only unrealistic but disastrously unhealthy. Consider the trap that American youth is maneuvered into: they are put off to a later and later sexual maturity and independence, and forced into an earlier and earlier career choice. There is no period for adolescence.

The community of youth must exist in a certain sociological isolation from the massive adult world, it must have its own rules. In principle this does not require the country or forest setting that is the usual image, though that has obvious attractions; a street gang isolates itself very well. We shall see that many youth-valuable and socially-valuable work projects require being in or near town, and therefore every effort should be made to devise an urban residential camp. A difficulty is the wildness and in-groupness intrinsic in any transitional stage. Hell-raising and the need for space are good things, but how to institutionalize them? (In Scheme I of *Communitas* my brother and I therefore locate all the high schools and junior colleges in the forest belt.)

A second interesting property is the mean size of the camps. One is struck by the unanimity of the writers. "A delinquent camp," says the latest manual (George Weber), "should be limited to a maximum of 60 boys, and fewer are desirable." By law, California delinquent camps "must not exceed 100 in population, including staff." (Lee Cary.) The two delinquent camps in New York number 50 and 60. The ccc nondelinquent camps averaged 110, but the discipline was admittedly too military. Senator Humphrey's proposed camps will therefore average 40 to 50. One is reminded of the kind of figure mentioned for a residential progressive school, 50 to 100. Clearly in this median figure, not too few and not too many, there is implied a face-to-face community where everybody knows everybody; and yet there is a complexity of social relations beyond cliques, or even gangs, so that a youth must learn to take himself also as a public person. Living together in such a community provides a continuum between intimate acquaintance and the public self, the citizen. In modern mass-society, this is the school of democracy, and possibly there is no other school.

It is relevant to leave home during *middle* adolescence. The youth is now past the anxieties of the onset of adolescence (age 11–14), which might still require, as our Mayor says, "the love and warmth of family affection." Now there is sexual and self-affirmation, and therefore fights at home. Contrast this period with the much earlier "separation from mother" (age 6). That was part of finding oneself in friends like oneself, ultimately in one's gang and uniform. But the break during 14 to 18 consists in finding oneself in the public real world.

The crucial question is this: *What can give structure to this new identity, to replace the parental identity?* And the answer I want to suggest is: *Objective productive work, leading to the discovery of unique vocation and career.* On such a view, a man's work and kind of work are as important to him as in Luther's religious view that "a man is justified by his calling." Yet our society does not think about it!

2.

Go back a moment to comparison with the primitive Youth House. This is a community of peers, but there is no need to provide for it an objective work, for *all* the work in such a community is cultural and useful and performed co-operatively or with a simply understood division of labor. From early childhood the youth has already been involved in it, trying out various skills.

Our nearest equivalent to such normal growing-up is, perhaps, middle-class youth going off to schools and colleges, continuing the academic work they have done since childhood and learning the verbal and symbolic skills of a bookish and technological adult world. They do not have a very communal Youth House in their schools; and their careers, and academic preparation, do not, for the most part, have much flesh and blood. Yet they are our model for the unproblematic in the "automated society."

For noncollege youth, however, merely "getting a job" is *not* unproblematic, it does not provide objective productive work. As I have pointed out above, it does not provide a normal next adjustment. For the wrong job, just to get a job, *prevents* growth. The job gives economic independence, but the employer turns into a substitute father, and the youth (and man) repeats the pattern of resentful dependency. Further, the job market being what it is, the job rarely has any relation to aptitude. If there is "guidance," it is of the sort that tests him to see where he can be useful in the economic machine, chopping off an ear or finger if necessary. No effort is made to find the job that will be useful for him, and there is no chance of trying out useful possibilities. (Why, at least, is the underprivileged or the nonbookish boy not given vocational scholarships, for exploration and training, if the college boy is given aid?) Finally, the job is not presented to the youth as a worth-while occupation with useful products to be proud of; often in our society the enterprise is not worth while, and the products are useless.

It is remarkable how both informed opinion and popular sentiment have insisted that the camp work have exactly contrary characteristics. The product must be publicly useful, manly, and admirable; conservation, planting trees, stocking ponds, etc., have this popular image. To say it wryly, the ccc jobs, like the wpa, were not allowed to compete with private "enterprise"; that is, the boys could not work for profits and be useless, but had to fall back on the worth of the products. One hears touching tales of the ccc boy returning twenty-five years later with his own son to point with pride to the park

167

pavilion he helped build. And indeed, in some cases, like the Red Rocks amphitheater in the Denver Rockies, he might well be proud, for it is a lovely thing.

Further, the notion that work is an "experience" and that skills should be tried out as part of education, is considered an advantage. Variety of work, such as domestic work and field work, is considered an advantage. The work is done co-operatively or in a division of labor arranged by the community; this helps make it one's own work. The youth is paid—typically, the army minimum for enlisted men—only so that he can have spending money; his support is his by right as a member of the community. How strange it is that the excellent things that the public insists on for work camps seem to be irrelevant to the ordinary jobs in society!

In all these ways, we can speak of productive work as providing an objective structure to replace the family authority. There is the background of a community of peers, but the work is something more than the interpersonal relations of the camp. It is a real project to grow on, to *project* on, in the real world, to find one's identity and hopefully one's vocation.

(We can see here the structural defect in the street gang. Being cut off from the adult real world, where the future values are, its enterprises are marginal and it has to make a structure of its own interpersonal relations: pecking order, enforced loyalty, and finally gang fighting with its similars.)

3.

There is a sharp distinction between the meaning of work in the delinquent and the nondelinquent camp. In the delinquent camp, work is a therapeutic discipline, precisely to impose an authority and "reality principle" where just these are lacking, perhaps in the so-called psychopathic personality. Such work must also be useful, not made, work, in order to build self-respect, for the youth says, "I have done that, therefore I am." Naturally I am speaking of good camps, not reformatories, where the work is likely to be either punishment .or slave labor. In a nondelinquent camp, however, the work is an end in itself, as process and product. The youth does not strengthen his ego against the discipline of work, but "loses himself" and grows into the work, to find himself new and larger on the other side. This entails, of course, programming great jobs of work. So far the programmers have not been very inventive; they are bureaucrats and haven't called on inventive people to help them. Even conservation, which is always first-rate, has usually not been made cultural and meaningful enough by scientific explanation and experiment led by the neighboring university.

Youth needs counseling and guidance, and here again we can distinguish between delinquent and nondelinquent guidance in terms the meaning of the work. The disturbed delinquent—let me hasten to say that many commit-ted "delinquents" are by no means disturbed but have gotten into trouble by influence of environment or even simply because society has foolish rules—the problem of a disturbed delinquent is likely to be inability to work at all, for he resists the objective demands of any job. He feels inferior and absents himself. A counselor will not then try to get him to work, but will use the lapse to explore his personality. Obviously in a good delinquent camp, the produc-tive work cannot be the goal, for, temporarily, not to do the work may be in the boy's interest. In a work-centered camp, however, counseling is the same as good work-supervision: it springs from the product and the process and aims at discovering further vocation. A young worker may lack interest in the product as worth while, and the therapy for this is cultural: giving information, showing meaning and importance. Or a boy may work badly; e.g., a boy who inhibits his aggression and has tight shoulders may not know how to drive a nail with confidence and beauty. The best therapist in such a case may be a master craftsman, who loves the making, the style. He will not need to explore problems of personality, for they project and heal themselves in the art and craft. After a while, more formal vocational guidance may be added, informing the youth what jobs are available for him in the future, how to get them, where to get further training. Perhaps he will want to return to school, for which he has now discovered his own use.

I have thus in an abstract way brought together the problems of a stage of adolescence with the need for residential camps with a program of real work. Leaving his family and choosing a community of his peers, a youth finds a structure to replace his parents in objectively valuable work, till he finds identity and vocation. So the youth camp is, in type, an institution of normal society.

4.

Paradoxically, the success of a great program of work camps designed for the advantage of youth depends on the worthwhileness of the work projects for the community at large, since only the community can give objective cultural norms. In principle, the invention of a master program of projects is prior to the location and staffing of camps, and provides their context. How topsy-turvy our thinking is! When we benevolently worry what to do with the mil-lions of drop-outs (35 percent of the high school population), we start with this "problematic youth" and try to find employment useful for them and useful for society; and perhaps we hit on the idea of forest work camps, postponing for a year the question what they will do when they "return to the community." Surely the normal procedure would be the reverse, to think what we need for a better quality of life and to rejoice that we have these new human resources to help meet the need.

There used to be an organization called the National Child Labor Committee, to protect youth from being exploited by parents and profiteers of industry. This organization has now changed its name to the National Committee on Employment of Youth, to protect youth from wasting away unemployed. We are in a unique dilemma. Given our "surplus productivity," we might do well to aim at a large *planned* paid unemployment, as Galbraith has suggested. No politician would dare this proposal, yet to judge from the lax boondoggling and expense-account "production," it seems to be the undercurrent of public thinking. And there is a general acceptance of the desirability, or at least inevitability, of automation involving unemployment grossly underpaid (by social insurance and dole). Yet it is also felt that especially for youth and the aged, who are the least employable, unproductive life is a moral and psychological disaster!

Consider our dilemma as a problem of administration and finance. Like any communities, the Work Camps are multipurposive. Their advantages are ecological, educational, moral, economic, judicial. Therefore it should be easy to get funds for them from several groups. But of course the opposite is the case: since many will be benefited, nobody is competent to administer or responsible to finance. This difficulty of coping with any multipurpose enterprise, any community, is a fair index of the state of our society. In a great city there is a plethora of community problems—housing, delinquency, traffic, schooling, unemployment, etc., etc. These are dealt with by a bewildering maze of departments, but there is no community plan—even though the problems *cannot* be solved in isolation, for the isolated "solution" of one problem (housing) in fact aggravates the other problems (traffic, delinquency). The normal approach, "This is irrefutably a fine thing, so let's get together and do it"—this is precisely infinitely difficult for us. And when by exception a great multipurpose enterprise like the TVA is implemented, with whatever crippling safeguards, it is a wonder of the age.

5.

We do not invent great programs, because not enough *mind* is put to the task. It is not to be expected that the departments of Labor and the Interior, or even a county administrator of Correction, will dream up remarkable work projects. A fine architect might, and might even do it gratis as a patriotic action, but we do not much rely on such men and such motives. Students of architecture at the university might think up something for youth to build; out of fifty of their inventions, one might be both remarkable and feasible. But the university is not on speaking terms with the government. Or in another genre, a social case worker might have a most vivid sense of some alteration or installation that would make all the difference to a harried family, and that youth could do. (This is the line of Carl May's Youth for Service; e.g., "The boys built a retaining wall at a neighborhood center. They scrubbed the kitchen and painted the bedroom and bath at the home of two elderly sisters.")

Camps have usually been located in a country or forest setting, for conservation, park maintenance, the construction of recreational facilities. But urban Conservation and urban renewal are equally important. And most important, to my mind, is that fifty thousand small towns in America are ugly, shapeless, and neglected—nowhere to belong to, nothing to be proud of. These will not in fact be improved by private promoters whose notion of a community center is not a green but a supermarket. Maybe some of them can be improved by artists and youth.

There is another valuable kind of work, the living theater, where youth can work as builders, stagehands, and actors. To offset the standardized mass communications, we need hundreds of Little Theaters throughout the country. These would not ordinarily be thought of as work-camp projects, but why not?

I am suggesting a very broad spectrum of projects; and this is why. We are at a crisis in America, when we must either improve the quality of our life or begin to give up. The idea of work camps as an adventure for all youth, as a normal institution of society, is itself a new quality of life. In such a ferment, of real community, real work, and real goods, bubbling up in every likely and unlikely place, we could tolerate the system we have. I am not sure that the youth "returning to the community" would tolerate it, having known better. But increasingly they do not tolerate it anyway.

Media and Culture

The Present Plight of
a Man of Letters

During the past twenty years, there have been a couple of hundred works of "social criticism" of American ways, of the cars, the hidden government, the physicians and funerals, cities and suburbs, schools and the growing up of the young, advertising and TV, the conflict of races, technology, ecology, management, popular culture, and so forth and so on. A score of these have been pretty good books. In my opinion, the writers may fairly be compared to the humanists of the fifteenth and sixteenth centuries and the philosophers of the eighteenth. They are men of letters exercising the specific processes of literature in times of religious, political, and cultural crisis.

Older worthies had their own frustrations. At present the plight of a man of letters is made hard by the following state of affairs: Those in power "co-opt" the critics, manage them so that they are rendered ineffectual (there is little direct censorship, though some). We are invited to be on panels or even task-forces to represent our way-out views, so the proceedings are well rounded; but, speaking for myself, I do not find that my critical insights are taken into account in any decisions or actions that ensue. The numerous and dynamic young do take the social critics more seriously; indeed, the bulk of their reading matter and most of their slogans come from them, and they are eager to act out what they have read. But they cannot read English very well: the conditions of modern life have so alienated them from history, from the professions, and even from the nature of things, that they do not understand what a humanistic writer is saying. Finally, there is a prevailing sentiment that literature itself is unimportant. It is mere entertainment, or confused sociology or psychiatry, or the posture of a new shabby elite. New media have made it moribund and it may pass away. What is useful in letters is only a noisy code that must be refined by other than writers, for purposes of science, technology, and social engineering.

Nevertheless, literature is humanly important. It is odd to have to say this at the meeting of an association dedicated to the modern languages, but evidently each era must write its own Defense of Poesy. Literature is not a "linear" unrolling of printed sentences nor an awkward code; it is artful speech. And speech is not merely a means of communication and expression, as the anthropologists say, but is a chief action in our human way of being in the world. And *pace* Marshall McLuhan, people will continue to speak for the indefinite future, as a chief way of being in the world. (The only alternative hypothesis is if technologists wire their brains; but at this point we would cease to classify them as human beings.)

Psychiatrists of aphasia, from Hughlings Jackson and Head to Kurt Goldstein, have shown that speech is a way of coping with the stream of experience and saves us from the catastrophic all-or-nothing reactions of aphasics. Speech is a peculiar use of symbols that both tell experience and are a substitute for experience, and the manner of speaking is how one is having his experience. To speak to someone not only communicates but creates community; for example, one can signal "Come" by snapping his fingers, but if he says it in words he makes the other into a person. To speak, as Buber and Kafka have said, is itself a primordial prayer to God and man. Passing from infancy actualizes and defines the self of a growing child; learning to speak is coincidental with, maybe the same as, the formation of the ego. And from Aristotle to Benjamin Whorf and the linguistic analysts, philosophers have repeatedly used vocabulary and grammar as basic hypotheses and world-views of reality.

All this is heightened by literature, oral and written. The habits, genres and tropes that have been developed in the long world-wide literary tradition constitute a method of coping with reality, different from science, religion, political power, or common sense, but involved with them all. (In my opinion, literature, although it is a method *sui generis*, is not a specialized department of learning but a good way of being in any department. The same is true of philosophy.) Literature brings to conscious awareness the folk wisdom that exists in vocabulary and grammar. It combines the subjectivity of personal experience and the objectivity of shared experience. Syntax, tenses, voices, moods, direct and indirect discourse, simple and complex sentences are the character of one's involvement in experience and with the others; they are a better diagnostic than Rorschach cards. Points of view, what the Ancients called "manner," are experiments in phenomenology. Rhythm, regular meter and the rhythm that modifies meter, is feeling; it is one's way of breathing, and being calm, forceful or languid. Plot structures and chains of syllogism extend the attention span and appropriate experience by reconstructing it with a philosophical beginning, middle, and end. Metaphor is surprise.

The ability of literature to combine memory and learning with present observation, need, and spontaneous impulse remarkably serves the nature of man as the animal who makes himself; for it revives the spirit of past makings, so they are not a dead weight, and yet is a making that is occurring now. Put psychotherapeutically, this process alleviates "inner conflict" and helps undo past trauma by bringing it into the public world of sharable speech.

The materials of literature are cheap and common. This is so with all the fine arts; they are made of mud, rock, gestures, tinkling, and babbling. Those who hanker after multimedia and overwhelming environmental effects should consider what is lost by using an expensive technology. Maybe only a simple and poor medium is flexible and subtle enough to lure the inward outward.

Yet despite its open access, literature is not democratic but aristocratic. Like any method, it lives by its own tradition as well as social causes or individual ability. But compared to other elites, the Republic of Letters has been a career open to talents and often classless. I venture that a disproportionate number of its stars have been persons socially despised, outcasts, convicts. There is truth in what Wordsworth said, that the speech of the poor and unschooled, if they have been brought up among beautiful scenes and simple affections—or if, I would add, they have been loving and passionate—is more literary than the speech of courts and capitalists. Recently, Baxter Bernstein has made some interesting studies of the differences of vocabulary, syntax, and attitude in lower class and middle class speech; and Wordsworth's model, as I judge, has the good points and avoids the defects of each; it is simply better human speech than either Bernstein's cockneys or his bourgeois.

The sentences and the stances of poets and men of letters have always seemed to provide an independent source or validation of ethics, and moral philosophers have cited them as evidence. In the Book of Job, for instance, the arguments of Whirlwind are logically no more cogent than the other arguments, but their poetry compels assent. (I interpret the beginning of the story to mean that Job is an obsessional neurotic, who can be cured only by being emotionally swept off his feet.) The Italians of the Renaissance used to say that only Eloquence, noble rhetoric, yields the "real" truth, just as only the real truth makes a man eloquent. The aim of literature is "to move and instruct"; in the later formulations of Dryden, this means that literature instructs by moving, by disturbing rigid or stereotyped responses. In our own time, Genet says it best when he confesses that his style soars only when he is describing his delinquents, and *therefore* they are good people; for he is a writer, and writing is his existential act and source of valuation.

So much for the praise of letters, the warrant by which a man of letters can be a social critic. Let me return to his present difficulties.

It is increasingly hard to fulfill one of the elementary functions of writers, to renew the speech of the tribe as it inevitably degenerates. Confucius said that speech reform was the first step of social change; these days I would sooner get rid of the atom bombs and the pollution, but maybe it's all the same. The trouble is that the rate of revolutionary change in important cultural aspects—urbanization, travel, schooling, communications, militarization, space exploration—is so rapid that it is impossible for any renewal of speech and style to mature and be assimilated. Good tendencies appear, but they are swamped by the flood of publications; and the over-all public style is wildly eclectic.

In principle, the omnipresent and powerful TV could have a good or bad influence—as the Canadian Broadcasting Corporation has, for better or worse, standardized the French of young Canadians. But the mode of operation of American mass media makes them almost necessarily corrupting. Since they aim for big audiences that have few serious interests in common, the subjects treated are trivial or trivialized; communication is quick and superficial; feeling is sensational or bland—or somehow both. Young people, brought up on this fare, become adept at judging the nuances and absurdities of TV commercials, but are quite unable to grasp other style or content. They, and most other Americans, cannot hear a line of reasoning if the premises are at all unexpected. Instead of assuming that the writer is saying something different and trying to figure it out, they decide that he is a bad writer. If the conclusion is not either of the two sides that an issue is supposed to have, they take the argument to be fuzzy. An editor of *Esquire* once objected to a line of argument in an article of mine because "the reader would have to think about that," too much to expect of anybody.

The surface of writing becomes swift and flashy, "cinematic"—the arresting lead, the startling statistic, the apt illustration; but the actual motion of intellect becomes excruciatingly slow; there must not be more than one poor thought to a page, for the readers cannot read. An editor of *Harper's* objected to a piece of mine because it had three ideas, and "an article in *Harper's*," he said, "cannot have more than two ideas."

For sufficient reasons, it seems to me, the young do not believe or understand the western tradition; but then the memory that is alive in humane letters is lost on them, either its allusion or its continuing dialogue millennia old. When I speak at a college, I pepper the discussion with references to Spinoza, Beethoven, and Milton, hoping that they will learn that former great men were real human beings, but the poignant effect is that they regard me wistfully because I seem to have a past and they are more forlorn than ever. If I try to analyze a text in its own terms, to find a human spirit coping with its particulars and *therefore* relevant to us, it is taken as an irrelevant exercise in order to avoid present gut issues. Naturally, inability to read a good book is cumulative. Since there is no belief in the tradition nor habituation in its ways it becomes a chore just to read the sentences, and why bother.

Ironically, the stepped-up schooling is literarily disastrous. Librarians have complained to me that children no longer have the time to browse and choose what interests them; but I venture to say that very few who can read and write have learned it by assigned lessons. Literature is both too complicated and freewheeling to be followed without spontaneous attention springing from within.

Without doubt, writers and readers can be encumbered by too much traditional baggage, as perhaps I myself am. This can prevent primary literature coping with the existential plight of the person and his community. Yet starting from scratch, without literary tradition altogether, writing and reading are imbecile and trivial; ancient errors are tiresomely repeated; platitudes are taken for ideas; hard won distinctions are lost; useful genres have to be reinvented, like reinventing shoes or learning to boil water. Unencumbered by history, when the young are discussing their immediate real problems, for instance, the draft, their rapping is fresh, direct, accurate, and inventive, excellently literary. When they are discussing politics, the institutions, or the professions, they become abstract and brassy. When the task is critical judgment or poetic affirmation of their own experience, they are embarrassed and inarticulate or full of clichés.

Needless to say, the lapse of a common background is grueling for a writer. He has to explain too much, beginning with academic synopses of First Principles that he ought to be able to take for granted. This present essay is an example: speaking to professors of modern languages, I start off with a lecture to prove that speech and writing are important in human affairs. It is like treatises of the fifth century that commence with Adam and Eve and ultimately get to the point. I *hope* that this analogy is not accurate.

Most painful is the need to repeat myself. I have written ten books of social theory and social criticism, trying to explore different relations of man and environment. But since there is no continuing community of readers and I do not know what I can take for granted, each time I have to establish my point of view and summarize things I have said before. Impatiently, to get it over with as quickly as possible, I have written some really hideous paragraphs of sociological and psychological jargon, as a kind of shorthand.

I have found that being misread can have boring consequences. For instance, in *The Community of Scholars* I criticized present university administration and pointed out that ten professionals and a hundred fifty students, the equivalent of most medieval schools, could provide professional education better and more cheaply than we do. So I suggested that some professors secede and try it. Somehow this made me the father, or Dutch uncle, of the Free Universities, and since I am sympathetic to the Movement in general, I have had to take part also in the Free Universities. Their curriculum is the psychedelic experience, sensitivity training, the liberation of women, and Castro's Cuba, which are fine subjects but not at all the Law, Medicine, and Engineering that I had in mind.

More serious in life-consequences for writers is the bland hypocrisy of those in power. When we are treated as court jesters or, worse, when our sentences are cadged for purposes the opposite of what we intend, then just to maintain our integrity we have to engage in follow-up actions that go beyond our skill or desire: demonstrations, picketing, civil disobedience, raising bail. I have written more leaflets and attended more press conferences than I like to remember. In order to say my say to the National Security Industries and be paid attention to, I had to summon students to picket the auditorium of the State Department. Writers and scholars spend long hours plotting with their fellows about ways to make trouble.

At any time, also, the contempt of learning can turn into direct censorship or the chilling climate of blacklisting. Consider the recent disclosure of blacklisting by the Department of Health, Education, and Welfare of scholars who actively opposed the Vietnam War. I can conceive of people honorably indecisive and silent about the policy of the Vietnam War, but it is hard to conceive of anybody talented in community medicine or the education of children or the welfare of the poor who would not be vehemently opposed to that policy. Thus, the effect of the blacklist was to doom the Department to mediocrity.

As a poet, I do not have these problems (though plenty of others). On the advice of Longinus, I "write it for Homer, for Demosthenes" and other pleasant company who somehow are more alive to me than most of my contemporaries, though unfortunately not available for comment. Anyway, in the best pages, I am not writing, but the spirit in me. But my trouble is that I have to be that kind of poet who is in the clear because he has done his public duty. All writers have hang-ups, and mine is To Have Done My Duty. It is an arduous taskmaster, but at least it saves me from the nonsense of Sartre's poet engagé, politically committed. How the devil could a poet, who does the best he can just to get it down as it is whispered to him, decide whether or not to be morally or politically responsible? What if the Muse won't, perverse that she is? What if the Truth won't, unknown that it is?

The most dangerous threat to humane letters at present, however, is none of the things we have been mentioning; it is not the ugliness and commercialism of corporate capitalism, nor the ignorance and alienation of the young, nor the hypocrisy or censorship of power. It is the same dehumanization of Modern Times that I have been discussing throughout this paper. Language is reduced to be a technology of social engineering, with a barren conception of science and technology and a collectivist conception of community. This tendency has been reinforced by government grants and academic appointments, and it controls the pedagogy in primary schools.

In this tendency, communication is taken to be the transfer of information from one brain to another, and all the rest, the expression, is noise or meaningless emotion. Linguists construct grammars of basic vocabularies of "factual" words connected by Russell's logic of relations to provide a pidgin for transferring information, or to allow for computer translation. These are useful purposes, but they are not what language, or English, is. In my opinion, speaking is an action and passion of speaking animals, directly affected by their speech encounter; the style of speaking is how the speaker *has* his information and is *with* the others, so it is intrinsic to the meaning. In most conversation, the non-informational part is by far the greater; a grammar of English should be drawn from common speech and the heightened speech that has proved interesting, literature. I doubt that there is a general basic vocabulary. What is "fact" depends on how one is in the kind of world one has.

For a long time, say from Francis Bacon to Neurath and Carnap, scientists resisted using the "unified language of science" that was periodically invented for them. It did not seem to fit the way each branch went about its enterprise; and Science as a whole was an indefinite number of wandering dialogues with the unknown carried on by brotherly cooperative (and competitive) researchers. But now Science is taken to be a central office in which new data are added, new theory is processed, and new projects are launched; and the convenience of calculating machines seems to be leading to the rapid adoption of a single language and method. To my lay understanding, this implies—doesn't it?—a likelihood of misinterpreting what cannot be easily said in the one language, and disregarding what cannot be coped with by the one method. Perhaps this danger does not exist in the physical sciences—anyway there continue to be important successes. But in the social sciences, the procedure of collecting and processing data and planning strategies has usually proved to be otiose or harmful, avoiding problems or creating worse ones. Evidently the essence has been left out, the language and method are not adequate. Similarly, the use of technology is proving to be disastrous. Technology is a branch of moral philosophy, but the language that is used is not the language of moral philosophy, which is literature.

It is the sign of an ignorant man, said Aristotle, to be more precise than the subject allows. There is more communication in a poem of Keats than in a scientific report, said Norbert Wiener, for the poem alters the code, whereas the report merely repeats it and increases the noise.

Society is increasingly taken to be a kind of machine directed by a central will, and in this structure the teaching of English is turned into social engineering. The purpose of learning to read is no longer political freedom, clarification, appreciation, and community, but "functional literacy," the ability to follow directions and be employable. The question whether a child can and will learn to read with such a purpose is not asked. At the level of Freshman English, the manuals aim to impart units of language skill necessary to perform various social roles. At the graduate level, the departments instill the style and format acceptable for work in the "discipline."

Thus, speech is increasingly reduced to a code to transfer information for increasingly narrow purposes. Conversely, the expressive part of speech, emptied of meaning and any relation to telling the truth, is reduced to ornament or shallow entertainment, as in the rhetorics of the Roman Empire. Or much worse, it is something to manipulate politically, to create thoughtless collective solidarity, like the Newspeak of George Orwell's *1984*.

I do not think this situation is the result of a conspiracy, although those who profit by the tide go along with the tide and have a vested interest in it. And it is not especially American, although our country is the oldest in Modern Times and is therefore the most mature in this way too. But this disease of speech seems to be endemic in Modern Times and has appeared in every advanced country, no matter what its economic system or political ideology. Mankind does not know, does not yet know, how to manage the exploding scientific technology and the collectivism, which are the conditions of the foreseeable future. I say does not "yet" know because we are an inventive species. But unfortunately we come across only when we are in trouble, and we may again have to go through something like the Thirty Years War.

Since I started by mentioning the humanists, let me come on at the end like Erasmus (perhaps it is his tri-centennial—his birth was "1469"?). Just now the method of literature is indispensable: to find and say the humanism in new science, the morality in technology, and the community and individuality in collectivism.

Format and Communication

1. Format and Empty Speech

By "format" I mean imposing on the literary process a style that is extrinsic to it. The dictionary tells the story very well:

> Format.—*n.* I. the shape and size of a book as determined by the number of times the original sheet has been folded to form the leaves. 2. the general physical appearance of a book, magazine, or newspaper, such as the type face, binding, quality of paper, margins, etc. 3. the organization, plan, style, or type of something: *They tailored their script to a half-hour format. The format of the show allowed for topical and controversial gags.* 4. *Computer Technol.* the organization or disposition of symbols on a magnetic tape, punch card, or the like, in accordance with the input requirements of a computer, card-sort machine, etc.—*v.t.* 5. *Computer Technol.* to adapt (the organization or disposition of coded information) on a magnetic tape, punch card, or the like, to conform to the input requirements of a computer, card-sort machine, etc.

Format has no literary power, and finally it destroys literary power. It is especially disastrous to the common standard style, because it corrupts it and takes the heart out of it.

Thus an editor chops a sentence here and there, and also my last paragraph because 3,000 words is the right length for the format of his magazine. An assistant editor rewrites me just to be busy and earn his keep. A daily column must appear though the columnist has nothing to say that day. An editor of *Harper's* asks me to simplify an argument because, he says, the readers of the magazine cannot digest more than two thoughts to one article. At another magazine they rewrite in *Time*-style. A young fellow writes his thesis in the style of professional competence of his department. Obviously, the effect of format is worse if the writer must adapt himself and write, rather than just having his writing mashed. Since writing is inherently spontaneous and original, a writer cannot produce what is not his own without a broken spirit.

American television is especially productive of format. The networks are a big investment of capital, so broadcasting time is cut up for sale to the fraction of a minute, and programs are tailored to the strips. A mass medium aims at a big audience, so the programs must be sensational enough to attract many and bland enough not to offend any. In the peculiar system of semi-monopolies, where a few baronial firms compete in such a way as to keep one another in business, if one network hits on a new show or newscast, the others at once program a close imitation. Legally the channels are public property, so the licensed stations must be politically impartial and present all sides of controversial issues; the most convenient way of handling this is to present no controversial issue. But there is another rule that a certain fraction of time must be devoted to public service, including political controversy; and a way of economically handling this is to have a panel of wildly divergent points of view debating an issue for the required twenty-six minutes. This sometimes produces heat, never light, usually nothing. It is a format. What is glaring in the whole enterprise is the almost entire lack of will to say anything, rather than just provide a frame for the ads.*

Format is not like censorship that tries to obliterate speech, and so sometimes empowers it by making it important. And it is not like propaganda that simply tells lies. Rather, authority imposes format on speech because it needs speech, but not autonomous speech. Format is speech colonized, broken-spirited. It is a use of speech as social cement, but it is not like the small talk of acquaintances on the street in their spontaneous style; it is a collective style for a mass. So in appearance it is often indistinguishable from the current literary standard. But in actual use it is evident from the first sentence that it does not tell anything.

Of course, empty style is nothing new. Diplomats, administrators of all kinds, and other public relators, who have to make remarks about what is none of our business, have always used a style to drain meaning from what they say. It can be a fine art—compare Proust on the virtuosity of Norpois. But modern society has unique resources of technology and social organization to separate speech from living speakers. I do not think that any previous era has ever worked up a universal pedagogy and a general Theory of Communications to sidetrack human speech as such. In Newspeak, George Orwell was shooting at not quite the right target. He was thinking of *control* of speech by the lies and

---

* In my fallible memory, the ads themselves used to have a more authentic style— more cinematic, more musical, even more poetical—because they had a real rhetorical purpose, to sell goods. But my recent observation is that they too have become lifeless. Is this because of the imposition of new extrinsic regulations, for instance, not to lie, not to sell carcinogens or dangerous toys, not to increase air pollution, and so forth? It is hard to be a frank huckster anymore.

propaganda of crude totalitarian regimes; but I doubt that this is humanly feasible. (In the end the State is bound together by simple fright, not brainwashing.) The government of a complicated modern society cannot lie much. But by format, even without trying, it can kill feeling, memory, learning, observation, imagination, logic, grammar, or any other faculty of free writing.

2.

The schools try hard to teach the empty style. There is frantic anxiety about the schools' failing to teach children to read and write; there have been riots on the street about it; the President of the United States has called the matter our top priority. But so far as I know, none of those who are frantic—parents rich and poor, nor the President—have pointed out that reading and writing spring from speaking, our human way of being in the world; that they are not tools but arts, and their content is imagination and truth. Occasionally a sensitive teacher pipes up that children might learn reading and writing if these were interesting and sprang from what the children wanted to know and had to say, if they were relevant to their personal lives and had some practical function. But mostly the remedies that are proposed are mechanical or administrative; there are debates between sounding out and word recognition and quarrels about who controls the schools.

The reason for anxiety is simply that if children do not learn the tools of reading and writing, they cannot advance through school, and if they don't get school diplomas, they won't get well-paying jobs in a mandarin society. Literacy is incidental, a kind of catalyst that drops out of the equation. To pass the tests really requires just the same verbal skills—nothing much else has been learned—and there is no correlation between having the diplomas and competence in any job or profession. School style exists for the schools. So some of us have suggested that if it and they did not exist, that too would be very well. (Rather, change the rules for licensing and hiring.)

In most urban and suburban communities, most children will pick up the printed code anyway, school or no school. (In ghetto and depressed rural communities, they might not.) It is likely that schoolteaching destroys more genuine literacy than it produces. But it is hard to know if most people think that reading and writing have any value anyway, either in themselves or for their use, except that they are indispensable in how we go about things. Contrast the common respect for mathematics, which are taken to be *about* something and are powerful, productive, magical; yet there is no panic if people are mathematically illiterate.

Thus, during the long years of compulsory schooling, reading and writing are a kind of format, an imposed style with no intrinsic relation to good

Speech. And this must be characteristic of any mandarin society, even when, as in medieval China, the style of literacy happens to be the standard literary classics. With us, as school reading and writing cease to have literary meaning, university study of Literature ceases to be about human speech, speech in its great examples. (It is a nice question, what university English studies are about.) And as fewer people read authentically, on-going literature may well become one of the minor arts, for connoisseurs, like rose gardening or weaving.

Naturally, when the imposing authority takes itself seriously as right and good, as in the Soviet Union, mandarin literacy is affirmed as excellent, the vehicle of all social and scientific progress, as well as the way to get ahead. Consider the following of the Russian pedagogue L. S. Vygotsky, which seems to say that it is necessary to *destroy* natural style:

> In learning to write, the child must disengage himself from the
> sensory aspect of speech and replace words by images of words. It is
> the abstract quality of language that is the main stumbling block to
> learning to write, not the underdevelopment of small muscles . . . . Our
> studies show that a child has little motivation to learn writing when we
> begin to teach it. Written language demands conscious work . . . . The
> concrete totality of traits [must be] destroyed through abstraction; then
> the possibility of unifying traits on a different basis opens up. Only the
> mastery of abstraction enables the child to progress to the formation of
> genuine concepts.

This odd view of writing and teaching writing is the precise opposite of a literary approach, for instance, Sylvia Ashton-Warner's, which tries to get writing from the child's spontaneous native speech, with all its sensuality and animal need. (We shall see later that by "genuine concepts" Vygotsky means the social ideology.)[*]

The use of words is already detachment from, control of, the stream of experience; to go the further step of Vygotsky is to control the speaker. It is a socially-induced aphasia.

In any case, the literature that is the fruit of this method of teaching writing is also taken very seriously, as the mandarin literacy is. It is carefully

---

[*] It is astonishing that Vygotsky can believe what he says. In another passage he shrewdly and accurately points out how the school set-up predetermines the child's responses: "Piaget's findings are valid only for his special kindergarten play milieu [encouraging] extensive soliloquizing. Stern points out that in a German kindergarten, where there is more group activity, the coefficient of egocentrism was somewhat lower . . . . The difference with Soviet children must be even greater." Indeed , in all cases a child must cope with the conditions that they impose on him, and readjust in order to survive. To do *this* is the child's nature

regulated in style, and it is reproduced in millions of copies. In Russia, writing that is more literary in a traditional sense does *not* become a minor art for connoisseurs, but is circulated in manuscript for a band of criminal conspirators.

3. The Resistance of Colloquial Speech

The forces of format, to conform to the input requirements of a social or technical system, can quickly debase public language and the standard literary style. Strong writers are less affected; society does not know how to produce them and it does not even know how to inhibit them, except by violence.

But colloquial speech is quite impervious to corruption by format. It has an irrepressible vitality to defy, ridicule or appropriate. It gobbles up format like everything else. There are too many immediate occasions, face-to-face meetings, eye-witnessings, commonsense problems for common speech to be regimented. People who can talk can be oppressed but not brainwashed. Modern cities are depressing and unhealthy, but the people are not mechanical.

Once out of bounds, children do not talk like school. In America, adults talk like school less than they used, because (I like to think) the school style has so little literary value that it's not worth adopting. Children imitate the TV, but soon do it sarcastically. Adults imitate the ads less than they used because there has been overexposure. The young are in revolt against the ads, so the ads lamely have to imitate the young. In totalitarian countries, even after a generation of benevolent instruction by all the schools, mass media, labor unions, and so forth., young Czechs and Poles, who have never known any other dispensation, have not learned what is good for them; apparently, they get their ideas by conversation with one another. American voters almost never repeat the sentences of politicians; rather, they tell you their own lay political theories and that they can't stand the personalities of certain candidates.

By and large, adolescents are the most susceptible to empty format. They often seem to take TV images for reality. In serious moments they often sound like a textbook in social psychology: A girl has a "meaningful relationship with her boyfriend," people are "consumed by negative feelings toward someone in the group"—I am quoting from *WIN*, the best of the youth movement magazines. And it is amazing how the language of underground newspapers, identical by dozens, is actually spoken by teen-agers. But this language is less format than it seems. It is filling the vacuum of adolescent speechlessness. The stereotypes serve as glue for ganging together, and the ganging is real though the language is spurious. A rock festival is usually a commercial hoax, but the pilgrimage to it is not.

More poignant is the speech of a highly articulate, but unread, militant *chicana* housewife, who declaims social worker Newspeak during a demonstration because she has no other public words. But her passion gives it life, if not sense.

The deep pathos of colloquial speech—with its indestructible good sense, eye-witnessing, communal vitality, and crotchetiness (including much private error and deep-rooted tribal prejudice)—is that in highly organized societies its field of operation is strictly limited. We can speak good colloquial where we have freedom to initiate and decide. When our actions are predetermined by institutional and political frameworks that are imposed on us, we necessarily become anxious, unconfident of ourselves, and we fall into institutional and ideological format and its mesmerized thoughts. Thus in our societies there is continually spoken a dual language: Intimately, people talk sense—about politics, the commodities, the schools, the police, and so forth—yet they also talk format, and act on it. In totalitarian societies, where a strong effort is made to re-form colloquial speech to official format, the effort cannot succeed, but people do begin to whisper and fall silent; finally, only a few brave writers, who have a very special obligation to honorable speech, continue to talk like human beings.[*]

In America, our colloquial is certainly not much improved by respectable literary models. It is a loss, because people would express themselves more clearly and forcefully if they could express themselves a little more literarily yet without sounding like a book, and they could thereby also extend the boundaries of their human expression into more public domains—at least somewhat (there would be conflict). A few of us writers do the best we can. Some of the young pick up our language—and turn it into *their* format!

There is a kind of style to our speech. It is the style of urban confusion: a Yiddish that chews up and can assimilate the ads, the sociological jargon, the political double-talk, the canned entertainment.

To achieve the controlled and accurate transmission of messages, it is necessary finally to dispense with human speakers altogether, and let us now turn our attention to this.

---

[*] Fortunately, there is hard evidence for my conjecture that modern people aren't "dehumanized." The Princeton Theological Seminary ran an ingenious experiment that showed that students stopped to help a (planted) man in need or passed him by not because of their gentleness or hardness of heart, but because they were told they had time or were late for an examination. Frederic Darley and Gregory Bateson suggest that the Good Samaritan of the parable was probably in a "low hurry" condition, while the priest and Levite were doubtlessly rushing: "One can imagine the priest and Levite, prominent public figures, hurrying along with little black books full of meetings and appointments, glancing furtively at their sun dials as they go. In contrast, the Samaritan, a man of much lower public status, would likely have fewer and less important people counting on him to be at a set place at a set time."

4. "Communications"

The primary idea of the art of communications is to open channels or provide technical means by which speakers can talk to one another, like couriers or telegraph or telephone. As the general Theory of Communications has developed, however—it is a new branch of philosophy—the idea has come to be to make the signals precise and perfectly transmissible by explaining away the speakers. I will briefly trace the steps of this curious outcome, quoting from some of the chief authors.

Most simply, and innocently, whenever we use any medium or technical means to convey our meaning, there must be some adjustment of the form of the message to be handled by the medium or the technology. An engineer of the telephone company who wants to improve reception of the signals will urge speakers to say the phonemes sharply, and he might suggest new pronunciations for very frequent words: "faiev" for "five," "naien" for "nine." The speakers must not speak too quick, too slow, too loud, too soft. In the fine arts, of course, the adaptation to the medium is what the whole art is about: The "object of imitation" must assume an entirely new form and live and breathe in the medium. From this beginning, the theorists at once take a giant step.

> Words [says Julian Huxley] are tools for dealing more efficiently with the language of existence; so that language is properly speaking a branch of technology."

Here the words are not adapted to the technology, they are themselves the technology. In this formulation, speaking is not to be considered as itself one of the free human actions—it is a means to expedite other actions. (One wonders what they are.) The study of language is suddenly no longer one of the humanities.

Regarding language as a technology, we can begin to refine what it must be.

> The communications engineer [says Roman Jakobson] most properly approaches the essence of the speech event when he assumes that the optimal speaker and listener have at their disposal more or less the same "filing cabinet of prefabricated representations"; the addressor selects one of these preconceived possibilities and the addressee is supposed to make an identical choice from the same assembly of possibilities already foreseen and provided for.

Needless to say, this is a very different doctrine from what I have been calling either the literary process or colloquial speech, where the speaker, drawing on many powers and expressing his needs, modifies the language to fit the unique situation. But if speakers cannot creatively adjust to the conversation they are having, Jakobson's requirement is certainly a technological necessity for accurate transmission. Otherwise, there will be guessing and sometimes not grasping what is meant at all, as if it were a foreign language.

It is in this sense that we must understand Jakobson's remark that

> the efficiency of a speech event demands the use of a common code by the participants.

The common code is not what the speakers have as a convenience, as they might have other common possessions; it is what they have as a law, that they must not tamper with. We have commented on many passages of Saussure and the cultural anthropologists, how this code is constant, supraindividualistic, and generalized. In the extreme view of Whorf, it predetermines what the speakers must think.

But next, according to Count Korzybski, we can make a more precise specification for the prefabricated representations that fill the filing cabinets and are the common code. They are, says the Count, the names of "facts" organized into classes and classes of classes, in levels of abstraction. Using abstractions

> integrates the cortico-thalmic functions [by] inducing an automatic delay of reactions which automatically stimulates the cortical region and regulates and protects the usually over-stimulated thalamic region.

On this theory, the use of right speech would preclude any forceful action or final satisfaction of life, for these always have concrete objects and become spontaneous. He seems to be describing what I call "acting in a chronic low-grade emergency"—see *Gestalt Therapy,* pp. 264–265. But he tells us,

> The socio-cultural developments of civilization depend on the capacity to produce higher and higher abstractions.

Freud called this *Civilization and Its Discontents.*

For the pedagogy to teach this common code of higher abstractions, we return to L. S. Vygotsky:

> We define "consciousness" to denote awareness of the activity of the mind, the consciousness of being conscious . . . . A concept can become subject to consciousness and deliberate control only when it is part of a system. If consciousness means generalizing, generalization in turn means the formation of a superordinate concept that includes the concept as a case. A superordinate concept implies the existence of a series of subordinates and a hierarchy. Thus the concept is placed within

a system of relationships of generality. In the scientific concepts that the child acquires in school, the relationship to an object is mediated from the start by some other concept. It is our contention that the rudiments of systematization first enter the child's mind by way of his contact with scientific concepts of the [teacher] and are then transferred to everyday concepts, changing their psychological structure from the top down. This is why certain thoughts cannot be communicated to children, even if they are familiar with the necessary words.[*]

Here at last is a prescription for transforming common speech itself into format. Just browbeat the child with verbal explanations that he cannot understand. Vygotsky spells it out in a remarkable example:

A child cannot use "because" in real life situations, but he can correctly finish sentences on social science subjects, for instance, "Planned economy is possible in the Soviet Union because there is no private property—all lands, factories, and plants belong to the workers and peasants." Why is he capable of performing the operation in this case? Because the teacher, working with the pupil, has explained, supplied information, questioned, corrected, and made the pupil explain. Later, in finishing the sentence about his bicycle, he makes use of the fruits of that collaboration, this time independently . . . . With the progressive isolation of speech for oneself, vocalization becomes unnecessary, and because of its growing structural peculiarities also impossible. In reality, however, behind the symptoms of dissolution [of common speech] lies a progressive development, the birth of a new speech form.

This new speech is not mandarin or format. Orwell was not thinking of anything nearly so sophisticated, in describing Newspeak. The trick of breaking the free spirit that is inherent in speaking is "to make the pupil explain." The way of breaking the spirit of a writer is to pay him to write what makes no sense to him in a style that is not his own.

I have quoted at length from the Russian savant partly for his dogged manner but especially because he adequately brings us to another great leap in the Theory of Communications—the elimination of speakers because they are supernumeraries. Since we have nullified the free action of speakers, their realm of choice, their individuality, their thalamic emotions, and their con-

---

[*] It is interesting, but not surprising, that Kropotkin, who was an anarchist, makes exactly the contrary point: You can teach anything to a child or an unlearned peasant *if you yourself* understand it concretely and can therefore follow *his* understanding and offer it by the right handle.

crete experience, and since their thoughts are internalizations of top-down instruction in a system of generalizations, it is possible to lop them off with Ockham's razor and to say that communication is the transaction of the system of general signs. This is what Sir Julian Huxley does:

> Language provides a new environment for life to inhabit. I shall call it the Noösphere, after Teilhard de Chardin. As fish swim in the sea and birds fly in the air, so we think and feel our way through this collective mental world.

The Noösphere, in Teilhard, is the network of signals which has evolved to brood over the world like the program of a universal computer—the Abbé identifies it with Jesus.

(It is remarkable how, pushed to the extreme, the technological approach to language converges so exactly, in content and rhetoric, with the anti-technological humanism of the phenomenologists, pushed to the extreme: compare Merleau-Ponty's "Speech is like an *être,* like a universe. It is never limited except by further language." In the end, it makes little difference if the "collective mental world" is man's new environment, or a project of freedom, or, as with Vygotsky, the internalized ideology of the State. But none of these describes what it is like to speak a language.)

It remains only for the physical world, too, to become Communications, and this step is taken by Norbert Wiener, with the synoptic elegance of a mathematician. The form or pattern of matter, the ordering of entropy (=disorder), is information; to cause such patterns is communication:

> When I control the actions of another person, I communicate
> a message to him, although the message is in the imperative
> mood . . . . The commands through which we exercise control over
> our environment are a kind of information which we impart to it . . . .
> Information is a name for the content of what is exchanged with the
> outer world as we adjust to it and make our adjustment felt upon it.

Putting it this way, moreover, we could say that a bat communicates with the ball it hits; there is no reason to take the point of view that "we," human beings, are the communicators; there is nothing essential to the metaphor "inner" and "outer." Indeed, a human being may well be the *message*:

> The organism is seen as a message. Organism is opposed to chaos,
> to disintegration, to death, as message is to noise. To describe an
> organism we answer certain questions about it, which reveal its pattern.
> It is the pattern maintained by homeostasis, which is the touchstone of

our personal identity—and this may be transmitted as a message, for instance, by wire. [To be sure,] any scanning of the human organism must be a probe going through all its parts, and will accordingly tend to destroy the tissue on its way. To hold an organism stable while part of it is being slowly destroyed, with the intention of creating it out of other material elsewhere . . . in most cases would destroy life. In other words, the fact that we cannot telegraph the pattern of a man seems to be due to technical difficulties—the idea itself is highly plausible.

Wiener does not envisage the man as a respondent or speaker who might interpret what is going on or object to it, for instance by saying "Ouch!" If he would say "Ouch!" however, would not this continually interject new information and put the scanner always one step behind?*

Thus, I have brought together half a dozen passages by important authors to show the kind of thing that sets my teeth on edge in modern theory of language. But I am sorry to conclude with a passage from Norbert Wiener, a real humanist who usually made a lot of sense and whom I have liked to quote on *my* side.

5. Avant Garde

The deliberate response to format is *avant garde*—writing which devotes itself, at least in part, to flouting the standard style, to offending the audience. *Avant garde* is different from other inventive writing. If a work is felt to be "experimental," it is not that the writer is doing something new but that he is making an effort to be different, to be not traditional.

In any period, powerful artists are likely to go way out and become incomprehensible. They abide by the artistic imperative to make it as clear as possible, but they are not deterred by the fact that the audience doesn't catch on. They do not want to shock the audience, but the audience just gets lost—and bored. Thayer comments on the first performance of *Eroica*:

> Some, Beethoven's particular friends, assert that it is just this symphony which is his masterpiece, that this is the true style for high-class music, and that if it does not please, it is because the public is not

---

* In his idea of sending the pattern of the man by wire and re-creating him out of other material, Wiener holds the ancient doctrine of Prime Matter—a position somewhat like that of Santayana, with his Realm of Essence and Realm of Matter. It is not a tenable doctrine. As Aristotle pointed out, "Only the flute has the song of the flute": in actuality, form is the form of its own matter, and we know matter only as the potentiality of that form. I am pretty sure that a man is not given by his homeostasis. Conversely, the matter that makes up that homeostasis, not to speak of the man, is not just any "other material elsewhere," but is highly preformed and might be the devil to collect.

> cultured enough artistically to grasp all these lofty beauties. After a few thousand years have passed, it will not fail of its effect . . . . A man shouted down from the gallery, "I'll give another kreutzer if the thing will but stop!"

Yet pretty soon, it made itself an audience, it taught people to speak, as Merleau-Ponty puts it well. On hindsight, the incomprehensible of genius almost always turns out to be in the mainstream of tradition, because the artist took the current style for granted, he worked on the boundary of what he knew, and he did something just more than he knew.

Avant garde artists do not take the current style for granted: it disgusts them. They do not care about the present audience: they want to upset it. Instead of trying to be as clear as possible, they are just as pleased to be incomprehensible, *fumiste* or *blagueur*. A sign of success, or success itself, could be to provoke a riot.*

Of course, such a disruptive attitude does not foster beautiful and finished works "exemplary to future generations" (Kant): the writer is too busy with making an effect to give himself to the literary process. *Avant garde* tends to be capricious, impatient, fragmentary, ill-tempered. Yet, except by raging and denying, a writer might not be able to stay alive at all as a writer.

As a style, *avant garde* is an hypothesis that something is very wrong in society. The icy objectivity of the Naturalism of the turn of the century said that people were hypocrites. The Revolution of the Word said that the values of the civilization that fought the First World War were not acceptable; one could not talk "their" way. Surrealism said that rationality was a sell. As the century has worn on and wears on, these startling literary guesses have gotten a certain amount of confirmation.

An ultimate step is always Dada, the use of art to deny the existence of meaning. A step after the last is to puff up examples of format itself to giant size, Pop.

But in a confused society, *avant garde* does not flourish very well. What is done in order to be idiotic can easily be co-opted as the idiotic standard.

Some artists use the cast-off debris of technological society as their raw material. My brother goes in for decorating styrofoam packaging. It is just the opposite of the dadaist impulse to paint a mustache on "Mona Lisa."

---

* But audiences are unpredictable. Sometimes—as at least the premieres of *Ernani* and *Le Sacre du printemps*—they are terribly sensitive in their philistinism and riot at works that were certainly not meant to offend. On the other hand, when recently my friends of the Living Theatre tried to get their goats with a determined *avant garde* happening, the New York intellectuals just sat there and enjoyed every boring minute.

A different direction altogether is to deny that literature as such is relevant—to say that writing is made honest only by its workaday and community use. In its philosophical form, which I remember hearing during the twenties (for instance *Gebrauchsmusik*), this is a profound doctrine. It is close to Goethe's great sentence that "Occasional poetry is the highest kind"—the poetry of weddings, parties, funerals, and dedications. Street theater and commedia dell'arte are the utopia of every playwright. Music and plastic art—though literature less—have certainly flourished in service to religion. It is a doctrine of happy communities.

Since the thirties, however, and very much nowadays, the irrelevance of literature has gotten to mean that the right use of literary speech is political action, like protest songs and guerrilla theater: we simply don't have the community necessary for celebration, occasional poetry, and commedia dell'arte. That is, the process of literature is not used in its natural power to find meaning and make sense, so that we can act in a world that has meaning and sense. It is claimed there is no time for this; there is too much suffering and injustice. And only by engaging in revolutionary action can one produce new thought and lively words. But in practice, I have found, this comes to not questioning slogans that are convenient for an immediate tactic or a transient alliance. The writers tell half-truths. "Action" becomes idiotic activism. The vocabulary and grammar are pitched to a condescending populism, about at the level of junior high school, including the dirty words. The thought is ideological through and through. By a "revolutionary" route we come right back to format.

6. What Is Communication?

A more interesting dissent is the distrust of language as a means of human communication. If speech has become an exchange between filing cabinets of prefabricated representations, to speak is to be oneself a cog in the International Business Machine. Verbal arguments are nothing but Ping-Pong games that tap the ball back and forth and avoid contact. Or they are ego trips to put one another down and confirm one's own conceited self-image. For people to know one another, it is better to touch, hold hands, make love, or manhandle. The only trustworthy words are emotional cries. These are the techniques of sensitivity training and group psychotherapy. Some believe that under the influences of the right drugs they share their thoughts and feelings. There is a revival of silent meditation.

This is the outcome of regarding language as essentially a constant code, not to be modified by its speakers, when people become alienated from all the institutions, including language. Long schooling increasingly attempts to socialize to the common code. Suburban life and mass consumption of mass-produced commodities extend the socialization into every detail of life. Communications engineers tailor speech to make transactions more efficient. Linguists devise ingenious formulas for the automatic translation of foreign languages. The general Theory of Communications asserts that noiseless exchange of accurate information is the order, value, and meaning of the universe. And people feel that by language one can no longer communicate anything.

But there is a meaning of "communications" by which we say, "They seem to be talking the same language, but they are not communicating"—that is, the speakers are not referring to the same situation or are not taking it in the same way; or even when they seem to agree, instead of thereby having an identity of purpose with one another and being able to cooperate, each continues in a parallel course in isolation; their speech has made no difference to them. Here, "communication" means that the speakers touch one another. Their speech has made a difference to how they organize their experience. A good sign of it is that they thenceforth use their own words differently. The essence is not the exchange of "information"; the information must form, re-form, the speakers. For this, the public constancy of the code is a disadvantage. To put it paradoxically, the aim of communication is to alter the code.

If I ask, "What time is it?" and you say, "Eight o'clock," and I go about my business using the information, my code is not deranged; I am set up for the information. Yet it is communication, because the information fills my need and makes a difference. But if I am surprised by what you say—I had counted on its being seven-thirty and I am late—there is *more* communication! Your response has made *my* language more for real. In most conversation, however, the speakers interpret one another's remarks according to their own habits in order to *avoid* derangement; information is exchanged—for instance, the sentences can be repeated later—but it is reasonable to say there has been no communication. But in the closer context of dialogue, as Buber calls it, there is resistance, vulnerability, reaching, excitement, and reconstruction. Since people's personalities are very much like their verbal patterns, communication feels like physical aggression or seduction.

Poetic speech, which drastically alters the code, communicates better than ordinary speech; one has to give in to it to get something out of it. The nonverbal contact of persons, if it wrenches their expectations, is usually more communicative than any speech—consider a stealthy sexual touch, or a slap in the face. As I have said before, a chief purpose of the speech of psychotherapy is to change the language, especially the syntax.

But I think that this is also the idea of feedback in the usage of wise cyberneticists like Wiener or Gregory Bateson: The communicators impart novelty in the exchange of information; stereotypes convey little and just increase the noise; the more speech approximates to an exchange between identical filing cabinets, the less the communication. But then we must say that the code of the exchange is always being reconstructed in use by feedback, there are no fixed counters. And the speakers cannot finally be dissolved into bits of information, because as originators of novelty they are whole, free agents in the sense that they are outside the system being considered, whatever it is.

I disagree with Vygotsky:

> Direct communication between minds is impossible, not only
> physically but psychologically. Thought must pass through meanings
> and these through words . . . . To understand another's speech, it is not
> sufficient to understand his words, we must understand his thought.

("Thought," we saw, was the internalized system of abstractions.) I rather agree with Merleau-Ponty that communication begins with people's bodies; this is by no means physically impossible. It is not minds that communicate, but people. The use of words is itself a creative act, somewhat physical, that produces meanings that did *not* exist in prior thought. People are more changed by changing their patterns of words than their thoughts. Good speech, colloquial or literary, is more meaningful than thought, not less, because it is part of a richer human situation, the dialogue of persons.

I realize that it is awkward and inelegant to define communication as I here propose; it is hard to build on it a precise Theory of Communications. It brings back the speakers and respondents as persons rather than exchangers of bits of information. If the speakers are free agents, we cannot know them through and through. What they do is probably not arbitrary, but *their* causes are outside the speech event and partly outside the realm of signs altogether. It is not possible to tell beforehand what sentences will be "meaningful" for communication. It is possible, even frequent, that it is some unnoticed nuance or connotation of the signs, or a fleeting gesture, even a "misunderstanding," that in fact communicates, rather than the common code or the prefabricated representations.

In this respect, a good conversation is like a unique artwork, unthinkable *a priori,* yet achieved, and then usually analyzable. It is only a literary or dramatic structural analysis of the actual speech event that can explain its functioning as communication.

The method of the linguist very much decides how "constant" the code is.

Like any other animal moving in a various and always somewhat novel field, a speaker must be able to say something new; coping with the environment, he will use neologism, metaphor, connotation, an exploratory word order. But to maintain his own equilibrium he must appropriate his new experience in a form traditional to himself, and he will favor the code, the dictionary meaning, denotation, formal word order. Thus, in linguistic research, if the speaker's response is restricted to his own judgment, as in the pair test or being asked what is grammatical, he will speak mostly code; but in spontaneous practical situations, he will speak with more variety and novelty.

Unless there is a fixed code, speaker and hearer cannot communicate; yet both speaking and hearing are active processes that shape speech for the occasion. If speech is too standard, it becomes an obstacle between speaker and hearer, like a foreign language; rather than speaking, the speakers have to translate. So in linguistic research, if language is isolated as an independent object of study, it will seem to be a constant code; but if we start from actual communication and ask what part language is playing in it, we will be struck by the flexibility of native speech. It will seem more a natural than a conventional behavior, more a creative adjustment than an algorithm or a pattern of culture.

The pattern of culture is itself ambiguous. A society determines the habits of its members; although there are always individual differences, the forces of imitation, cooperation, and conformity are overriding. But society is in more rapid flux than we usually judge. (Consider that the grandfather of a reader of this book may have conversed with George Washington.) If only because of unequal development during rapid change, most societies consist of a complex of small sub-societies. This and many other reasons make for intimate communities of speech. And also for much creole speech. Thus, it is not to express his individuality, but just to cooperate and conform, to form himself on a social model, that each speaker must continually alter the code he has learned. So in linguistic method, an instantaneous cut will reveal a constant code; but a more plausible historic stretch, that allows for subgroups to impinge on one another, will show much more modification as the individuals adjust to one another and to their own changes.

Whether to assert or communicate or serve as a social bond, language must both be definite and have wide leeway. To be meaningful, it must also take the risk of being delusory or mere word-play.

The Shape of the Screen and the Darkness of the Theater

In a controversy some ten years ago on the best shape for the cinema screen—the occasion was the abortive introduction of the Grandeur screen—Sergei Eisenstein contended for the Square as against the Flat Oblong (5:3, 8:5, and so forth). His interest was to give the director more latitude for "vertical compositions." In practice, as it turned out, he lost the argument, for although a few theaters have square screens, all film-frames remain oblong. Partly to explain this outcome, so far as it can be done on merely psychological and esthetic grounds, I should like to discuss the Screen-shape in a more fundamental context than was at that time proposed.*

To begin with, let me add a few notes to the old discussion. Eisenstein summed up the arguments for the oblong under three heads, which he then refuted: theatre-structure, physiology, and esthetics.

(1) The overhung balcony requires a screen lower than the square in order not to interfere with the line of sight of the rear seats; but the new theaters, argued Eisenstein, could dispense with such balconies (which were indeed invented for audition without amplification, for reasons of rent, and so forth). But other architectural considerations must also be kept in mind, namely the pitch of the seats to insure a good direct line of vision, and the avoidance of obstruction from the heads in front.

(2) More crucial are the physiological arguments: that the field of stationary vision is broader than it is high and that the moving eyes cover a wider angle horizontally than vertically. It seems to me that these are refuted too cavalierly by the great Russian when he says that the head itself can be moved; for it is all very well to look up and down at a painting, but for the ninety-minute-long attention to a movie, every cause of strain or effort must be absolutely minimized before any other consideration.

---

* Quite apart from this entire discussion, I should say that a sufficient explanation for the oblong shape for average use is the physiological one that the *field of vision* is broader than it is high, so that the flat oblong presents a larger easily visible area than the square.

(3) Thirdly, the esthetic arguments are twofold: that the majority of paintings are oblongs, and that the oblong (for instance, the golden rectangle) is demanded by dynamic symmetry. Let us pass over the discussion of dynamic symmetry. As to the other point, first he denies the statistics, then goes on to say that it was not the influence of painting that made the screen oblong, but of the stage-opening. But cinema must cease to copy the stage (this was of course just at the commencement of the calamitous retrogression of the talkies). Whereas the stage must be an oblong because human action spreads out horizontally, since men don't fly, the cinema, he argues, is not restricted to action in this sense.

These points are capital and certainly true; but the question must still be asked whether there is not a basic affinity between the style and most cinema as spectacle as well as action. The entire question of how the screen is and is not like the stage-opening, and again the relation of the screen-frame to a picture frame, is just what I want to go into more fundamentally.

1. The Illusion of the Total Field

Reverting to the physiological fact of the field of vision: since this field is a kind of broad ellipse flattened at the top and bottom, the question must first arise why the screen, or again the picture-frame or the stage-opening, is not elliptical rather than square or oblong.

Now of course the scene, whether in cinema, drama, or painting does not fill the whole field of vision, but only the center of attention. The scene is not identical with our spatial reality, but is an object in the space, which also contains the walls, other spectators, and so forth; and there is no doubt that the restriction of the audience to psychological participation in the scene rather than overt participation, and to a kind of psychological participation rather than the total psychological participation of dreams, depends on the persistent sense of this spatial discontinuity.

At the same time the scene is not a *mere* object in our vision, as a man or a chair might be an object, for the scene is (in most cases) an *imitation of the whole visible field*. If this were not so, we could not project ourselves into its world without asking ourselves, What other objects are there *alongside* the scene? and such a question would be destructive of dramatic illusion and the self-containedness of the spectacle. That is, *the illusion, the self-containedness of the spectacle, and the discontinuity of the scene-reality with the physical reality are mutually involved*; and an artist bent on *avoiding* one of these, must also do something about the others.

The original ellipse of the physical total field to be imitated, therefore, must always bear some influence on the shape of the screen or frame. The *degree* of this influence, however, will be great where the real space and the action of the actor in it is a major object of imitation—the case in most landscapes or in presenting the world of the drama; but the degree will be less where a more particular body is a major object, as in the portrait of a man or in the recitation of a soliloquy. There are thus three cases: On the one extreme, where total and even overt participation of the audience is required, as in the "audience-participation theater," the ellipse broadens out to become identical with the physical space; there is no frame or proscenium. On the other extreme, where the attention is to be centered on a particular object in itself, the ellipse is irrelevant. In the middle, where the illusion of a world is required, there is a frame and it is elliptical.

But why the flat oblong then (as nearer than the square to the ellipse) rather than the ellipse itself?

In the second place, granting that in a given case the illusion of the total field is the effect aimed at, nevertheless the visible arts in general exploit *interesting objects as their most immediate presentation.* These are for the most part men, animals, trees, buildings all seen with relation to the horizon and the foreground, that is in a system of verticals and horizontals. A composition whose members have no rectilinear relations—for instance, a group of shapes by Miró—at once seems to be in the vacant sky or in the depths of the sea, and such a picture often seems more "real," to hang together better, in an irregular oval frame. But to the degree that the horizon-line and its system of perspective belongs to the objects of interest, and these objects are the immediate presentation, the scene as a whole will come under a rectilinear influence; the frame correspondingly—for in the end the function of the frame is to confirm the spatial system of the scene—will be square, vertical oblong (as in the portrait of a man standing), or flat oblong.

If we would then require the *combined* effects of illusion of the total field and immediate presentation of terrestrial objects, perhaps the flat oblong is the most serviceable simple shape. Given a single problem, a peculiarly appropriate shape is always most expressive, for instance a little upright oval for a miniature of a face; but the movie-screen, we must remember, is the common-denominator of an indefinite number of usual problems. For a very special effect we may work *within* the common-denominator, for instance mask the screen to isolate a figure or iris down to a detail.

2. The Square and the Synthetic Montage

When I speak of the "illusion of the total field," I do not mean that the scene-space must be illusory in the sense of reproducing the very same spatial properties of the physical space. For instance the scene may have different laws of perspective, as in many Chinese paintings, or be the space appropriate to fantastic space-time juxtapositions quite different from the world we are used to seeing. And in all painting, in abstract painting especially, the illusory space tends to become two-dimensional and none other than the space of the canvas itself.

Nevertheless, all these scenic arts, which begin from the real space and either reproduce it relatively unmodified (the case where the frame is like a window), or distort it to create effects of unreality (as in *Caligari* or the paintings of Chirico), or abstract it to the two-dimensional conditions of the canvas—all these are to be distinguished from those arts which from outset disregard the existence of a persistent space and *construct* objects and designs without determining their space at all. Léger's *Ballet Mechanique* is of this sort and the so-called non-objective paintings like Kandinsky's (as opposed to abstract paintings). And to understand Eisenstein, I think it is in this direction that we must look. Consider the following series of effects in cinema: Scenes of cinema often achieve the pictorial, for instance, much of Murnau's *Sunrise* is Dutch landscape or chiaroscuro interior, and the poses in Dovzhenko's films are certainly portraits. In such cases the screen-shape is not unlike the corresponding picture-frame, and it has the pictorial function of bounding the determined space, guiding the eye back into the composition, and completing the static whole. (By "static" here I do not exclude motion across the scene but only the movement of cutting from scene to scene.) Such active preoccupation with a single shot as a completed whole, however, tends to destroy the temporal flow of the *sequence* of scenes, and is therefore eschewed in most cinema, for instance in any ordinary story-telling film. Here the screen-shape is looked *through* rather than looked *at*; it offers the means for looking out, so to speak, at the world behind; that is, it acts purely as a window. But now supposing no illusion of the total world is desired at all: then the screen-shape may simply be disregarded as a part of the spectacle, and the composition may be formed of objects succeeding each other as if in an indeterminate space or even in no space. This effect, most obvious in the light-play films, sometimes moves so far from the conventions of ordinary vision as to be analogous to music— compare the efforts of Scriabin. But if the presentation is not to be mere play of lights, but objects determined by an horizon, then the Square shape might be just the most suitable space, for, as Eisenstein insists, it allows the greatest quantity of expansion in the relevant directions; as a rectangle, it supports the design of each shot of objects; as *not* an ellipse or flat oblong, it neutralizes the sense of an actual visible space. Now anyone who has admired the marvelous synthetic montage of this director, which is not the turning of a scene before the camera (illusion of the actual total field), nor yet the posing of a static composition (picture-frame), but a unity of cutting and synthesizing a sequence of images of objects by means of their psychological and philosophical associations, will easily understand why Eisenstein asks for the Square. *The square is the convenient screen for synthetic montage.*

The square neutralizes not only the illusion of the actual visible world, but also the sense of visible spectacle altogether, for it does not play to the visual potentialities of the spectator, but retracts from the largest area that he could conveniently rest his eyes in. This leaves the way open to the *non-visual* play of attention, unconscious, visceral, and theoretic, that Eisenstein so much delights in exploiting. He does not speak to the sight. It is then in this double sense, first as getting away from the limitations of physical visible reality and secondly from the sentiment of spectacle altogether, that Eisenstein says the cinema must not copy the stage. But expressionist staging tries at the same freedom—let me mention the expressionist dictum that "vertical motion is more interesting than horizontal," so that actors somewhat "fly" after all.

We now ask, however: How are the *sequences*, whether of pictorial images, synthetic montages, or dramatic episodes, organized into the ninety-minute-long film? In answering this, we shall again have to return to the relation of the screen and the stage-opening in a more fundamental way. But let me first indicate another possibility.

The *ideal* for Eisenstein would no doubt be that the whole should be one vast synthetic montage of parts of synthetic montage. This result is even somewhat achieved in *Old and New*, where the overall changes of tone and rhythm are a direct expression of the general theme, while the narrative is reduced almost to a story-framework for the montage. But certainly for the most part in Eisenstein, Pudovkin, Trauberg, or any of the others, the organization of the sequences of montage is not itself montage but either narrative or drama. As such, it draws again on the illusion of a whole visible world. Do not misunderstand me: the narrative and drama may themselves be symbolic and not the chief expression, which may be an idea; but the point is that this idea is not presented directly by the montage, but indirectly through the narrative and drama, with their sense of a self-contained illusory world.

3. Some Kinds of Stage

Let us now broaden our scope from the screen or stage-opening itself to the more inclusive whole of the scene-opening in the theater, with its conditions of light or darkness, silence or music, and other spectators. My contention is that the flat oblong screen and the ordinary dark cinema-theater are conditions for the same kind of illusion. But I can analyze this out better first in terms of some kinds of stage.

The argument against the against the peephole or absent-fourth-wall stage has generally been wrongly proposed as an absolute rejection, but the correct formulation should be: The peep-hole has an expression incompatible with the theme or attitude that we now wish to express; or again, the peep-hole produces a psychological state in the audience that makes impossible such and such a communication; or again, putting it formally, such and such a state and theater-conditions are good for such and such a plot or probable sequence.

Consider some properties of the peep-hole theater. The house-lights are dimmed, the audience is silent. Not only are the stage-lights always brighter, but they belong to an independent system of lighting and they illumine an independent space. The stage-space is made distinct from the audience-space in other ways also: is raised above it, framed in a proscenium, and so forth. Further, the sense of an absent fourth wall gives the stage-incidents an independent time and causality, for the stage-events can in no wise act on or be reacted on by the physical audience. But since the dimly-lit and silent audience has no life of its own, its entire activity must consist in mental projection into the stage-world. There, of course, it has the liveliest interests, interests which are indeed intimately personal to each member of the audience; but these interests assert themselves and are gratified under the conditions of fantastic projection. In short, we might say the following: (1) The peep-hole stage expresses an illusion of the total visual field. (2) It keeps the audience all eyes. (3) The probability of the plot on such a stage seems to be given entirely through the actors, who are self-subsistent and on their own, for there is no other continuous reality. (4) The scenery must also add up to a self-subsistent reality, though of course it need not be realistic; but bare stage-boards will not do. (5) The audience-interest is given under the psychological conditions of projection, as in day-dreams.

Now contrast such a stage with a daylight performance (of, say, a masque) on a lawn or in an amphitheater. Here there is a continuity between the visible audience and the stage and actors; and this might express, depending on the ethical tone of the plot and the occasion, the sense that the actors are amateurish neighbors, subject to running comment; or that they are heroic surrogates of the audience, perhaps in a religious act like the mass; or that the play is a mere spectacle or pageant, an interesting object *alongside* the other sights in the total field of vision. The unit of the whole, we must then say, is partly given by the audience's sense of its relation to the play. (I do not mean this to be a description of the Greek theater, where the Chorus *both* unified and divided the play and the public.)

Consider, again, the Elizabethan stage with much of its action on the apron—I am speaking more of the stage of Marlowe than of Shakespeare, and more of the chronicle-plays than of the tragedies. Suppose on this stage the poet violates the unities of space and time at will, brings forth his speakers on the apron or on the inner-stage as suits his purpose, and so forth. Such a stage makes more indirect the illusion of a presented world, it introduces effects of narration into the drama. (At the same time there is still the illusion of a world, though with indefinite geography and perspective.) Psychologically, there is a more direct communication between the poet and the audience; the unity is partly in the poet's interventions and juxtapositions, better for rhetoric or lyrical effect, or reportage, or to tell a story. Here elaborate asides to the audience and topical jokes do not seem out of place. It is interesting to observe how the conventions of the Living Newspaper, like vaudeville before it, have tried to adapt the architecture of the peep-hole stage to the direct communication of the Elizabethan platform.

The expressionists, as I have mentioned, sometimes neutralize the sense of all (imitated) physical world entirely. The revolving stage, the spiral stairs that rise from the flat on which men ordinarily converse, the timeless masks and costumes—these all speak in terms of theory or inner perceptions; there is still a self-contained visual pattern and therefore the imitation of a total field, but the pattern is more abstract and indeed tends to spread out to include the architecture of the theater itself, which is preferably styled according to the same canons.

Quite another effect, again, is that of the audience-participation theater, for here not only are the play and the public physically and psychologically continuous, but—in the ideal case—the overt reactions of the audience ought to alter the events of the play. Strictly speaking, this is not a "theater" at all. Here we enter the realms of political meetings, religious revivals, and parlor conversations; and have come a long way from the hush, the three knocks, and the footlights lit, before the curtain rises.

I have introduced these few remarks only to demonstrate that the flat oblong of the peep-hole stage is by no means due merely to the fact that human beings do not fly, but especially to the fact that its peculiar properties, which are not the properties of the Stage in general, strongly call for imitation of the total field and illusion of the physical space.

4. The Darkness of the Theater

The movie-theater is darkest of all. The movie audience consists preeminently of *individuals in isolation*. And the *discontinuity* between the audience-space and the space of the scenes is of course absolute. If the effect of the brightly lit stage is a controlled fantasy, the flickering lights of the screen working on the ninety-minute attention unrelieved by intermissions produce what is nearer hypnosis (where it is not perfect sleep). Certainly, especially in a small theater, the stage is warmer and more intimate in appeal than the screen, so long as the fantasy is more nearly like what we are used to or consciously desire; the actors are flesh, the shadows are only shadows. But let the cinematic attention become fascinated, as it does as the minutes flow by, and these huge shadows press in closer to the mind at this deeper level than the sight of real flesh can penetrate. The disjoined and composite space created by cutting from scene to scene is more like the space of dreams than the quiet stage can hope to imitate.

These circumstances explain easily enough why cinema has devoted itself almost exclusively to the excitement of ordinarily repressed feelings and even unconscious connections; and why, though clearly visible and therefore more patently absurd than literary fantasies, its world of desire is not immediately rejected. Adding the mass-production and the enormous audience, we have the principle of selection of these feelings and we understand the usual plot, the star-system, the surrealist interiors, and so on. Indeed the real difficulty is to see why the movies have not more directly imitated the actual technique and contents of dreams—consider for instance, the extraordinary compulsion of *Le Sang d'un Poète*, where this is done. But the reason for this abstention may well be audience fear and modesty which are even stronger than audience desire. To put this another way: the *public* moving-picture that the audience talks about after the performance or reads about before it in the reviews is not the same as the actual experience of the solitary spectator; but this actual experience is hinted at in the advertising.

How far this tepid bath is from the intellectual synthetic montage of Eisenstein! His constructions are passionate and rich with dream-symbolism to be sure, but like other artists he gives these in effortful stabs to a *disturbing* depth, at which the audience cannot rest.

It would be further still from a "film of political participation" whatever such a thing might be. (Does it not seem to be impossible in principle?)

The hypnotic absorption, again, was immensely aided by the continuous and not independently interesting musical accompaniment of the old films. This music neutralized the audience noises, lulled the muscle-jitters, and restricted the only possible field of sensuous interest to the eyes. Its continuity provided just the matrix needed for the scene-space to keep it one despite the often kaleidoscopic cutting; when the music stopped the mechanism at once became apparent.

The fact that both the peep-hole stage and the movie-screen imitate the total world in conditions of fantasy is a chief cause, it seems to me, of the remarkable phenomenon of audience-interest in the personalities of the actors themselves, a phenomenon not apparent with respect to other arts and spectacles, even musical performances or oratory. The conception of "Hollywood" is of course pat for this argument: here is a distant and paradisal world inhabited completely by the beings of the world of fantasy but come to "life." And the machinery of Hollywood publicity is designed precisely to controlling that life so as not to jar with the properties of the other world.

Let me make still another sociological observation, a point of the highest importance, but almost completely disregarded by the critics of stage and screen. I have mentioned the "drama of political participation." Now certainly the most determined essays in both stage and cinema have been made towards direct rhetorical appeal, for ends both high and low. By "direct rhetorical appeal" I mean both the rousing of feeling and the presentation of arguments, especially by dramatic example, for or against something with the end of producing appropriate overt action of the part of the audience. But first: is it the fact that the excitement roused in the theatrical condition of fantasy can bridge the discontinuity and survive in the public world? might not the *contrary* be partly true: that the energy attached to such theatrical symbols is thereby fixed at that level, permanently submerged beneath the political level? (This is the old story of the women who exhaust their function of benevolence in the esthetic splendor and sexuality of religious ceremonials.) Secondly: is it likely that the desired reactions, whether of horror or enthusiasm, when fixed in the fantastic world, reappear in the public world with the same positive or negative value? Perhaps with even the opposite value! as a child frightened by a gangster film or by images of the horrors of war may retain, when he "awakes," the sentiment of a forbidden thrill. Certainly the American public, presented with the usual images of filmic luxury (still, in 1941, in the style of the Paris Exposition of 1925), does not react with either emulation or resentment, but rather with a dream-delight in these *ideals*, which exist in the mental world somewhere near the ideals of honor and divinity. What then? Am I arguing that these arts can not or ought not to aim at rhetorical ends? Certainly not; but that from such rhetorical calculations we must not omit a dimension which may turn out to be absolutely vital. A necessary safeguard is the analysis of the expressive medium.

5. Conclusion

To sum up: I have tried to distinguish between artistic imitations of the seen world as a whole, discontinuous from the self-conscious spectator, and seeming to exhaust the field of vision, and those other imitations which are merely part of the total field and present a certain continuity between the object and the spectator. I have touched on a few differences of the two types in plot and psychological appeal. I have argued that the flat oblong of the screen was not taken over from the stage merely by an historical influence, but that there is a common cause in the medium of expression of both. And I have tried partly to explain—the chief explanation, I would maintain, is physiological—the almost universal success of the flat oblong by the somewhat simplistic formula that it is a compromise between the imitation of the total field of vision and the rectilinearity with which we compose the terrestrial objects within the frame.

Again, what then? The conclusion of this line of argument is by no means that cinema can not or ought not aim at effects of synthetic construction, or participation, or anything except spatial illusion—God forbid that a critic should argue for the status quo, and what a status quo! Rather, that such non-illusory effects require the invention of new technical resources and manners of handling, the work of creative directors. We have seen, for instance, how Eisenstein's Square is one such invention, more far-reaching in its expression than one might have thought, intimately related to the achievement of a non-illusory effect. An invention along another line is Herr Gropius' "Space Theatre," a plan to project films simultaneously on several different screens. The exact expressiveness of such a medium would have to be discovered by exploration, but it seems to me—on the analogy especially of the Grandeur screen—that at least an effect of pageantry could be directly achieved by this means, for the several spaces would destroy the illusion of the unique illusory space, restore the relation of the spectator to the spectacle as spectacle, and give the spectacle great magnitude. Another technique for overcoming illusion—but one which seems to me to sink even *deeper* into illusion—is the employment of newsreels or newsreel atmosphere in documentaries. Another, thrice-familiar, technique is the direct address to the audience by a huge close-up of a face—but almost always this particular sequence in the film merely clashes with everything that has gone before; let me give no examples.

Designing Pacifist Films

1.

I am asked for my thoughts about the content and style of anti-war films, and how to make such a film.

First of all, such a film must at least not do positive harm by predisposing its audience towards war. The images of senseless violence, horror, and waste that are usually employed in the commercially successful "anti-war" films do have a titillating effect and remain in the soul as excitants and further incitements. Let me show how this works.

(1) In cinematic conditions of bright screen and dark theater, lasting for many minutes and tending to fascination and hypnosis, images of horror easily detach themselves from the kind of intellectual and ethical framework in which they are usually presented, and they attach themselves to quite different subliminal ideas. We must bear in mind how a child wakes up screaming with his nightmare of the animated cartoon he has seen, the nightmare now expressing a kind of wish.

(2) Also the response of a theatrical mass audience is different from the more intellectual and ethical response of a small company or an individual reading. (Perhaps TV is a special case.) What a theater audience experiences most vividly is how it has, anonymously, shared in breaking a taboo, in witnessing with accomplices the forbidden and shocking. The "message" of the spectacle is then employed as a rationalization that is mentioned outside the theater or in the reviews, though the advertising hints at the shocking.

(3) This dual process is specific for the heightening of guilt: a forbidden stimulation with one's censorship lowered by crowd feeling, disapproved by one's ethical and social self. Now, the effect of guilt is not reform or, finally, deterrence; but inevitably resentment for having been made guilty, and perhaps then clandestinely or unconsciously choosing more congenial buddies. (Pacifist propaganda in general, let me say, is prone to arouse guilt just because it is irrefutable and on the side of the angels. This is an important reason why accompanying persuasion some immediate *action* must be available—just as a loving sexual seduction must lead to acts or it does harm.)

(4) The arousing of lust and self-disapproval leads to the specific porno-graphic effect of wished-for punishment (the hallmark of popular sexual art). The image of punishment is often provided in the film itself, as its poetic justice. Such self-punishment is evil in itself; but worse is that usually it is projected far and wide as vindictive hatred of scapegoats. And alternatively, it seeks for allies in mass suicide, as if to say, "*We* are not worthy to live."

(5) Especially in cinema, the conditions of fantasy and the habits of the audience are so discontinuous with behavior in the waking public world that the shock of strong images is sentimentalized: the rationalizing sorrow and regret is used to *insulate* the experience from any possible action. The energy of revul-sion turns into pity, a pornographic emotion, rather than active compassion or political indignation—not otherwise than with Christians who exhaust their neighbor-love in the sentimentality of the Cross. The next step is for the senti-mentalized horror to be taken as matter-of-course in the public world, just as for those Christians the poor *must* always be with us, so Christians can be charitable.

(6) Finally, bad audiences cannot be relied on to respond to a whole work of art; they will select from it what suits their own repressions, and interpret according to their own prejudices the very fact that they have been moved despite themselves. The lovely is taken as dirty, the horrible as sadistically thrilling. This derogation is partly revenge against the artist. Bad audiences follow the plot as a story; they do not identify with the whole work as the soul of the poet, but they identify with the actors of the story and take sides. Given a film about capital punishment, for instance, a Camus will notice, and be steeled in revulsion by, the mechanism of execution: he will deny the whole thing the right to exist because it is not *like* us (this is the reaction-formation, denial, that is characteristic of active compassion); but a vulgar audience will identify with the victim, get involved in the suspense, thrill to the horror, and weep with pity. The effect is entertainment, not teaching or therapy; and to be entertained by such a theme is itself damaging.

2.

By a good audience, of course, a work of genuine art cannot be easily taken amiss and abused in this way. By definition, the images of genuine art do not allow themselves to be detached from its idea, for the whole is solidly fused in the artistic activity. But this standard of excellence is useless for our present pur-poses, since such works are not conveniently had for the asking. And when they do occur, they are just as likely to be embarrassing to our rhetorical purposes. For example—I choose classics of literature that are beyond debate—both Homer's *Iliad* and Tolstoy's *War and Peace* are infused by, and teach us, a profound pac-ifism, a lofty and compassionate dismay at the infatuated violence of men in their armies. Yet they certainly also express, and even celebrate, the demonic in war, the abysmal excitement of mankind gone mad. This was interesting to these artists and it *might* be to any contemporary artist—how could one know? The counter to such demonism in a great artist would have to be a kind of saintliness. We are here clearly outside the context of planning pacifist films.

Again by definition, in a work of genuine art the images of horror, and so forth, do not have a pornographic effect and do not incite to repetitions, for the experience is finished and cathartic: the fearful images are purged, transcended, interpreted, or otherwise integrated with the rest of life. An art work leaves its audience with a saner whole philosophy (more congenial to pacifism in so far as pacifism is truth); and it has taken some of the venom from the cruelty and arrogance in the soul. But such a re-creative "finished" experience is precisely not rhetoric; it does not lead directly to action or any *immediate* policy. The Athenians seeing Euripedes' *Trojan Women* were no doubt wiser and sadder about the very course of folly that they continued plunging along. (I do believe, however, that great art, forcibly confronting us with a more meaningful universe, does *initiate* conversion, and pacifists do well to perform these achieved monuments of their tradition.)

My guess—I judge from my own art-working—is that a serious modern artist who happens to be a pacifist (and how could he not be, if he once attends to these matters?)—if such an artist begins to move artistically among the scenes of war, his art action will soon lead to the exploration and expression of his *own* horror, rage, pain, and devastation. The vegetarian will disclose his own cannibalism, the pacifist his murderousness. Such works, for instance, *Guernica*, are monuments of how it is with us; they have no leisure for a practical moral, nor even for the luxury of indignation. The eye lamp flamingly thrust forward over *Guernica* does not light up the deed of Nazi bombers, but the violent soul of Picasso, brought to a salutary pause.

If we consider spurious, *kitsch,* or propagandistic antiwar art, on the other hand, its actual pornographic and provocative effect is equally to be expected, for the fantasy and the art-working convey the disorder of the weak artist and speak to the underlying wishes of the bad audience.

We thus have, by and large, the ironical situation that precisely the best cause, which has irrefutable sense and common humanity, ought to avoid psychological, "artistic," and mass-rhetorical effects.

3.

What, then, are the available resources of pacifist persuasion that can be used for a pacifist film? They can be roughly classified as:

(1) Factual education

(2) Analyses of character-neurotic and social-neurotic war ideology, and the withdrawal of energy from the causes of war spirit.

(3) Opportunities for positive action, and pacifist history and exemplars.

(I. a) As a strictly prudential argument, pacifism has an easy case, perhaps too easy a case, so that people do not take it seriously, it is too obvious. People have always known that war is a poor expedient, inefficient for any plausible purpose. And "present-day war," not only *our* present-day war, has long been out of the question. It is best if the facts, of the senselessness of it, are allowed to speak for themselves, without admixture of moral or emotional appeal or any grandiose references to saving the human species. The matter is much simpler. War talkers are pretty close to fools or else not a little crazy; their postures and remarks are not proper to normal grown men. This can be simply demonstrated, relying on logic, statistics, and history. The framework must be an irrefragable and unmistakable structure of verbal proposition, even printed subtitles, however "uncinematic"; for we are dealing with a deeply neurotic and even schizophrenic phenomenon, and the *reality of ordinary reasoning, and ordinary dismissal of stupidity*, must be strongly affirmed.

(b) On the other hand, the dangers of pacifist action—for instance, the risks involved in unilateral disarmament—should also be dispassionately and fully presented, so far as they can be fairly estimated. *It is not necessary to have an answer for every argument*, even grave arguments, for we cannot do what is senseless and unworthy of men anyway. Pacifism is a decision. The "serious" position is not, as Niebuhr, for instance, seems to think, to choose a lesser evil; it is to realize that we cannot have been so wrong for so long without purgatorial suffering.

(c) The facts of war policy, war makers, and war economy ought to be exposed with unsparing honesty and detail, at the risk of inevitable censorship. For instance, delineating the personalities—a Teller, Kennedy, or J. Edgar Hoover—on whom so much is allowed to depend. But further, the immense network of the power structure must be made clear and diagrammed, so that a person comes to realize how nearly every job, profession, and status is indirectly and directly involved in making war.

(II. a) Psychologically, our "tough" warriors live by a conceit of themselves as strong, to ward off the anguish of their spirits broken by authorities they could not face up to; and a conceit of themselves as hard, to ward off loss of love and fear of impotence. A film might profitably analyze the military posture, pelvis retracted, belly kept hard, exhalation restricted; the military ethos of inhibited feeling; the conceit of superiority by slavish identification with authority symbols. For comparison, analyze the social and family genesis of an underprivileged gang tough. Explain the details of Marine discipline as a means of destroying manliness. The system of griping fostered in armies as a means of maintaining childish dependency and avoiding mutiny. But further, show how in our times the classical sociology of the armed services as a substitute for civilian responsibilities is combined with the use of the services as complements of, and training for, organizational civilian life. The soldier seeks for ratings like a junior executive, while the Organization Man has a tough as his secret ideal. A thorough social and psychological analysis of these types might immunize the young.

(b) Analyze the notion of the Enemy as a projection (scapegoat) and also as a political red herring. Show in detail how Enemies have been manufactured and miraculously reformed by techniques of press and promotion. Show also how foreign nations have thus manufactured the Americans as the Enemy and assigned to us Enemy traits and wishes.

(c) But probably the chief factor of war spirit that must be analyzed is not the military character nor the projection of the Enemy, but the paralysis with which the vast majority of people of all countries accept the war that they oppose both by conviction and feeling. This must betoken an inner, fatalistic attachment to the feared disaster, and it is best explained as "primary masochism" (Reich): the hypothesis that, because of their rigid characters, people are unable to feel their pent-up needs, especially of sexuality and creative growth, and therefore they dream up, seek out, and conspire in an external catastrophe to pierce their numbness and set them free. The prevalent conditions of civilian peace and meaningless jobs tend to heighten this lust for explosion. (My experience, however, is that in analyzing this factor of war, one is opposed precisely by the more moralistic pacifists themselves. Rather than condone normal homosexuality or encourage the sexuality of their children, they would apparently accept the brutality of armies and see people blown to bits. One is dubious about the sanity of their pacifism, which seems to be rather a defense against their own hostile fantasies.)

Social and psychological subject matter of this type is sufficiently interesting in itself and is only confused by attempts at drama or case history; a straight classroom approach, the illustrated lecture, is most quietly effective.

(III. a) Factual exposure of the political and corporate operations of war society, and psychological and social analysis of its war ideology and spirit ought to disattach and release the energy that has been bound up in conventional symbols and habits of life. We must then have uses for this energy and opportunities for pacifist action. In principle, any animal satisfaction, personal self-realization, community welfare, or humane culture will draw energy from the structure of conceit, projection, and fatalistic masochism of the war spirit.

"Waging peace" is the best means of preventing war, and pacifists do well to invent and support programs for the use of our wealth and energy freed from the expense, fear, and senselessness of war. In my opinion, let me say, there is also natural violence that diminishes war, for instance, the explosion of passion, the fist fight that clears the air, the gentle forcing of the virginal, the quarrel that breaks down the barriers to interpersonal contact. War feeds on the inhibition of normal aggression. (Of course, many pacifists disagree with this point of view.)

(b) Specifically pacifist action—usually in the form of refusing—is called for when people are required to engage directly in war-making, for instance, by the conscription, the civil defense, working in war science or war factories. The defense of civil liberties, also, seems to be congenial to pacifists, because the libertarian attitude goes contrary to the power state.

(c) Finally, the preferred pacifist means of exerting social force has gotten to be nonviolent direct action, shared in by the group. Any instance of this, even if it fails, is proof of the feasibility of the pacifist position, for it shows that sensible and moral individual and small-group action is possible, and thereby it diminishes our masochistic paralysis in the face of an approaching doom "too big for men to cope with." (The history and the heroes of civil disobedience and nonviolent direct action, achieving or failing to achieve happiness, social welfare, or cultural progress, constitute the mythology of pacifism. They have the heartening exemplarity and the, perhaps, sentimental irrelevance of any mythology.) To my mind, pacifism is like Rilke's unicorn, it "*feeds on the possibility of existing*." For the resistance to modern warfare is natural and universal; the arguments against pacifism are weak; and the spirit of war is reducible by analysis; but what is needed is stories, examples, and opportunities for action concrete in the experience of the audience.

Factual and analytic handling of images of war can neutralize their pornographic effect. My bias is that even the exemplary images of pacifist action are best handled in a documentary fashion, avoiding audience identification with their heroes and keeping the real situation in the foreground. The purpose of the film is not so much inspiration as to point to opportunities in the audience's real environment. *It is better to err on the side of dryness. The heart is already enlisted.* Emphasis on the pacifist "movement" with its charismatic symbols and "leaders" betrays us into the field of public relations, where we are swamped. The charismatic excitement that gives courage and solidarity must emerge in each concrete occasion of pacifist action, and it will emerge, if it is really a man's own occasion. We are in the tradition of bearing witness. It was just the genius of Gandhi to notice faultless occasions.

The kinds of theme I have outlined could be the substance of a useful series of documentary pacifist films. Developed forthrightly and in particular detail, they would certainly prove offensive to many audiences, including some pacifist audiences, but they could hardly fail to hit home. They would rouse anxiety both by the character analysis of the audience and by the need for the audience to make decisions in their actions. The shared shock of the truth and of possibility is, in our society at present, equivalent to breaking a taboo. For most, I guess, the effect of such films would be uneasy silence, a dangerous but transitory state of feelings. The hope is that some of this feeling would be mobilized to decisive action, just as some would surely result in ugly reaction. Perhaps most persons would be made deeply thoughtful.

For its makers, such a document would certainly be a pacifist action, a commitment, and a bearing witness.

Reflections on Literature as a Minor Art

I am setting down the following melancholy reflections not with any hope of a remedy, but because the matter is important and nobody else seems to be saying it.

In many ways literature has, in this century, become a minor art, more important than pottery or weaving, perhaps less important than block-printing or other graphics. Firstly, it is no longer an art of either the mass-audience or an elite audience. Cinema and radio-television, journalistic photography and series of illustrations, and persistently architecture and a kind of music: these are arts of the great public in a way that books, even best-sellers, have ceased to be. For the elite, the policy-making, audience there is no particular art as such; in its artistic taste and needs this group does not distinguish itself from the rest of the people. (To be sure, rich people collect objects of paintings and sculpture and thereby support artists, but these artists do not produce their works for the collectors any more than poets write for them.)

To the extent that in metropolitan centers the stage is still a popular art, it is not a literary stage, the emphasis being rather on the stars, the spectacle and music, and the production.

The diminution of letters is especially evident to those of us who write very seriously, who try for the classical literary functions of subtle ideas and accurate distinctions, ingenious and cogent reasoning, distilled learning, poetic expression. These functions are not easily or often adapted to the major modern media, to cinema, photography, or television, for in the adaptation they are blurred, blunted, curtailed, and lost. We are not then deceived, like other writers, by the illusion of finding ourselves in the swim; we cannot be made use of; we practice a minor art and occupy a minor place. The comparison to pottery and weaving is apt, for what we are doing is analogous to individual handicraft, no doubt rare and beautiful, compared to the major media of the present which tend to be produced by teams with a standard technique, not unlike machine-production.

These are, I suppose, the first decades in the western tradition that letters have not been a major art. It is a situation so peculiar that it is not noticed. Now the shift to other media is not necessarily a cultural misfortune. It happens that, on the whole, cinema and television, and so forth, have so far produced pathetically inferior works that cannot pretend to compare with the masterpieces of book and stage over 2500 years; but it is not inconceivable that the new media will get hold of themselves (I do not say "mature" since, in cinema at least, the works of a generation ago were much more promising than those today). Naturally, for men of letters our new status is personally unfortunate. We were trained in a tradition where letters had a quite different ambition and scope; our adolescent fantasies of becoming major artists are doomed to be fantasies; and ironically, just because we are too good for the current scene—for we draw on a tradition better than the current scene, but that tradition is irrelevant—we find it hard to adjust to the realities. Also, when, as often, we are called on to teach our English and our Literature, we find ourselves like curators in a museum; the average student (like the average editor and publisher) no longer reads English like a native. This is lonely-making. But as Trotsky said, "History fells the dead wood and the chips fly off."

2.

A second way in which literature has diminished is that it is no longer the source of ideas important for social policy and moral behavior. Such ideas as now get influentially abroad—I am not often impressed by their wisdom or brilliance—originate among economists, social scientists, administrators and businessmen, and technologists. Now this lapse of letters from a major position is not a new thing. When Shelley spoke of poets as "unacknowledged legislators," he should have meant not merely that they were unofficial but also, by his time, unaccepted. By the nineteenth century, compared to the preceding 500 years, although men of letters still had respectable positions in the homes and palaces of the policymaking elite, they certainly had ceased to function as important first sources of ideas that would eventually shape practice. The exceptions stand out and illustrate my point: the social-revolutionary ideas of the Russian writers that brought nearly every major Russian man of letters to jail or exile, or the moral ideas of the European and American writers that at once awakened the censorship. These writers were thinking up ideas not for the makers of policy, but against the makers of policy.

(In general, through the ages we can estimate the importance of letters as sources of policy by the negative test of the censorship of letters. Where books are heavily censored, books are important for social policy and moral behavior; and throughout the high middle ages and in modern times there was always a heavy censorship. But through the nineteenth century, except in Russia, this decreased, and in our own days it is trivial. Of course in America it is not from the government that we would expect the important censorship of ideas or expression, but from those who control the capital-means of communication, the owners of radio stations, publishers, theatrical producers. Let me then suggest the following possibility: since what these persons do diffuse is not important, policy-making literature, if there exists any important literature at all, it must be in what they refuse to diffuse, what they censor. It is possible that that exists. Note that in our times the question of the quantity of diffusion of ideas is essential. Since there is little legal censorship, it is possible for nearly any idea to get itself printed; but our country is swamped with printed matter—more than twenty books a day are printed in large editions and literally tons of newsprint and magazines—and there is no difficulty in muffling any idea at all by refusing to spread it widely. Indeed, we have the interesting paradox of precisely the overworking of printing presses being a possible cause of the reduction of literature to a minor art.)

So far as the subtle, learned, reasoned, and persuasive treatment of ideas is a function of letters, our present shift to other major media, and literature becoming a minor art, is socially unfortunate. Cinematic and pictorial arts do not treat ideas adequately; that is a verbal business, it is specifically literary. Moving pictures can powerfully determine norms of behavior and style of life. The picture-coverage of an event in an illustrated magazine can powerfully direct what people feel about it. But subtle and learned explanation, the application of history and experience, the play of thought and hypothesis, the effort toward the truth under the surface that does not leap to the eye, everything Matthew Arnold meant by "criticism of life," these things are not skillfully accomplished without letters and training in letters and a high expectation from letters. In the earlier and hotter days of thought, Socrates complained that a book was a poor thing compared to a man because you couldn't question it and reason with it; he would have taken a dim view of audio-visual education.

3.

In one important respect, however, literature cannot become a minor art, for it is the art of language. In every generation, the art of letters renovates and codifies the style of speech, assimilating what has sprung up new, inventing new things itself. This is far-reaching, for the style of speech is our interpersonal attitudes, which are largely patterns of rhetoric and syntax; and also the style of speech is a good part of our philosophy of life, for a point of view proves itself viable and gets abroad by being able to tell a real story in a new way. (So the plastic arts, drawing and painting and sculpture, cannot become minor arts for they demonstrate perception, how people can see and are to see; and so a people's music is its kind of feelings.)

Speech is not going to stop changing, and so men of letters, marking down the speech, relating it to character, and developing the characters, are always indispensable. And the strong and subtle writers are fulfilling this function as always. But the mass of speakers are faced with the dilemma: on one horn they must get their style from the writers; on the other they have ceased to follow writing, or expose themselves to it, as major artistic experience. The result is that the ever-new speech is not strongly characterized and explored into its poetry and ideas and assimilated with a great humane tradition; people get their speech, in low-grade letters, as a caricature and a stereotype, with the conformism and thin conversation that we hear.

The Chance for Popular Culture

For a decade now the critics have told us about the unfortunate state of popular culture, the culture of the mass-media. Previously this culture was attacked by the acute for particular political and moral tendencies, commercialism, esthetic ineptitude. The difference in the later, usually socio-psychological, analyses is that the culture is now told off en bloc, as a hopeless state of mind, a general character-symptom of the social disease; the culture is inauthentic, superficial, falsely professional, coordinated, and so forth; there is no point in singling out for attack details or trends or individual works. The critics are of course merely explicating in theory the longtime attitude and practice of most of the best artists of the twentieth century; indeed the artistic attitude of rejection and withdrawal goes so far back that its earlier rebellious insults are now, in reproductions, a great part of popular culture.

Much, even most of this recent criticism is correct. But the critics do not sufficiently feel, I think, what a bleak and lonely prospect they envisage. To put it bluntly, if the critics were more frequently creative artists they would not so blithely observe, and annotate, the disappearance of a popular audience for good work; they would suffer anguish and shrink inward, as most artists have done, or fight back for our audience, as I hope we all shall do. The coldness of the critic toward this calamitous loss is itself a phenomenon of the superficial culture they assail; perhaps it is just this that is needed to sting the creative man to revulsion, to make liars of these wiseacres.

In the following remarks I am myself, as a poet, looking for a way out. First, to see the situation as it is, I summarize the gist of the usual, correct criticism of popular culture; but by looking at the case a little more simply than is usual, I think I can view it more charitably (more hopefully for myself). It is a maxim of our psychology that every symptom of disease is a sign of vitality.

1.

There is more art—more art-works and more experience of them—in America at present than at any time or place in history. By "art" I mean simply the communication of feeling through images, stories, tones, and rhythms: the evoking and displacing and projecting of dormant desires by means of some representation. Half the population sees a two-hour drama every week; the radio nightly presents long hours of vaudeville to millions; records beat out music everywhere; there is no measuring the floods of printed matter, merchandising pictures, cartoons, that have, whatever else, an artistic purpose.

Now this sheer quantity itself is the first thing to explain. But the explanation seems to me to be obvious: people are excessively hungry for feeling, for stimulation of torpid routine, for entertainment in boredom, for cathartic release of dammed-up emotional tensions, and so forth. The life the Americans lead allows little opportunity for initiative, personal expression, in work or politics; there is not enough love or passion anywhere; creative moments are rare. But they are still feeling animals; their tensions accumulate; and they turn to the arts for an outlet. (I say they are "excessively" hungry for feeling because feelings alone cannot satisfy the lack of creative life, still less can the feelings released by even the noblest art.)

They are a passive audience; they do not strongly or overtly react, nor do they artistically participate themselves. There is, of course, no point in overtly reacting to a movie-screen or radio; but it is the audience passivity that has made these canned arts become so important. They dance to music but do not make it; they hardly sing; and less and less frequently do they participate in religious or other ceremonials. Contrast, for instance, the musical spirit of a dancing party with a live pianist, where sooner or later people gather round and sing, with that of a dance where the music is supplied by a radio or phonograph. There is, again, less and less place in the mode of economic production for the expression of artistic feeling, craftsmanship. It is possible to conceive of a society equally rich in art-works where the art is active, for instance in the society described by William Morris in *News From Nowhere*; but our America is drowned in passive art.

And this passive reaction is superficial—this is why it is perpetually sought for again. It does not unleash, like the tragic or comic theater of old, a violent purgation of the deepest crises and thwartings, death, lust, scorn. These things are not purged every morning and night. Rather, *the American popular arts provide a continual petty draining off of the tensions nearest the surface.* Their working can be fairly compared to chewing gum as a means of satisfying an oral yearning for mother love and sustenance.

The social role of this gum-chewing is not obscure: it is to make possible an easier adjustment to the air-conditioned world by quieting the nerves. The very conveniences and comforts of the American standard of living, the quarantining of suffering, and the lack of physical danger, are an emotional disadvantage, because they prevent the occurrence of real objects of effort, anxiety, and passion. The arts give imaginary objects. (The war, again, gives a real object.)

Lastly, works of popular art have the following form: they present an important emotional situation, of love, danger, adventure, in a framework where everything else is as usual. The detailed routine of life, the posture and speech-habits of the actor (and the audience), the norms of morality, the time-table of work, these things are not deranged by the plot; they are not newly assessed, criticized, X-rayed, devastated by the passional situation. Therefore the esthetic experience remains superficial; the passional story releases a surface tenseness, but there is no change in character, habit, or action. One does not sink into these works or return to them, for what is there to sink into or return to? and therefore again there must be more and more. (In the popular music the form is that the outer limbs are moved, even violently agitated, but no visceral sentiment or tenderness of the breast is touched.)* By definition art of such form can have no style, for style is the penetration of every least detail by character and feeling. Somehow the popular arts have won the reputation of having a "slick," professional style; but this is false, because the least scrutiny or attempt to feel the meaning with one's body or experience makes one see that the works are put together with preposterous improbability. It is a Sophocles or a Shakespeare who is professional and workmanlike; in comparison with the style of *The New Yorker*, Dreiser is slick and neat.

2.

In this ambience of too much art, what faces the good artist, the artist who draws on a deep dream and alters his character, the artist who means it, who has style, who, that is, experiences a world starred with his truth? His outlook is bad. (I do not mean, of course, so far as his creation is concerned—for this, at least in the limits of a discussion like this one, is simply mysterious—but so far as his action and happiness as a social animal are concerned.)

To begin with, he sees his productions swamped and drowned in the mighty flood of art-works; how can his win much notice? Among all this printed matter, how to win attention for what could be called a book? Also, quite apart from economic deprivation, which is likely not so appalling to a person who is daily justified in his work, he cannot fail to see that the stupid and preposterous are rewarded, and unless he is rarely philosophical this makes him bitter and envious and, by reaction, foolishly boastful.

---

* An important part of the popular culture is the large audience of concerts and records of Beethoven and Mozart. Let me say, angrily, that this is a cheap and safe emotion. What would those masters say of programs made up, as ours are, of work not written last week, of works whose passion has being absorbed and made safe by a century of habit?

But then, more important, he sees that the elementary passionate themes and the popular idiom have been preempted and debased by the multitudes of art-works, not to speak of advertising and journalism. Simple stories are "corny" and the language of the heart is devaluated. So in recent history we see that the good artists have turned to subjects and methods not immediately and directly communicable to average audiences. (I do not mean "private" subjects and language, for it will prove in a generation or so that just these works were the communicable and important ones of our day; certainly I mean "personal" subjects and language, but these belong to all good work of whatever kind or period.)

Let me hasten to say that if serious artists have avoided corn and directness, we are justified, for we work by an inner necessity. In my own case, because of the chances of my life and the twists of my character, I most often find it so hard just to say what I mean and what presses uppermost, that I have no energy left to bother also about whether you understand it or it is immediately important to you.

3.

Well, all this is fairly familiar. This is the mass-culture analyzed by the critics and this is the plight of the honest artist. Everybody is blameless all around and we are all wretched.

The situation is outrageous and intolerable! I do not choose to endure it any longer. Why should we have robbed from us our elementary passionate themes? And why should we not dare to speak our dear English tongue? And what! are we never to get the heartenment and glow of pleasure that comes from our words being greeted by a roar of laughter, hushed attention, and gleaming tears?—but these greet only what is elementary and direct. The animal proof of the demonstration in the theater or the buzz that follows hard on publication. In this animal warmth it is possible to go on, next time, to what is more daring.

The question is this: how can the artist express himself, have style; and yet communicate to most people the elementary "corny" situation in a popular way? The answer is easy, easy in theory. No! it is easy in fact, easy to do. (If we do not in fact do it, it is because of a moral defect.) What is necessary is to love the popular audience, a few members of the audience; to want to entertain them and to move them. Then the work is both the expression of deep feeling and is aimed to communicate directly to the few and the most. If then the work fails to communicate, the situation is distressing and terrible, but it is not a cold distress.

When I tell a story to my child, I express my best feeling and use my best language, yet I carefully follow her comprehension, interest, and excitement (she is an active audience); there is no incompatibility because I am here concerned, in love. But I do not in fact feel the same toward the corner grocer—I speak of him as the type of person with whom one has daily dealings, friendly but defensive, this is the average audience (of course there is no average audience). Now if I tried, this moment, to entertain and move him, I should likely begin talking down to him and I should certainly bore him; but this is neither my fault nor his; it is simply that my relation to him is not concern, love—nor hot hate, which would serve almost as well. Therefore my subject and words would be not mine, but a presumptuous guess at his.

That one feels concern or not is a fact; but it is this fact—however caused—that determines whether or not one can be a popular artist, have style, and also be greeted by an audience; it is not considerations of debased language, corny themes, corrupted audiences.

Presumably there was a time when the artist turned to his audience as a matter of course, on a basis of love, respect, and fear, as one tried to please and show off to parents or wooed a notoriously fickle beloved. Concern existed as a matter of course, how strange that seems! just as the words communicated by convention. What is the case now of myself as an artist? I see no grounds for an intelligent man to respect the American public in its mania; yet thinking about it, I do not really take their mania seriously, *nor do I think they do* (if I'm wrong I'll get rapped for it); and this mania aside, I respect my brothers and sisters pretty well. What I find lacking in me is the desire to please; I want their love without giving myself to the wooing. Aha! it is the fear that is too strong. I do not love the audience because I am afraid of the corner grocer! Fear of rejection? fear of blows? fear of contact?

4.

"The audience is corrupt." This statement must mean two things: that the audience is so accustomed to the stereotyped use of language that it cannot hear the ring of urgent presentness, and that the audience is so fearful of any feeling that might work a change that it freezes against giving in to unsafe-guarded experience. Both these things are true of the popular audience. Yet if we state them thus, we see at once that the audience cannot be much corrupted. An art-hungry public is not unfeeling; in fact the Americans are too vulnerable because of their passivity (and ignorance), so that small novelties effect crazes and fads. When a man, or an audience, freezes against the deepening of feeling, the threat of its working a change, the problem is a simple one: to find at just what point the freezing occurs and to sensitize that point. Surely the artist can recognize that point, *he* is not insensitive there, otherwise how is he an artist? And as to the language of communication: ultimately it is the English language of childhood and of occasional adult passion; the musical rhythms are those of walking and skipping, for those who still walk somewhat and used to skip.

Suppose a delegation of the taxi-drivers came and asked me to write a vaudeville to entertain the taxi-drivers. This would not be difficult; one could always, at least, have recourse to pornography. If one felt concern for this audience, the work would be beautiful and releasing (the pornographic raised to beauty and understanding). Suppose a couple of sensitive and intelligent gentlemen on the radio directly and feelingly expressed their convictions, without making it nice? Would not the effect be electric?

5.

There is an obstacle in these pleasing fantasies. Between the artist and the public stand those who control the mass-media, the publishers, impresarios, and so forth.

It is important to remember that from time immemorial an essential characteristic of the great art-media (architecture excepted) is to be cheap: paper, mud, rock, tinkling, humming, talk, agitating the limbs. It is on these poor nothings that great spirits have lavished endless labor toward their immortality. The media of communication served as means, not as obstacles. But now suddenly, because of our peculiar social arrangements, a feature of the mass-media is expense; and expense is controlled by, let us say, "social policy."

Thus, if I want to move a million people, I must also persuade the editor of the *Saturday Evening Post* to let me. It is not a question of moving him esthetically, as one member of the audience, but of stirring him to *practical approval* of the way he has been moved. This persuasion I could never accomplish. As an audience, he is a human being; but as a controller of capital means he is an intermediary something, not a human being at all. For instance, he maintains a policy, and I don't give a damn for his policy. As a responsible agent he looks into my credentials, but I trust my poetic act has no credentials. As a businessman he has an empirical notion of what will appeal to many readers; but by now this empirical test is meaningless, for the readers get nothing else in the mass-media except what he gives them, so perforce they like what they get. But what they get and take demonstrably does not move them, make any difference to them, for we see that with so much art we have the society we have. In fact he does not know what will deeply move people, nor do I; but he can never know, whereas I might find out by inventing it. How to get by this fellow? He, like any member of the audience, is afraid to be moved; but because of his role he holds on to himself very tight, much tighter than they. No doubt he is afraid to have the audience be moved. (This is called "the storm of angry letters" and "cancellations of subscriptions." Is it the case that magazines have foundered in such storms?) He seems to me to have a certain lack of daring; there is no reason why a profitable institution should be daring, but at least let us not talk about "what the public wants."

In the whole dilemma of popular culture, this difficulty of proprietary control of the media by the tribe of intermediary bureaucrats is, I think, the only fixed reality. The natural problems, of themes and language and taste, solve themselves by natural means. If the audience and artist are brought in contact, concern must follow, and following concern a deepening of communication. To the extent that editors, impresarios, and so forth, are human beings, they too are a part of nature; but most often one has to do with them as dummies of public policy and profits.

So we come, finally, to a hackneyed political issue. And frankly, as an unreconstructed anarchist, I still must consider the solution of this issue easy, easy in theory, easy in practice; if we do not apply it, it is for moral reasons, sluggishness, timidity, getting involved in what is not one's business, and so forth. The way to get rid of dummy intermediaries is by direct action. Concretely, in the present context of popular art (I am always fertile in little expedients): let actors get themselves a cellar and act and forget about the critical notices; let writers scrape together a few dollars and print off a big broadside of newsprint and give it away to all likely comers on 8th Street; forget about Hollywood movies—they don't exist—and how surprising it is to find one can make a movie for a couple of hundred dollars and show it off in a loft. I don't want to lay stress on such particular expedients; but it is ridiculous to gripe about vast socio-psychological labyrinths when what is lacking is elementary enterprise and belief.

You see, I myself am waiting for my friends to open a little nightclub where the talents that we know galore can enliven us, instead of our frequenting idiotic places that bore us; and where I myself, setting myself exactly to this task, with concern and love (and a little hot hate), can move an audience to the belly and be greeted by a roar of laughter, hushed attention, a storm of anger, gleaming tears.

"What's this? he speaks of popular culture, mass-media, the state of society, and he ends up pleading for a little nightclub where he and his friends and their hangers-on can display themselves!" Listen, here is my concern: I want to be happy; I am an artist, I'm bound to it, and I am fighting for happiness in the ways an artist can. If you, audience or artist, take care of yourselves, the intermediary somethings will get less take at their box-offices, and we'll have a popular culture.

Literature

Western Tradition and World Concern

Now that in technique, economy, and government the world is fast becoming a unity, a unity not only of great ideas like the brotherhood of mankind or of great movements like Christianity or social revolution, but of daily habits and manners—at such a time a self-conscious artist who is aware of the sources of his style and his themes is faced with a terrible dilemma. Either he abandons the western tradition he has been brought up in and patiently absorbed, and tries, a late-learner, to adopt a new outlook (but what outlook and how to absorb it?); or he persists in his ways and feels that he is somewhat parochial (but a conscious sense of parochialism is fatal to high seriousness or high comedy, for these are incompatible with any suspicion of merely relative value). The following reflections spring from my own awareness of this dilemma; but unfortunately they do not solve the problem.

1.

How can we speak more precisely of the "western tradition" or the "oriental tradition"? Let us use as an earmark the following consideration: to have a literary tradition means that in thinking of the most basic human relations and human conflicts, a writer pictures them dramatically to himself in a few ancient exemplary stories. The most basic relations are those of child and parent or other exemplar, of kin and friends, of ruler and subject, of sexual love, of death, of man and God. In the western tradition these are conceived fundamentally as Greek and Biblical stories, to which are added a few medieval national cycles. Thus, the tragedy of the family is the story of Oedipus or Orestes, the murderer is Cain, the dominant father is Abraham expelling Ishmael and sacrificing Isaac, the lover is Phaedra, the poet-king is David, the premier among peers is Arthur. Then, the tradition is alive when in each generation these stories are retold: not simply told again, but revived, dreaming through the old story to the moral of the current wisdom. In the past thousand years the Greek and Biblical stories have always been so revived, and the authors include, of course, the greatest names in western letters. On this criterion we see how Goethe, for example, is the very embodiment of the western tradition—so that he is almost a myth himself:—whereas Shakespeare is less so, but also in the tradition. (The reason is that Shakespeare did not pose to himself the basic problems as such, but started from current theatrical excitement.) Further, when a radical social and historical change brings people to consider a new human relation as basic, as basic as the other continuing basic relations, then an occasional new story is added, e.g., Tristan or Faust. From a sophisticated point of view we may consider that the new relation, e.g., sex-death, is not really fundamental but is a secondary perversion; but it is preferable to consider it as basic in the socio-psychological situation into which the people have been maneuvered.

Psychologically there is no mystery about the fact of such a continuing tradition, revived and revised from generation to generation. A small child is instructed and entertained with stories, and these are the stories. Then grown-up, when he is face to face with the expression and interpretation of his deepest thoughts, the old stories recur to him as compelling formulae because they are energized by the thoughts of childhood, which were unconscious in childhood. (To be sure, only stories with a certain formal greatness can carry such energies to begin with, and this is why a tradition is long in developing, for it requires the inheritance of stories already greatly told.)

It follows that if, as we find today, these stories are no longer told to children—I mean the Bible stories and the Tale of Troy—then the tradition must lapse, no matter how deep and accurate the comparative literature may become. By "comparative literature" I mean the adult collation of great stories not necessarily energized by the thoughts of childhood. In fact the situation is fast becoming as follows: (a) There ceases to be a large public aware of the stories. (b) The learned and intellectual poets to whom the stories are deeply meaningful cling to them all the more closely and defiantly. (c) But their handling becomes increasingly private and hectic, lacking the centrality of common wisdom, for it is only a common standard that can keep a story clear and grand in form. (d) What was originally human fate comes more and more to be the private case history of the poet. (e) And the larger public, having not yet learned other stories, now has no basic stories at all, but is condemned to shallow literature.

Every step of the way could be easily demonstrated by examples.

2.

Now we are entering a time of world awareness and world concern, in politics, economy and communications. What is the deepest possible relation between the western tradition and this world concern? for it is obviously not possible in every way both to use the traditional culture to communicate one's new concern to vast new audiences, and at the same time to have a simple and integral style. But we must seek for the deepest possible relation, because only a deep memory can invent humane letters.

It must be pointed out at once that the expansion from a western to a world concern is not analogous to the expansion from a national to a Great-European point of view. For intrinsically the Great-European point of view is culturally prior to the separate national cultures; it is everywhere apparent in the great national works; even in the most limited political meaning, it is a late historical phase of the western tradition, not something added to that tradition. Is there any sense in which world awareness is similarly apparent in the western tradition?*

I do not think that there are important world stories in the sense that there are important western or far-eastern stories. On the contrary, it seems that the same fundamental human problems have been pre-empted in the different cultures by precisely different classic stories, with corresponding differences in style. For the most part, in the west the eastern stories have been employed exotically; sometimes, as we shall discuss at once, they have been handled with deep earnestness; but there are no positive world stories. If the world concern is to be related integrally to the western tradition, it cannot be on the basis of the myths directly, but in some way on the attitude and handling.

During the Enlightenment and in the time of Goethe, great western writers, interesting themselves in the near-eastern and far-eastern traditions, drew the inspiring moral of universal brotherhood: namely that it is the same human nature that speaks out in different stories. Among the *philosophes* this meant generally a thinning out of their own stories into rational fables, and no profound intuition of the eastern stories. But in Goethe the western dreams are told with undiminished depth, and he does not misread the foreign dreams, for he saw both that all the traditions belong to one humanity and that they differ in the most radical way possible in style. A few Great-Europeans of the 19th Century, e.g. Nietzsche, likewise reached beyond the European tradition without losing all tradition whatsoever and degenerating into comparative literature, philology and history. What a beautiful ambassadorial role these poets had! imposing nothing, but communicating the universal philosophy and natural science that by definition belong to all intellect.

World concern has developed beyond this ambassadorial relation of mutual respect and communication: first, into the imperialism of the west over

---

* Yes, perhaps just in the negative stories of calamity and irreparable exclusion, like the Tower of Babel; or in the Hellenic awareness, proud and guilty, of the existence of Barbarians. And in the Mission of Paul to the Gentiles we read how one such irreparable breach was healed.

the east, and then into the present stage of either superficial tolerance or international social revolution.

3.

The classic pattern of imperial culture (when once it is beyond the stage of brutal parochial imposition) is the amalgam of traditions, tolerant of all, and lightly blurring differences in style to facilitate urbane intercourse among the literary masters. Soon there ceases to be any fundamental tradition at all, yet superficially nothing is lost and a great master either can invent a hybrid story (which often becomes classic: for the mixture also, e.g., Christianity itself, may be fundamentally humane); or he can return to a sophisticated purity of tradition, with the appropriate audience. One aspect of the Paris International Style of the twenties was just such an amalgam; but, as we shall see, it had also a profound and traditional aspect. But there are strong reasons why just the Americans could be the leaders of such an imperial amalgam: (a) Having aborted their national culture into a technology, they have weaker ties to the western tradition. (b) Their history has given them a cultural humility, the guilt or conversely the boasting of major American writers at having cut loose from Europe in 1776; but now they can joyously atone, in new circumstances, as the literati of the world: the Americans would be quick to adopt any number of styles if once they could learn to read. (c) And they have the wealth to finance a world academy. On a vaster scene they could repeat the relation of Rome to Greece and Syria.

The chief American locus of this tolerant amalgam, so shiny to think of, is not in the seaport cosmopolitanism of New York, but in the cornfed cosmopolitanism of the west coast. The Californian (*homo californiensis*) could become the perfect variety to bear such a broad culture vitaminized, for the first time, with a universal high standard of living. Radiant in body, accustomed to material success, without idiosyncracy, acquainted with the ideas of the two worlds but unembarrassed by the cultural lag that comes only from trouble or vocation, and impenetrable by any earnest word. A remarkable beginning has already been made there by the best type of refugees (academicians and Nobel Prize winners) who seek out the climate.

Against this (but unfortunately exploited by it) is the worldwide communication of the ideals of social revolution: humane labor, physical security and freedom, mutual aid; and among more thoughtful revolutionaries, the humanizing of technology and the ethical measure of production and consumption. These social ideals are simple and integral, not an amalgam; they are close to every concern and causally grounded in the universal spread of the techniques and economy; but of course they are not yet fundamentally cultural at all. It

is only in the fantasies of the political press that they even make such a pre-
tension. They are largely concerned with secondary relations; they are as yet
aimed at overt action, rather than profound practice or thought; they do not
even recognize the simple psychological sources of their own energies——and
fiascos. Nevertheless, such as they are, they are compatible with the humane
culture of the world and they partake of its spirit, though no master has made
them part of its content. The notion that as merely mass ideals they will con-
tinue to blank out our deep personal and social concerns is mere desperation;
it comes from the cultural accident (no historical accident)* that the genera-
tion of world concern happens to be the generation distraught by a technical
revolution.

It is in this direction that the Americans can make a true contribution.
The heirs, through the Dissenters and Franklin and Jefferson, of the English
and French political philosophers, they have had the historical chance to make
many great experiments in what an independent man can do with material
resources. (But we see that this living line is sidetracked into sociolatry and
Lincolniana.)

4.

One aspect of the Paris International Style was the amalgam of cultures that
we have already referred to; bringing together all times and places as if these
things were neighborly here and now. But another aspect was the concentra-
tion on literary method, the abstraction from the content, everything that goes
by the name of the Revolution of the Word. And this development, it seems
to me, has been the greatest achievement thus far (a) within the stream of
western tradition, and (b) towards the integral culture of the world.

If we return a moment to the 19th Century masters, we see that there is
a curious contrast between the Parisian way and the national ways of being
a Great-European writer. Byron, Tolstoy, Nietzsche, Ibsen, Dostoyevski were
Great-Europeans; the ideas they represented and their powers of expression
overrode the national boundaries (even when they were nationalists!) in a way
that the works of equally great writers such as Keats or Gogol, did not. But with
the French, surprisingly, we find that Flaubert, Mallarmé, or even Zola have a
European importance quite beyond the scope of their ideas. Their power, of
course, is that they are the inventors of literary methods, and these methods

---

* I say a "cultural accident" simply because it is logically conceivable that America, for
instance, could have completed its technical revolution (it had the intentions and the
resources) before going overseas; but historically, of course, the technical revolution,
and its economy, and going overseas, are all causes and effects of each other.

carried their fame and spirit abroad wherever a young writer made use of what had been invented.

It was not necessary for them, in order to achieve the most humane communication, to have a philosophic or revolutionary content, for they at once touched the deepest possible of meanings, a new style. In the nature of the case, however, a literary society that habitually seeks such a level, soon ceases to be France or any other country, and becomes—precisely—Paris.

Artistic method, when it is the grappling of the artist with his attitude toward the subject-matter, is his most integral act qua artist; it is his way of neutralizing the ego and drawing freely on the common immortal energies of life. To say it again: artistic methods, e.g., naturalism, expressionism, or cubism, are fundamental theories of the universe, the perception of it, the place of personality in it; and they are proved by the successful creation of the unity of a work, for you cannot create a work with a false attitude. Now such an increased self-consciousness of method and style is not a break with tradition so long as the author does not and cannot forsake his fundamental stories, but is driven by the refinement of the habit of art and by skepticism of those stories that he still cannot but believe, to get behind those very stories to express what is more humane still. But there *is* a break with tradition in so-called experimental writing, which is preoccupied with technique as such, apart from the analysis of the stories. I am referring in poetry to exactly the contrast in painting between abstraction and non-objectivism: abstraction is traditional; non-objectivism is exotic.

At the same time, however—and this is the capital point—abstraction and every other self-conscious method are potentially traditional in several traditions; for they are a passage beyond the stories themselves to the artist in every man universally; they are a passage to the fundamentals of feeling and perception that all men share as brothers. Thus it seems to me that in the abstract handling of his deepest stories learned in childhood, the traditional poet contributes also to a world culture. His *deepest* stories, because only these have the tension of the most humane feeling and perception; and *abstract* handling, in which he is most free. But thus we have come to the hackneyed aphorism that classic art is universal, for classic art has been always just this self-conscious expression of fundamental stories, where neither the expression nor the story calls attention to itself alone and nothing can be added or omitted, for it is like nature.

Consider lastly such a work as *Finnegans Wake*—I say "such a work" as if there were another such!—where there is not only a stubbornly abundant invention of method, perfecting whatever was invented in Paris for 100 years and in England for 500, but also an exploration beneath the stories themselves toward the sources of image, myth and language. These sources are of course a more universal content than the western stories, just as the dictionary of inherited dreams (if these exist) is more universal than a man's dream. But the enormous complexity of Joyce's detail follows from the unlucky naturalism with which he starts ("unlucky" relatively, in that naturalism belongs toward the end of a tradition, not toward the beginning); but no doubt with a different method to start with, similar primordial stories will be presented more simply, and be like the images of Picasso or Klee.

Literary Method and Author-Attitude

In ancient criticism the word "Manner" is applied only to the distinction between narrating the story and acting it out. In modern usage it often covers the whole topic of literary methods, such as the naturalist manner, the symbolist manner, the surrealist manner. Such questions are hardly touched on by the ancients, except in the contrast of the so-called Attic and Asiatic styles; yet if one were concerned to prove the catholicity of the ancients, I think it could be argued that their distinction of narrative and dramatic is a right introduction to the entire study of literary method. The distinction is explicitly not one of means or medium; nor is it like the distinction between comic and tragic (which is discussed under subject-matter). A possible interpretation would be that it deals with the author's approach or method in relating the subject-matter to his verbal and rhythmic means, keeping in mind his attitude toward his own role and his relation to the audience.

In any case, by the time we come to Goethe and Schiller we find that the distinction of narrative and dramatic has blossomed into a perfectly modern discussion of the different possible kinds of authorship, with different attitudes toward the subject-matter and different rapports with the audience.

Now every kind of manner, whether dramatic, symbolist, naturalist, or their combinations, has structural properties discoverable in the mere formal analysis of the works themselves, apart from either their creation or their communication. Thus, the immediate objective presentation in the dramatic manner is formally the unities of time and place; the formal property of symbolism is the existence of a system of metaphor over and above the particular uses of metaphor in the literal story. But here I want to deal not with this structural part of literary manners, but with their meanings as author-attitudes, a branch of psychology and social-psychology.

At the same time, let us not directly discuss the author's relation to the audience (the problems of communication), but precisely the author's freedom, that is his ways of being a creative author. In general in criticism, we can talk about the author's action or the structure of the work or the experience of the audience.

In talking about the author's action, it is useful (though of course not essential) to draw upon his own concrete experiencing of it. So now I, having written many works in different manners, will tabulate briefly what seems to me to be the attitudinal meaning of my own use of five or six different manners. These remarks are drawn from my own experience as an author; it is unlikely that they apply to many other authorships, and without doubt my reading of my own behavior is often incorrect. But that there is in general a relation between attitude and manner seems to me quite certain.

1. Symbolism, Naturalism, Realism

When in a period of acute consciousness of dissent from the political and moral values of my society (America 1941) I came to revise a little novel I had composed several years before (1935), I found, as is common enough, that it was written in a manner I could no longer master. The difficulty was twofold. The incidents, descriptions, thoughts, and characters of the story were continually and consistently overdetermined by a symbolic idea, growing in body throughout the work but at no point directly expressed. But in 1941 I was seeing things (and dismissing them) in terms of simple causes—not necessarily correct. Secondly, the earlier work consisted largely in a naturalistic presentation, accurate as I could make it, of an experienced environment—for the immediate story had not been used as a framework for a symbol, but other meanings had forced themselves into expression while I was trying to transcribe certain incidents that I remembered. But it was this naturalistic detail even more than the symbolic overtones that was impossible to me in the period of dissent: I was now too impatient to describe in detail scenes of a society which as a whole had no fascination for me.

Then I realized that the naturalism and the symbolism were parts of the same attitude, and that this attitude was itself a previous stage (certainly not the primary stage) of the social-estrangement that I later came to suffer in actual consciousness.

The formula of the symbolism was that: *it is intolerable that this scene should be merely what it seems, it must have also some other meaning.* But the other meaning was of course not apparent to me, in 1935, or I should have used it as the subject-matter of the work. Nevertheless! clear or confused, I was willing to regard the scene and the society as *my* scene and my society, rich in interest, still possessing the potentiality of life, worth transcribing with fidelity: this was the naturalism. It was my society and I felt uneasy in it; I felt that if I could reach toward other meanings I could resolve the uneasiness and achieve the unity of a work of art. Yet since the meanings were not to be attained it was inevitable that the subject-matter of this novella and numerous tales of the same period should incorporate hitch-hikes, canoe-trips, and other chancy travels, *in which one becomes involved yet intends to go away.* (And structurally: new beginnings and ambiguous or dual-paralogistic resolutions.)

Going further into the past of my writing (1931), I found examples of the naturalism pure, unrelieved by symbols, yet always expressing the latent estrangement by a malicious or indignant selection of the pointless or unsavory, though usually softened by youthful compassion. These were copies, of course, of the formula of High Naturalism: *To bring home the grim facts to the complacent,* as if to say, "*This* is our world, damn you."

I should now say (1945) that such youthful, unsophisticated naturalism, whose formula seems so conscious and rational, is the expression of a quite unconscious cleavage, between the innocent, frustrated effort to be happy in the big Society and the fact, in which the personality is grounded, that the Society has inhibited natural drives from the beginning and therefore one does not really dissent to be happy. This is then not simple *dissent* or withdrawal from the social values; it is *alienation,* socially-caused estrangement from the natural values.

The expression of simple dissent is probably nothing but a kind of Realism: the interaction of the author's sense of what is meaningful and at least the potentiality of the scene accurately described: on both parts there is a free passage of potentiality to act, the activity of authorship being one of several efficient causes. But this attitude, this confidence, I could rarely find in my early tales.

The emergence of the symbolism in the naturalism, then, may be taken as the deepening awareness of the author's alienation; but this is the same thing as the stirring of natural drives, though in a personal arena withdrawn from the big Society.

2. Expressionistic Naturalism and Miracle

Let us turn to the author in the full consciousness of alienation. The key to his method is his conviction that *their* world is not his world, and the forming of a literary defense against them. (At the same time he does not yet know what is *his* social world, or he would not expend himself in defenses.)

At this period (1940–42) the method that I habitually employed was a kind of expressionistic naturalism. Literary expressionism in general proceeds by abstracting from the scene concepts and ideas, and activating these as character, most often in a kind of dialectical drama. But I preferred to abstract what I took to be the true causes of events, both sociological and psychological, and to activate these in imitation of the likely interplay of causes in the world. Then in these stories, since the emphasis is so strongly on the causes and their interplay, the acts and characters are reduced almost to X-ray pictures or schemes. But I intended them to be scientific X-rays, without my own—and certainly without their—mythology; the picture was to add up to the actual world. And if it was a somewhat dry and empty scene, so, I thought, were the lives of the people.

This was the last stage of the withdrawal that was already apparent in the innocent naturalism. But now the scene was not even admitted to be *my* scene; its living details were meaningful only to them, but I was impatient to present anything but its schematism, which I analyzed and abstracted with the more ferocity in order to put it in *its* place, and what had that to do with me? As if to say: *There* is what *they* think reality is, that error, America 1940, compelled this way and that, and *comically* compelled, by causes that in themselves have no special value (except that they are clear and beautiful). Far from having a larger, symbolic significance than those people suspect, these incidents have even less significance than they believe, and they are feeble believers. But I, thanks be to God and my ill-luck, am sufficiently withdrawn to portray those things in their proper little places in the reality in which I have my secret faith.

"Secret" faith, because in the naturalistic portrayal of the scene, no hint could be given of the author's position which therefore seemed nowhere to have a place. And yet the author himself knew, if not where he stood, at least that he stood somewhere: for we are describing not a self-centered ego but an active author. Therefore the tone of the schematic naturalism, which could easily have been horrible and grotesque, always turned out to be cheerful and comic. The characters were indeed rushing to their disastrous ends, but to the unsympathetic author those ends were indifferent one way or the other as against quite other (unexpressed) values; and comedy is the representation of "destruction without pain or harm." (This is the contrary of Shakespearian tragedy where the characters are likewise rushing to disaster, but since the author respects the motives and the forces at work, there is everywhere, as Bradley puts it, the sentiment of "waste.")

The schematic naturalism, impatient of detail, was the means of defense against the scene, of the author who had confidence in his private position.

The author was alienated not absolutely (it is impossible to be alienated absolutely and be a creative author), but only relative to the social institutions and mores and his own habits and fears. Against these he could place his own natural existence, proved by his activity; and also, as an author—I think I speak for every artist on this point—a familiarity with the creator spirit in whom his works have been again and again completed (for it is the completion of a work that confirms the artist). Yet the natural causes, both sociological and psychological, for instance the origin of his food or his erotic desires, which would ordinarily serve to interpret and heighten, if not explain, these vantage-points of nature and creativity—these causes were for him already trivialized, because they were the public explanations of the very life from which he was alienated.

To solve this dilemma, of being confident without a cause, I boldly adopted the device of introducing angels and other miraculous incidents to open out again the dead-ends of worthlessness into which the characters' 1940 dispositions had betrayed them. The angels speak unintelligible syllables; the incidents are causally improbable, though not necessarily artistically improbable. The themes are crime, drunkenness, gambling. This kind of plot satisfied the author that the desperate view of the scene, which he was complacently demonstrating was nevertheless somehow adequate to the reality he knew intimately. *Miracle is confidence without a cause.*

So, as the estrangement of the scene became acute, the earlier symbolism was thinned and intensified into miracles.

3. Abstraction, Cubism, and Heroic Portraits

We turn now to the attitude of such an author vis à vis what he is sure of, nature and creativity, quite apart from the blight of alienation. (A "blight," though I would not for a moment question its truth or necessity.) First let us discuss the attitude of creativity in alienation.

By an artist as opposed to a dilettante I mean, with Goethe, one concerned not with his own feelings or the effect on an audience but with the structure of the work; and by an artist as opposed to an amateur I mean one who brings projects to completion. But the repeated experience of artistry forms in the artist an habitual attitude, namely confidence in the medium and the plastic devices, whether conventional or original, that have not failed him; and invention.

Now in my own case, through the last half dozen years, I have found that since the conventional patterns of artistry—for instance the well-wrought 3-act play—are so bound up with the very subject-matter from which I have been estranged, it is in inventive play in the medium itself, more or less abstracted from the represented scene, that I have most freedom. The abstraction of literary expression is to the "means of signifying": making a plot out of acts of denotation and connotation, demonstration, exclamation, etc. Such a method of abstraction in my case, then, has been the expression of *artistic confidence under the conditions of alienation.* One can easily see genetically how the passage from method to method must lead to abstraction if (a) the art seemed more and more worth the trouble and (b) the scene seemed less and less worth the trouble.

Yet in fact I have rarely been able to generate sufficient interest in pure abstraction to energize complete works by this method. (Obviously, for to an alienated person such abstraction is maintained only with effort, it is not free play; in a sense the abstraction is a natural defense against the forces of personal and social nature that must storm to the surface when the big Society is at least effectually dismissed.) Then I resorted (1936–1943) to a kind of cubism, that is an abstract handling of a concrete subject. But what were these subjects? Portraits of ancient and classical heroes: as the madness of Saul, the pleasures of Tiberius, or the non-violence of Alcestis. We see—omitting always the pathological factors that are no doubt also active here—that just these heroes are exempt from the estrangement of the social scene; they are proved by time and enduring significance, there is no need apparently to relate them to the present concern. Further, the portraiture is static: it is a cluster of concepts, images, and symbols; far from imitating the dramatic action of conscious desire; close to the unity of dreams. Thus the author could find in these heroes the natural forces and motives that in himself and in the contemporary scene he could not find.

In general, the freedom and confidence expressed in the abstract and unconventional handling of the medium sought out such subjects as were free, in the author's mind, from the trivializing bondage he saw roundabout. But he had not (and I have not yet, in 1945) attained the freedom and power to see as such every subject whatever.

These works are affirmative in that I found myself able to present the characters and their motives without hedging, without pervasive irony and ambiguity, and without miracles. I do not mean they are optimistic; on the contrary, most of the cubist pieces tell the tragic story that such and such a motive leads to a bad end or is in itself a bad end, for instance that the music of a certain composer is the same as bouncing a ball in a little courtyard of an asylum. But the motives are the true motives of the characters and the characters are really what they are presented as, and this is far different from calling precisely this into question, as I was forced to do in the naturalistic works. But it was easier to maintain such an affirmative attitude in writing of heroes mythical or long dead. The power of Saul, for instance, "to do as his hand should find," was impossible to describe in a contemporary scene, as in *The Grand Piano*, without humor and sarcasm; and without the classical example of Tiberius, I should have been unable to represent my own little pleasures with a straight face.

4. Dramatic Manner

This little study was sketched out in 1942. Writing now in 1945 I cannot but see that such an analysis is nothing but a kind of schematic naturalism applied to my authorship itself: it is a defense against that authorship, as if to say, What has that to do with *us*? That *craft idiocy*! to the band of our natural friends. But of course we do not thereby impugn the power of the creator spirit, given to us and not made by us (certainly not made by me); these poems, such as they are, are also among our social inventions and realize our capabilities. But the author who understands this will no doubt have a different attitude and a different manner.

(But one cannot foresee the manner of works according to a previous program, for it is only the work that explores and proves the existent power of authorship.)

In writing a play in 1942, I found what it is that has always brought me back to the dramatic manner: the glorification of simple overt acts—the finite physical reality of a few actors on a little stage. The dramatic manner is *the celebration of a natural existence with which one is acquainted, without exhibition of the power of the author himself at all.*

The classical property of the dramatic manner is the unity of time and place, both for verisimilitude (formally speaking: the expressiveness of the medium in its material characteristics) and for concentration on the single passional act. For the most part the drama itself has never strayed far from the spirit of the unities. But let us consider a play in which the unities are in fact absent: where between two scenes there is a change of place and there is a discontinuity in the presented stage-time. Then the world in which the audience is absorbed is no longer the one directly presented, but is somewhere poised between the imagination of the audience and the intention of the poet. If the scenes are juxtaposed for special esthetic effects, such as contrast, we see that the stage is being manipulated extrinsically from the world of its characters: we have passed over into narration. The dramatic manner, then, properly belongs only to the single scene, and to the degree that the audience is absorbed in the scene.

Simple overt acts are serving a cup of coffee to a stranger, a fight, the play of an old man with a child, the juxtaposition of colors, the standing of a tree. To present such matter without the intrusion of the author, because it is felt as simply important in itself.

Perhaps the single scene is the extreme limit of natural, unalienated authorship *within the possibility of isolated authorship altogether.* (The little poems of introspective monologue that many of us are in the habit of writing are nothing but such single scenes.) But it must be said that the isolation of the act of authorship from other natural powers is itself, *if insisted on*, a sign of alienation: of withdrawal from natural society, of craft idiocy. The very insistence on pure authorship which vis à vis the big Society is a sign of honorary revolution and of refusal to be treasonable to nature, is in natural society a sad relic of our childhood blasted by coercion.

The man of letters, with his special gifts and the habits of a craft, is one of the band of natural friends, a poet rarely, a spokesman sometimes, not often indeed a man of letters. But just in this band of freedom we do not prejudge occasions: when the poet in the grip of a strong dream will utter it, or the dramatist decorate our common behavior, or tell us stories, or the expert exercise himself for his joy and solace, or plead for us in their courts.

5. Further Remarks (1942)

I have thus given a little lexicon of the literary methods answering my own occasions. It is personal, limited both in extent and definition. I am even surprised to notice, for instance, how such a major method as Impressionism has not been valuable to me as a poet when it is so delightful to me as a reader. It is personal, yet inasmuch as I have not drawn on the material causes of the attitudes, socio- or psychopathological but have restricted my remarks to the formal relations between attitude and method, even this list attains a certain generality.

Stating these formal relations by no means prejudges the causal question: which is prior, the method or the attitude? though non-creative people will always think of the attitude as the cause and the method as the effect. But especially among artists we must often expect that a certain inward bent rules *both* their lives and their works, so that it is as true to say that they experience what they will write as that they write what they have experienced.

It is not by wishing, nor because it would be convenient to write in a different way, that an author can alter the attitude on which his style feeds. A man would be glad not to write what expresses his misery or the evil of the world; yet write in this way he must. But who would deny that *disgust* of a style is a powerful life-sign for an author?

Because of biographical accidents, an attitude and method are tied to certain images, themes, and scenes. (One hardly realizes how restricted he is by such associations.) To give a personal example: I seem to remember that a kind of accurate, hostile, and somewhat standoffish observation was most dominantly my conscious attitude during some seasons at the seashore during my middle adolescence. (The causes were both psychosexual and associated with a fear of drowning.) Now much to my surprise I find that the stories I have written in a naturalistic method gravitate inevitably to such seaside-resort locales and incidents, even when—as in a novel about the economic depression—there would seem to be no intrinsic connection. And contrariwise, the symbolist parts gravitate toward a childhood memory of the mountains (another vacation environment!) And I find scenes of realism referring back to an in-between period of boyish games—which I would, again, refer forward to 1945 bands of natural friends. But the result is that the associations are severely limited: discomfortable weather is always hot weather, never wintry weather or storm. And without doubt the naturalistic handling of personal relations is restricted to the suspicions and ironic insights of the age of 16. The understanding treatment of children will be imbedded in prose of one method, of adolescents in another method, of adults in another method, and of old persons in another method! And the same holds for the critical situations of life. But we can see exactly the same limitation in a master like Balzac, whose handling of virtuous young women is in a blurred Lamartine manner that might be enormously effective if done in extenso, but it is overwhelmed and made pallid by the strong naturalism and realism of the rest.

But freely handled, the great literary methods ought to be powerful world-outlooks that could find meaning anywhere!

A literary method, as the critic rather than the creator would view it, is a moral hypothesis completely general in its scope, far more general than any theme or subject-matter could hope to be. And from the point of view of the creator, it is more than an hypothesis, it has the reality of necessity.

Method is close to the heart of writing, Style. It is Style that most confirms an author in the secure consciousness of being an artist, of being able to fuse the details that press on him inwardly and outwardly into a whole work. I have mentioned various attitudes, but there is above all this one attitude, of being a free artist rather than something else. To speak by analogy, Style, could be called the method of this attitude of being an author.

Wordsworth's Poems

To make some kind of sense of the everyday, just to live on a little. My way of being in the world is writing something, to remain with my only world when, as is usual, she doesn't come across for me; or if by exception she does come across, I accept also that event by celebrating it in verses. Last year I suffered an event too hard to bear, but I coped with that also by repeating many times, in verses, the one grim fact. But it would be impossible to live on by versifying if we did not have a tradition of it.

From my teens I hit on three poets who coped in this way with both their everyday and their extreme chances, and who have served me as supportive proofs and models. Catullus, whose little book I learned by heart at City College, has been my model of saying with well-born frankness the sadly comic vicissitudes of my own arrested adolescence, but he died much younger. Tu Fu, the T'ang poet whom I studied in the translation of Florence Ayscough, said the everyday of exile, grieving and complaining, but fortified by the beauty that is nevertheless in the nature of things. There is a joy we writers get in formulating just how it is, however it is. When we are saying it, we do not notice that we are unhappy, so perhaps we are happy; and I sometimes wonder how other people manage who do not have this recourse. But especially the poems of Wordsworth have served me; they are in my English tongue: not very different from how I have it myself, an educated speech deliberately cut back toward the colloquial.

Wordsworth was tireless in making do, or staying in there pitching anyway. Distracted by timid inhibitions and fatigue itself, he remained fairly sane and pretty good by continually saying into being some meaning or other. Maybe this is not a high achievement, but it stirs my sympathy and admiration. Critics judge that he was humorless, and it seems so. His work has a solemn seriousness, like an animal's face, so lacking in irony or tragedy that, for an intellect of his scope and depth, there seems to be some human screw missing. But instead, he lets himself wander into fugues of fantasy, often to the edge of being dreamy, and surely there is a kind of mischief in being so odd with a dead pan. It is British. Yet he is never grotesque like Dickens, for he had a good childhood, and he does not mock himself like Lewis Carroll, who had to satirize him, for he was not despairing about his life.

Poets who cope with everyday vicissitudes by saying them do not tend to produce fully formed, self-standing "poems." We have neither the luxury to be detached craftsmen nor the divine grace to lose ourselves completely in great imitations. Rather, it is each one's persistent attitude that is his poem; the whole book is a more objective poem than any of the poems. Even so, in the helter-skelter of English poetry since 1800, Wordsworth's "Resolution and Independence" is still the most classic performance, with the sobriety and controlled terror—and deadpan strangeness—of Sophocles. It cannot be accidental that its theme is Staying In There Pitching. It was precisely the virtue that moved Wordsworth to bitter grief of himself and to celebration of an old leech-gatherer as if he were a victorious athlete of Pindar.

I still cannot read it through without breaking down and sobbing. (I have just again put it to the test.) "I thought of Chatterton, the marvellous boy," is the verse that begins to get to me. "We Poets in our youth begin in gladness," he wrote in 1802, "but thereof come in the end despondency and madness"; but he had a better recourse than he feared, and it served him out. "Such seemed this Man, not all alive nor dead, not all asleep—in his extreme old age . . . a flash of mild surprise broke from the sable orbs of his yet-vivid eyes." "Once I could meet with them on every side," says the old man, "but they have dwindled long by slow decay; yet still I persevere, and find them where I may."

Let me insist. It is not in his majesty or astounding moments, though they are frequent, that he is Wordsworth for me, but in his pervasive saying his kind of speech as a way of being in the world. What is always emphasized, of course—and it is important—is his simplification of vocabulary, and the connection of this with the speech of unsophisticated people and the expression of feeling. But even more effective, though hardly mentioned, is his exquisite syntax. In my opinion Wordsworth is the most knowledgeable grammarian among the English poets, except maybe Milton. Syntax—tense, mood, voice, agreement, sentence structure—is the immediate expression of disposition and character; it is the way of seeing, grasping, giving. Wordsworth's so-called "theory of perception," indeed, is identical with his syntax and sequence of exposition. (I will illustrate this briefly in a moment.) But I do not mean that the kind of perceiving determines the syntax, or vice versa; rather, for these poets of mine saying is the *same* as finishing experiencing, closure of experiencing. Goethe put it wryly when he explained that he did not write from his experience, for instance his love affairs, but that he tended—unconsciously—to experience what he would come to write.

Consider "There Was a Boy." Mainly, the poem is a description in past tense of a boy hallooing in a valley. But toward the end of the descriptive part there occurs (my emphasis):

> Then, sometimes, in that silence, while he hung
> Listening, a gentle shock of mild surprise
> *Has carried far* into his heart the voice
> Of mountain torrents . . .

The present perfect here is grossly ungrammatical, even shocking, as if it were a misprint. Nevertheless, that tense is the fact—of how one hears in the silence, the non-anxious surprise of insight, the fixing of permanent character by childhood play, making poetry by spontaneous recollection; and because it is these facts the erroneous present perfect tense is crashingly right. Almost immediately there follow the lines:

> This boy was taken from his mates, and died
> In childhood, ere he was full twelve years old.

Those past tenses return like a blow in the pit of the stomach. Ay! "Pre-eminent in beauty is the vale"—we are now making do in the terrible dispassionate present—"where he was born and bred . . . there a long half-hour together I have stood mute—looking at the grave in which he lies!" In which he *lies*! *Has* carried! *This* boy! I have stood.

Or notice the tenses in the divinely *faux naif* sonnet "With Ships the Sea Was Sprinkled Far and Nigh." The octave is again a description in past tense, of the harbor and of one vessel. Then the sestet,

> This Ship was naught to me, nor I to her,
> Yet I pursued her with a Lover's look;
> This Ship to all the rest did I prefer:
> When will she turn, and whither? She will brook
> No tarrying; where She comes the winds must stir:
> On went She, and due north her journey took.

That's a mighty brave and tearfully looking past tense in "went." The capital letters are here just right, though Wordsworth is usually too free with them. Those who charge this kind of poetry with committing the pathetic fallacy, projecting human feelings upon nature, do not know what experience is and that the best speech is saying just how it is. Both things: oneself is part of how it is, and also Thou art That.

It is interesting to contrast the two anthology poems, "The Solitary Reaper" and "I Wandered Lonely as a Cloud." In "The Reaper," the description is in the present tense, then Wordsworth suddenly shifts to a peculiar kind of past, qualified as lingering: "Whate'er the theme, the Maiden sang as if her song could have no ending. . . I listened . . . long after it was heard no more." Yet in the daffodil poem he tells a seemingly similar experience in the opposite way, going from past to present: "And then my heart with pleasure fills, and dances with the daffodils." How is it with him? Is it because the strain of the maiden is melancholy, but the dance of the daffodils is sprightly? I mean, phenomenologically, that he cannot *now*, while actively making a damned good poem, be *with* the sad song, he must alienate it, but he can be with the gay dance. In any case, there are few poets—Rilke is one that comes to mind—with whom it is plausible to raise such a question.

The Wordsworthian "moment" of experience is easy (in our times) to define. It is what Freud called fore-feeling, inattention, and the return of the repressed. One is attracted by something interesting; one is slightly distracted either by one's mood or the circumstances; the full meaning of the object, and of how one is, is revealed. "Revealed" means behaving in a new way, doing something in the "environment"—for instance, reforming one's relation with others by new poetic saying, and then there abides the poem. Freud puts it: "The art-work solves an inner problem." But notice that the psychologist uses terms like "repressed" and "inner," whereas the poet does not need to make metaphysical assumptions about outer and inner. Anyway, from where the poet breathes, how would he judge?

With Wordsworth, it is his way of saying that has influenced me, consoled or made me cry—they come to the same thing. It is not what he says about. His subject matter has gaps: he avoids what is sexual, what is political, and even much of what is humanly noble, e.g., in high civilization. Yet in concluding this little essay, I want to assert that, in my opinion, his idea of pedagogy is true and primary: it *is* the beauty of the world and simple human affections that develop great-souled and disinterested adults. A few years ago a professor of astronomy at Yale explained to me that his students were superb mathematicians, they had mastered the subject; they would fly to the moon—but they would never be astronomers, because, he said, "They don't love the stars." How to produce disinterested and magnanimous people, whether scientists or artists or physicians or statesmen? But I have not heard that the Office of Education, or the National Science Foundation in its curriculum improvements, or the Congress when it votes billions for schooling, cares about these things at all.

Notes for a Defense of Poetry

1. Summary of This Book

Language is not a congenial scientific subject matter; it does not lend itself to a simple converging theory that explains what goes on. In order to make mathematical models, structural linguists disregard the influence of meaning, which is what the speakers are after. Theorists of Communications save the meanings, the patterns of information, but they tend to leave out the speakers and hearers, so that the theory of language becomes a branch of physics or physical biology. To get their fixed counters, positivists disregard the continual variation and invention in use. Anthropologists identify the language with the pattern of the culture, so that the universal human and animal functions of language that cross boundaries and change culture become inexplicable. In general, to make their simple theories work, all these rely on artifacts, like postulated expressions in ellipses or a constant code; or they use a method which freezes actual speech, like the pair test. But on the other hand, in order to affirm the freedom and meaning-making of language, phenomenologists disregard its conventionality and instrumentality; they stretch the meaning of "words" till the whole world is made of words.

By and large, older philologists did not come on as scientists or philosophers, but as naturalists, historians, and men of letters, and so they could allow the various aspects and uses of language to live and breathe together, with no systematic order. There would be chapters on the physiology of the speech organs, history and geography, etymology, semantical changes, syntax and comparative syntax, magic, logic, culture and literature, dialects and pidgins, artificial languages, etc. To bind it all together, they might use a convenient definition like "language is the chief means of conveying thought." The advantage of this definition was that, except for a few who were very psychology-minded (and fanciful), they did not bother with it further. And anyway, "thought" has as many various aspects and uses as language itself, so it imposes no order, sets no limits—and provides no explanations.

Colloquial speakers, of course, do not need to explain what they are doing when they speak their language. They use their inherited code and modify it.

They try to be clear to the hearers, but they rely on them to make sense of what is being said. They use language to say propositions and to say nothing, to be sociable, to command, reveal, and deceive. They have their own style, they are culture-bound, they speak scientifically and with broad perspective. They use the words accurately as signs, and they get lost in words. They try to be correct, but they say their say any way they can. They adjust to dialects, they use language as a badge. They use language as a means for their ends, but their personalities and purposes are largely made of language. They speak complete sentences, shortened forms of complete sentences, redundancies beyond complete sentences, and forms that have not gotten to be complete sentences. They say the phonemes accurately; they miss the phonemes to a degree that should be confusing, but they are understood anyway; they use all kinds of "para-linguistic" noises as part of their language. They imitate like parrots, and they derive grammatical sentences which they have never heard. They communicate mostly speaking, mostly not speaking, and speaking and not speaking in combination. Finally, any of these may occur not in exceptional cases but with very many speakers in many situations. There is no good reason to exclude any of it as essentially not language. For special purposes, an investigator may abstract this or that use for concentrated study; but in my opinion he will make false statements about his abstracted part if he does not keep the rest in mind, as what speakers do when they speak language.

Instead, I have tried to stay with a few observations that are *prima facie*. Speakers speak to cope verbally with a situation when it is more appropriate (in their fallible judgment) than not speaking. The transaction of speaker and hearer is fundamental, though the hearer may not respond nor even, as in poetry, be a real person. For this transaction, the speakers use an inherited code (which could be called a "means"), but it is not constant, and the actual language is a tension between the code and what needs to be said. Communication is not the conveyance of meanings from one head to another by means of language; it is the language itself being said and understood. Finally, I have suggested that the wisest method of exploring language is to analyze how it operates in actual concrete situations, rather than deciding beforehand what "language" is. This is similar to the literary analysis of particular works; and, as in literary criticism, conversations and discourses fall roughly into genres, such as small talk, intimate talk, gang talk, public exchange of information, talk of different social classes, poems, journalism, dialogue, neurotic verbalizing, scientific exposition, etc. Each of these might have, roughly, certain distinctive characteristics of pronunciation, grammar, lexicon, concreteness of denotation, assertion of propositions, personal engagement of the speakers, modifying of the standard code, tone of voice, interplay of speaker and hearer, intermixture of the nonverbal, order of exposition, etc. I may be mistaken, but I think that a reasoned description of such genres would tell us something about language that we have not been getting from linguists, anthropologists, and philosophers.

2.

Deliberate literature, oral or written, is not spontaneous speech, but it has compensating advantages in providing samples for exploring language. In the process of making literature, an author finds his structure in handling the words, and he does not exclude any aspect or use of language—at any turn he may resort to precise denotation or metaphor or syllogism or a dramatic colloquial scene, or say his feelings. And he has to make the words fill out what the ordinary speaker relies on non-verbal means to do. There is no active respondent, so a literary work has to incorporate both sides of the dialogue. This inevitably produces a certain amount of idiolect—the writer's whim or delusion of what English is or should be—yet writers are also more than average respectful of the tradition and genius of the language: They are its keepers. An artist organizes a whole work, with beginning, middle, and end, so it is usually possible to figure out what the various parts are accomplishing—whether the choice of words, the syntax, the metaphor, the connotations, the tone and rhythm, the narrative or dramatic manner. And of course a literary work is a concrete whole of speech that stands fixed, is repeatable, lets itself be examined closely.

In general, a stretch of good colloquial speech is a better example of the power of language than most writing. But there are thousands of literary works that are beyond comparison, just as there must be innumerable cases of excellent colloquial speech constantly occurring, apt and dramatic, beyond comparison. My bias is that we best catch the essence of a coping behavior like speech when it is operating at its best: Good literary works are good samples; excellent moments of common speech are even better samples, but they are elusive.

It has been argued, however, that the literary use of language is simply outmoded in modern times. It is neither the common speech that the anthropologists are after, and the linguists say they are after, nor is it the speech for good communication that the language reformers and the people in Communications are after. There is a famous analysis of the history of poetry and human speech that makes literature now quite irrelevant. On this view, poetry was the inevitable and appropriate speech of primitive ages, as the only available way of saying reality when not much was known and before the division of labor; these were ages of myth, when people living in a fearful and uncontrollable environment could not distinguish magic and science, nor saga and history, nor dream and empirical experience; the poets were the prophets, historians, philosophers, and scientists. In the course of time, poetry was replaced by philosophy and history; and these in turn have given way to special physical sciences and positivist sociology. In our time, literature can be merely decoration or entertainment or exercises in emotional noises. This was the line of Vico (on one interpretation) and of Comte. And prophylactic empiricist languages, like Basic English or positivist logic, carry it out as a program.

Apologists for literature have tended to regard exactly the same development of language as a devolution rather than an evolution. In his *Defence of Poesy* Philip Sidney argues that history and moral philosophy are ineffectual to teach the man of action and the warrior—he comes on strongly as the Renaissance scholar-poet who is also soldier-statesman. History tells us only what has been, poetry what should be; moral philosophy is dry analysis, poetry motivates to emulation and action. He would certainly not have been happier with the "value-neutral" language of present departments of sociology. In its high Italian form, Sidney's argument goes so far as to deny that scientific or philosophical sentences are true at all; only Eloquence is true, for truth resides in right action, not in propositions, just as Nietzsche holds that the only true science is the *Gaya Scienza* that makes you happy if you know it.

Shelley, in his *Defence of Poetry*, takes the same tack. He sees the world of his time as fragmented, quantified, rule-ridden; it is only poetry that can liberate and bring the parts together:

> The great secret of morals is love, or a going out of our own nature
> and an identification of ourselves with the beautiful which exists in
> thought, action, or person . . . A man, to be greatly good, must imagine
> intensely and comprehensively . . . Poetry enlarges the circumference
> of the imagination by replenishing it with thoughts of ever new delight,
> which have the power of attracting and assimilating to their own
> nature all other thoughts.
>
> We want the creative faculty to imagine that which we know:
> our calculations have outrun conception. The cultivation of those
> sciences which have enlarged the limits of the empire of man over the
> external world has, for want of the poetical faculty, proportionately
> circumscribed those of the internal world.

In my opinion, there is a lot of truth in this—it is grounded in Coleridge's post-Kantian epistemology. It *is* odd, however, that as a philosophic anarchist after Godwin, Shelley should end his *Defence* with the fatuous sentence, "Poets are the unacknowledged legislators of the world." What does he intend? That they should be acknowledged? Then what would they do?

Depressed by the passing of Faith, Matthew Arnold—in *Literature and Dogma, Culture and Anarchy,* and the debate with Huxley—deplores the language of the churchmen, the Liberal and Radical economists, and the scientists, and he turns desperately to literature to give a standard for "Conduct" for the majority of mankind. Astoundingly, this view has condemned him as an elitist—in a speech by Louis Kampf of M.I.T., the president of the Modern Language Association! But Arnold is explicitly drawing on the Wordsworthian doctrine that uncorrupted common speech, heightened by passion and imagination, binds mankind together, whereas the utilitarian speech of the Liberals or the ideological speech of the Radicals destroys humanity. Professor Kampf singles out a passage of Marx on the miserable education of poor children, to show the virtues of a political radical who wants to change society. It is a fine humane passage. But I am sure the professor of English knows that it can be paralleled by, for instance, Arnold's blistering attack in *Culture and Anarchy* on the Philistine journalism of that same society for its account of "the woman Smith" who had been arrested. What is pathetic about Arnold, however, is his delusion, shared by both Liberals and Radicals, that good speech can somehow be learned in schools. Wordsworth did not make this mistake.

Nearer to our own times, bureaucratic, urbanized, impersonalized, and depersonalized, Martin Buber could no longer rely even on literature, but went back to face-to-face dialogue, the orally transmitted legends of the Chasidim, and the psychotic experiences that underlie the text of the Bible. And we have seen that, in the present deep skepticism about specialist sciences and scientific technology, the young do not trust speech altogether, but only touching or silence.

In this dispute about the evolution of positivist language or the devolution to positivist language, both sides exaggerate (as usual). It is for quite reasonable human purposes that we have developed languages that are more accurately denotative and analytic and simpler in syntax than poetry. But the broader function of literary language, including poetry, also remains indispensable, because we are never exempt from having to cope with the world existentially, morally, and philosophically; and there is always emerging novelty that calls for imagination and poetry.

Consider the world-wide unease about the technology, the social engineering, the specialist sciences and their positivist value-neutral language. Suddenly, the line of dissent of Blake, Wordsworth, Shelley, William Morris, the symbolists, and the surrealists no longer seems to be the nostalgic romanticism of a vanishing minority, but the intense realism of a vanguard. I have found that I can mention even Jefferson and ruralism without being regarded as a crank. To try to cope with modern conditions by the methods of laboratory science, statistics, and positivist logic has come to seem obsessional, sometimes downright demented, as in the game strategies for nuclear warfare.

As in a dream, people recall that technology is a branch of moral philosophy, with the forgotten criteria of prudence, temperance, amenity, practicality for ordinary use; and they ask for a science that is ecological and modestly naturalistic rather than aggressively experimental. But one cannot *do* moral philosophy, ecology, and naturalism without literary language. It was only a few years ago that C. P. Snow berated literary men for their ignorance of positive science, and now it is only too clear that there is an even greater need for positive scientists who are literary. Unfortunately, since men of letters have for so long let themselves be pushed out, we don't have relevant literary language and topics to say right technology and ecology; our usual literary attempts are apocalyptic, sentimental, out of date, or private.

A physician, for instance, is faced with agonizing dilemmas: euthanasia when novel techniques can keep tissue alive; birth control and the destiny of a person as a human animal; organ transplants and Lord knows what future developments; the allocation of scarce resources between the vital statistics of public health and the maximum of individual health, or mass practice and family practice. How does one spell out the Hippocratic oath in such issues? How can anyone by his own intuition and individual ratiocination, usually in crisis, possibly decide wisely and without anxiety and guilt? Yet there are almost no medical schools that find time for the philosophy of medicine. And we do not have the linguistic analysis, the reasoned description of precedents, the imagined situations, in brief the literature, for such philosophy.

The social sciences have been positivist only during my lifetime, though Comte talked it up a hundred fifty years ago. Marx was still able to say that Balzac was the greatest of the sociologists. Comte himself was energized by a crazy utopian poetry. Sir Henry Moore, Frederic Maitland, Max Weber, and so forth were historians, humanists. Geddes, Dewey, and Veblen were practical philosophers. Freud and Rank came on like a kind of novelists and fantasists and posed the problems for anthropology. It is, of course, a matter of opinion whether, after so many lisping centuries, the brief reign of mature sociology has been brilliant.[*] My hunch is that, despite a few more years guaranteed by big funding, it is moribund, done in by the social critics and the politically

---

[*] A recent study captained by Karl Deutsch, emanating from the University of Michigan, points to the great advances in recent years made by big teams of scholars heavily financed; and it refers sarcastically to those—namely me—who claim that we don't know much more than the ancients did about psychology, pedagogy, politics, or any other field where they had adequate empirical evidence. When I look at the list of great advances, however, I find them heavily weighted toward methodology and equipment: stochastic models, computer simulation, large-scale sampling, game theory, structural linguistics, cost-benefit analysis, etc., etc.—in brief, an enormous amount of agronomy and farm machinery and battalions of field-hands, but few edible potatoes.

engaged of the past decades, who have had something useful to say. As one of the social critics, I can affirm that we are *philosophes*, men of letters.

Humanly speaking, the special sciences and their positivist language have been deeply ambiguous. At their best—it is a splendid best—they have gotten (and deserved) the pay-off of the theological virtues of faith, selflessness, and single-minded devotion, and of the moral virtues of honesty, daring, and accuracy. In Chapter vii, I singled out the operational language of Rudolf Carnap's *Testability and Meaning* as an exquisite vernacular. Such science is one of the humanities; its language is difficult because what it says is subtile and strange, minute in detail, sweepingly general. At their worst, however—and it is a very frequent worst—specialist science and its value-neutral language are an avoidance of experience, a narrow limitation of the self, and an act of bad faith. It is obsessional, an idolatry of the System of Science rather than a service to the unknown God and therefore to mankind. Needless to say, such science can be easily bought by money and power.

Its language is boring because what the men do is not worth the effort, when it is not actually base. Being busywork and form-ridden, it has no style.

Psychology
and Theology

Anthropology of Neurosis

1. The Subject-Matter of Anthropology

In the previous chapter, we discussed the importance of the recovery of "lost," that is inhibited, childhood powers in the mature individual. Now let us broaden the view and talk a little about what is "lost" in our grown-up culture and in the present use of the powers of man, for here, too, in the altering fields given by new powers and new objects, many feelings and attitudes are by-passed or inhibited that should healthily be continuous and employed.

This is a chapter in abnormal anthropology. The subject-matter of anthropology is the relationship between man's anatomy, physiology, and faculties in his activity and culture. In the Seventeenth and Eighteenth Centuries, anthropology was always so studied (climaxing, probably, in Kant's *Anthropology*): for instance, what is laughter? how does it culturally manifest itself for man's well-being? More recently, anthropologists lost sight of the relationship as their special study and their books display a quite astonishing split into two unrelated sections: Physical Anthropology, the evolution and races of man; and Cultural Anthropology, a kind of historical sociology. For instance, it is an important proposition of Cultural Anthropology that technical innovations (e.g., a new plow) diffuse rapidly to neighboring areas, but moral innovations suffuse slowly and with difficulty. But this proposition is left groundless, as if it were part of the nature of these cultural objects, rather than shown to be part of the nature or conditioning of the animals involved, the men carrying the culture, these men, in turn being shaped by the culture they carry. Most recently, however, owing mainly to the impact of psychoanalysis, the classical animal/cultural interrelationship is again being studied, in terms of early child-training, sexual practices, and so forth. And from the point of view of abnormal psychology, we here offer some biological/cultural speculations.

2. The Importance of This Subject for Psychotherapy

We can see the importance of the anthropological question: "What is Man?" if we consider that medical psychology owes a difficult double allegiance. As a branch of medicine it aims at "merely" biological health. This includes not only healthy functioning and absence of pain, but feeling and pleasure; not only sensation, but sharp awareness; not only absence of paralysis, but grace and vigor. Dealing with a psychosomatic unity, if psychotherapy could achieve this kind of health, its existence would be justified. And in medicine the criteria of health are fairly definite and scientifically established; we know when an organ is functioning well. This aspect of "human nature" is unambiguous.

But there is no such thing as "merely" biological functioning (for instance, there is no such drive as "mere" sex, without either love or the avoidance of love). So medical means are insufficient.

Once beyond medicine, however, the very aim of therapy, the norm of health and "nature," becomes a matter of opinion. The patient is a sick man and man is not finally known for he is always changing himself and his conditions. His nature is surprisingly malleable. Yet at the same time it is not so completely malleable that the nature can be disregarded, as some democratic sociologists and fascist politicians seem to assume; it is also surprisingly resistant, so that suddenly there are neurotic reactions of individuals and a stupidity, torpor, and rigidity of the average.

In psychotherapy, moreover, these changes of condition are all-important, for they are what engage a patient's interest; they involve his fears and guilts and his hope of what he will make of himself. They rouse his excitement—they are the only things that rouse excitement—they organize awareness and behavior. Without these peculiarly "human" interests there is no biological health and no way of achieving it by psychotherapy.

3. "Human Nature" and the Average

So the doctor beats about for models and theories of what is humanly enlivening. (In Chapter 4 we discussed several such theories.) This is why Freud insisted that not medical men, but, with medical collaboration, literary men, teachers, lawyers, social-workers make the best therapists, for they understand human nature, they mix ideas and people and have not been content to waste their youth acquiring a specialty.

The task would, of course, be immensely easier if we enjoyed good social institutions, conventions that gave satisfaction and fostered growth, for then these could be taken as a rough norm of what it means to be a full man in the specific culture; the question would not then be one of principles but of casuistical application to each case. But if we had reasonable institutions, there would not be any neurotics either. As it is, our institutions are not even "merely" logically healthy, and the forms of individual symptoms are reactions to rigid social errors. So, far from being able to take fitness to social institutions as a rough norm, a doctor has more hope of bringing about the self-developing integration of a patient if the patient learns to adjust his environment to himself than if he tries to learn to maladjust himself to society.

Instead of dynamic unity of need and social convention, in which men discover themselves and one another and invent themselves and one another, we are forced to think of three warring *abstractions*: the mere animal, the harried individual self, and the social pressures. The normal person either keeps himself unaware of this raging war within his personality, does not notice its manifestations in his behavior, and keeps it fairly dormant, or he is aware of it and has concluded an uneasy truce, snatching at safe opportunities. In either case there is much energy spent in pacification and valuable human powers are sacrificed. In the neurotic person, the conflicts rage to the point of exhaustion, contradictions, and breakdown—nor can it be concluded that he was therefore in some way weaker than the normal, for often precisely stronger gifts are socially disastrous. There is an important difference between the normal and neurotic, but it is not such that when a neurotic comes as a patient and poses an earnest *practical* problem for the doctor, the doctor can set as his goal a normal adjustment, any more than he could give an arrested tuberculosis a clean bill of health, though he might have to discharge the patient. Rather he must hope that, as patient begins to reintegrate himself, he will turn out to be more "human" than is expected, or than the doctor is.

Further, we must remember that in the present run of patients of psychotherapy, the distinction between normal and neurotic has become less than irrelevant; it is positively misleading. For more and more of the patients are not "sick" at all; they make "adequate" adjustments; they have come because they want something more out of life and out of themselves and they believe that psychotherapy can help them. Perhaps this betrays an over-sanguine disposition on their part, but it is also evidence that they are better than the average, rather than the reverse.[*]

4. Neurotic Mechanisms as Healthy Functions

Neurosis, too, is part of human nature and has its anthropology.

The split of personality—breakdown as a form of equilibrium—is probably a recently acquired power of human nature, only a few thousand years old.

---

[*] We have mentioned above that the selected run of patients is an intrinsic factor in the various psychoanalytical theories, for they are both the observed material and the confirmatory evidence of response to the method. Obviously the trend of patients toward the "well enough" or even "better than well enough" is an important factor in the trend of recent theories toward those like the one in this book. In this way psychotherapy is taking over the functions of education, but that is because the customary education, in home, school, university, and church, is increasingly inept. What we would hope for, of course, is that education would take over the functions of psychotherapy.

But it is one in a long line of evolutionary developments that are worth briefly reviewing in order to recognize where we are.

If we consider organismic-self-regulation, the process by which the dominant needs come to the forefront of awareness as they arise, we are struck not only by the wonderful system of specific adjustment, signals, co-ordination, and subtle judgment, that go to maintain the general equilibrium, but also by the devices that serve as cushioners and safety-valves to protect the contact-boundary. We have mentioned blotting-out and hallucinating and dreaming, and regarding as-if, and accepting instead-of; and there are also immobilizing (playing dead), isolating, mechanical trial and error (obsessive re-doing), panic flight, and so forth. Man is an organism of great power and efficiency, but also one that can take rough treatment and bad times. The two sides go together: ability leads to adventure and adventure to trouble. Man *has* to be malleable. These safety-functions all, of course, play a chief role in mental disorders, but they are themselves healthy.

Indeed, without being paradoxical one could say that in the neuroses just these safety-functions—of blotting out, distorting, isolating, repeating—that seem so spectacularly "crazy," are working fairly healthily. It is the more respectable functions of orientation and manipulation in the world, especially the social world, that are out of kilter and cannot work. In a finely-adjusted whole, the safety-devices are made for trouble and continue working while the more usual functions rest for repairs. Or to put it another way, when the orientation is lost and the manipulation is failing, the excitement, the vitality of the organism, expresses itself especially in autism and immobilizing. And so again, if we speak, as we must, of a social or epidemic neurosis, it is not the symptomatic social eccentricities (dictators, wars, incomprehensible art, and the like) that are pathologically important, but the normal knowledge and technique, the average way of life.

The problem of abnormal anthropology is to show how the average way of a culture, or even of the human state, is neurotic and has become so. It is to show what of human nature has been "lost" and, practically, to devise experiments for its recovery. (The therapeutic part of anthropology and sociology is politics; but we see that politics—perhaps fortunately—does not devote itself to this at all.)

In reviewing the steps of evolution leading to modern man and our civilization, therefore, we lay the stress contrary to where it is usually laid: not on the increased power and achievement gained by each step of human development, but on the dangers incurred and the vulnerable points exposed, that then have become pathological in the debacle. The new powers require more complicated integrations, and these have often broken down.

5. Erect Posture, Freedom of Hands and Head

(1) Erect posture developed along with differentiation of the limbs and ulti-mately the fingers. This had great advantages for both orientation and manip-ulation. A large upright animal gets a long view. Established on broad feet, it can use its hands to get food and tear it, while the head is free; and to handle objects and its own body.

But on the other hand, the head is removed from close-perception, and the "close" senses, smell and taste, atrophy somewhat. The mouth and teeth become less useful for manipulation; as such, in an intensely manipulating animal, they tend to pass from felt awareness and response (e.g., there can be a gap between disgust and spontaneous rejection). The jaws and muzzle degen-erate—and later will become one of the chief places of rigidity.

In brief, the entire field of the organism and its environment is immensely increased, both in largeness and in minute intricacy; but the closeness of contact is more problematic. And with erect posture comes the need to balance and the danger, so momentous in later psychology, of falling. The back is less flexible, and the head is more isolated from the rest of the body and from the ground.

(2) When the head is freer and less engaged, a sharper stereoscopic vision develops, able to appreciate perspective. The eyes and fingers cooperate in drawing outlines, so that the animal learns to see more shapes and to dif-ferentiate objects in his field. By outlining one differentiates experience into objects. Perspective, discrimination of objects, ability to handle: these greatly increase the number of connections among impressions and the deliberate selectivity among them. The cerebrum grows larger and likely the brightness of consciousness increases. The ability to isolate objects from their situations improves memory and is the beginning of abstracting.

But conversely, there is now likely to be occasional loss of immediacy, of the sense of ready flow with the environment. Images of objects and abstrac-tions about them intervene: the man pauses, with heightened consciousness, for a more deliberate discrimination, but then may forget or be distracted from the goal, and the situation is unfinished. A certain pastness that may or may not be relevant increasingly colors the present.

Finally, one's own body too becomes an object—although later, for this is perceived very "closely."

6. Tools, Language, Sexual Differentiation, and Society

(3) When things and other persons have once become outlined and abstracted objects, they can enter into useful deliberate fixed and habitual relations with the self. Permanent tools are developed, along with the *ad hoc* objects that

were spontaneous extensions of the limbs; and denotative language is developed along with instinctive situational outcries. Objects are controlled, tools applied to them, and the tools too are objects and may be improved and their use learned and taught. Language too is learned. Spontaneous imitation is deliberately intensified, and the social bond tightens.

But of course the social bond pre-existed; there was communication and the manipulation of the physical and social environment. It is not the use of tools and language that brings persons together or workmen and objects together; they have already been in felt organized contact—the tools and language are convenient differentiations of the contact that exists. The danger that is incurred is this: that if the original felt unity weakens, these high-order abstractions—object, person, tool, word—will begin to be taken as the original ground of contact, as if it required some deliberate high-order mental activity in order to get in touch. Thus interpersonal relations become primarily verbal; or without a suitable tool a workman feels helpless. The differentiation that existed "along with" the underlying organization now exists *instead* of it. Then contact diminishes, speech loses feeling, and behavior loses grace.

(4) Language and tools combine with the earlier pre-verbal bonds of sex, nourishment, and imitation, to broaden the scope of society. But such new intricacies may upset the delicately balanced activities that are crucial to the animal's welfare. Consider, for example, how from remote phylogenetic antiquity we have inherited a sexual apparatus exquisitely complicated, involving the senses as excitants, and the motor responses of tumescence, embracing, and intromission, all nicely adjusted toward a mounting climax. (The so-called "adolescent sterility" [Ashley Montagu], the time between the first menstruation and fertility, seems to indicate a period of play and practice.) Besides its advantages of sexual selection and cross-breeding, all this complexity requires at least temporary partnerships: no animal is complete in its own skin. And the strong emotional bonds of lactation, suckling, and fostering care tighten the sociality. Also, in higher phyla, the young animal acquires much of its behavior from imitative learning. Then consider how much depends on what delicate adjustments! Consider that the function of the orgasm (Reich), the essential periodic release of tensions, is bound with the workings of the finely-adjusted genital apparatus. It is clear both how important is the social manner of reproduction, and how vulnerable it makes the well-being of the animal.

7. Differentiations of Sensory, Motoric, and Vegetative

(5) Another critical development of fairly remote antiquity has been the separation of the motoric-muscular and sensoric-thought nerve centers. In animals like the dog sensation and motion cannot be much disengaged; this

was long ago pointed out by Aristotle when he said that a dog can reason but it makes only practical syllogisms. The advantages of the looser connection in man are, of course, enormous: the ability to survey, hold back, cogitate, in brief to be deliberate and muscularly hold back the body while letting the senses and thoughts play, along with immediately spontaneously moving in smaller motions of the eyes, hands, vocal cords, etc.

But in neurosis this same division is fateful, for it is seized on in order to prevent spontaneity; and the ultimate practical unity of sense and motion is lost. The deliberation occurs "instead of" rather than "along with": the neurotic loses awareness that the smaller motions are taking place and preparing the larger motions.

(6) Primitively, the ties of sex, nourishment, and imitation are social but pre-personal: that is, they likely do not require a sense of the partners as objects or persons, but merely as what is contacted. But at the stage of tool-making, language, and other acts of abstraction, the social functions constitute society in our special human sense: a bond among persons. The persons are formed by the social contacts they have, and they identify themselves with the social unity as a whole for their further activity. There is abstracted from the undifferentiated felt-self a notion, image, behavior, and feeling of the "self" that reflects the other persons. This is the society of the division of labor, in which persons deliberately use one another as tools. It is in this society that taboos and laws develop, bridling the organism in the interest of the super-organism, or better: keeping the persons as persons in interpersonal relationship as well as animals in contact. And this society is, of course, the bearer of what most anthropologists would consider the defining property of mankind, culture, the social inheritance surviving the generations.

The advantages of all this are obvious, and so are the disadvantages. (Here we can begin to speak not of "potential dangers" but of actual surviving troubles.) Controlled by taboos, the imitations become unassimilated introjections, society contained inside the self and ultimately invading the organism; the persons become merely persons *instead* of also animals in contact. The internalized authority lays open the way for institutional exploitation of man by man and of the many by the whole. The division of labor can be pursued in such a way that the work is senseless to the workers and is drudgery. The inherited culture can become a dead weight that one painfully learns, is forced to learn by the duteous elders, yet may never individually use.

8. Verbal Difficulties in this Exposition

It is instructive to notice how, in discussing this subject, verbal difficulties begin to arise: "man," "person," "self," "individual," "human animal," "organism" are sometimes interchangeable, sometimes necessary to distinguish. For example, it is deceptive to think of the "individuals" as primitive and combined in social relations, for there is no doubt that the existence of "individuals" comes about as the result of a very complicated society. Again, since it is meaningful to say that it is by organismic-self-regulation that one imitates, sympathizes, becomes "independent," and can learn arts and sciences, the expression "animal" contact cannot mean "merely" animal contact. Again, "persons" are reflections of an interpersonal whole, and "personality" is best taken as a formation of the self by a shared social attitude. Yet in an important sense the self, as the system of excitement, orientation, manipulation, and various identifications and alienations, is always original and creative.

These difficulties can, of course, be partly avoided by careful definition and consistent usage—and we try to be as consistent as we can. Yet partly they are inherent in the subject-matter, "Man," making himself in different ways. For instance, the early philosophic anthropologists of modern times, in the Seventeenth and Eighteenth Centuries, spoke usually of individuals compacting society; after Rousseau, the Nineteenth Century sociologists returned to society as primary; and it has been a great merit of psychoanalysis to restore these distinct concepts to a dynamic interaction. If the theory is often confusing and ambiguous, it may be that the nature too is confusing and ambiguous.

9. Symbols

We have now brought our history down to the last several thousand years, since the invention of writing and reading. Adapting himself to the vast accumulation of culture, both knowledge and technique, man is educated in very high abstractions. Abstractions of orientation, distant from concernful felt perception: sciences and systems of science. Abstractions of manipulation distant from muscular participation: systems of production and exchange and government. He lives in a world of symbols. He symbolically orients himself as a symbol to other symbols, and he symbolically manipulates other symbols. Where there were methods, now there is also methodology: everything is made the object of hypothesis and experiment, with a certain distance from engagement. This includes society, the taboos, the super-sensory, the religious hallucinations, and science and methodology itself, and Man himself. All this has given an enormous increase in scope and power, for the ability symbolically to fix what one used to be fully engaged in allows for a certain creative indifference.

The dangers in it are, unfortunately, not potential but realized. Symbolic structures—e.g., money or prestige, or the King's peace, or the advancement of learning—become the exclusive end of all activity, in which there is no animal satisfaction and may not even be personal satisfaction; yet apart from animal or at least personal interest there can be no stable intrinsic measure, but only bewilderment and standards that one can never achieve. Thus, economically, a vast mechanism is in operation that does not necessarily produce enough subsistence goods and could indeed, as Percival and Paul Goodman have pointed out in *Communitas,* proceed in almost as high gear without producing any subsistence at all, except that the producers and consumers would all be dead. A worker is crudely or skillfully fitted into a place in this mechanical symbol of plenty, but his work in it does not spring from any pleasure of workmanship or vocation. He may not understand what he is making, nor how, nor for whom. Endless energy is exhausted in the manipulation of marks on paper; rewards are given in kinds of paper, and prestige follows the possession of papers. Politically, in symbolic constitutional structures symbolic representatives indicate the will of the people as expressed in symbolic votes; almost no one, any more, understands what it means to exert political initiative or come to a communal agreement. Emotionally, a few artists catch from real experience symbols of passion and sensory excitement; these symbols are abstracted and stereotyped by commercial imitators; and people make love or adventure according to these norms of glamour. Medical scientists and social-workers provide other symbols of emotion and security, and people make love, enjoy recreation, and so forth according to prescription. In engineering, control over space, time, and power is symbolically achieved by making it easier to go to less interesting places and easier to get less desirable goods. In pure science, awareness is focused on every detail except the psychosomatic fear and self-conquest of the activity itself, so that, for instance, when there is a question of making certain lethal weapons, the issue debated is whether the need of a country to get superiority over the enemy outweighs the duty of a scientist to publicize his findings; but the simpler reactions of compassion, flight, defiance are not operative at all.

In these conditions it is not surprising that persons toy with the sadomasochism of dictatorships and wars, where there is at least control of man by man instead of by symbols, and where there is suffering in the flesh.

10. Neurotic Split

So finally we come to a very recent acquisition of mankind, the neurotically split personality as a means of achieving equilibrium. Faced with a chronic threat to any functioning at all, the organism falls back on its safety-devices of blotting-out, hallucination, displacement, isolation, flight, regression; and man essays to make "living on his nerves" a new evolutionary achievement.

In the early stages there were developments that the healthy organism could each time merge into a new integrated whole. But now it is as if neurotics went back and singled out the vulnerable points of the past development of the race: the task is not to integrate erect posture into animal life, but to act on the one hand as if the head stood in the air by itself and on the other hand as if there were no erect posture or no head at all; and so with the other developments. The potential "dangers" have become factual symptoms: contactlessness, isolation, fear of falling, impotence, inferiority, verbalizing, and affectlessness.

It remains to be seen whether or not this neurotic turn is a viable destiny for our species.

11. Golden Age, Civilization, and Introjections

We have been generally defining the neurotic adjustments here as those which employ the new power "instead of" the previous nature, which is repressed, rather than "along with" it, in a new integration. The repressed unused natures then tend to return as Images of the Golden Age, or Paradise; or as theories of the Happy Primitive. We can see how great poets, like Homer and Shakespeare, devoted themselves to glorifying precisely the virtues of the previous era, as if it were their chief function to keep people from forgetting what it used to be to be a man.

And at best, indeed, the conditions of advancing civilized life seem to make important powers of human nature not only neurotically unused but rationally unusable. Civil security and technical plenty, for instance, are not very appropriate to an animal that hunts and perhaps needs the excitement of hunting to enliven its full powers. It is not surprising if such an animal should often complicate quite irrelevant needs—e.g., sexuality—with danger and hunting, in order to rouse excitement.

Further, it is likely that there is at present an irreconcilable conflict between quite desirable social harmony and quite desirable individual expression. If we are in such a transitional stage toward a tighter sociality, then there will in individuals be many social traits that must appear as unassimilable introjections, neurotic and inferior to the rival individual claims. Our heroic ethical standards (that come from the inspiriting dreams of creative artists) certainly tend to look backward to the more animal, sexual, personal, valorous, honorable, etc.; our behavior is quite otherwise and lacks excitement.

On the other hand, it is also likely (even if the different likelihoods are contradictory) that these "irreconcilable" conflicts have always been, not only at present, the human condition; and that the attendant suffering and motion toward an unknown solution are the grounds of human excitement.

12. Conclusion

However it is, "human nature" is a potentiality. It can be known only as it has been actualized in achievement and history, and as it makes itself today.

The question may quite seriously be asked, by what criterion does one prefer to regard "human nature" as what is actual in the spontaneity of children, in the works of heroes, the culture of classic eras, the community of simple folk, the feeling of lovers, the sharp awareness and miraculous skill of some people in emergencies? Neurosis is also a response of human nature and is now epidemic and normal, and perhaps has a viable social future.

We cannot answer the question. But a medical psychologist proceeds according to three criteria: (1) the health of the body, known by a definite standard, (2) the progress of the patient toward helping himself, and (3) the elasticity of the figure/background formation.

The Tree of Knowledge and the Tree of Life

1. Introduction

To explore the truth in the thought of Kafka, I deal first, at perhaps surprising length, with what he said in his own person in a few aphorisms and reported remarks, although, in the end, that truth must be found in the more extensive sayings of the romances and dialectical lyrics. In the case of most romancers this would obviously be the correct method, for the thought of the impersonations in fiction is dramatic thought, appropriate to the plot, and is the author's thought only indirectly. Yet though I pursue the same method with Kafka, it is for just the opposite reason. Not only are his impersonations never far from himself but, what is more important for religious thought, their dramatic plight mirrors his own plight in the pressing present moment, even too closely for art—there is not sufficient projection: so, he says, Writing is a form of Prayer. Certainly such existent thought, wrung from its conditions, is worth more than his generalities. But it is too immediate, dense, and difficult; one cannot at first see the truth in it; to say it darkly, one cannot see what is real anxiety and what is nervous anxiety. Therefore I start with his generalities—such curiously personal generalities!—just because speaking in his own person he offers a more projected impersonation of himself. His character. Now, the truth of religious thought is the same as the underlying structure of a man's character. So for half this book I am looking for the underlying character. But true religion, like happiness (it is the same as happiness), exists in the act; the act in the plight; so we look in the romances, and the dialectics of the animals. Then many things which would have seemed miserable (false) now seem true and free, in his plight, considering his character.

By religious truth I mean the expression of relations among the ego, the soul, and the world that can lead to happiness.

Again, all art is prayer, as well as the final, the temporarily final, satisfaction of dream. It is prayer of the audience and of the ideal audience—the "good" elders. In a given case, how much of this appeal is self-justification? how much is a plea for approval or punishment? and how much is humility, "the firmest relation to our fellow men, a relation, too, that is instantaneous"? And of this prayerful humility, what is the crooked claw of *begging,* that is really a clutching and a tearing? and what is the offering and asking hand of sociality, that will come to giving and taking and release the powers of the soul and the world?

In the religious aphorisms of Kafka there are warring strains of truth and falsity. There are sentences that seem to me (in my plight) true without condition: I can see no further; there are others that express only his misery and weakness, that are the subject for psychological analysis and are demonstrably religiously false (though it is already a great thing that he can express his own, and our, misery so definitely); again, there are sentences true on one interpretation, false on another, and where it can be shown that he himself vacillated from one interpretation to the other.

The admirable character picture, *"He,"* shows us the kind of man who cannot but make the errors and erroneous interpretations of the *Aphorisms.* It is a self shut off, shutting itself off, from every source of energy, and then finding that it has no energy to draw on, but who also recognizes how it is with the self. (But this recognition itself seems to him to be another and perfect defense against the threat of happiness.) Kafka is not *He,* but *He* exists in Kafka; and in a sense it is the energy imparted to *He* by what is not He—for *He* has no energy—that is the characteristic note of Kafka's writings. Or to say it another way: it is the war between the true and false strains in the religious aphorisms, both strains of the same voice, that explains the effort, the hopelessness, and the persistent effort of the romances.

"He" is a character picture; it is not an analysis of the genesis of such a character, nor a narrative of his acts in the world. But in the imaginative works, where *He* is given energy by what is not *He,* we may learn a good deal about how *He* came to be and by what devices he strives to maintain himself. For the most part, though less in the end than in the beginning, *He* seems to wreak a stubborn and melancholy triumph; a bad ending or a worse endlessness. We see, too, that these works are partly a high jump for *He* to practice on, so that what is not *He* can live on, and we can live on. And the artist Kafka can always begin another work, as if nothing had happened, not quite as if nothing had happened, and once more express the war between *He* and the soul.

This is a very earnest artist; we must pay him the respect—that critics, alas, rarely pay—of asking whether what he says is true and freely said or false and miserable; remembering always that what may be false as a general aphorism may be true and necessary in particular ("certainly such freedom as is possible today is a wretched business"). For lesser artists it is sufficient to show the biographical and institutional conditions in which they were able to make whole works. At the other extreme there are the magisterial creators who disturb our humanity deeper than we readers know it, who create conditions for us, so that there is no use in our questioning because we are persuaded beforehand by major force. But with Kafka one fences—against him, and *for* him against possible error. Also *with* him, for ourselves.

2. The High Jump

> APHORISM 1. The true way goes over a rope which is stretched not at any great height but just above the ground. It seems more designed to make people stumble than to be walked upon.

He means that the way is easy, it does not require gymnastic feats; but you must be aware, for perhaps it is dark or you are rushing headlong. On the other hand, one cannot notice everything, the blow falls unlooked for. Especially if it is secretly longed for, it falls unlooked for. We shall see that *He* has long since fallen under the wheels, "comfortingly enough." And K. says that if you can keep your eyes open you can notice much—but he is so drowsy. Nevertheless it is true! that the way is easy.

When we meet this rope in *The Castle*, however, it is as the apparatus of a gymnastic feat. K. is looking at the photograph of a Castle messenger:

> "It seems . . . he's lying on a board stretching himself and yawning. . . .
> No, he's floating and now I can see it, it's not a board at all but probably
> a rope, and the young man is taking a high leap." ". . . That's how the
> official messengers practice . . ." " . . . He's obviously making a great
> effort, his mouth is open, his eyes tightly shut."

He seems to be asleep; the gentlemen of the Castle sleep a good deal, and K., too, finds it hard to keep awake.

Awareness is a gymnastic feat. No, more deeply, sleep is a gymnastic feat. More deeply still, asleep you can perform a gymnastic feat with ease: I am later going to argue that this is the theme of *The Castle*.

Once you see the rope as designed to make you stumble (*whether* you do is a question of fact, it is your plight), then you attend to the rope, you perform on it, you do not attend to the way. It is better to stumble on it and be done with, and fall asleep.

This high jumper is the Knight of Infinity of *Fear and Trembling*:

> The knights of infinity are dancers and possess elevation. . . But
> whenever they fall down they are not able at once to assume the
> posture, they vacillate an instant, and this vacillation shows that after
> all they are strangers in the world . . .

> But to be able to fall down in such a way that the same second it
> looks as if one were standing or walking . . . that only the [Knight of
> Faith] can do.—Kierkegaard.

The Knight of Infinity is not a Knight of Faith; the question, for Kierkegaard, Kafka, and ourselves, is whether that exercise is the way to become a Knight of Faith or is not precisely not the way. If the feat is so prodigious, as Kierkegaard thinks, then the performer is indeed a stranger in this world and the way is extraordinary. But Kafka thinks, truly, that the way is easy.

It is, I think, from these dancers of Infinity that Kafka drew his seven musical dogs:

> From my hiding hole I saw . . . that it was not so much coolness as the
> most extreme tension that characterized their performance; these
> limbs, apparently so sure in their movements, quivered at every step
> with a perpetual apprehensive twitching; as if rigid with despair the
> dogs kept their eyes fixed on one another, and their tongues, whenever
> the tension weakened for a moment, hung wearily from their jowls . . .
> Why were they afraid? Who then forced them to do what they were
> doing?

It was the impression of this performance that robbed the dog of "the blissful life of childhood." It does not seem to the Old Dog, remembering, that these strange dogs are on the way to joyous faith but that they are miserable and forced; they are the serfs of despair.

But if we omit the conditions of sleepiness, of estrangement, of being forced, and of seeing the rope as designed to make you stumble (these are questions of fact), then it is easy to step over the rope. What is hard about stepping over a low rope?

3. Patience and Method

> 2. All human error is impatience, a premature renunciation of method,
> a delusive pinning down of a delusion.

> 3. There are two cardinal sins from which all the others spring:
> impatience and laziness. Because of impatience we were driven out
> of Paradise, because of laziness we cannot return. Perhaps, however,
> there is only one cardinal sin: impatience. Because of impatience we
> were driven out, because of impatience we cannot return.

Stated negatively, as concerning impatience, this is miserable; for to say "stop being impatient" is as useless as to say "stop being nervous." But say it positively; "Be patient, return to Paradise"—then it is true. For patience is not a restraint of action, but a recreation in some action deeper than the action you temporarily do not commit yourself to. You are not holding back but drawing strength from time and place and from the energy of all the time of the world. Thus, a convalescent recovers by patiently resting in bed, negatively by not agitating himself, but positively by the healing forces in the organism, the air, nourishment. Many great sentences could be cited to show that this is what Kafka means. He says:

> 66. Theoretically there exists a perfect possibility of happiness: to believe in the indestructible element in oneself and not strive after it.

> 24. What is laid upon us is to accomplish the negative; the positive is already given.

With what astonishing optimism he says in the last Aphorism,

> You do not need to leave your room . . . be quite still . . .
> the world will freely offer itself . . . it will roll in ecstasy at your feet.

Obviously this is not because of the habits of the world but because of a power in the still soul.

Patience is a stillness that releases the energy of time and the world. It is impossible to abstain from striving, to accomplish the negative, unless you draw on a positive energy that is not striving. In *The Trial* Joseph K. cannot be quite still and let the Court freely offer itself, but he seeks it out at the first business hour, although no hour was set, to precipitate the decision—so strongly does *He* want to die!

What is usually called "sitting still patiently" is a thousand small distractions trying to use up the one striving. These are the heaviness of the body and its habits: we now see why he speaks of impatience *and* laziness. He conceives that even Alexander the Great

> 36. . . . might have remained standing on the bank of the Hellespont,
> and never have crossed it, and not out of fear, not out of indecision, not
> out of infirmity of will, but because of the mere weight of his own body.

Alexander the Great is the imperial ego; to the ego, shut off from the energy of time and the world, there is no action and power in the life of the body, but the body is a dead weight.

What is required is a powerful patience. Now, the question is whether this is the same, as he says, as the persistent application of Method? Yes, if method is accomplishing the negative by drawing on the positive—in the tao-word, creating a Void and then into it there flood the life of time and the world. Yet all the characters in all the romances of Kafka seem to be methodical, excruciatingly methodical, and do they return to Paradise? Method is the means they employ to cut themselves off from help wherever it freely offers itself or even forces itself, for happiness is too terrifying. (I do not mean that, in their plight, they are unjustified; on the contrary, they are justified, for by method they bring to a pause the imperial ego.) The logical form of their method is the Infinite Regress: we shall see how they develop it in pursuit, in constructive will, in hunger-art. Develop this method awhile, and after a while you sink down with the mere weight of the body.

> [K.] was not to relax in his struggle but was to die worn out by it . . .
> and from the Castle itself, the word was to come that though K.'s legal
> claim to live in the village was not valid, yet, taking certain auxiliary
> circumstances into account, he was to be permitted to live and work
> there.
> [The reported ending of *The Castle*.]

But the powerful patience, that rests in the indestructible element and does not strive after it, can indeed return us to Paradise. Patient in this way we have never left Paradise—

> 62. . . . we are continuously there in actual fact, no matter whether we
> know it here or not.

The way is easy—whether we know it or not.

4. The Infinite Regress

> 5. From a certain point onward there is no longer any turning back. This
> is the point that must be reached.

Good. That is something positive, that we draw on without striving, for it is given. Now, "a point is that which has no dimensions."

But what shall we say of the machinations of *He* who by an infinite regress prevents us from ever reaching such a point, just as Achilles never catches the tortoise? The Knight of Infinity!

5. Antinomianism

Let us place in conflict two sayings:

> 7. One of the Evil One's most effectual arts of seduction is the challenge
> to battle. It is like the fight with woman which ends in bed.

20. From a real antagonist boundless courage flows into you.

These are both matters of everyday observation. First, to succumb to the battle is just to be impatient, for why should one commit oneself on "their" conditions rather than on the right conditions? (The history of radical politics, for instance, consists almost entirely of such erroneous battles.) Second, if courage flows into you from a real antagonist, it is that he is your partner in heightening the battle; the ego is sacrificed to the battle, and from the depths flows unknown strength. The exchange, that seemed at first competitive and self-defensive, releases play that surpasses the players.

Yet, if the two sentences are brought together, is there not a contradiction? But let us try to resolve it. First, there is a superficial resolution: that the Evil One is not a "real" antagonist; and this is a line that Kafka often takes:

52. . . . What we call evil is only a necessary moment in our endless development.

There is no strain more characteristic in the romances than the argument that justifies, sympathizes with, and friendlily embraces the obvious injustice, partly masochistically, partly because it is a necessary injustice, really an act of love and justice under complicated conditions. So the horrors of the Penal Colony are justified; and so he says,

39. The disharmony of the world seems, comfortingly enough, to be merely an arithmetical one.

What then? does it not follow that just to succumb to the Evil One is the necessary moment, etc.? it is from *that* embrace that boundless courage flows into you. Not because he is not a real antagonist, but just because he is real. The important thing is to make sure that he is *your* evil, not some general evil; then this battle is the point from which there is no more turning back. What harm if it ends in bed?—I think this is what Wilde meant when he said that the only way to resist temptation is to succumb to it, for the evil lies in the continuing temptation. And Goethe said: We willingly commit some folly just to live on a little longer.

That is to say, the Evil One is a real antagonist from whom—if you end with him in bed—boundless courage flows into you. This is the extreme antinomian position: from evil comes good, if it is *your* evil. Is it a hard position? Kafka goes on! *Leopards*,

17. Leopards break into the temple and drink the sacrificial chalices dry; this occurs repeatedly, again and again; finally it can be reckoned on beforehand and becomes a part of the ceremony.

(It is impossible to write more beautifully.) These leopards are, for instance, lusts of the flesh, if these are in fact a man's evil. When they come again and again, shall we not say that it is a divine omen and part of the ceremony? That is, first we come to realize that character is destiny; the religious step is to recognize that this destiny is providence. This is faith. But if these leopards are providential and the objects of faith, why is it any longer appropriate to call them leopards? We must call everything by its right name. If the Evil is a necessary moment, is it any longer appropriate to call it Evil? It does not follow to embrace every evil, but to embrace the one from which boundless courage flows. This is a question of fact.

"There is a goal," he says falsely, "but no way; what we call the way is only wavering." On the contrary! there is a definite way, but the goal is a matter of gossip and of little concern. The goal we discover as we go along, and that is also how we discover the way.

6. The Ground Underfoot

21. Grasp your great good fortune that the ground on which you stand
cannot be greater than the two feet that cover it.

Why does he say it ironically rather than simply: "the ground fits precisely the two feet that cover it." Is it not, usually, a good sample of all the ground there is? This good sample of the ground—almost every stander has a good sample—is the indestructible element; one need not strive after it; to rest on it is patience; and Antaeus found that from it boundless courage flowed.

But if he says it negatively and ironically—"Thank God we have only thus much to worry about?"—then he tries to accomplish the negative without resting on the positive that is given. It is a false method, as if, for instance, it made no difference to the next step that I am standing on a good sample of the ground; then we are back to Alexander's body, unsupported by anything. But the right method is to let the ground take care of the ground; what is given for us to do is to create a void roundabout: that is, not to be where in fact we are not. The positive is given, not in the sense that it is given altogether, but that it will create itself if there is a void, but this is not for us to accomplish. So in politics, for instance, if we undo the State and relax the repression of the children, then the good society will flourish.

There is a passage in the *Diary* (1913): "This strength of life—to put one's foot joyfully on the right place. He sits in himself like a master oarsman in his boat." This is better; yet even here there is a fatal error. For like Plato he speaks of the soul as a man, a steersman, in a ship; but next it will be like a man in a jail (so indeed *He* says it). But the right analogy of the soul is Aristotle's:

It is like the song-of-the-flute and the flute, only the material flute has such a song.

7. The Ground Underfoot and the Physical World

52. There is only a spiritual world; what we call the physical world is the evil in the spiritual one . . .

53. All is deception . . .

81. Evil is a radiation of the human consciousness at certain transitional stages. The physical world itself is not really an illusion, but only its evil, which, however, admittedly constitutes our picture of the physical world.

63. [A man is fettered to both heaven and the world, and if he heads in either direction he is throttled.]

Let us say it bluntly: Kafka is floundering among these alternatives; there is only a spiritual world, neither a physical nor a spiritual, both a physical and a spiritual—they are incompatible. Poor country doctor!—"naked, exposed to the cold of this world, with an earthly carriage and supernatural horses, I wander about."

What he should say, what he wants to say, what I shall try later to prove he does say by implication, is this:

There is only a physical world and what we take to be its evil is our illusion of a spiritual world.

I do not mean it as a materialistic novelty, but as a literal statement of the old mystery of the incarnation. It is only God that is perfectly incarnate, all the rest of us are suffering from spiritual delusions. Suffering from this angelism, these angelic goods and angelic goals, inevitably we are throttled when we seek to move on earth, but if we move away from the earth we are throttled. That is, we throttle ourselves, the gorge rises—but this is a familiar psychological mechanism of protection against the repressed instinct. It is especially the mechanism of speakers and writers; like the silent dogs they will not speak it out.

Suppose we follow this formula and look at the incidents of, say, *The Castle*, the doings of Klamm and Sordini and Sortini: then we find that just the ordinary acts that seem offensive and to constitute their inferiority, if one could allow himself to conceive of their inferiority, really constitute their superiority and justify them; but the mysteries that constitute their supposed superiority, these are nothing but the delusions that constitute our misery. I should not say it so positively if we could not see it, grossly, glaringly, "writ large" as Plato said, in the social institutions that fetter us: they are our social institutions, made by our belief in them. Who can deny that it is we who throttle ourselves?

There is a passage in *Repetition* that expresses the problem (not the solution) of *The Castle*:

> How did I obtain an interest in this big enterprise they call reality? Why should I have an interest in it? Is it not a voluntary concern? And if I am to be compelled to take part in it, where is the director? I should like to make a remark to him. Is there no director? Whither shall I turn with my complaint? Existence is surely a debate—may I beg that my view be taken into consideration?—Kierkegaard

Must one not make a formal reply to such questions? That what else is the meaning of anything being profitable for you, except just the creativity of the reality? That, to be sure, the reality is not what "they" call the reality, but what is the reality (this is a question of fact)? That naturally one feels "compelled" if he adopts the ludicrous view that there is a director; that it is *precisely* existence—the one only universe in the universe!—that is not a debate, though concerning one's delusions there can be plenty of useful debate. (Kafka was too wise for much of this idiocy.) Here in Kierkegaard speaks *He*; and *He,* the Individual, is raised to a first principle of hopelessness.

And so, a few pages later in *Repetition*—for these romances are bound up with one another—we come to *The Metamorphosis*:

> Or, if I am guilty, then surely I must be able to repent of my guilt and make amends

—why?—

> shall I perhaps repent furthermore of the fact that the world takes the liberty of playing with me like a child with a June-bug?

We are here in the full world of Kafka's small fry, the vermin, and moles, and the condemned men, and *He.*

But the resolution is not the same for Kierkegaard as for Kafka. Kierkegaard's reply to the complaint is—the reply to Job: It is a personal "trial of probation" between the child and the father, and ends with the child's accepting the loving buffets and, it goes without saying, identifying himself with the superior strength, so he himself will deal the buffets later (as Kierkegaard did with a certain notorious charity). This trial is transcendent and has no scientific explanation. Oh!—"If this is what we come to," said Freud, "we could have got there sooner and much more directly."

Kafka is stubbornly unwilling to accept such a solution, self-aggrandizing, and, it seems to me, blasphemous (for why is God invoked in what is no doubt some error of our own?). If *He*, if, for instance, Joseph K. in *The Trial*, more and more, indeed from the beginning, accepts the verdict of the Court—then something is wrong with that *He*. Let him perish—"like a dog." The question is, then, whether, having accomplished the negative and made so terrible a Void, our Kafka took pleasure in the flowering of the indestructible?

"The physical world is real—evil is a radiation of human consciousness": so Kafka tells us that it is just our spirituality that is evil, the contrary of his first thought on the subject. Now, if he did not have the grace to be a little more incarnate (and this is simply a fact), not a Christian living in the Last Times, these misfortunes a good many of us share in common. But what is astonishing is that, as a Jew, he deviated for a moment into the error of questioning the Creation, the work of the Six Days.[*]

51. One must not cheat anybody. Not even the world of its triumph.

8. The Ground Underfoot and Awareness

52b. In a light that is fierce and strong one can see the world dissolve. To weak eyes it becomes solid, to weaker eyes it shows fists, before still weaker eyes it feels ashamed and smites down him who dares to look at it.

The weakest eyes are those of the fearsome child spying on the parents copulating. The weaker eyes are those of the adult unconsciously straining to see the old scene again. The weak eyes—these are our interest—are those mentioned by K. in the famous deleted passage: "If you have strength to look at

---

[*] One more word on Kierkegaard, Kafka, and Job. Kierkegaard's interpretation contains, it seems to me, only the husk of the reply to Job, a reply so far false. But the kernel is true: It is that the image of the Horse and Leviathan do in fact break through the defenses of the ego, they stop the questions, as Kafka would say, "by an operation of nature." Without the poetry the reply to Job is nothing but a false identification with power; with the poetry it may be for certain people a true release of power, in faith. Now, Brod, who is not such a person, strongly criticizes the reply (*Kafka*); he calls it Fetishism (this proves that he understands that there is a mystery in the nature images); and he wittily compares the monsters with the "*dumm-bürokratisch*" wonders of *The Castle*: Kafka, says he, is not impressed by such. But I shall argue at the end of this book that Kafka's solution is nothing but such music after all; except that, by a necessity, not an advantage, of our historical institutions, the song is milder, more "humane." Further, it is strange to call Kafka not a fetishist when it leaps to the eye that he is a totemist!

things steadily, without as it were blinking your eyes, you can see much; but if you relax only once and shut your eyes, everything fades immediately into obscurity." The bother here is that the man does not blink, that is, as any doctor will tell you, he is straining his eyes and making them weaker; the much that he sees will never be enough, and it is probably better for him, like the Officials of the Castle, to fall asleep. Perhaps in the obscurity he will see a bright dream.

Kafka needs, and hopes for, too much from awareness. Must we not say that it is because of a primitive fear that he wants it to accomplish no less than to think away the world and leave him in the hell of spiritual delusion? He fixes his eyes in order *not* to see something he knows is there. And what a savage destructiveness! But the attempt is hopeless; one cannot fix one's eyes on everything and explain it away.

Let us turn off that fierce light and go into good daylight. Awareness is an auxiliary, to help us on the way, for instance to help us leap over a rope which is stretched at no great height above the ground: but we jump with our feet and not our eyes or head. The role of the ego is to provide for us, not to explore; it is to help satisfy desire, not to seek out the desirable; not to rob the soul by eating up the world beforehand.

9. The Operation of Nature

> 54. There are questions which we could never get over if we were not delivered from them by the operation of nature.

This is the nub of the whole matter. If only he said everything so!

He means to say merely—but how far the saying takes us!—that a man begins to question, he establishes a paralogism and sets in motion an infinite regress: for instance the arguments pro and con a marriage. But then because of imperious sexual desire he gets married anyway, or the roof caves in and settles another question.

What! Do such operations of nature *answer* the question? Is it worthy of a human being to be so answered? Yes! yes! For if it is a question altogether unconcerned with such operations of nature, then it is not a very serious question; or if there happens to be a serious question wholly unconcerned with the operations of nature—which I doubt—then it belongs to a part of the soul that could not be delivered by an operation of nature, and it is not such questions that we are talking about. But if it is then a serious question in some relation to the operations of nature, what kind of consideration would a man be giving to the question if he did not look for an answer in the relevant operation of nature? If a surprising operation of nature does not provide new evidence, then he has surely wrongly phrased the question. Thus, a man is torn between alternatives as to his child's education; each way there are insoluble practical difficulties; then one day the child falls deathly ill; the insoluble difficulties fall into a different importance; for instance, the imminent fulfillment of the wish common to parents that the child will die marshals the forces of love, and the parent now first seriously considers what is good for the child itself; a much more "difficult" solution, hitherto unthought of, now seems eminently practical.

Now suppose a man, like Kafka, observes this to happen with a certain regularity (like the leopards breaking into the temple); ought he not then to begin to rephrase his questions? In such a case he would no longer feel impelled to write, "There are questions which we could never get over," but that "it is only the operation of nature that compels us to put the question rightly." And suppose this fails to happen with a certain regularity, must we not conclude that he is avoiding the operation of nature, blinking at it just when it occurs; that he is questioning himself into an infinite regress—until he is astonished by an operation of nature that gets him over the question?

10. The Operation of Nature Is Not Identical with the Visible World

> 82. . . . The whole visible world is perhaps nothing more than the rationalization of a man who wants to find peace for a moment. An attempt to falsify the actuality of knowledge [of Good and Evil], to regard knowledge as a goal still to be reached.

I have never seen this acute, this devastating observation elsewhere in this form. He means to say that such a man fixes the world and his being in the world—his being *against* the world—as "those things out there," that "visible" world, not immediately felt as his concern; he must still investigate, he still has the leisure to investigate whether or not they are his concern, and indeed to discover what his concern is. The liar! This is what he really knows beforehand and is trying to forget.

The saying is of course peculiarly applicable to the men who have now abrogated the name "scientists." In another context Tolstoy makes a similar excellent remark:

> What occurs is something similar to what the result would be if a man, desiring to understand the nature of an object before him, should, instead of approaching it, examining it on all sides, and handling it, removes farther and farther from it, finally removing to such a distance that all details of color and unevenness of surface should disappear, and there remained only the outline which detached it from the

horizon. And from such a distance the man might begin to describe this object in detail, imagining that he has now a clear understanding of it.

Must we not say that the man is afraid of the object?

It does not follow that the world is a rationalization, nor that visibility is, but only the definition of them apart from concern.

On the contrary! it is equally fatal—and Kafka is prone to it—to use the "indestructible element" as a rationalization in order to exclude the visible world; this is to punish oneself with an impractical concern, instead of taking joy in the concernful world. It is only because the world (not the "visible world") is *not* a rationalization, that knowledge of good and evil is actual. That is, knowledge is given sufficient for our living concern in the world.

There is a confusion in it when he says,

> 82. . . . We [are] essentially equal in our capacity to recognize good and
> evil . . . [but] nobody can remain content with the mere knowledge . . .
> but must endeavor as well to act in accordance with it. The strength to
> do so, however, is not likewise given him.

I am going to show almost immediately that this is not the best strain of Kafka on this subject, but it is a characteristic strain. Yet a moment's reflection as to how knowledge comes to us, in the act itself, proves that what he alleges is impossible: it is impossible that if we know in the act we do not have the strength to act the knowledge. But the case is that we prevent ourselves and are prevented by obstacles that are mostly our delusions; and soon, out of practice, so to speak, we forget even the knowledge we used to remember. But it is not lost once and for all, for the next moment we can begin and be happy.

11. The Weariness and the Harness

> 31. His weariness is that of the gladiator after the combat; his work was
> the whitewashing of a corner in a state official's office.

Shall we say that this man did not have the strength, so artfully turned against himself? (Though admittedly the wall in an official office is very black.)

> 42. You have harnessed yourself ridiculously for this world.

I Samuel 17: 38–39: "Saul clad David with his apparel and he put a helmet of brass upon his head, and he clad him with a coat of mail. And David girded his sword upon his apparel and he essayed to go, but he could not; for he had not tried it. 'I cannot go with these, for I have not tried them.' *And David put them off him.*"

12. The Tree of Knowledge and the Tree of Life

Attend to what he says now:

> 78. Why do we lament over the fall of man? We were not driven out of
> Paradise because of it, but because of the Tree of Life, that we might not
> eat of it

> 79. We are sinful not merely because we have eaten of the Tree of
> Knowledge, but also because we have not yet eaten of the Tree of Life.
> The state in which we find ourselves is sinful, quite independent of guilt.

Are not these sayings lovely and terrible? More lovely than terrible, for he says, "Why lament?" "We are continuously in Paradise in actual fact," he said—is it a question of fact?—*therefore* we can eat of the Tree of Life at any moment, at any moment that we stretch out a hand and take the fruit and eat; at any moment, that is, that we can lift a hand to stretch it out, etc.—What! Do we fail to, not out of fear or indecision, but just because of the weight of the hand, like Alexander's body? On the contrary, the hand is vibrant with anticipation. He says, "We have not *yet* eaten," not, "we did not eat," because indeed we shall eat of it.

How astonishing it is to read these sayings by the man who described the monstrous bug, and the doctor astray in the night, the machine for punishing, and the fatal mistaken knock at the door. On the contrary, it is just this author who must say them: "Here as elsewhere," as Kant said, "the human spirit has first tried all possible wrong ways before it succeeded in finding the one true way." It is because it is Kafka who says it that this urgency, to mere life, otherwise perhaps somewhat banal, is authoritative and compelling.

It is a characteristic of such thoughts of our existence that if another man says them (if perhaps I say it to myself), I can still shrug my shoulders; but if they are said by the author of *The Burrow* and *The Dog* they are nearer proved.

What does he mean by the Tree of Life? We may know it by what he says of death:

> 82. [. . . The final attempt to act in accordance with the knowledge
> of good and evil, even at the risk of not achieving the necessary
> strength . . . is the original meaning of natural death.]

But to eat of Life is to have this necessary strength. Here he brings close together the knowledge and the strength. To know and not to strive to do, but to live and easily to do. That is, if it is possible to stretch out your hand and eat, then it is easy to act in accordance with the knowledge of Good and Evil. He seems to say the contrary:

15. If it had been possible to build the Tower of Babel without ascending it, the work would have been permitted.

But this is because Babel is an arduous and impossible enterprise; it is, shall we say, methodical; only a sinful man engages in it, precisely in order to fail (masturbating and withholding the orgasm). But the Knowledge is not sinful and not arduous; it is not even a goal to be reached (sufficient for the next step). But what is sinful is not to take the next step, that is a step: to eat of the tree of Life and thereby have the strength.

Spinoza said: "Happiness is not the reward of virtue, it is itself a virtue."

But Robinson Crusoe is our model! this example makes the meaning quite clear:

Had Robinson Crusoe never left the highest . . . point of his island . . . he would soon have perished; but since without paying any attention to passing ships and their feeble telescopes he started to explore the whole island and take pleasure in it, he managed to keep himself alive and finally was found after all, by a chain of causality that was of course logically inevitable.

There is, to be sure, a terrible bitterness in the expression "we were driven out that we might not eat of it," in the expression "permitted if we could toil at it without ascending it"—the sentence writhes with hatred; who prevents us? The expression that knowledge is the source of our guilt, the innocent knowledge that is so easy to act in accordance with, when you have the strength. But it cannot be helped; we have here the distinction between the Old Law and the New, the Old Law that cannot be fulfilled except that in the New Law it is fulfilled. The writer is under the Old Law (this is a question of fact); he still has not eaten of the Tree of Life, and

98. . . . . Every stage seems unattainable to the previous one, whether in fear or longing.

Nevertheless it comes to be! by a natural operation.

Then let us review the cluster of sayings in the order in which he wrote them down, so the reader may not think that I am forcing his thought into this hopeful way, but rather that I am forcing it in the way that he wants to go:

77. No one can desire what is fundamentally harmful to himself.

78. Why do we lament over the fall of man?

79. We are sinful . . . because we have not yet eaten of the Tree of Life.

80. We were fashioned to live in Paradise, and Paradise was destined to serve us. Our destiny has been altered; that this has also happened with the destiny of Paradise is not stated. [That is, the Tree of Life still stands there waiting.]

81. The physical world itself is not really an illusion, but only its evil.

Is this a "wavering way"?

13. Community and the Tree of Life
The community of mankind is our means to life:

67. The indestructible is one: it is every human being individually and at the same time all human beings collectively; hence the marvelous indissoluble alliance of mankind.

71. Test yourself on humanity. It makes the doubtful doubt, the believer believe.

101. Humility provides everyone . . . with the firmest relation to his fellow men, a relation, too, that is instantaneous. . . . It can do this because it is the true language of prayer, at once worship and firmest union. Our relation to our fellow men is that of prayer, our relation to ourselves that of effort; from prayer we draw the strength for effort.

The indestructible in oneself is not the self understood as the willful ego. Our relation, through the indestructible, to our fellow men is the reliance on strength that is not the strength of our willful selves. This is prayer. And as for effort, the act of the willful self, its proper use is to accomplish the negative, that is, simply, to put the willful self out of the way of the strength that springs from the indestructible, an inexhaustible fountain. Here at last we find Kafka saying, in thinking of our social nature, what he apparently could not say as an individual: that the negative depends on the positive, effort draws its strength from prayer.

Psychologically, it means that the basis of our sociality is prior to the formation of the ego. Sociality is not an "interpersonal" agreement between individuals; it is intrapersonal, grounded in love, fraternity, infantile dependency, the ability to communicate. *Therefore* we can draw on it for energy that the sick ego, constituted precisely against the instincts, tries to starve us of; but face to face with our fellows the ego lowers its guard. The relation is instantaneous, in the sense that it is unmediated by the plans and calculations of consciousness; a man is surprised to find that he is given strength just when, in humility, he forgets himself. Humility is the by-passing of the ego ideal that paralyzes us by binding our energy to the willful ego.*

Taking these sentences with the novels, we see that to Kafka there are two types of society: the interpersonal state, bureaucratic, business, and industrial society, and the intrapersonal community of life. On the one hand a structure of egos, in which the ego never finds expression but always its menacing self as in a Hall of Mirrors—how deeply it wounded him we may read in so many of the romances. (It is the most immediate impression that the reader gets.) Except that finally he was redeemed by his ability to remain

> 28. . . . passive in simple astonishment at the tremendous complex, and . . . take away . . . nothing but the strengthening power which that spectacle gives by contrast.

On the other hand the libidinous community that pours energy into the will, if only, as among the Mice Nation, the energy of rest and solace, or, better, the creative communalism of pioneering Zionism that he looked toward in his last years.

(There is not in the romances much expression of this strength-giving creative community, but what a romance Kafka could have written about this very Zionism, as Hawthorne, the novelist who is most like Kafka, wrote of Brook Farm. I mean the action of such a simple communalism in the framework of vast State and Imperial structures, of financial connections with distant bourgeois, and deadly strife with natives who are also essentially simple farmers who love them. The history is more Kafka-like than *The Castle*.)

And because we attribute to the physical world the relations familiar in society, we may find there the same two types, of hopelessness or hope: to say, on the one hand, "the disharmony of the world is merely mathematical," like the business cycle, or to say, on the other hand, with Goethe, "This poor old earth—but see, a little sun, a little rain, and everything is green again."

"It makes the doubtful doubt," for the ego sees in his fellows only other egos, choosing between the trap and the cat. "It makes the believer believe," for the instantaneous relation floods the heart.

---

* This is creative humility; but in speaking of Kafka—of the complex of humility and hunger-art, willed poverty—we cannot altogether omit a darker aspect, the aspect of humility that Nietzsche so particularly made his target; that humility is sometimes a kind of *begging*, and that these beggars, we beggars, do not hold our hands without consciously clawing and grasping, in hatred and resentment. We destroy ourselves the easier to destroy the happy; we ask difficult questions in order to make the happy uneasy.

Here, in the indissoluble alliance, Kafka is a far superior theologian to Kierkegaard, who in fact pursues his protestant individualism to the suicidal length that the very existence of a church is impossible, and therefore impossible also the tie that supposedly binds him to the historical incident in which his faith is grounded. Says Kierkegaard:

> . . . it is beautiful to be born as the individual who has the universal as his home, his friendly abiding place, which at once welcomes him with open arms when he would tarry in it. But higher than this there winds a solitary path, narrow and steep; it is terrible to be born outside the universal, to walk without meeting a single traveller.

These are uncharitable, presumptuous remarks. Certainly if he believes that a man is "born" as a self-contained individual, taking comfort in his hypocrite similars, then surely the universal will lead up no lofty way, whether narrow or broad; though if he had taken, like Kafka, a more concerned look at mankind, he would have seen that there is no comfortable tarrying for such either. But in heaven's name, you Dane, to whom is one to give his neighbor-love, as is bidden? But Kafka could take the golden words in their plain sense: "Humility provides everyone with the firmest relation to his fellow men, a relation, too, that is instantaneous." It means that love, faith, grace are the same act; surely this is the plain meaning. But are we to fancy the Dancer of Infinity, quivering with tension, as saying, "Our relation to our fellow men is that of prayer"?

14. Profane Love

> 75. Profane love can seem more sublime than sacred love; of itself it could not do this, but as, unknown to itself, it possesses an element of sacred love, it can.

By profane love he means sexual love, and the sense in which unknown to itself it frees the spirit is clear from what we have said before. Sublimity in the Kantian meaning is the significance forced on the consciousness beyond its own power to organize experience at all. One smiles to put in Kant's mouth the statement that sexual love is a source of the "dynamical sublime," but it is so nevertheless.

The problem in the saying of Kafka's is in the first part: that profane love can seem to be *more* sublime. To explain this puzzling seeming we would have to turn to biographical conditions. (In general, one cannot explain the truth by the conditions, for the truth is implicitly a statement *of* its conditions; but an error omits something and is corrected by adding conditions.) Now there is evidence, of which we shall eventually amass a good deal, that for sexuality Kafka had a special guilt, beyond the guilt of the willful ego altogether. He tends to think of it in a special sense as the Evil One—as if when he says the fight with the Evil One ends in bed, he meant that to end in bed is to succumb to the Evil One. Therefore in sexuality he finds an extra mystery; therefore he says "*seems* to be *more* sublime."

The saying, involving both the freedom and misery of the author, is of immense importance for the interpretation of the great scenes in *The Trial* and *The Castle* where the heroes find themselves forever enlisting the aid of women, the Lenis, Friedas, Olgas, and Fräulein Bürstners. The relevance of such aid is the sacredness of all love, but its defect lies not in its profanity but in the fact that it is being used and not given in to: that is, these persons and their author still will not first simply eat of the fruit of Life; they have plans and aims. These higher aims are partly a secret device to avoid, by an infinite regress, the explosive virtue that springs from only life. He says,

> 92. The joys of this life are not its own, but our dread of ascending to a higher life; the torments of this life are not its own, but our self-torment because of that dread.

It is a great, deep and subtle saying, that we must turn this way and that; but here we may give only its crudest interpretation: it is pleasure-anxiety, the fear to give oneself freely to those joys, else one might "burst" (Wilhelm Reich).

15. Psychology

> 89. For the last time psychology!

No, no, yet another time! Precisely if it is religion and our existence that we are concerned with, would it not be blasphemous to assign such dignity, and invoke such help, in what is conceivably some little sickness of the soul, where we could get help from a human physician? By psychology he means psychoanalysis, of which he had a deep suspicion. But this is to depart from the tradition of Maimonides, the physician, who did not question the divinity of created nature.

In another sense, of course, the saying is simply true, for as he says in the *Meditations*,

> Psychology is the reading of a mirror writing: in *actuality* it avails us nothing.

It is only in the present, passing into the next moment, that our providence can fulfill our destiny. For the concern of the present moment, surely no more psychology (whose value as a Tower of Babel I think I know well). "Just once!—

without looking back at the past, without looking back at the future!"—But the truth is that Franz Kafka, a champion of our concern, often *could* not attend to the present moment; and therefore yet another time, psychology!

The Existent Moment

The present concern in one's existence. . . . I have been trying, if only out of respect for our friend, to take his sayings seriously and ask whether they are true or not, in general. But this is also not to be serious with him, not asking how it was with him at that actual moment, our past but his present. Thus, it is serious enough to say that Kafka had the conviction of a saving possibility in Life and in Community; but this is also frivolous—and callous. For in fact it does not seem in his writings that Kafka is stretching out his hand, finding fulfillment in love and friendship, and will eat the next moment. Perhaps the moment after the next moment. But in that present moment passing into its next, it is clear what he felt his existence to be: suffering; suffering and sin the same thing, the suffering being the sin (for he did not believe in punishment or penance); but also humility, as we have mentioned, and detached astonishment, and laborious creation.

Proceeding to the last group of these sayings, let me try harder to interpret the pressing sentiment.

16. Suffering and Dread

> 92. The joys of this life are not its own, but our dread of ascending to a higher life; the torments of this life are not its own, but our self-torment because of that dread.

> 93. Only here is suffering suffering. Not in the sense that those who suffer here are ennobled elsewhere because of that suffering, but in the sense that what is called suffering in this world is, without any alteration except that it is freed from its opposite, bliss in another.

> 99. You can hold back from the suffering of the world, you have permission to do so and it is in accordance with your nature; but perhaps this very holding back is the one evil that you could have avoided.

The joy is the dread. . . . Let us think of a man who experiences a simple joy of this life, perhaps seeing a lovely contour, and the immediate effect of it is to draw to his eyes the tears of loss and mourning. He is mourning for himself. It is that the joy expresses a best self that is also his deep self: all bygone desire both fulfilled and justified. But in fact no desire has been fulfilled—though at this moment he sees that all were justified; time has lapsed away; it is himself that he is grieving for. A forepleasure loosens the ice of resignation, makes that alien loss his own. At that moment he is no longer *wasting* his loss, "We, wasters of Woes"—

> —how we look away into the duration beyond them, but they are our
> wintry foliage.—Rilke

But now Kafka says that the joys are not the forepleasure of mourning but of dread; his heart is pounding and he is trembling, with dread. (34. "His reply to the assertion that he *possesses,* but never *is,* was only a trembling and heart-pounding.") Surely one must say, first, as I interpreted it above, that he has been escaping to the joys in order to avoid a deep pleasure that is dangerous; but now, pleasure being a forepleasure of pleasure, he is trapped in dread: the joy that belongs to the self has failed to serve as a refuge from the joy that would unmake the self. Or closer: the symptomatic defensive joy is a real one—for we must say that if a man moves toward something he really wants it in a positive, not merely a negative, way—but he can only enjoy it if it is masochistically ransomed by the dread: as in many religious rites a man atones for the presumptuous self in order to satisfy the self, the atonement and the pleasure being sometimes the same rite (we are back to the Leopards). Or contrariwise: that the joy is a forepleasure for the punishment which stands for a deeper pleasure. It would be easy to produce evidence that Kafka feels all this. But still closer, and I think we here hit the religious meaning: he feels that the joy is not justified enough, certainly it does not justify itself, because it does not fulfill the whole desire, childhood longing, but he *strains* to justify it, for it is all the joy there is: the dread is the dread of failure, that the world will be annihilated if he does not fulfill it, but he cannot. Thus, primarily, to be sure, the anxiety of "bursting" and surrendering the self, ascending to a higher life; but religiously, the fear of *not* "bursting" and not being able to justify the world and its joys. This is the religious addition that Kafka makes to the ordinary pleasure-anxiety.

Such a thought would occur to a man who with inflexible honesty and determination forces himself to become aware of how it is with him, but who nevertheless does not abreact the repressed contents in feeling and action. Such a man is Kafka.

Throughout we hear crying the lost child: "Eternal childhood, again a call of life" (*Journal*, 1922).

Aphorism 93 must be taken as a correct introspection of Freud's old principle that the energy of anxiety is the libido belonging to the repressed content.

By the "opposite of bliss" he cannot mean anything but repression, for how else could the freeing from this opposite give bliss without any other alteration; and then by suffering he must mean—as every one of the romances could tell us anyway—nothing but anxiety. Nevertheless he does not relax the repression! (It is beyond admiration for insight to be pushed so far by sheer will, without the aid of emotional release; if Kafka were not the author of the tales of Kafka it would be unbelievable.) What is the secret of this energy of insight? must it not be that there is an extra energy, expressed in the repressing itself, beyond the simple bliss transformed into anxiety? The situation is this: supposing he would surrender to the bliss, to the orgasm, and *thereby* justify the world, then he would fall asleep and lose the sense of it: he would no longer have the sense of the justification of the world as his possession, but he and the world would *be* justified. This is the prescription of health and is enjoined on us: to lose ourselves in order to find ourselves; but it is not the way to be Kafka. He cannot bear it that, at the very moment when the world justifies itself, he—falls asleep; and yet he knows that it is inevitable and says it plain:

> 76. Truth is indivisible, therefore cannot know itself; the man who desires to know it must be false.

Nevertheless he will keep his eyes open; *He* is false; he will not release the libido that is bound to the ego's awareness and self-sense. Primarily, to be sure, in order to prevent the orgasm; but religiously, just in order to justify that little blissful orgasm, which is what it is.

(I cannot feel that religiosity at this depth is the opposite of neurosis, but of psychosis. With most of us, our selves are so securely grounded that we can take the risk; but with Kafka, the self seems to feel that, if it temporarily relaxes, the entire order of the world will fly in pieces. Then the art of Kafka, resolving the tensions near to psychosis, reveals a different reality of our natures from the projected ego-immortality of most great art.)

The worst sin is not to suffer at least the greatest anxiety—not to expose oneself to one's temptation, as Joseph K. in *The Trial* refuses to open the door of the lumber room, behind which the fateful beating is unfolding. This self-torment is the "one suffering that could be avoided." Primarily, 99 means that the repression is weak and the breakdown imminent, but a total cure therefore all the easier; religiously: to glorify the world even if I must create out of my own flesh and blood a world to glorify.

Beyond the masochism, that leaps to the eye, to come close to the use of the masochism that constitutes, not the strength, but the unique witnessing of Kafka. His strength is clear: The Tree of Life, the prayer to humanity, the refusal to be deceived, accomplishing the negative. His weakness is clear: the need for punishment, the fear to surrender, the survival of certain taboos, and the practical acceptance of social institutions. But the witnessing is the dogged courage with which he will not extricate these strands, yet will not give them up: this calls into question my own convictions, not seeking to refute them. It is an artist who by dogged courage justifies the world. It is the one great artist who disheartens and bores every reader yet whom we do not dismiss with anger and contempt; but we come to love his dogged courage.

17. Laborious Creation

> 94. One's idea of the infinite extent and fullness of the cosmos is the reward of a combination of laborious creation and perfectly detached self-consciousness, both pushed to their uttermost extremes.

Is this not admirable, beautiful, and—dogged?

He complicates and extravagates the world in order to prove its glory and justify it; he detaches himself in self-consciousness in order to prove that it is the world that is glorious, no creature of his. In order to glorify the world, keeping his eyes open, he fails to justify himself, to release himself from his own willfulness. Is not this something new in religiousness: to be willing to endure in Hell in order that, for God's sake, there should be a Paradise? Will there be a Father who can endure this child, who makes allowances for him? Let us compare the child with another God-justifier, Job: presented at last with the infinite extent and fullness of the cosmos, Job is released from his weakness: partly identifying himself with the father, partly liberated from willfulness by the surge of images and dreams; the profundity of the drama is that it is *both* these, the poetry being great enough to combine them. But this dry little child, just by presenting to himself the infinite extent and fullness of the cosmos, becomes strong—and solitary. By this method he will not identify himself. To reach such an attitude, as I shall argue later, there is required more than an authority of the father, but also a fearsome destructiveness of the child. Except that if there is love in the world, he will—all unknowing, despite himself!—sink into it, as the drop into the sea.

We come now to a very characteristic business of Kafka: to push the opposites to their uttermost extreme. He well knows—though most of the critics seem not to know it—that this creates a convenient space-in-between, humorous, easy going, large enough in which to swing a world. It is made beautifully explicit in the vastness and absolutism of China. (*The Great Wall*):

> . . . If one should draw the conclusion that in reality we have no
> Emperor, he would not be far from the truth. . . . There is perhaps no

people more faithful to the Emperor, . . . but the Emperor derives no
advantage from our fidelity. . . . The result of holding such opinions
is a life on the whole free and unconstrained; by no means immoral,
however . . . but yet a life that is subject to no contemporary law. . . .
This attitude . . . is certainly no virtue. All the more remarkable is
it that this very weakness should seem to be one of the greatest
unifying forces among our people; indeed, if one may dare to use the
expression, the very ground on which we live. To set about establishing
a fundamental defect here would mean undermining not only our
consciences, but what is far worse, our feet.

The intolerable tension of absolute contrary demands is—the simple ground
under our two feet, the indissoluble alliance of our natural morality, the inde-
structible: freed from those alien laws.

But in order that we, we Chinese, we dogs, we mice, may enjoy the joys of
this world, it is necessary that some one, our Josephine, our singer, our Kafka,
study the laws for us and demonstrate their contrary absolute demands, and
explore with laborious creation the infinite fullness and extent, and maintain
himself in perfect self-detachment with neither surrender nor identification.

This easy going antinomianism, this justification *à bon marché*, is capital
for the concern, the unconcern, of Kafka. We *are*, he says,

We are nihilistic thoughts arising in God's head.

The inhabitant of the simple ground is pre-eminently Sancho Panza, and
Kafka tells us about Sancho as follows: He succeeded

. . . in so diverting from him his demon, whom he later called Don
Quixote, that his demon thereupon set out on the maddest exploits
which, however, for the lack of a preordained object, which should
have been Sancho Panza himself, harmed nobody. A free man, Sancho
Panza philosophically followed Don Quixote on his crusades . . . and
had out of them a great and edifying entertainment.

And again, there are *Parables*:

All these parables really set out to say merely that the
incomprehensible is incomprehensible. . . . But the cares we have
to struggle with every day: that is a different matter . . . "Why such
reluctance? If you followed the parables you yourselves would become
parables, and with that rid of all your daily cares." "I bet that also is a
parable." "You have won!" "But unfortunately only in parable." "No, in
reality: in parable you have lost."

In reality, rid of cares! in parable they are absolute, hopeless, intolerable. I submit that this is the most delicious statement of antinomianism. It is by the author of *A Penal Colony*, of *The Trial, The Metamorphosis*, and *The Burrow*—those parables.

Then I think we can add to the witnessing of this author, to his dogged courage in the hopeless fettering that he wills not to extricate, the easy-smiling world that he opens for the rest of us, as he laboriously creates: a region wide enough to live a life. But *only* a life, without angelic presumptions.

18. The Process of Life

> 98. We, too, must suffer all the suffering round us. What each of us possesses is not a body but a process of growth, and it conducts us through every pain, in this form or in that. Just as the child unfolds through all the stages of life to old age and death (and every stage seems unattainable to the previous one, whether in fear or longing), so we unfold (not less deeply bound to humanity than to ourselves) through all the sufferings of this world. In this process there is no place for justice, but no place either for dread of suffering or for the interpretation of suffering as a punishment.

This contains no error. We can learn each phrase of it with confidence.

To the extent that a man is in a state of sin, quite independent of guilt, he will read suffering as it is written; to the extent that he has eaten of the Tree of Life he will read for it "bliss." The extent is for each man simply a question of fact.

19. Faith

The last aphorism contains two parts:

> 104a. "No one can say that we are wanting in faith. The mere fact of our living is in itself inexhaustible in its proof of faith." "You call that a proof of faith? But one simply cannot not live." "In that very 'simply cannot' lies the insane power of faith; in that denial it embodies itself."

The mere fact of living is the present experience of existence: it is an omnipresent question-resolving "natural operation," with whatever structure and content it happens to have in any case. The argument is not dissimilar to Descartes' *Cogito ergo Sum*, except that it is not limited to thinking. But indeed, if we go further and read for "living," "eating of the Tree of Life" (however sour and puny a sample of the fruit), then we see why the proofs can be called "inexhaustible," for this life is invention itself.

What he means by faith is not clear. It is possible that he means the faith that one has the strength adequate to the knowledge, therefore one can be justified. But such a faith is very dubious, whether with regard to one's freedom and courage or by inference from experience. (Kafka, par excellence, knows this.) Such probabilities, and improbabilities, are not made a metaphysical certainty by the experience of the present moment.

But the conclusion follows if we define faith other-wise: Faith is the consciousness that destiny is providence. Different persons have a greater or less awareness of destiny, for instance, that their character is destiny and always leads them into the same situations. And some persons notice the operation of providence, for instance, that God takes care of fools and drunkards. In general most persons (I myself) have no persistent awareness that destiny is providence. But if I am aware of my present moment, must I not bear witness that it is the end result of the long process of time; and that it has brought me—safely, so to speak—to not less, and not more, than I am? These two are brought together in my experience of the present moment, not without thanks and praise.

> 104b. You do not need to leave your room. Remain sitting at your table and listen. Do not even listen, simply wait. Do not even wait, be quite still and solitary. The world will freely offer itself to you to be unmasked; it has no choice; it will roll in ecstasy at your feet.

By listening he means silencing your questions and demands and letting come to you the experience for which conceptions rise in the soul, as a melody rises from one knows not where in response to a contour of the hills. And by not listening he means to silence even these conceptions, for they are the ideas that generate willful demands. To be quite still means to accomplish the negative, to create for the living moment the fertile vacuum. ("Solitary" is not true in general but only for his weakness.) You do not need to leave your room, it is a good sample of all the space there is.

The world will freely offer itself, for there it is. It will roll in ecstasy: that is, with all the violence of the creation from the beginning of time, blooming, in freedom, into the next moment.

20. Concluding Remarks

Such is, according to my judgment, the strength and weakness in Kafka's *Aphorisms*.

The strength is in: 1. Patience that draws on the in-destructible element. 2. The Tree of Life, the natural operation, the certainty of the ground underfoot. 3. The indissoluble alliance of mankind. 4. The dogged glorifying of the world while not succumbing to any identification. 5. Accomplishing the negative by drawing strength from the positive.

All these are coiled into one strength.

The weakness we can pass by; it is the subject of much of the rest of this book.

Franz Kafka was not a master theologian, yet a very remarkable one. He was not great because he makes too many errors inconsistent with his strength; therefore he lacks authority, his least word does not command respect and predispose to assent. (Where we want not reasons but help it is a disadvantage to have to maintain an open mind.) It is not that he is lacking in system; some of the greatest, like Socrates, Paul, or Pascal, are lacking in system, necessarily, because their daily lives and emotions, of which religion is nothing but the form, were not bent to method and literature. It would be absurd to look for system in the tentative formulas of Kafka; yet he is systematic enough. But he is inconsistent; in the most important issues he contradicts his strength and would mislead.

Yet remarkable. His theology is original—I do not mean that he says something novel; in first philosophy novelty is not exactly a merit. He is original because his theology is the outcry of his own existence. But in this there is nothing remarkable, for all important religious writing is the cry of existence. Yet remarkable and original in the language, the occasions, and the concepts: as if he were an amateur—he was not an amateur—who had never seen a book. But this is again his refusal to make an identification, not to speak of a submission. If he comes to an agreement with traditional wisdom, this must be shown afterwards by a glossator. Is even this remarkable and important— for many modern writers reject traditional language?

Yes! because in our times if religious writing does not, for a time, start afresh so, in language and concept (of course not in the problems), and only at the end come to bear a resemblance to traditional theology—writing that does not do this proves useless to us; and whatever its intention as scholasticism, it does not help us read the traditional theology. Surely the fault here lies completely with the traditional theology, that is with the modern formulations in that language: because here as everywhere we must judge by the fact, and those formulations are not heard as the cry of existence. Yet existence cries out, nevertheless.

Kafka, though feeling, as he says, "a certain melancholy, uncertainty, unrest, a certain longing for vanished ages, darkening the present" (this longing itself is a thrice-familiar cry)—nevertheless Kafka writes religiously, and in the depths of a superego plight, and will not use the concept God, hardly the concepts Father and Master, Grace, Creature, Penance. In *The Castle*, for instance, there is a single mention of the Count West-West (what is our concern with such distant powers?). Indeed, his most common traditional terms, Diabolical and Evil One, belong precisely to the strain of his weakness; not that the problems do not exist, but that in these very problems he betrays that he was not free, and therefore he did not face the occasions with his customary "laborious creation."

I am not saying that it is a convenient thing that we must rely on such individual language, but heavens! if in this field we do not affirm the facts, where will they be of any use whatever?

So Kafka and Rilke, to name another, are remarkable and important religious writers for us, where Barth or Schweizer, who are almost masters, are not (and this is why they are not masters). The *occasions* of the writings of Kafka and Rilke are common to us; it is our familiar existence that they are the cry of: the proof of it is the extraordinary attention that is paid to such puzzling and private songs, much as the Mice Nation listen to their Josephine.

Post-Christian Man

It is evident that the Americans are no longer a Christian society in any important sense. Their vital dogmas, tinged with superstition, are scientific; their ethics, rapidly changing, are the product of economic and urban institutions that are already only distantly related to Christian ideas. We are Post-Christian men. This must be a very important fact, and yet not much attention is paid to it—what more striking proof that people are not Christians than that they don't bother much whether or not they are Christian or Post-Christian! And perhaps this indifference is one of the striking characteristics of being Post-Christian! Ministers of religion in their sermons of alarm usually speak as though they were speaking to Christians, or sometimes, more luridly, as though they were speaking to pagans, backsliders; but their sermons are irrelevant, because they are speaking to Post-Christians.

To delineate this interesting state of being, let us ask what it was to be Christian and what has become of that. The term "Christian" was applied to a complex of attitudes and notions that became signal at various periods and that always formed an uneasy unity which theologians organized in various ways. It was a complex infinitely rich, composed of personalities and social movements, literature and controversy, laws and buildings, etc., etc. But for our purposes let us single out half a dozen important articles of belief, which we might arrange in a rough chronological order as follows: Christianity has held that:

(1) There is a new heavens and new earth. (Mark and Paul.) A Christian is a man reborn in a new flesh, and bearing witness by his presence, his affirming, and his acts of love. He lives by waiting in the last days.

(2) The history of the world is a theodicy unfolding the City of God. (John to Augustine and Erigena.) Jewish history, Roman history, and cosmic history have been parts of this process. A Christian acts in this world in imitation of the patterns of paradise.

(3) Dreading death, man has an immortal soul, and a Christian is personally ransomed to live immortally happy. (Romanesque period and Anselm.)

(4) Through the Church a Christian belongs to a universal community of Christendom, which inspirits and gives meaning to society in all its parts and

is destined to embrace the world. This involves converting the heathen abroad, and the interpenetration of sacred and secular at home. (Period of the "medieval synthesis.")

(5) An individual man, by his resolute will against sin, demonstrates himself to be a Christian and a member of the Church. (Later Reformation and Counter-Reformation.)

(6) Besides these, Christianity has importantly mediated into Western civilization such attitudes of the old Roman Law and the Hebrew prophets as universalism, philanthropy, and the tempering of personal violence. A Christian is the loving brother of all mankind.

Through the centuries of Christianity these almost incompatible notions have managed to cohere, uneasily but always recognized and respected. They have been theologized as if they were all implicit from the beginning; and sometimes they have been as if miraculously united in saintly persons.

In recent times, however, there has been a change. Some of these properties of Christianity have so strongly and universally established themselves in our culture that there is no point in attributing them to a special group of believers—the Church is no longer militant—and indeed they have come to look strangely un-Christian. Other properties, however, now seem archaic, eccentric, and even to be disvalues, so that the expression "a Christian" almost connotes, as Dostoevski foresaw, an idiot. I think that this parting of the ways increasingly characterizes the past century. By "Post-Christian" I mean the *falling apart of the complex of Christian notions,* so that they no longer balance, limit, and inspirit one another. Some Christian attitudes have historically fulfilled themselves and have begun to seem anti-Christian. Others have begun to seem irrelevant. Nevertheless it is assumed, without inquiry, that the old global unity still exists. It is the tensions and the paradoxes of this situation, rather than any new idea or image that we experience as Post-Christian.

2.

Consider first some Christian tendencies that have fulfilled themselves in anti-Christian form.

The conception of Modern Science, which I have described in a previous essay, as an infinitely self-accumulating and self-improving system, is, I think, a Christian one. It is like the old Augustinian theodicy, the notion that the history of the world is a process unfolding the City of God, and it is the part of a Christian to inhibit or otherwise detach himself from natural satisfactions and to imitate the abstract patterns. God's purpose is replaced by the consensus of scientists, but this does not make their activity any more humanly pragmatic, for scientists are interested in solving the problems of Science. The psychology of both scientist and priest is objective and obsessional, frowning on spontaneous responses and rejecting other methods than the proper ritual discipline as essentially irrelevant if not wicked. Both nobly propose Truth and Beauty as absolute aims and models, and promise happiness for mankind; but these goods are attainable only through strict observance. Among the folk, modern science has replaced Christianity as the chief object of superstition. The transformation from "idealism" to "materialism," in which the revolution-ists of the eighteenth and nineteenth centuries had such high hopes, has not mattered much for true believers; for our empiricism is detached from ordi-nary experience and its products are imposed on ignorant people. We can say that both priest and scientist give forth matter sacramentally improved; the Church, having a religious background, has given psychological techniques for well-being, whereas Science, with a background of industrial arts, abundantly produces scientific technology.

In the heroic age of science, in the sixteenth and seventeenth centuries, the scientists, as natural philosophers, were in rebellion against the ritual order and turned, as a band of rebels, to personal contact with personified Nature who provided them a new ethic. But when the enterprises of science combined with the "Protestant ethic" and became bureaucratized, and then became the dominant system of ideas, the theodicy and its service again came to the fore. It would be absurd, of course, to call modern science Christian—indeed, the scientific miracles have beat out the Christian miracles and have destroyed Christianity—but the present attitude of both scientist and folk is comprehensible only on a firm foundation established by one successful ten-dency of Christianity: belief in the progress of an objective abstract entity.

Another closely related example of anti-Christianity established by the fruition of Christianity is our economic relations of production and con-sumption, in the line of development famously traced by Max Weber as the Protestant Ethic and the Spirit of Capitalism. I do not think that Weber gives enough weight to the psychological factor of the individual anxiety felt by the pre-Lutheran and early Lutheran saints when reduced to a simply per-sonal relation to God, unmediated by old institutions, and therefore to their need to internalize a new abstract system. Losing their community organs and their local intercessors in heaven, men fall back on Augustinian, imperial, Christianity to cushion the new individualism.

But when we extend the line of economic development further than Weber did, to the present system of semimonopolies and state collectives, and when we find that the Calvinist virtues of asceticism, rationality, individual self-help, etc., have been transformed precisely into their opposites—a high standard of living, various kinds of boondoggling and feather-bedding, and the morality of Organization Man and bureaucrat—nevertheless the under-lying moral demands of attending to business, righteously one-upping one's fellows, and disciplining one's animal and communal self, are the same as when it was the Lord's work that was to be done. At least from Adam Smith on, the system of rational business accommodations has again been seen to be a theodicy working itself out independently of any human wishes. And outside the strictly business world, we can go back a century earlier and see the lineaments of our mature corporate system and its mores. Pascal's satire on the Jesuits sounds exactly like a description of the techniques of Madison Avenue. He rightly called this system anti-Christian, but it certainly grew out of Christianity.

Still another example of anti-Christian results of significantly Christian tendencies is the development of modern national and world-wide conform-ity. Nationally, the modern style of conformity began in the sectarian exclu-siveness of Protestant or Counter-Reformation small towns, with their stern disciplining of animal expression. In the course of time, this Christian norm has become the national norm of behavior—as men's business suits seem to carry on a clerical cut; (but of course on a national scale it has become non-Christian and nonascetic, simply a respectable coloration, without sacramen-tal community meaning. On a world-wide scale, the European conformity has spread also by the proselytizing and crusading zeal endemic in Christianity from its early days. The spreading empires of Christendom have been differ-ent from the other empires of history, which either let be and taxed or wiped out and resettled or forcibly enslaved; but the Christians have had to convert by various means. Under modern conditions of economy and communica-tions, however, this Christian universalism has sloughed off its other Christian content as irrelevant, and what we export is our machine tools, mass culture, and other secular goods. (Faiths we tend rather to import.)

The contrast is striking when it is a subordinated minority that promotes Christian universalism, as in the sit-ins of the Southern Negroes and their friends. Then nearly the full spectrum of Christian attitudes is carried along, including brotherly love, singing of hymns, militant pacifism, personal purity of motive, and almost millennial expectations.

It is worth mentioning that in the very long run Christian pacifism has not had the effect, as Nietzsche claimed, of shackling the strong in the interests of the resentful weak. Rather, it has subordinated all persons and local commu-nities to the concentrated power of the constituted authorities that alone bear arms. We have little personal violence, but only big wars with plenty of slaugh-ter of noncombatants. Correspondingly, philanthropy, grounded in Christian charity for the sick and poor, has in modern conditions been taken over by social welfare, which precisely insulates the giver from the creaturely facts of life.

So Christian universalism, Christian pacifism, and Christian charity have ironically fulfilled themselves in Antichrist.

3.

Perhaps superficially, perhaps essentially—it is hard to know—mankind seems to be galloping toward the condition of a social beehive or termitary, in which individual uniqueness, creaturely contact, neighborly charity, the satisfactions of local community, and the high culture of real cities, are all increasingly irrelevant. In this process the tendencies of Christianity have certainly been influential. A conformist and universal population, working to keep running a busy economic machine, and controlled by an abstract and normative science: this is socialized human nature. One cannot help thinking of Auguste Comte's remarkable simulacrum of Christianity in his Positive Religion.

Yet such a religion of socialization is, of course, also the very contrary of Christianity; for Christianity is a personal relation of the creature and his creator, it is individual saintliness and neighbor love, existential commitment, the folly of the Cross, spontaneous illumination. In its history Christianity has known love feasts, speaking with tongues, martyrdoms, chivalric honor, and militant conscience.

To be sure, whether man can be essentially socialized or not, forming almost a new species from anything we have known, is a question for future history. If essential socialization is impossible, what will become of our present gallop toward such an absurd state? There seem to be two alternatives: either the unbearable heightening of anxiety, total apathy and anomie, and catastrophic violence; or the revolt of nature, existential disgust, conflict, and new religion.

4.

Let us consider, now, a couple of important Christian notions that have become eccentric or archaic, and no longer belong to Post-Christian man.

For the first time in nearly two thousand years Western people are losing their belief in the personal immortality of their souls. It is astonishing how little this extraordinary change of opinion is mentioned by the writers, as if there were a tacit agreement to overlook it. In the Old Testament there is not much belief in such immortality, nor evidence of longing for it—the Resurrection in Ezekiel is a different matter; but from Rabbinic times it has been a fundamental article, and the apocalyptic resurrection of Jesus was rapidly transformed into a theory of after-life in heaven. In some periods, as during the building of the great Romanesque crypts, the dread of death, the cultivation of relics, and the longing for immortal personal salvation seemed to be the chief business of Christian society; as again during the waning of the Middle Ages, with greater emphasis on black spirits and damnation. These wishful thoughts of survival and the intercession of dead saints were an important cause of the immense efflorescence of Christian plastic art; and our Western poetry, from medieval times deep into the Romantic movement, is marked by the fear of dying and the esthetic triumph over death. I doubt that love-death would have been so sought if it did not promise immortal bliss. So, too, Augustinian theodicy and modern both, imitating their abstract patterns, have been vivified by the sense that the thinker, the image of the Creator, is also a creator of images and in them proves his immortality. Among religions, Christianity has most cultivated the Holy Spirit, infuser of life into the dead. It could be said that Christianity extended to all folk the immortality of Fame and Muse that in antiquity had been reserved to heroes, emperors, and poets.

What can it mean that in recent times this energy of despair, and of reaction by denial, is waning? One does *not* have the impression that it is because of animal satisfaction and self-fulfillment in meaningful action, which would be the normal means for draining energy from impossible wishes. On the contrary, one has the strong impression that death is being kept out of mind and out of feeling. This appears clearly in our urban arrangements and entertainment, our hospitals, our funerary institutions, our popular optimistic philosophy. We seem to have here a character-neurotic repression of a psychoneurotic fantasy; this may be regarded as a technique of socialization, and perhaps also our peculiar American socialization is needed to make this repression stick.

But even more absent from contemporary ideas is the primary notion of Gospel Christianity, that there has *already* occurred, in the incarnation and resurrection, the transformation of the physical and psychical worlds into a pneumatic new heavens and new earth. This psychotic belief bloomed in an apocalyptic climate. (I say "psychotic" technically, without valuation, to mean contrary to the evidence of the senses. Whatever else it is, religion is, as Freud said, a socially acceptable psychosis; but I need hardly point out that the deliveries of some psychotic states are pragmatically truer and better than usual "reality" and "prudence.") As early as John, this material belief began to be toned down to the psychological reality of love or the metaphysics of otherworldliness plus allegories; nevertheless, through two millennia it has always revived in evangelical and millennial movements, especially in the face of vast natural and man-made calamities, and has been attended by miracles with their peculiar pneumatic physics. Now, here again, it is astonishing how in the face of our recent and threatening calamities, there have been so few and tiny millenarian impulses. The mass-evangelism of Graham or Buchman is entirely moral and sentimental; it is uncosmological, no miracles are reported. The psychological Christianity of confident living and positive thinking is even less messianic. So total, apparently, has been the victory of the rival scientific superstition, thin as it is! To my mind, *this present failure of millenarian nerve is an irrefutable proof that Christianity has ceased to exist as a living world faith.* If a Christian has not been reborn, he is nothing at all. But the religiously lifeless institutions of Christianity still do plenty of emotional damage to children and adolescents.

In our Post-Christian times, we have a vacuum of religious expectation; one would assume that in this vacuum people would be frantically busy about political changes toward a satisfactory reality to replace the vanished dream; or at least that the institutions of modern science had accomplished something, or promised something, in that direction. But no such thing. It is amazing. Can it be that the standard of happiness has fallen so low that the present-day "reality" seems better than a flight from reality? I prefer to believe that people are simply temporarily too confused by the complicated technology and social changes in which they are wandering, to be able to dream awake. Also, we have not yet recovered from the shell shock of the wars and the continuing colonial upheavals that have taken away the traditional world.

5.

In America, the vacuum left by Christianity is perhaps a new and promising factor. Especially among Protestants there is dismay at how the establishment of Christian notions has resulted precisely in anti-Christian life. Since the Reformers were more progressive theologians to begin with, their doctrines have come to the abyss sooner; being less relevant, the Catholics are now smug, and the editor of *America* has recently proclaimed that we are in "Post-Protestant" times and can enthusiastically share "in this fascinating thing we call America."

Conversely, the best of the Protestants are willing to conclude that the Christian notions most dear to them might be better served if they are no longer thought of as Christian, though nobody knows *how* to think about them. This is not a new story. Kierkegaard was saying it in the time of Hegel and Pastor Moeller. But Kierkegaard is first being heeded in the past thirty years, and Nietzsche, Gide, Wilhelm Reich, and other voices of Antichrist, including even Communists, have come to sound like truer Christians.

If I may judge from my not-extensive experience, there has been also a marked change of personnel. When I was young, a minister of religion was likely to be an ass, and seminarians were little better than morons, comparable to the military. Nowadays, many clergymen are brighter than average, and the theological students are among the salt of the earth. Rival secular careers, in law, science, teaching, politics, no longer seem more enlightened nor eminently relevant to an earnest and honest lad who consults his feelings about the world we live in. The ministry makes as much sense as psychiatry. And often on issues like pacifism, racial and social justice, or even attacking censorship or bad narcotics or sexual laws, the churches are the *only* traditional groups to speak up for common reason. This does not follow from their orthodox Christian tradition, but simply because, as Christians, they are more serious and therefore less afraid to be unconventional.

Indeed, some honest pastors can be said to be carrying on a holding operation. Rather than giving over their valuable real estate to secular hands that will use it worse, they are holding onto it, hoping that they will learn *what* to do with it. Creator Spirit come.

Beyond My Horizon

It's a rudimentary experience I choose as mine, as if I were a simpler animal who doesn't have a long human memory, nameless yearning, creature anxiety, synoptic vision, and abstract language. How do I fill the gaps and make sense to myself? There are things that I do and say ritually, that go beyond experience. I can read them off as sentences, but they are empty of content. They are not perceptions, meanings, or feelings. They are theological, "the substance of things unseen."

I do not "believe" these theological sentences, that is much too intellectual a term. Not that I am skeptical by disposition; I am rather gullible. I entertain as likely almost any esoterica that people tell me with conviction, whether telepathy, orgone boxes, the Eucharist, or the revelations induced by psychedelic mushrooms. Having no wonders of my own, I marvel at other people's. Writing this, I have a sudden fellow feeling for Hume, who said he would walk a mile to hear Whitefield deliver one of his revival sermons. Except that we won't use these ideas as premises for anything that we might responsibly say or do.

I don't have a "faith," that is much too factual and erotic a term. I think of Karl Barth, one of the few modern writers whom I always read with empathy and pleasure, surfing on the wave of his thought, and his beautiful style speaks right to me. But he had a kind of substantial love affair with Jesus; and either Jesus made him happy or his faith did. My experience contains no such fact or feeling and I am tolerably unhappy.

Rather, I go along exactly with Kant in his little book on religion, "within the limits of mere reason." What I say here was already well said by him, that sticking to finite chunks of experience, it is inevitable to say words that go beyond their horizons and relate them to what surrounds them. But there is no sense to the spatial metaphors of "beyond" or "surround" any more than to other prepositional metaphors like "above" or "within," or to Kant's own nominative metaphors "things in themselves" and "symbols." Conversely, however, there is nothing in my finite experience that *prevents* me from saying such words! This gives me a crazy freedom of speech that I otherwise lack. Freer and crazier than if I were superstitious or had a faith. But of course nothing follows from this freedom empty and crazy.

The agnostic way of being of Hume and Kant is out of fashion these days, so people do not remember the positive exhilaration of it. (Today, nonbelievers are atheists.) Since the theological sentences of agnosticism are empty, it is possible to pick and choose and shape them, as the Deists, Unitarians, Universalists, and Ethical Culturists did, to be edifying. Or for poetry. Or just to live on a little.

Let me say again what I don't mean and do mean. "*Le coeur a ses raisons que la raison ne connaît point.*" This is crashingly true, but it is not what I mean. Pascal meant deep impulse, specifically his Christian impulse, as when Lawrence said, "Follow your deepest impulse." It was high romance for a mathematician like Pascal to make Pascal's wager.

"*Credo quia absurdum.*" This is a powerful defiant idea, underlining the quite certain folly and Pharisaism of human judgments and moral values, and preferring to throw oneself on the Wholly Other. Writing about Ishmael and other outcasts in my twenties, I used to affirm the antinomian version of absurdity: let us rebel and sin in order to be touched by something divine, if only God's wrath.

> ANGEL: Hypocrite! do you not live and breathe by the daily gifts here and here given you?
> ISHMAEL: So *You* say! when this mask of the world is stripped away, then shall we have full joy!

Nevertheless, though I am still not impressed by the wisdom or morality of righteous society, I am no longer tempted to deny what I think I do know, nor to act imprudently on principle.

But I like the safeguard of the Negative Theology of Jewish and Islamic philosophers—and from a different angle, of the Taoists. That whatever we say, is not true of God, nor is the contrary true. Simply, God is not a body and I know only about bodies, including myself. I mustn't take them as idols, including myself.

And yet—and yet—Why should I be fastidious of idols? What difference does it make? "Manlike my God I make." It makes no difference. But idolatry is stupid, and try as hard as I can, I cannot be stupider than I am.

Psychoanalytically, the obvious interpretation of inevitable but empty religious ideas is that they are obsessional rituals, like hand-washing or touching lampposts—their real meaning is repressed. I agree. Kant himself was the type of an anal character, with his scrupulosity, his routine, his sometimes amazingly harsh and strict sense of duty, his classifying, his aversion to instinctual feelings.

Yet it was Kant. Through middle age and a good old age, his work flowed on spontaneous, vigorous, brave, endlessly inventive and continually maturing, minutely attentive and boldly synoptic, and with a fine rhythm of style. We have to ask if Kant's way of being obsessional is not a good way to cope with the nature of things, in order to live on a little. I repeat it: the proof of a sage is that he survives, he knows how. "To work out your allotted span and not perish in mid-career: this is knowing." (Chuang-tzu).

And there is something sweet in religious routines, once drained of the virulence of belief. The cozy religiosity of the Danes, benignly ineffectual, is a good background for guiltless sex and common-sense pacifism. Every human child is necessarily brought up among tribal myths old or new. We must of course use our wits as best we can and strictly affirm and act our best judgment; but it is harsh and imperious toward oneself to try to root out one's archaic symbols. Especially since in the field of myths, new is almost invariably worse.

Finally, there is a wide divergence between the agnostic Enlightenment and what has proved to be the history of positive Science. But from the beginning they had different aims. It was the idea of humanism and the Enlightenment—of Erasmus and Montaigne, Hume and Kant—that the purpose of philosophy is to get rid of superstition so that life can go on; philosophy has no content. But the idea of positive Science—consider the program and utopia of Francis Bacon—was to accumulate a system of self-correcting natural philosophy by which we can live happily, with a useful scientific technology.

Naturally, during the sixteenth and seventeenth centuries, when humanism and heroic science were undermining the orthodox dogma, they were close allies. Indeed, before and during the French Revolution, they were for a time disastrously identified; together, they seemed to *be* the Enlightenment. But the Rule of Reason enthroned at Notre Dame was bound to disappoint, if only because the scientists did not yet know enough.

Now two centuries later, however, when positive Science does know a wonderful and fearful amount, it has itself become the worldwide system of orthodox belief, heavily capitalized, recruited by a million trained minds—"there are more scientists alive today than since Adam and Eve." And it is hand in glove with the other powers-that-be.

It still disappoints, though its futurology promises infinite blessings. But to us threadbare men of letters, heirs of humanism and the Enlightenment, it is again the entrenched system served by a priestly caste, and it is again our duty to show how it is a superstition, so life can go on. (Oddly, the agnostic critique of Hume and Kant has become an intrinsic part of the orthodoxy, as conventional positivist logic.)

In his swan song, *The Conflict of the Faculties,* Kant spoke of philosophy as the "loyal opposition from the Left," whose duty was to harass the three positive Faculties of Law, Medicine, and Theology. I have no doubt that at present he would he criticizing the Faculties of Law, Medicine, and Scientific Technology.

For us who are thankful that we occupy only the ground that we cover with our two feet, the primary theological virtues are patience and fortitude, so said Kafka. (I think also of the comic portrait of Socrates firmly planted during the battle, not going out of his way to look for trouble, but every now and then giving a hard knock.) No doubt those who have a different kind of experience require different virtues.

Patience is drawing on underlying forces; it is powerfully positive, though to a natural view it looks like just sitting it out. How would I persist against positive eroding forces if I were not drawing on invisible forces? And patience has a positive tonic effect on others; because of the presence of the patient person, they revive and go on, as if he were the gyroscope of the ship providing a stable ground. But the patient person himself does not enjoy it.

In a passage that I often repeat, Goethe speaks of that patient finite thing the Earth. "The poor Earth!—I evermore repeat it—a little sun, a little rain, and it grows green again." It has a tonic effect on us, So the Earth repeats it, Goethe repeats it, and I repeat it.

Kafka himself, to be sure, was not persistent in his finitude. He was invaded by terrible paranoiac abstractions. (I take him as what he wrote.) Then his serene obsessional defenses broke down and he could not finish his stories.

Fortitude is to persist in one's task with an extra ounce of strength, after one has exhausted one's resources. As we say it in American, fortitude is to stay in there pitching. As I recall how often I have done it in bleak ball games and I have seen others do it, I realize it is a mystery.

But it must be a man's own ball game, exhausting his own natural powers, otherwise I will not get the extra ounce of strength, more than I have.—I learned from the most grievous event of my life, Matty's death five years ago, that it is useful to persist in doing what *is* one's own thing, exhausting one's natural powers very quickly when, in such a case, one has little grip on his own life. I wrote repetitive little poems about the one subject. And I was upbraided by an uncharitable lady for making literature out of the death of my only son. (My eyes are suddenly full of tears, but I will write down this *too*.) So I venture to give advice to other people in mourning: be sure that what you are doing is yours and persist in doing it; in everything else, willingly break down, suddenly bawl, run away if you feel like it.

Plato's Socrates defines courage as having an idea, and I suppose this helps one transcend his natural fear. But my hunch is that Socrates—it is in one of the early dialogues—said something less abstract: if one is *in* the situation, identifying with its meaning, he does not have a structure for running away; it does not occur to him, he is occupied. Then he will have an extra ounce of strength. He doesn't know from where; he has no leisure to ask.

I notice that I keep recurring to my authors of the concrete, the finite, the intrinsic: Socrates, Goethe, Kant, Kafka when he was well. It shows me again that I cannot learn anything different, and it shows that what I say is mine to say.

But I could spell it out as "developing" and it would come to the same thing. In my teens I was a Platonist and I wrote a long paper on the place of myths in the Dialectic Method: the plot was that it is the purpose of dialectic to bring us to a pause, paralyzed by the *narke*, the man-o'-war, and then there is a myth to revive us. But the form of Platonism to which I temperamentally gravitated was Leibniz: the concrete monad and its molecular *petites perceptions*,

—the dainty noise of drop on drop
accumulates to be the ocean's roar.

This seemed to me compatible with Freud whom I was also reading, as my only pornography.

Soon Berkeley and Hume, however, seemed to me even more like home. They were matter-of-fact. And I went backward from Plato to Socrates and Heraclitus and Parmenides. Kant, "of course," solved all the problems. When I was subjected to a heavy dose of McKeon's reading of Aristotle, for my purposes it was the same philosophy. Evidently, in these notes, I still think so.

I later learned just enough from the positivists and phenomenologists to steer my middle course between them, in the wake of William James, who was real American.

Meantime, I was a hungry reader of the neo-Protestants—I remember Nygren, Otto, Schweitzer, and Barth; and Maimonides, and Lao-tzu. These have somehow permitted me to say the magic I need, like Kant or William James or Rank, but unlike Aristotle or Freud.

No. As I now think of all of them, and scores of other great authors, what stands out is the common enterprise: how to explain (or explain away) the matter-of-fact, the erotic, the abiding, and the unknown. How it is and what to do. It is possible that being a philosopher sets it up this way; or it is possible that it is this way for everybody and philosophers cope by spelling it out. I don't know.

Faith is having a world-for-me. That my experience is given. That it will continue to be given: the Next is not the brink of a precipice. Its structure has consequences that I can draw; there might be evidence to clarify the meaning if I attend. By faith I am not caged in my finite experience; it has an horizon rather than bars; so I speak of it as "roomy enough." I am not alone, only lonely.

It is a latitudinarian notion of faith, like being sane. Nearly everybody behaves as if he had a world. A child runs headlong as though there will be gravity and ground, though he does not have nearly enough experience to believe this as certain as he acts it; it is built into his constitution. A speaker has a hearer in his language community, he does not think about it. Noah planted a vineyard because the Lord promised with his rainbow that something would come of it, there wouldn't be another flood. A scientist pursues his method as though the evidence was not planted to deceive him. I go to an orgasm by faith, I will not fall apart or not come down. We fall asleep by faith. I suppose there is nothing we do that we do not do by faith. "We live by faith."

I am paraphrasing Anselm's or Descartes' ontological argument: however we do proves faith. But there are no grounds for the faith. I cannot find anything in my experience that I would call faith. It is like Kierkegaard's Postman: one cannot tell, looking at him, that he is a Christian.

Perhaps the animal feeling of faith is trust, and perhaps at first, faith and trust are the same, like a child's trust in grownups or a dog's trust. These look animal. There is feeling on the face of the Adam of Michelangelo, trust already clouded with melancholy. But it is the genius of our families and institutions to destroy trust. Only God can destroy faith.

The Reformers seem to be right in saying that faith produces works but there is nothing that we can do to give faith. We can certainly do a good deal to remedy institutions that destroy trust.

"To them who have shall be given; from those who have not shall be taken away even that which they have." Yes. The muscular lad plays rough and gets still stronger. A lovable person is loved and becomes still more open, radiant, and lovable. A person who is not anxious profits from psychoanalysis; an anxious person can afford to profit very little. And faith yields works. But the error of Geneva is to institutionalize this unfair distribution, coming on like God, deciding who is elect.

Theological hope is expecting the impossible. It is a terrible risk; as Goethe said, "By acting as though the impossible were possible, you soon make the possible impossible."

Certainly, for unlucky people like myself, natural hope—imagining, wishing, expecting—is an utter curse. It is disappointment. This has so often proved itself to me that I have almost come to understand how it works. I entertain a wild hope before I have laid a groundwork, or even *instead* of making a practical plan. My fantasy is an abstraction not in touch with the real situation, and it keeps me out of touch with it. In the order of my wishes, a random promise becomes a heated vision; in the order of other people's behavior, it has been quite forgotten. Most often when I am hopeful, nothing at all eventuates. If something does happen to eventuate, I am overwrought and act foolishly.

I do better, and suffer less, if I act with nonattachment, doing what is technically correct, expecting nothing; or acting generously, casting bread on the waters, expecting nothing. And if anything eventuates, if I cope with it like a present fact rather than the fulfillment of a wish.

Yet my extraordinary ineptitude contains a clue. A man could not possibly succeed so poorly unless he needed to fail. Either I am afraid to get what I wish for, so I see to it that I don't; that is, my excessive hope is a built-in prudence. Or I have despaired beforehand that my wish is what I want, and therefore I do not go about it practically to succeed. Yes, for the crazy glow of my hope, not its substance, is the color of what I really want, which is not possibly in the offing. And the horrible sinking of my disappointment is not for what I wished for, but because I am again reminded that I am not in paradise.

Theological hope is not delusory but blind. It is for a new heavens and new earth and I do not know the content of such a change. As I live from day to day, I do not feel any such hope, yet I live as if I had it.

> What do you want, my captain? what you want
> is impossible, therefore you must want nothing.
> "No. I am looking for the Northwest Passage to
> India; *if I had made the world,*
> *that would exist.*"

Love is the experience that takes me beyond experience. Love has a concrete object and feeling, but it exists by promising to continue beyond Here Now and Next. As Rilke's Unicorn "exists by the possibility of being," love exists by the possibility of becoming. Thus it is the only theological virtue that is not empty of content, and from which something follows in my behavior. And I think this is why it has a privileged position in orthodox theology: it incarnates the god. He who will come.

To make a familiar distinction, sexual lust is experienced as Here Now and Next, it does not include an indefinite hope. But this difference, though real, is transient, for happy lust very soon turns into sexual love or into love without sex. Conversely, I doubt that one can have a good time lusting unless he is prepared to risk loving, losing himself. Orgastic pleasure is already a risk that needs both trust and faith. We love what has by-passed our blocks, so unfamiliar energy is released, that feels like risk.

Theologians make too much of the distinction between *agape*, self-giving self-losing love, and *eros,* love that tries to satisfy oneself and complete oneself. For also the latter is self-losing. And common language has always refused to make the distinction. Simply, the beloved fills the field of experience—"I am That"—and because I am diminished, new energy wells up, undomesticated, indefinite in meaning. It is crazy hope, except that now it seems to be practical, possible, having something to work at.

All love, whether sexual, parental, communal, or compassionate, is delusional. There will be no such ever-new world, if only because my anxiety reasserts me and protects me. (Saints, of course, can keep going.) But whether it is delusional or not, love is psychotic. It can be quietly psychotic, as I reasonably and prudently give myself away piece by piece.

Love creates new faith. Faith is given by grace, and love does the work of grace. It does so by actively making, or making up, a world for me in which I trust and where hope has substance; paradise, where there is no difference between grace and everyday practical action.

I notice, as I write this, how well it is all told by the Christian myth of Jesus incarnate as love and redemptive by giving himself, instituting a new heavens and new earth. But by my character I naturally prefer a literal analysis to the beautiful story.

I say "I love you" more than I do, not lying,
it's an hypothesis I hope will be surprisingly confirmed.

But there is no rime or reason for you to love me too.
Don't you say anything at all. Just be.

I like to announce my intentions with a fanfare of six trumpets.
I'm tickled when I sound like an old book.

The type of self-giving love is grown-ups' love of children. The unique gift that children give us is the opportunity to do for them, with no claim of return, therefore no resentment, therefore no guilt. It is depressing that this glaringly obvious fact is not told in the stories of God the Father, that *He* has a lot to be grateful for because of His creatures. Instead, He is represented as paternalistic; His guidance is very like a command, exacting obedience; His feeding seems to expect thanks.

On the other hand, those who, unlike the Creator of the animals, want to limit the number of children born, so that children may inherit an uncrowded Earth—they also tend to overlook that caring for children is one of the few things that make life important from day to day, and there ought to be enough opportunity to go around. Friendship and neighbor-love are pretty complicated to manage. The ideal love of the artist or scientist is a daily fact for only a few. Love of society or mankind is abstract and begins to stink of idolatry. But everybody can love children.

Compassion, the virtue of the physician, is another spectacularly self-losing love. It is psychotic denial; the physician denies that the patient is really as he is. (Psychoanalytically, the compassionate man refuses to accept his own maiming.) And like other lovers, the physician sometimes transforms the world by making his denial stick. He puts it into question, which is crazy after all, finite experience or love? But in my observation, physicians are deeply angry people: "How dare you walk into my office in that condition?"

—A lifeguard, when he rescues someone, curses.

He has nothing to show for having lost himself. It was just remedial.

When Isaac was saved on Mt. Moriah, Abraham must have gone into a towering anger. The Bible, written as God's history, tells us nothing about this. All that heartache for nothing.

Beauty too proves something beyond experience, but it is not practical. The forms of paradise without the matter. As Kant put it, if the forms are adapted to our experience, we cannot experience the adaptation but only the pleasure of it. The forms seem purposeful for us, but they have no purpose. Plato speaks of beautiful forms as memories, of the jewels in the court of Jove.

Beauty mild is lively, but strong is terrible. When a strong beauty is just to see or hear but not desire, it makes me cry because paradise is lost—and there is nothing to do. If it is something to desire, then it is at peril that I resist what attracts me, however dangerous, unavailable, inappropriate, or perverse I may judge it to be. I must love it and suffer rather than be bored and caged as the horizon closes in. I cannot choose my paradise to be convenient, moral, or prudent. Pursuing the beautiful, I become still more inept.

And then it is notorious that the beautiful appears only at the right esthetic distance and nearness. With art works, a good critic chooses the distance at which they show to best advantage. But with beautiful people, it is hard to attain the right distance, and impossible, I have found, to maintain it. One cannot eat beauty or fuck it. I have often lapsed into orgasm because the tension of beauty became intolerable for me. I have to sign it off.

The beautiful is not abstract; I cannot believe it is a delusion, and must respond with grief or desire; but it is only an esthetic surface, not practical for me.

It is like King Macbeth in the play: he is not an illusion of a king, he is a real king; but he is made of words, and one must not jump onto the stage and join in the battle. On the other hand, those contemporary plays in which I am supposed to join in, are not beautiful, and I get more excitement from action on the streets or with my friends. An artist can stage my beauty, but he cannot stage my paradise. A politician tries to stage my paradise, and it is the same purgatory.

I notice that I sometimes use the language of psychoanalysis and rarely a few terms of existential philosophy, but on the whole I prefer the language of orthodox theology to talk about the invisibles. Using words like faith, hope, love, paradise, purgatory, nonattachment, vocation, Way, Creation, koan, holy spirit, mana, Messiah, idol, Void, God, Karma, incarnation—mostly from the West, with a scattering from the East or from primitive religions.

These theological terms have been in use for thousands of years far and wide. We must assume that they have met a need, and they have certainly been polished by handling. Naturally they are resonant in a poet's vocabulary. They are very ambiguous and have been tormented by interpretation—though perhaps not more so than recent psychoanalytic and philosophical terms—but the contrasting interpretations are themselves ancient and have been spelled out in schisms and heresies. Hundreds of fine brains have been busy about it, with millions of adherents, and much bloodshed to show that they meant something or other.

If I use this language when I talk to a person brought up in a Christian sect, we often quickly come to an earnest conversation about important matters of life or death. Using the other languages with no matter whom proves to be pedantic, cruder, and more polemical. To be sure, some Christians are puzzled and disappointed that, since we understand one another, I do not come out where they do. Richard McKeon, the Aristotelian, used to have this trouble with the neo-Thomists at the University of Chicago during the thirties; they charitably called him the Anti-Christ, because by making better sense of the texts he sometimes cooled off prospective converts.

Needless to say, the ones who are irritated if I say "holy spirit" or "Messiah" are the Unitarians and Ethical Culturists. Having (once) struggled to get rid of superstitious beliefs, they cannot tolerate even the language of theology.

But young people these days like this palaver, which seems meaningful to them, though their language is rather more eclectic than mine. There is a difference from my own youth when such talk was considered moronic and we had no language at all to describe our hopes or troubles. (I hit on psychoanalysis.) In the peculiar historical crisis they are now in, some of the young are so alienated that they finally germinate crazy ideas and will add to the history of theology, if there is any further history of anything.

Paradise is the world practicable. I do not mean happy, nor even practical so that I can make it work, but simply that I can work at it, without being frustrated beforehand. A task to wake up toward. If I work at something, I am happy enough while I am doing it—I don't think about whether or not I am happy. And if I have worked at it, if I have tried, I sleep well even if I have failed.

This is a very modest criterion of paradise. To many people (how would I know?), there might be no reason to call such a world miraculous rather than the nature of things. For instance, John Dewey, who must have been a happy man, describes the nature of things as pragmatic through and through. But though I have faith that there is a world for me, I am foreign in it, I cannot communicate my needs, I do not share the customs, I am inept. So it is like a new world, I am as if resurrected, when the world is practicable. Therefore, until that moment, I put a premium on patience and fortitude.

The difficulties of the world, said Kafka, are mathematical. Given the spreading of space in all directions on a plane, it is infinitely more probable that our paths will diverge than converge. That you will be out when I phone and I will be out when you ring my bell—indeed, as Kafka points out, I was on my way over to your place. If several conditions are necessary for success, and each is moderately probable, the likelihood of their combination is wildly improbable. At every relay the message is distorted, and we did not speak the same dialect to begin with, but just enough of the same language so that we thought we were communicating. An unexpected stress, a lapse of attention, makes me vulnerable to other stresses, breakdowns, and accidents, so the rate of mishap is exponential. You get a flat tire and pull over, and step out over the edge and break a leg. These are the facts of life, no?

They are the facts of life for those who cannot abstract, who have only concrete and finite experience, like Kafka and me. We cannot take the vast numbers of possibilities as collective facts to manage, assigning them the infinite numbers Aleph, Beth, and Gimel. We cannot soar off the ground covered by our own two feet in order to survey the landscape. Since we have no values except in the tendency of what we are doing, we cannot make a plan of action to a far goal; we have no such goal, just the reality that we are dissatisfied. Then except by the miracle that events happen to converge in my poor Here Now and Next, my world is impracticable.

Fortunately, I have low standards of what is excellent as happiness.

In my politics—anarchist, decentralist, planning to leave out as much as possible, strongly conservative of simple goods that in fact exist—I have hit on a principle: Given the mathematical improbability of happiness, for God's sake don't add new obstacles.

In my morals, the cardinal sin is waste.

Consider the logistics of sexual satisfaction, a major part of happiness for most of us. Starting with the odd notion of sexual intercourse as a way of reproducing species, there is a rough carpenter's logic in dividing the human males and females equally, 50–50, to maximize the couplings; and then to attach a strong instinctual drive so that the animals will seek one another and persist in accomplishing the complicated operation of approaching, getting an erection, finding the hole, being receptive, and so forth. But a desire that is attached can become detached. The 50–50 possibilities are immediately drastically reduced by notions of beauty, inevitable childhood nostalgias and tabus, insecurities caused by factors that have nothing to do with sexuality, fetishism of other poles and holes. Since it is a complicated mechanism, Murphy's Law will certainly hold: if the parts can be put together wrong, they will be. And the machine has to operate in the frame of the rest of life and social life: being hungry and sleepy, sick, maimed, hampered by institutions and laws, poor and disadvantaged. Of course, since nature always operates with prodigal generosity and calculated waste, with a factor of safety in the thousands and millions, in spite of everything the human species is reproduced. The chances of personal happiness are trivial.

I have had half-a-dozen too brief love affairs (I am past 60), and in every case our virtue was to be practical, seizing chance opportunities, creating no obstacles, having no ideas in our minds, and trying hard to make one another happy. Or put it this way: I offer myself all at once as a package, with the absurd conditions of my ineptitude, my fantasies, my perverse needs, and my crazy hope. I must be either frightening or ludicrous. But the one who became my lover was not put off and took me at face value. *Then* we were practical. And I say proudly, when we could not continue indefinitely as is the essence of love, the causes of our separation were not our doing, they were mathematical.

This world is purgatory. I have plenty of proof that I am not damned—I understand that it is heretical to say so—but I am being tried, I have no notion why. Maybe that's what I'm supposed to learn. Faith, having this-world-for-me, means that I am not tried beyond my capacity. The Lord will keep me alive, until He won't.

I spoke of myself as "unlucky," but it's not exact. Rather, my destiny has been to be continually hungry, balked, and deprived, but never starved, a total failure, with nothing. Continually in pain and handicapped by it, rarely incapacitated. Since I cannot believe that God is playing games with me, He must be testing me for my own good. Perhaps He is protecting me from the excesses of happiness, but gives me enough to keep me alive. If this is the case, He doesn't understand me well. For I do not become foolish, lazy, or arrogant, but sensible and grateful when I am happy, whereas this purgatorial regime keeps me inept and griping. Maybe I am wrong and if I were very happy I would be arrogant. I can't conceive what that would be like.

Sometimes I have the thought that God means to provide for me better but He can't. There are shortages. He doesn't have the technique to deal with difficult cases like me. He does well, considering.

Or I have the bitter, but not hostile, thought that God is an impatient artist. His conceptions are sublime beyond anything, like War Horse or the Big Dipper. Or they are deliciously odd, like wrapping up a bundle of levers, tubes, and wires—mechanics, hydrostatics, and electronics—to be an animal. The execution is usually exquisitely minute. Yet there are clumsy or unfinished sentences, missing transitions, characters left hanging.

However it is, since I am in purgatory, I sing "Lead Kindly Light—one step enough for me." I often hum variations on the tune of it, half a dozen, a dozen, twenty, as I walk along.

There is a Creation, given to me. In which "everything is what it is and not another thing" (Bishop Butler).

I have tried to experience this givenness by dumb-bunny experiments. For instance, I am in the waiting-room, roughly aware of the rough structure of my chunk of experience. Can I notice the new that occurs that is not in that structure, and that will be given? A side door opens and a Puerto Rican woman in a green dress emerges. The effect is paranoiac; her appearance is portentous, a "delusion of reference," more tightly structured than all the rest. I dare not let the new be new.

The givenness of experience is what I do *not* attend to as I walk along, and there is always new space for it coming into being. Or when I pay attention to a meaning, and there is surprisingly more meaning, or less meaning, than I thought. Or I open my eyes, and I must take up from where I have been thrown. To Adam, I conjecture, the givenness of Creation was more apparent; everything happened to him for the first time. He lived in surprise. The givenness of Creation is surprise. But one cannot be surprised in the way one chooses to be surprised.

Kant, like Aristotle, held that existence is not a proper predicate that makes a scientific difference. There is no property of a real thing that may not be assigned to an imaginary thing and yet not make it real. Givenness is essential to any experience, but it cannot be experienced as such, nor scientifically measured. I must respect this opinion. Yet it is hard not to speculate that there is some extra energy in what is real rather than a possibility, a wish, or a dream. There are such heavy consequences from the reality of the real. Why could not this extra fire be measured, like the heat that changes water into steam? Possibility is one "phase"; add the elixir and wish is another "phase"; and existing is another "phase."

I cannot think something into becoming real. But a reality can certainly make me think.

The present, says Whitehead, is holy ground. It is strange. It not only has the crashing weight of reality, but, unlike the immobile real past, it is frothing into indefinite possibilities. It is the Burning Bush of Moses that was not consumed, out of which God named Himself "Who Am."

It is the aim of Zen Buddhist exercises to know presentness as an experience, and it is said to be a mighty revelation. But of course the koan that brings infinite enlightenment is just the specious present: "What is the Buddha?" "Pass the salt." I have not been enlightened. (How would I know?)

In our Western tradition, however, both of the Jews and the Greeks, we have methodically won a mighty revelation of the Creation which we sum up by saying, There is a nature of things. "*Felix qui potuit rerum cognoscere causas.*" By methodically studying the present appearances, we come to know, not the present, but the reality.

The Easterner seems to say that the present is God, the Westerner that it is the sacred text.

In *The Galley to Mytilene* I tried to distinguish the Actuality that weighs down the ship carrying the message of doom; the Reality of the confusion of the sailors in which the ship is foundering; and the Existing Moment on whose wings the new ship is bringing the message of clemency. But it is the same ship. I wrote, "Try! and I shall never be able to distinguish them."

History, what has happened and happens, has a privileged position over possibilities, noble ideas, lost causes. It is Creation, and thenceforth the given. And I can understand why Vico, Hegel, and the others have taken it to be God or His demiurge. But I think that these philosophers too much mean by history the history of institutions, nations, great men, Society. If God is history, it includes the history of me.

The Creator Spirit visits me and treats me as a familiar, but I have not experienced this. I have never felt inspired. (I think of Cupid and Psyche.)

After a work is finished, I can usually show in fine detail how it is made, how the parts hang together, and why it works; and I can often offer shrewd guesses as to why I made it, what it has done for me, and what it is for. But none of this is experienced by me while the work is in progress. And indeed, the words and their relations, and the choices to be made, are so indefinitely numerous that it is mathematically impossible that I could manage them, except to keep at it and to steer.

The coming of spirit is new creation. From nothing. In fields where I have any firsthand acquaintance, literature, social institutions, therapy, the relation of master and apprentice, the conservation of energy is not *prima facie*; it is farfetched. Nobody in such fields would think of it. The weight of evidence is overwhelming that there are continual flashes of creation, order made from nothing, against entropy. There are initiative, invention, and insight, and there are routine, falling apart, and entropy, but the entropy does not look like the dominant trend. We would not see the passage of the prophetic into the bureaucratic if we were not struck by the prophetic. Sudden and interesting. My bias is to deny the theory of conservation.

The question is if the physicists who affirm conservation are not using it as an *a priori* principle, proving beforehand by their language of equations and by their attitude toward the matter they work on, which is always *natura naturata*, never *natura naturans*. If they included themselves presently experimenting in their operational account of the experimental situation—as indeed the operational language requires—maybe they would come out differently. I don't know.

I think that a physics without the conservation of energy would look like Taoist magic. It might even be technologically productive. They say that the Master rode the whirlwind, the only one motionless in the storm.

I do not know of any sacraments that take me beyond experience. Love takes us beyond experience, but we love by grace, and I am puzzled at those who urge me to love my neighbor (though I think I ethically understand what it means to be a sociable, considerate, and cooperative neighbor).

Yet there are two religious exercises that confront the invisibles: confusion and prayer. It is odd to call confusion an exercise.

Experience is torn by confusion, and the darkness seeps through. "All have smiles on their faces, as if going up to the Spring Festival," says Lao-tzu, "only I am murky and confused." Murky, with the solemn face of an animal, not much in its mind. But confused because, unlike the animal, the sage has little grip on life, so his experience doesn't make sense, it has no tendency. He is standing out of the way.

The sage is at a loss on ordinary occasions; he does not need "borderline situations" in order to go blank.

Buddhists and Western contemplatives attain clarity by their nonattachment. Therefore I say they are abstract; by concentration they have willed themselves out of the stream. The Taoist sage is scattered—drowning—as he relaxes his grip on life. His insight becomes still dimmer than it was, and he is face to face with the void. Which may or may not yield up a treasure.

For those of us who are used to making sense, however, it takes a big deal to be baffled. Typically, we have tragic dilemmas, the clashing of absolute duties. To carry these through is very much a Western plot. In the *Gita*, when Arjuna is in a tragic dilemma, the Lord advises him to act with nonattachment, and evil will not cling to him any more than water to the lotus leaf. But the recipe of our Greek tragic plots is decently to affirm both contradictions, to sink into them deeper, till the protagonist becomes exhausted and then confused and then goes blank, all with a good conscience. As Kant says, it is one of the functions of God—not my business—to see to it that, if I do my duty, I can nevertheless be happy. "You do not need to finish the task," said Rabbi Tarfon more gently, "neither are you free to leave it off."

When we are baffled on a grand political, national scale, we hope for the coming of Messiah. For instance, the probability is high (95 percent) that atom bombs will destroy my friends and children. Our statesmen are not going to solve this (100 percent). Yet we persist in our institutions because of the coming of Messiah.

Statistically, as I grow old, I inevitably see more and more the death of my colleagues and dear ones, and I am confused. I understand that all flesh is as the grass, and very good. I see, too, the ever unique woe the survivors suffer—what we knew as moving and responding and initiating movement, is a worthless corpse, and it is too late for many things; yet I understand, I understand that we must try to mourn it through. I *understand* these two ideas but I cannot grasp them in one vision. It is too sublime for my finite experience and I become confused.

Prayer is the opposite exercise. I gather together my finite experience that is scattering in confusion. Here it all is, like an offering. Thus I disown my experience and again come face to face with nothing.

I do not pray for anything; whom would I ask? When I am not needy but happy, there is also no one to thank. But I pray by saying just how it is with me, and that is my prayer.

If we pay close attention to an isolated word, instead of scanning it in use in an ongoing sentence, it becomes odd and crazy. It is the same with any object that we gaze at intently, unless it is something beautiful and loved that keeps meeting us with new meanings. (But even such a thing soon becomes exhausted and looks monstrous.) So, by publishing my chunk of experience as literally as I can, I get rid of it.

Unfortunately, I have then thrown it to you, like the Orthodox confession in the village square.

When I do what is called "thinking," muttering to myself, I never use words like God or Faith, and they are in no way premises for my behavior. When I talk to other people, I sometimes use them, but not authentically; I might use such language, as I have said, to facilitate earnest conversation with a believer, though I am not a believer; or I might use it to cut short a boring conversation with an unbeliever, when I am too tired to explain myself better. When I write, however, I readily use this vocabulary and apparently seriously. How is this?

In "*Defense of Poetry*," I suggest a possible reason: "Maybe it is that when I think or talk to myself, I am embarrassed; but when I write, I am not embarrassed"—since writing is my free act. But there could be a simpler reason, more *prima facie,* more what it feels like; I use this language because it is a poetic convention, a traditional jargon, like wearing old clothes because they are comfortable. It means nothing. A free act is an empty act, except as an act. It means what is the genius of the language of billions of human speakers—not my business. As a writer my business is only to be as clear as possible and say a work that has a beginning, middle, and end.

Fiction

Iddings Clark

Lo! on every visage a Black Veil!

— Hawthorne

1.

In the assembly-room of the Northport High School they were celebrating the day before Christmas. All the children were present in the seats and a crowd of parents in the rear, and many graduates—some of whom were parents and some collegians home on vacation. The greatest hilarity and yet decorum prevailed, as always (so that many held that "the best part of the holiday season is the High School celebration"). This year was given a pageant of the Nativity, but only half-reverent, for at intervals a great burlesque Santa Claus rolled in, did tumble-saults, and so forth, while two end-men bandied jokes. All this was invented and directed by Mr. Iddings Clark, M. A., a teacher of English, a mind so spirited and original, with modern notions of Art (considering the community); and these masques have since been collected and printed. He was also in charge of the singing. To see him high on the platform, waving his arms, lifted everybody to enthusiasm; ordinarily a shy, almost reserved man, on such occasions he was red with pleasure and crowned with joy. Recent students of his, home from college, crowded beneath him to the platform. The song rang through the hall:

> Jingle bells! jingle bells!
> Jingle all the way!

—when suddenly, in the midst of a note, the conductor fainted away, and fell from the platform on his face. A cry of horror rang through the hall. The young men who had been at his feet now bore him up; they laid him on the platform and loosened his collar—he was pale—and dashed a glass of water in his face. His eyes fluttered open and he came to. "It's nothing," he said. "I see you all clearly. I am so happy having around me my friends so bright and close. Everything is exactly as it was."

The fact is that at the moment he was about to faint—perhaps because the blood rushed from his head, or that the electric light faltered, or for some other reason—at that moment he beheld over everything a cast of dark-ness. He saw on each face a veil. It was the Black Veil in the harrowing story of Hawthorne (from which I have taken the motto for this story). At one instant all faces were lit up—the lights overhead ablaze and the falling snow outside—and all printed with an indulgent smile at the well-known song; the next instant, though their mouths were open wide, the sinister shadow was everywhere apparent! A teacher of literature, Iddings Clark was only too well acquainted with Hawthorne's unnatural romance; twice a year for eight years he had read through with his classes the tale of the Minister's Black Veil. But although each time he came to that awful outburst "Why do you tremble at me alone? tremble also at each other!" he was so moved that the sweat appeared on his brow, he hardly thought that it would come to this. As if we experience works of art with impunity! The next instant he fainted away.

He sank in the dead faint and the light came and went. Then there was no more light and his soul was profoundly torn—accompanied by violent trem-bling and shaking in all his limbs, so that the students among whom he had fallen felt the body quiver in their hands. Thus quietened, he began to rise again through the zones of light, and he had a dream: that he was walking on Hooker Street in the snow and he saw, with a sense of appalling loneliness, that all the passers-by wore half-masks like highwaymen; then he entered the school and stark naked stood before his class. With a cry, he awoke.

2.

That night, Christmas Eve, Iddings Clark went to the home of Otto, an instruc-tor in chemistry, to trim the tree for his five-year-old daughter. To spend the night thus had become almost a custom. "Yet soon," said Otto, "she will be beyond the age for Christmas-trees."

"I am all right," said the English teacher in a strained voice. "Anyway there is a compensation for everything! How well Emerson put it!"

He was famous as a decorator of trees! For here also—as in the clever masques he composed—sparkled such fancy and originality, in the dramatic contrast of white lights and the deep boughs, not without a touch of wild wit, such as a jack-in-the-box in the heart of it. People dropped in at the house where he had decorated the tree.

"How strange your tree is tonight, Iddings!" cried the chemist. "It looks almost sinister; you can't mean to leave it so. All the tinsel, the silver globes, the dolls, candy-canes, and lights are crowded down in one corner, pellmell, without beauty or order. The rest of the tree is black. Why have you cut out a little recess in the dark boughs, and there put, so lonely, the silver star that is supposed to ride so brightly at the top? And around it four upright candles, one above, one below, on the left, and on the right, so rigidly?"

"We must snatch at least this much order from the riot."

"But the star itself is not balanced; it leans to one side . . . . Why did you arrange the candles in a cross? It doesn't fit Christmas."

"They are four soldiers."

Frau Otto looked attentively at the young man and said, "You are feverish—I can see by your eyes."

"Remember this afternoon—" said Otto.

"I've been neglecting a cold; it's nothing. Perhaps you could give me an aspirin tablet."

She dosed him with two, and a cup of hot milk to wash them down. "You can't go out now in a sweat," she said. "We must put you up overnight."

"Oh!"

"We'll sit up just a few minutes."

At the opportunity to stay and talk the English teacher was overjoyed. He smiled and at once started to talk about himself, saying, "I remember when I was a boy, I lived in Boston, and at night I used to walk on Washington Avenue, among the bright lights, and look in the faces of all the people! Dr. Otto, did you ever do anything like that? I mean, not necessarily in Boston. . ." He sped on in the same vein. After a few moments, Frau Otto rose and excused herself—— though indeed there was nothing scandalous that he had to say; for what could a person so young and sober have to confess?

"You're strange, Iddings!" said Otto, thinking of the uncanny tree, which, he felt, would frighten his child.

"Maybe I ought to call the doctor."

"A different person exactly!" said Clark. "I don't apologize for talking about myself because nothing is more important than that we understand one another."

"I understand you less and less."

Soon it was past midnight. The chemist began to foresee that the Christmas in his house was ruined; in the morning he would not be up to greet his daughter; and what a rude fright was in store for her when she saw the Christmas tree. He speculated on the possibility of putting his guest to bed and then stealing down to redecorate it. He could not foresee that this tree would be the merriest his daughter ever had; for throughout the morning, her newly-gotten toys—dolls, a house and furniture, a mechanical fire-engine—all lying neglected, she kept climbing a chair to right the lopsided star and then, dancing for joy, knocked it away again with paper balls aimed from across the room.

In the afternoon, several visitors, teachers, dropped in at Dr. Otto's—Messrs. Bell and Flint; Dr. Croydon, the dean; and Miss Cohalan, the registrar. Iddings Clark continued, in the same nervously intimate strain; his sleep had been only moderately feverish, enough to generate almost pleasant dreams—and these he now proceeded to expound in minute detail.

Otto took Dean Croydon aside. "He's not well. I tried to keep him in bed but he won't stay."

"What is his temperature?"

"Normal."

"You see," cried Clark, "there is nothing we're not capable of!"

"Nothing is more false!" said the Dean sharply. "Nothing is falser than when we think ourselves creatures of any chance fancy, not as we really are—just as, brutally frank with rage, we tell our friends what we think of them in a rage, not what we really think."

The situation rapidly became strained; the social atmosphere spoilt. Each of the friends cast his eyes upon the ground to avoid looking at the others; only Iddings himself eagerly sought them out with his eyes.

"When all know too much, all are ashamed," thought Otto.

"It's lucky he's taken ill during the holidays; he'll be better by the start of school," thought Dean Croydon.

3.

On New Year's Day, which fell on a Tuesday, Iddings Clark was scheduled to deliver the annual Hooker Lecture on Literature, in the auditorium of the High School. And this year an extraordinary audience had gathered, for not only was Clark always a treat as a lecturer, but every one remembered the dramatic incident that had befallen him the week before, his dead faint in the midst of the singing. Many children, as well as the grown-ups, came to stare at him in curiosity; the ushers were given orders to shunt those boys not with their parents up into the balcony—and there they sat, staring down, their lips pressed against the shiny rail.

Dean Croydon introduced the speaker as their "beloved friend who occasioned so much anxiety on the day before Christmas, but who has since quite recovered." The subject of the lecture was "The Incentives of Poetry."

When the English teacher stepped to the front, however, he seemed the opposite of quite recovered—thin, white, with somber eyes. Everywhere there was a leaning forward to see him better. He said in a strained voice, "I had intended to speak of poetry as objects and forms, and of the excitement of *inventing* something: for there is a pleasure in creating a new structure, or in elaborating a living plot, as if a man were Prometheus. But instead I shall speak of it as communication, and why it is that one person talks to another.

"But talking to you, as Meyer Liben said," he cried suddenly, "is like talking to a wall!"

As he spoke the pink color mounted in his face, and his dark eyes burned. He made no gestures, but with white-knuckled fingers gripped the edges of the lectern, and his voice came forth over his hands. "*Come alive Galatea!* cried that famous sculptor, *that I may talk to you!* and he kissed a statue not yet free of the formless rock. What a sad pity that the centuries of evolution could not create a human friend for him!"

People looked at each other.

"Very lonely," said the lecturer. "Such exact symbols—but only poets pay close attention, and they adopt this language for their very own. The poets speak only to the poets. To talk to you is like talking to a wall!"

"Our friend Iddings," whispered Miss Cohalan, seated behind the speaker, leaning across to Dean Croydon, "he seems beyond the bounds of order. His sentences come in gusts."

"I have not heard more moving eloquence," said the Dean sharply. (One would not have expected him to say this.)

"The French poet, Charles Baudelaire, wrote:

Le bourdon se lamente, et la bûche enfumée
accompagne en fausset la pen dule enrhumée,
cependant qu'en un jeu plein de sales parfums,
heritage fatale d'une vieille hydropique,
le beau valet de coeur et la dame de pique
causent sinistrement de leurs arnours défunts—

'in a game full of dirty perfumes, the handsome knave of hearts and the queen of spades, gossip sinisterly of their dead loves.' Why did he say *this*?

"And he wrote:

Et le printemps et la verdure
ont tant humilié mon coeur
que j'ai puni sur une fleur
l'insolence de la nature—

'the springtime and foliage humiliated me so, I took punishment on a flower for the insolence of nature.' Why *this*?

'*J'ai plus de souvenirs que si j'avais mille ans*'—'I have more memories than if I were a thousand years old!'"

At this sentence many in the audience started.

In the balcony the children began a whispered debate.

"He says he is a thousand years old!"

"No. He says it was as if he was a thousand years old."

"Mr. Clark is a *thousand years old!*"

"Quiet! quiet!" said the usher.

The afternoon growing late, the snow outside falling thicker—the hall became dim. Yet all, straining their eyes in the dusk, thought that they saw the speaker clearly.

"This is a common experience," he said, "young people in love are unable, no matter how hard they try, to keep from talking about the person.

"But when they are *out of love*; still wounded, not yet healed, hopelessly hunting around in every direction for sympathy—then they *still* talk (making all ashamed)."

Suddenly—just as he had begun, and as he continued—he stopped. His voice no longer came in separate gusts across his white-knuckled hands. But the faint light that seemed to play on him on the platform persisted.

They began to clap and abruptly found themselves in pitch darkness. The applause grew loud. There was a hubbub of people trying to put on their coats and galoshes in the dark. At last the lights came ablaze. Blinded, the people took this opportunity to add to the infectious applause, but the speaker had slipped away during the darkness.

"Would the young man have us go around confessing each other?"

"No. It is only that we read poetry more sympathetically."

"Come alive, Galatea! cried that famous sculptor."

"How pale he looked at the beginning; then how flushed he became."

"I thought that he was going to keel over again."

"How was he at the end?"

"You couldn't tell, it was so dark."

4.

The next day, it was a Wednesday, school reconvened. The snow lay deep on the ground, but the sun shone brightly; it reflected from the snow and sky, and poured into the large-windowed classrooms. At nine o'clock, flushed and damp from a snowfight, the boys and girls came trooping in.

Out of his little cubicle off the English lecture-room, Mr. Clark stepped to face his class: he was stark naked except for his spectacles and a Whittier in his right hand.

With cries of fright the young people fled up the aisle and through the doors they had just entered; before the period-gong had finished sounding, the classroom was emptied—except of one small girl who sat spellbound in the front row, and a boy who stopped near the door on his way out.

"I'll tell Dean Croydon," he said, and left.

Now Rea, the small girl, and the teacher of English were left alone, facing each other, she seated behind a desk, he standing naked beside his table.

"Why don't you run off with the others, child?" said Iddings.

"I'm hot and tired with playing; I'd rather stay here for the class."

"They have an unexpected holiday out of me."

"Won't there be a class, Mr. Clark?"

"The assignment was *Snowbound*, by Whittier."

"I read it all!" cried the girl.

"It's not a great poem. What the devil prompted him to write it?"

She stared at him closely, from head to foot, and said, "Is it true, what they say, Mr. Clark, that you are a thousand years old?"

"A thousand years! Heavens no."

"They say that you said you was a thousand years old, and I see that in some places you're grown all over with hair."

"I am 31," he said smiling.

"I'm 13, just the opposite," said Rea. She kept looking up into his face.

"What's your name, girl?" he said sharply, "my glasses are sweated over and I can't see you clearly."

"Rea."

"Rea! That's a strange name. It means the guilty one. Rea. Is there any of the boys you love?"

"Donald Worcester."

"Come here, child," he said in a tight voice. "Have you told him that you love him?"

"I wrote on the school-wall with chalk," she cried, "REA LOVES DONALD W. Just as if somebody else wrote it."

She rose from her bench and came beside the teacher.

"That's *right*!" he said. "Now he must tell you."

At this—as if for no reason—she burst into sobs. At the same time the door in the rear opened, and in came the Dean with a posse of instructors summoned from their classes for this extraordinary occasion. With a cry of fright the girl fled across the bars of sunlight out of the room.

"She's crying. What did you do to her?" asked the Dean.

"I did not!"

"Iddings! What's the meaning of this?"

"It's the story of Hawthorne's, *The Minister's Black Veil*."

"I don't remember. It's many years since most of us read Hawthorne," said the Dean.

"I at least shan't wear a black veil!" exclaimed Iddings Clark exaltedly, and a wave of color swept over him, from his feet to his forehead.

The Dean took off his coat and flung it round the shoulders of his trembling friend.

"This is serious; this is awful, Iddings Clark," he said.

"We won't hear the end of it. Where are your clothes? Get dressed. It's *my* fault; I knew it was coming. At least we'll try to hush the matter up. It won't come before the School Board. But how can I answer for the consequences?"

New York City

1933

A Cross-Country Runner at Sixty-Five

The list for the X-country run was tacked up in front of the Post Office; the small boys crowded round, looking for only one name, and there it was:

No. 6—Perry Westover—

"He's going to run again!"

"Look, is the old man going to run again?"

"Let *me* see."

"They say he has run a thousand times."

They crowded up close to the bulletin board, staring at the one name.

"How could he run a thousand times when the race is only a hundred years old?"

"I saw him run last year and before that. I saw him run twenty times!"

"What! you little liar; you're only eight years old."

"He *used* to run, my mother told me so."

"Why does he run; he's too old to win."

"How do you know he can't win? He takes it easy, he's just kidding around. He could win any time he wants."

"I saw him running once in the woods when nobody was watching, and he went like a streak; you couldn't see him—"

"How did you know it was him?"

"If he once put on the steam! They say he has so many silver cups that the whole cellar is full, and there's no place to put the coal. Isn't that so, Danny?"

Danny was the runner's grandson. "My grandpa has lots of cups and medals," he said.

"He must be a hundred years old!"

"My grandpa is sixty-five," said Danny.

The Winchester Borough X-Country was one of the oldest races in the State; it was forty-five years old. Runners from all the neighboring boroughs and even from neighboring counties came to run in the event. Perry Westover, however, had run all forty-five times, ever since the inception of the race; he had not missed one year. In his prime, he had once won three times in a row, and twice besides that. Even now he always came home among the first third, probably because of his experience of the course. Other entrants came back eight or nine times; but this was his forty-sixth! A X-country runner at sixty-five!

Mrs. Perry Westover disapproved of her husband's racing.

"I hear that you have again handed in your entry," she said sharply.

"Yes," answered the old athlete.

"Why do you do it, running with a lot of boys! You act like an old fool. Don't you see that you are an old man?"

"I used to run to win; now I run just for the race."

"Running under the broiling sun—you don't know how it aggravates me or you wouldn't do it, to see you come home worn-out and panting. How long do you think your heart can last? One day they'll bring you home on a stretcher. What a shame it is that *my* husband is the one all the neighbors laugh at!"

"Naturally! living close to us and having known us for so many years, they regard us in every respect in the same class as themselves; so I seem eccentric and even comic," said Perry Westover. "But to people farther off, perhaps, there's nothing ridiculous in my devoting myself to a race, again and again; perhaps it's even admirable."

"Do you suppose I care what people say, Perry?" said the white-haired woman. "I am thinking only of yourself. What a pity it is that a person of your intelligence should waste his life away in preparing to run across the fields. Almost every morning you are out before breakfast. The closet is crammed with discarded hobnailed shoes and dirty running-pants hung up forever. And half a dozen tarnished silver cups. Are those proper relics of a life's work?"

"Do you think you could name me a career that is obviously preferable, that everybody would rather choose?" said Perry excitedly, for it was a point much thought of by him. "Don't you believe it! In the long run, the X-country runner is as wise as the banker or doctor—seeing the countryside in rain and shine. One life is as good as another; mine is no worse. Anyway, haven't we done well enough and brought up three children?"

Perry had evolved this doctrine of the indifference among careers partly by a long reading of the book of Ecclesiastes. He kept this book by him so often that it began to infect his speech, and he sometimes bewildered a person talking to him by saying, suddenly, out of nowhere, like the memory of a dream: "Time and Chance happeneth to them all," or "Ere ever the silver cord is snapped asunder, and the golden bowl is shattered, and the pitcher is broken at the fountain . . ."

The Westovers were well fixed, for the village of Winchester, almost rich; this despite the fact that, all his life, Perry had never chosen a career, unless to be a X-country runner for silver cups be regarded as a career. He was "lucky," always falling into money-making ideas, "hunches," "windfalls." One time he saved the State a quarter of a million dollars by demonstrating that a new bridge ought not to be built where they intended building it, at the road, but farther upstream, since the road would have to be made over anyway within a year or two. For this he was paid $10,000 as a "consultant-engineer." Again, he set up his eldest son in a prosperous hardware business by inventing a patent can-opener, sold by mail-order. The secret, of course, was that he alone was not tied down to anything, but could look about him disinterestedly; in a freely competitive society (such as this rural country used to be in his youth) a person like that could always make money.

"I used to run to win," said Perry; "now I run to see the countryside!"

At this moment, Cummings, the eldest son, entered the house—an alert, well-groomed, rather portly gentleman of forty. Like his mother, he disapproved of Perry's running in the race. So did his brothers, and so, aping their parents, did all the grandchildren excepting little Danny. No one could see any *sense* in it, in being a X-country runner at sixty-five! Perhaps they would have felt less ill at ease if he were guilty of some criminal mania, kleptomania or a lust for little girls; then at least one could condemn him. Now, what could one say to him?

"To see the countryside!" cried Cummings. "If you want to see the countryside, papa, I can drive you high and low in a yellow Stutz, and from here to Denver!"

"One need not go so far; a little territory thoroughly explored is sufficient."

"By God, you've had time enough to do that."

"Listen, Cummings," said Perry Westover, "to know one typical thing, it is necessary to return to it again and again, so that each time you change your mind, you also see the countryside afresh. You would not trust to your childhood reading of a poem, would you? Most often, when asked for a judgment about anything, we have no clear present idea of it, but judge it with the same words we once used, although they have lost their meaning; and this is why we so often contradict ourselves, trying to harmonize past words and present knowledge. But luckily we suffer that vague uneasiness of conscience, which tells us (though nobody else knows) when our words are opinion and when they are knowledge. By running across the country again and again, I hope to keep my judgments up to date," said the old man smiling.

"What!" cried Mrs. Westover, "is all this philosophy behind a X-country race? I should never have thought it."

"You intrigue me, papa," said Cummings. "What is there to see in the environs of Winchester? Perhaps I have been missing something all my life!"

"Not very much."

"For instance?"

"There seem to be at least five temporal layers of the countryside. When you first pass by, different patches of land seem to have completely different dates—a spot beside Beaver Brook has not changed since the time of the Cayuga Indians, whereas the macadam highway, Route 4W, seems exclusively of 1930. But the more you look at each, the more you see all the others emerging from it."

"What are the five?"

"In tabular form:

"1. The rough brook poppling among the green rocks, and under the high pines roundabout, the quiet carpet of brown needles: this is a hunting ground for the ghosts of Indians (since they believed in ghosts).

"2. A stony field baking in the sun, a few cattle penned in with a wall of stones and a wooden fence; the land cleared but full of stumps, planted with wild grass for grazing and four trees where the cows can lie down.

"3. A cultivated field with tomato vines, a sow lying in the mud nuzzled at by seven sucklings; a barn with a nag, a well with a windlass. (You see how crowded the scene now becomes.) A wire chickenhouse strewn with corn grains, and loud with the four sounds of clucking, cackling, crying, and crowing; and a post-box of the RFD.

"4. Next is the tarred road, the tar spattered on the brittle leaves of the huckleberry bushes, and the reek of gasoline; a road turning and bumpy—the wreck of an old Packard with the door in the back; telegraph poles leaning in different directions; a red gasoline filling-pump (painted over for the third time) outside a hut of corrugated iron. (This Age of Iron is the most crowded of all.) The billboard CASTORIA, 'children cry for it.'

"5. And most recent is the concrete speedway, Route 4W, bright buff broad way across the State, crossing valleys and hills with hardly a rise or fall; the road-signs are made of little mirrors that catch the headlights or the sun and burst into brilliance; the bridges are of gray steel. Lying on the road, like a metal jewel, is a smashed radio-tube, the plate, grid, and filament all entangled."

"Bravo, Perry!" cried Mrs. Westover.

"Look, Cummings," said the old runner, "when you skim by in your yellow motor-car, you see all these in a flickering succession, as in a moving-picture: woodland, steel bridge, farm, woodland, pasture, rapidly coming into being and vanishing. But when I break my way through the woods and emerge suddenly on the concrete speedway, a viaduct arching over my head, I am cast bodily into a different time. That is, I am compelled to look. Indeed, sometimes, at the end of a long, hot run, fagged, a little sunstruck, it seems as hard for me to drag my way from a hunting to a pastoral economy as it was for our famous ancestors; I break forth from the forest like a tired replica of the Race of Man!"

"Is it true, what they say, grandpa," said little Daniel, "that you sometimes run so fast among the trees that a person can't see you?"

"Who said that?"

"Alec van Emden."

"Watch out, Perry!" cried Mrs. Westover, "you are becoming a ghost in your own lifetime, and after death you'll haunt the country like the Legend of Sleepy Hollow!"

"What else do they say, Danny?"

"They say you must be one hundred years old."

"What else?"

"They say that the cellar is so full of silver loving-cups that we have no place to keep the coal."

An automobile drove up to the porch. Cummings looked out the window to see who it was.

"It's Roy Wiener of the *County Recorder*."

The reporter came in without knocking, explaining that he was after an interview with the famous X-country runner.

"Is it true, Mr. Westover, that this is to be your forty-sixth annual race?"

"Just so."

"Do you mind if I take a picture?" he said, setting up his apparatus.

Perry likewise gave him a photograph of himself snapped over forty years before, when he was twenty-two or twenty-three. A blond, curly-headed youth stiffly posed, with a serious face, in the manner of that time, and holding up an absurd little silver loving-cup in his right hand. The reporter thanked him profusely; this was of course just what he was after. Little Danny kept looking away, fascinated, from the white-haired old man to the boy in the photo.

"In the course of years, I suppose there have been many changes in the itinerary of the race, isn't that so?" said Wiener. "What was the course of the Winchester X-country forty-five years ago?"

"Substantially what it is now. Then also we started at the Post Office, went as far as Hemans Hill, and came back by way of Gaskell. There has been only one considerable change, and I was the one who suggested it."

"What was that?"

"When the road was built through Chapone, I suggested that we run along the road for a mile or two, rather than go out of the way across the fields. It was a X-country race, I argued, and it would be a strange view of the countryside indeed that failed to take in the roads as well as the fields."

The old man searched in a trunk and brought forth a complete set of charts of the course, dating from before 1890 and indicating all the minor variations. The first drawings were rough, blurred pencil-sketches on brown paper; the later ones increased in elegance even to the point of having the printing in red ink. (It was clear that with the passage of the years, the old man had lost not a whit of his interest in the race, except that now he paid more attention to the formalities and perhaps less to the actual running.) Wiener noted the marginalia: "If a warm day, cross at M; if not, at N." "'Ware of the bull in this field; sprint to get here in the first half dozen."

"You see, there is a certain science to it," said Perry.

"Tell me, Mr. Westover, are you always consulted by the sponsor when there is to be some change in the course or the regulations?"

"Yes."

The reporter thought that this was a good opportunity to ask his most difficult question.

"Do you mind if I ask something a trifle more intimate, Mr. Westover?"

"No no. Go right ahead."

"The readers of the *Recorder* would like to know just what you see in X-country running, just what is its peculiar attraction, that you have devoted so many years to it."

Perry laughed briefly. "What crust!" he thought. "How do you mean?" he said.

"Why, I mean, some men go into a thing for the money in it, others because they want publicity—"

Suddenly, for no cause at all, Perry became cross and excited. What infernal crust, he thought, to ask a man for *reasons* for what he has devoted fifty years to!—as if we lived for some ulterior end outside the act of living.

"'He that observeth the wind shall not sow!'" he quoted, "'he that regardeth the clouds shall not reap . . . In the morning, sow thy seed; in the evening, withhold not thy hand—for thou knowest not which shall prosper, this or that—'"

"Where is that from? it sounds like the Bible," said Wiener.

"'Enjoy life with the wife whom thou lovest all the days of thy vanity. . . *Whatsoever thy hand attaineth to do by thy strength, that do.*' That *do*. That DO!" DO!

"My husband is a little tired; couldn't you come back some other time?" said Mrs. Westover discreetly.

"Oh no, thanks, thanks. Thanks very much, you've been too kind," said Wiener, hastily packing up his camera.

"'Veteran Athlete Quotes Scriptures,'" he thought viciously, as he climbed into his roadster.

"Is it really fifty years?" thought Perry anxiously.

Next morning, practicing, he slowly jogged over the entire course, glad of the opportunity to move his limbs; he was very disturbed inwardly, very nervous. (He had lost his temper at Wiener's brass and had not yet recovered his mental balance.) At the same time, the realization that he had become an old man made him very thoughtful. He kept withdrawing from the surrounding countryside to the thoughts and memories inside himself, and then moving back to the environment as if awaking, shuttling back and forth until the two regions became inextricably mixed. Running year after year over the same course and carefully noting, as he did, the slow transformation of every part of the countryside during two generations, the houses demolished, built, moved from place to place, again demolished, brick replacing wood—it had still not really occurred to him that he also was being slowly transformed. Now, as by a flash of light, he looked at himself with the eyes of all the children of Winchester; he realized that he was not just a runner, but an old institution, extremely ancient, almost fabulous. Likewise, an old man. "Perhaps after all," he thought, "I ought to be thinking about getting ready to die, rather than running across the country again and again." All these ideas obsessed him successively, and kept recurring in various combinations—as the idea that he was a kind of institution led to the thought of Wiener's brass and this to the thought that it was contemptible for such an old man to run across the country again and again; but again, the idea of Wiener's interview led to the thought that he was a kind of institution, an institution something like a house, more permanent than those that had been moved away, soon to be demolished in turn—so that he soon realized that they were all expressions of one basic idea, and it made no difference which one of them he proposed to his mind, anger at Wiener's brass, or bewilderment at having grown old in a second, or the strange humor of being a ghost while still alive. Thus, without a thought of the road, he ground away mile after mile.

But suddenly, in the heart of Winchester Wood, in a little clearing, he found himself in front of a small house of logs that seemed strangely familiar to him; for instance, he knew, without counting, that it was so many logs high, and, without looking, that the fourth log in the rear was pointed on one end as if cut for a different purpose. Then he realized that he himself had built this cabin: he had sharpened the log to drive it into the ground as one of the corner posts, but had finally decided for a different mode of construction. How many years ago, he had absolutely no recollection. During the past twenty years at least, he had apparently passed the house by without even seeing it, as he ran by (unless indeed he had now missed the trail and was lost in the wood!), without regarding it even as a milestone to identify the course. But now when he looked at the cabin, the memory of all the intervening years vanished away.

He pushed open the door—which was provided with new brass hinges—and he went in. The room was in the best of repair and very clean. There was an unpainted deal table with a book and a couple of cans of tomatoes on it. The fireplace had been several times rebuilt; now it was cemented and mostly of brick; but the two big conical stones, almost twin, which he himself had built into the front, stood there still, after many years, the andirons, wardens of the fire. Perry picked up the book from the table, half-expecting to find it a Bible; but it was a tattered copy of an old edition of the Boy Scout Handbook, with a boyscout on the cover in khaki shorts and a flat-brimmed hat, signaling semaphore with a pair of red-and-white flags.

The back wall was thick with carved initials:

Some were fresh and yellow on the varnished logs, or stained red, or some were dark, worn, and painted over. Among these, the 85's and the 92's, Perry looked vainly for some carving of his own. Quite by accident he lighted on

```
CW · GW
   LW
  1911
```

Cummings, Gerald, Lawrence Westover, his three boys. But there was no P W, no Perry Westover; either he had never thought of carving his own name in the wall, or—what was inconceivable—somebody had scratched out his initials (as the oldest and most worn) to carve over them. To be sure, it was he who had built the wall! . . . To Cummings and Gerald, evidently, this cabin must have seemed part of the immemorial wood; how could it have occurred to them that their own father had built it. P. W. Struxit—Perry Westover built it! For a few moments he became passionately absorbed, fascinated, in the contemplation of each separate carving in the wood—so that he could hardly drag his eyes from one to the next.

On the way to Chapone, he again lost all sense of his surroundings; he clambered over stone fences, his thoughts 240,000 miles away.

"Were Wiener to ask me again," he thought, "I should again quote the passages from Ecclesiastes: *There is a time for every purpose and for every work.*"

"But Perry," Mrs. Westover said (he thought), "all the same, perhaps some works are more proper than others." "All are the same! all come to one end!" he cried. He quoted, "'He hath made everything beautiful in its time; also *He hath set the world in their heart, yet so that man cannot find out the work that God hath done*, from the beginning even to the end.' Even a wise man can't find it out! What does this mean? It means that one thing is as good as another!—

> Strange things I have in head, that will to hand;
> which must be acted ere they may be scanned."

"Is that how you interpret Ecclesiastes?" asked Roy Wiener, arranging his apparatus to take a picture. "The book is a long sermon against idolatry," said Perry; "some men experiment, as it is said, 'how to pamper the flesh with wine'; others make great works, houses, vineyards, gardens, and parks; they gather gold and silver and servants. Others, again, try to become wise. All this is vanity. 'Let me point out,' says the Preacher as I read it, 'that to put your trust in such works is idolatry and vanity. Yet it is proper to turn to something or other,' he goes on to say, 'whatever your strength is capable of, for "to everything there is a season, a time to every purpose under the heaven"—only do not put your trust in *it*.'" "In what shall we put our trust?" asked the reporter. "In God," said Mrs. Westover. "Is this the meaning of the book?" asked Wiener wonderingly. "'Then,'" quoted Perry, "'Then I beheld all the work of God, that man cannot find out the work that is done under the sun; though a wise man *labor* to seek it out, yet he shall not find it; though a wise man seek to know it, yet shall he be unable to find it out. Chapter ix. For all this I laid to my heart: that the righteous and the wise and their works are in the hand of God; whether to be love or hatred—man knoweth it not; all is before them. All things come alike to all. . . . *This is an evil that is done under the sun!*'" "'Whether to be love or hatred—man knoweth it not,'" said Mrs. Westover. "Yes, yes," said Wiener approvingly, "'the race is not to the swift, nor the battle to the strong'—I am a reporter, I have seen it often!—'neither yet bread to the wise, nor yet riches to men of understanding; but time and chance happeneth to them all.'" "Ah," cried Perry, "I see I have convinced you!" "Who would have thought that there was so much philosophy behind being a X-country runner at sixty-five!" said Mrs. Westover.

"On the other hand," said Perry Westover, "although it is certain that one career is as good as another—I mean to say that this can be established by incontrovertible proofs—yet sometimes it is clear to me that the reverse is true. Isn't the Governor superior to his stenographer? If only I, if all of us, had turned to something else—" "*No no!*" cried the Reporter; "Everything seems whole and strong when you look at it from afar; it is only when you take it in your hands that it falls to pieces. It is only when you take it in your hands that it falls to pieces." "Meantime, as you try each thing, you grow older," said Mrs. Westover; "and this goes on from day to day. Perhaps my husband has been right to stick to one thing." "What a snare!" cried the old man, about to burst into tears; "finally you get to be sixty-five years old and ought better to think about dying than about living."

Suddenly, emerging from a copse of birch, he found himself at the white fence of the State Road, 4W. A green roadster, with flashing glassware, shot by at eighty miles. Perry sat down on the fence for a breather. On the road was lying a broken spark-plug, the porcelain insulation broken. There was always some such broken relic on the unending speedway—just as Perry had previously described the shattered radio-tube on the concrete. He kept staring at this spark-plug. He knew from experience that by staring long enough at one spot, and thinking hard, he could revive in one timeless vision the whole history of the place—the steam rollers would return and the tar-men light their fires; the salvos of dynamite leveling the hill; and before that, a nag dragging a peddler's cart up the grade. He ran on a few yards, along the road. On the right hand was a battery of signposts: GASKELL 2½ miles. MIDDLETON 10 miles. MALORY 15 miles. CICERO 125 miles. From the lowest of these signs could be seen dangling an old shoe that Perry, having found it on the road, had hung there, in case the owner ever drove back that way; but by now it was spoiled by the rain and shine. The fancy struck Perry that, just as these signs marked the distances of different towns, it would be a natural thing, and not useless, to set up signposts of the passage of time: 5 years ago. 50 years ago. 150,000 years. (As if abruptly, on a local signpost, there should appear: THE MOON ↑ 240,000 miles!). . . At the signpost, the course left the road, and once again Perry plunged into the wood.

It was the fall of the year, the beginning of October. In the wood, four urchins, playing hooky from school, had built a fire among the brightly-colored trees. They were telling dirty stories and were playing cat's-cradle, passing the intricate cord from one set of fingers to another.

Perry sped out of a scarlet thicket nearby; his white form appeared and vanished among the tree-trunks.

"Look! there is Perry Westover, practicing for the race!" cried one of the kids in an awestruck voice.

"Where? where? I don't see him," cried the others; they were unable to point because of the game of cords between their hands. "Where is he?"

Perry kept appearing and vanishing in the wood.

"*There* he is!"

"There he is!" they cried one after another.

New York City
[January] 1936

A Ceremonial

Oui, le culte promis à des Cérémonials, songez quel il peut être!

— Mallarmé

1. Viola and the Alderman

A breezy May morning (not long after the establishment among us of reasonable institutions), a section of decrepit billboards along the highway was called to the attention of Alderman Manly Morison. He was out walking in the breeze when he came on a small black girl, Viola, letting fly with a rock at the sheet-metal billboard: *Bang!* After this percussion she kept time with her forefinger: "1–1–1,2,3–1–1–1,2,3"; then she screeched at the top of her voice:

"*Eeeeee! Iiiii!*" and then again let fly with a rock: *Bang!* while antique flakes of paste and paper showered to the ground.

"*Bang!*" said Alderman Morison.

"Oh," cried Viola, surprised out of music, awakened out of music, "you spoilt the rhythm." She was about to burst into tears, so rudely awakened out of music and dancing; but curiosity prevailed and she asked, "Hey, what all wuh them tin fences for?"

"Those?" Now suddenly it came to the Alderman's memory that they had been billboards for advertising, to make profits by persuading people to buy certain products. As he thought of the advertisements, those curious works of painting and poetry, and of the institution, the Alderman turned pale and lifted his hand to his brow in dizziness, at the ancient madness. The fact was that he could not think of those times without becoming confused. "Oh those," he faltered, "were just used for pasting up paintings and things."

"Paintings!" said Viola contemptuously, thinking of louder and more wonderful noises than the *Sacre du Printemps*.

—One of the billboards had shown a huge sexy pirate naked to the waist carrying off a smirking girl in a gossamer nightgown. Above, in italic type, was the legend: *Nature in the Raw is Seldom Mild*, Below: Lucky Strikes (a brand of cigarettes)—"It's Toasted!"

Another billboard had displayed a farmer leaning on a rake with glasses on the tip of his nose and symmetrical patches on his overalls, reading to his pink-cheeked white-haired wife holding in her hands an apple-pie, a letter from their son: "... *Am doing swell! just bought a Ford V-8.*" And below: "CONSULT YOUR LOCAL FORD DEALER."

The third billboard at Christmas season had borne the poster of a mother in a mauve dress with newly marcelled blond hair and just the faintest suggestion of a halo (perhaps only a highlight), gingerly holding a darling baby with face taken from a contemporary infant cinema-star, Baby Kelly. Against the deep rose background shone two golden candles. Underneath in tasteful Gothic letters was the legend:

"Sheffield Farms (milk products) wishes you a Merry Xmas and a Happy New Year."

The fourth billboard merely said peremptorily: BUY REM (a kind of cough syrup).

"What are yuh *cryin'* about?" cried Viola, astonished to see tears rolling down the Alderman's cheeks.

"Look here, black girl," said Manly, "suppose a huge sign there said 'Chew Juicy Fruit!' what would you do?"

? ? ? ? ?

"I mean, supposing the sign jumped up and down and did acrobatic exercises—" cried Manly, and he broke into a peal of laughter.

"What are yuh *laughin'* about?" said Viola. But she was not unwilling to join in, first uncertainly, then with a high clear peal of laughter. She let fly another rock: *Bang!*

"It's all right, kid," said Manly, "we'll have the fence knocked down this afternoon; it blocks the view along the road."

"Yes, it does," said Viola judiciously.

"We'll have to get together some kind of program," said the Alderman.

"*Program!* Just to knock down the tin fence—"

These historic sentences, which I have imitated somewhat crudely, I fear, were first spoken on the morning of May 9, 19—.

Manly Morison and Viola clambered through the hedge to see what was behind the billboard. From tatters of paper hanging from the metal Manly could see that one of the advertisements had been the following, founded on an evil sentiment of fear:

A young girl is shown in tears, because no boy could call her, because she had not rented a telephone from the Bell Telephone Corporation.

What should there be in the field behind the antique billboard but the meadowflowers?

—the white-eyelashed daisies and gold buttercups
and devil's-paintbrushes in fire dipt.

There was a linden sapling we must refer to again below. The wind had swept away the last wisps of cloud, and the sky was what one might call a *breathing* blue. So blue, day of lovely glory. The grass and weeds, so early in the year, were almost knee deep. With an exclamation of delight, Viola picked up an antique milk-bottle, full of soil.

"What do you want with that, girl?"

"It has a *squeak* note," said the girl, making it tinkle.

"Don't you have any regular instruments to play, girl?" asked the Alderman.

"Oh yes, I play the viola," said Viola.

2. Address by Meyer Leibow

The afternoon's program began about 4:30. Almost a hundred chairs were set up in front of the billboards on the now little-used highway. The children, for the most part, were playing a ball game in the field a few hundred meters off, but they silently returned whenever anything was of interest.

Three of the billboards were to be pushed down; the fourth, on the right, was to be preserved and it was draped with a yellow curtain.

Our good friend Meyer Leibow made an address somewhat as follows:

"Spinoza said there's no use upbraiding the past. Yet I'd like to point out just how insulting these old signboards were; and I guess I'll have to induce, therefore, that some of us were very undignified to take so many insults without being offended. Finally, perhaps I'll make just a remark about the color yellow.

"All of these advertising signs operated on an hypothesis of how we'd react. Namely, the advertisers believed that if they merely brought a certain name to our attention, we'd pay out money for something. Quite apart from any reasonable persuasion, mind you, but just: Stimulus! Response! Can you imagine such a belief? It was, of course, an *insult*.

"Furthermore, some of the signs used to scream *Buy! Buy!* Yet how many of us ever stopped to say: 'I beg your pardon, are you addressing me? Would it not be more polite to say 'If you please—or wait till you are asked, or even, perhaps, to wait till we are introduced?' But a citizen would walk along the street and jump out of his skin when something shrieked at him, 'Hey you! Do! Don't! Give! Buy! Use! Hurry!'

"Other signs became even more insulting by adopting a familiar attitude: 'Listen, Buddy, let me give you a tip' or 'Say, don't miss it on your life' or 'Ain't got time for loose talk, folks, but they got taste and plenty to spare!' The theory here was that if we'd develop a chummy attitude to Campbell's soup, we just couldn't help pay out money.

"But this brings me to what to my temper was always the most irritating insult of all. The idea being to make people well-disposed, the advertisers had a theory as to what would make people feel well-disposed. For instance, one thing that could not fail was to show a picture of a blonde little girl or an apple-cheeked boy with torn pants. As Delmore Schwartz once remarked, whenever a baby appears on a movie-screen everybody says '*Ah!*' (something like the end of the skyrocket cheer the young men do). Therefore folks would pay out money. Another sure way to attract attentive observation, so the fateful name of Hennafoam Shampoo could sink into the soul, was to display some secondary sexual activity, such as the exchange of ardent looks. Therefore folks would pay out money. It was the belief of advertisers that the mind worked in this simple way.

"It was essential in putting the buyer in the right frame of mind to suggest to him the right social status, namely just one grade above (as they used to say) what he could ever attain. The theory was that a person would feel that if he bought such and such an article he as good as belonged to the next economic class. Therefore he would pay out money. This was a sad insult.

"Besides this, there were catchy rimes, such as:

Cooties love
Bewhiskered places,
but Cuties love
the smoothest faces—
USE BURMA SHAVE!

And there were many deep-thought mottoes and slogans, such as: 'Not a Cough in a Carload' or 'Next to myself I like B.V.D.'s best' or 'Eventually—Why not Now?' It was likewise considered good by these theorists of our common human nature to use elegant diction, such as 'Always Luckies Please.' And to give credit where credit is due, it was they who invented a remarkable usage of grammar, the comparative absolute, as to say: 'I *prefer* Tasty Bread,' or 'Kraft Cheese is *Superior*.'

"Aware that we were rational as well as passionate, they made philosophy, too, the handmaiden of commerce. 'Nature in the Raw is Seldom Mild,' posited one product that had a patent process. 'Nature's Best after All!' countered its rival, displaying the effigy of a miss in riding togs (as they used to wear) feeding sugar to a thoroughbred horse. Therefore people would pay out money.

"Science and common-sense were not exempt. It was believed that by sufficient repetition, assertions in the teeth of the most ordinary experience would come to be credited. That is, it was a cardinal principle of the advertisers that they could instill in people a habit of lies. Habit of lies—habit of publicity—This, I take it, was a great insult."

As Meyer declared that this or that theory of the advertisers was an insult to our common nature, some of the older men and women shifted in their seats and their eyes flooded with tears; for sometimes they had not been proof against these very advertisements. They therefore listened with the greater attention to the simple speech.

"What a sad case!" exclaimed Meyer, "that science, ordinary sentiment, painting, our dear English tongue—should all have been made to serve so ruthlessly. Everything, to be sure, must be made to serve—I mean to serve life as a whole and our freedom—but not so ruthlessly.

"We often find, I think, that things serve best by being enjoyed in themselves.

"What a nervous time it was when every perception along the road was designed to influence some far-off behavior! I am surprised that there were not more automobile accidents. But we most often have peace, I think, in enjoying each thing in itself."

He turned to the draped billboard. "This color—this color yellow—this yellow—" he said, turning to regard the yellow curtain with attentive sensation. "No, do not consider it too attentively—it is not important enough.

"But before I begin to wander," said Meyer, "I'd better bring my remarks to a close. When I'm sitting down I can let my mind roam as much as I please; there is no problem of communication then! Then to conclude: I have of course touched only a single aspect of this ancient evil of advertising. For instance I have not spoken of unproductive effort and the expense of the creative soul; I have not touched on the creation of immoderate desires, the fixing of the habit of publicity, and so on. Yet even with so much alone as I have mentioned, how is it that these advertisements, so insulting, so nervous, were able to survive? The answer, my beloved comrades, is that they *did not!*

"Therefore today we are demolishing these boards."

Hereat Meyer again took his seat in the audience.

There was, of course, no applause for these remarks, since what was there to rejoice in such remarks?

3.

The next number on the program was the purpose of it all, and the boys came drifting in from the field. It being nearly five, tea and cakes were passed around.

"Will the gentlemen carpenters please come forward and take charge, and explain the proceedings," said Alderman Morison.

Three fellows rose, rolling up their sleeves, and came forward. Two at once disappeared behind the billboards. Their spokesman, a short stout type, wrapped his cigar in a piece of paper and put it in his breast pocket. He said "Well, we first sawed through the supports in the back, leaving a few props. Then we cut through these posts here in front, down on the bottom here." He indicated where wedges had been cut from the posts, just as lumberjacks do with great pine trees "Now then, when I push in front, at the same time they'll pull away the props in back with cords—and down she'll go! all except that end one that's being kept." He indicated the one on the right, draped with the lemon-yellow curtain.

When he finished this explanation, the people broke into a volley of applause—until the two in the back reappeared at the edge, grinning.

"O.K., boys—" said Tony Bridges, the spokesman. All the children had gone around the back to watch. "*Ready?*" cried Tony.

"Ready!" cried they.

"Here *goes!* One—two—and *three!*" and with a great shove he gave his weight to the billboard.

With a crack, that made the audience jump, it went down, sounding a dull *bunnnnng!* as it landed, amid a cloud of dust, disclosing the grassy field and the meadowflowers.

But there in the field, center of all eyes, the two young carpenters standing on ladders were holding stretched a maroon curtain. What was behind it? This was the question every one asked himself. (It was of course the linden sapling.) Some observed with pleasure the maroon curtain and the lemon-yellow curtain.

"Our friend—Gregory Dido—" announced Manly Morison, his voice broken with emotion.

And in fact, when this great artist and poet and statesman, this philosopher, came to the front, all stood up for a moment, in token of respect.

"I just thought," said the aged man in his beautiful easy tone, "that when something appears from behind a curtain, or when there is a frame round it, we consider it more easily, peacefully, more in itself, as my friend Meyer was just saying. All right, lads, drop the curtain," he said to the lads on the ladders.

They disclosed the quiet tree with its heart-shaped leaves and a few cream-colored blossoms in the sunlight.

This tree, at first, excited only wonder, almost disappointment; until it became apparent, just by looking at it, that the utmost tiny leaves and petals were expressive, were organs, of the invisible roots. Such as it was, this tree in seclusion had come to its present being, behind a fence. Here it was, this linden tree, when the maroon curtain dropped.

Loudly enthusiastic, the plaudits broke forth. "Bravo! bravo!" cried some. There was thunderous hand-clapping. Even Dido and Meyer Leibow, who had spent a long time considering the tree in the morning, were deeply moved anew. The children, in the field, did not fully understand the occasion for it, but they added their cheers and joyous clapping. This continued for three or four minutes, during which time the linden-tree stood appreciative.

"I see," cried Gregory Dido, "that we'll have to incorporate this as a new act in the theatres: I mean displaying a tree alone in the middle of the stage."

"Perhaps the tree wouldn't be so handsome," said Meyer, "taken away from its natural meadow."

"I am not so sure of that!" exclaimed Gregory.

Many of the audience leaned forward expectantly, hoping to hear a further exchange of ideas and arguments between these two.

But no! The next number on the program was not a dialectical skirmish, but more fittingly a little poem of gratification composed that day by Harry Walker, 14. Dark-haired Harry, dangling a fielder's glove from his wrist, unfolded a soiled sheet of paper, which he took from his hip-pocket; and although the other boys made a few sotto voce remarks, he read in a firm and manly voice, as follows:

Today in center field although
   I shouted to the others playing ball,
   there was not any sound at all.
The meadowflowers softly grow

in the knee-deep grass; the meadowflowers
   grow softly in the knee-deep grass;
   I do not know how many hours pass;
I do not know how many hours

the meadowflowers grow softly in
   the knee-deep grass; there is not any
   sound at all; I do not know how many
hours pass; there is a present din

of baseball; is no sound at all;
   I do not know how many hours pass
   the meadowflowers in the knee-deep grass
grow softly without any sound at all.

There was no applause for this effort, except from the children, for it was not considered convenient to applaud young boys (all were without the habit of publicity). Having used up his courage, Harry awkwardly stuffed the paper in his pocket; but as he was going away, Dido drew him near and said in a low voice, "It is true, it is true!—the meadowflowers grow softly in the knee-deep grass"; so that the boy blushed deep red, and when the others wanted to know what Dido had said, he wouldn't tell.

"All the same, it's a sad way to play ball!" said Meyer to Gregory Dido; "he probably can't field."

"No no, otherwise he'd be put in right-field, not center-field."

"Hm. Tell me, Joey," Meyer asked one of the kids, "what position does Harry Walker play on his ball-team?"

"He? He holds down the hot-corner for the Bears!" said Joey.

Dido roared.

"Little liar!" said Mike.

And now the members of the famous string-quartet, who had traveled over a hundred miles to come to this ceremonial, were already setting up their music-stands.

For it was a principle (one of those established by this very Gregory Dido) generally followed throughout the land, that there was never a public gathering without excellent music of some kind.

But since the music was this afternoon of so serious a kind—namely one of the later works of Beethoven—the children and several of the adults went to occupy themselves elsewhere for half an hour. Tony Bridges took his cigar from his pocket and lit it, hoping to enjoy the music and his cigar both.

The quartet tuned their instruments, dropping the plucked notes and the premonitory strains into the deepening silence.

They played several deep, slow chords—major and minor triads—until the spirit of simple harmony spread among the listeners in the late afternoon: for what advantage is it to surprise with complicated music the unprepared soul? (This also was an idea of Gregory Dido's.)

4. Cavatina

The four began now to play the long quartet of Beethoven, opus 130, in B-flat major. And while they are playing let us withdraw from representing their real activity (for there is no describing these tones in words); but just represent the performers, and a few of the auditors, and the power of music.

The second violinist, Dickie M'Nall, was a youth in the period of form and fire. That is, after endless study, taking his work to bed and for long walks with himself, and expounding it in discussions, he would arrive at a formal analysis of the whole; and now, in executing his part, he attacked this form, outline and details, with the utmost passion and precision. Self-centered, centering on this imagined ideal, he sat as if alone, constructing carefully the edifice of the second-violin.

The violist, Maritimus, was a profound intelligence; it was he who was the synoptic soul of this famous quartet, who, in a sense, played the four instruments. Indeed, there was nothing like the experience of seeing Maritimus look up, with a profound glance of dark eyes, at M'Nall or Mrs. Troy—and moderate. It was he who gave the broad lines of what M'Nall studied. (Between the youth and Maritimus subsisted a difficult sexual friendship.)

Mrs. Troy, the cellist, was a heroine of the civil war, the mother of two grown daughters and a small son, a strong and simple musician. I do not mention these other characteristics at random, for she held her instrument between her knees and bowed it in a firm and matronly way, as part of life, playing music as if it were drawing breath, and sometimes joking with Maritimus (whom she had first met when he was a sailor!). About such a person as this, one can *say* very little.

The first violinist was Herman Schneider. About such playing, in which there is no distinction between the playing of the sounds and the preconceived form, one can never say enough, for it is like anything in nature growing, as a tree. A strange illusion grew from this playing, namely that after a piece was over and the other sounds faded, the line of the first violin seemed to persist in the air, almost visible, like a kind of ghost. There is a legend that once the other three broke off in the middle, to hear Herman Schneider alone.

So these were the four who were playing: Herman Schneider, 1st violin, Dickie M'Nall, 2nd violin, Charles Maritimus, viola, and Martha Aaron Troy, cellist.

Dido, with head bent haggardly on his chest, was hardly listening. He was thinking altogether, with horror and fatigue, of his blighted life. And, I fear to say it, when the quartet came to the smiling, morosely repetitive Dance, *alla Tedesca*, tears began to stream down his lined cheeks. But the next part, *Cavatina*, would free and relax—and make this poor soul's breath more formal with the song.

At the Dance, *alla Tedesca*, small black Viola, who had been painfully following the score in a book, now laughed and hummed so loudly that Mrs. Troy smiled to her with a queenly air.

I, too, was there, this author; but I have never been less attentive than on that day to my master Beethoven. For besides my task of remarking so many details both inner and outer, I was perplexed by a problem of art: for it sounded to me, although I *knew* that I was in error, that the other players were more musical than Herman Schneider. "So to an incompletely formed taste, the good always seems more powerful than the perfect," I thought. But if I had listened only and not thought at all, I might not have erred; and so it came about when they began the *Cavatina*.

Tony Bridges, with moving finger, intently hearing, was a true critic, his attention *crowding* into his ears.

After the fourth movement there was a pause, a half minute of unusual attentiveness. The glance of Maritimus held us all. (I think now that it was a *kind* glance, one with the feeling of our kind.) When he lowered his eyes, they played the deathless *Cavatina*.

Then any one might, if he came by, have observed the power of music. For the people were as if asleep or dead—relaxed—some with open sightless eyes, as if they had been slain with great violence and suddenness. An arm in an awkward position; no grace left to these mere bodies. Indeed, a passerby would have been amazed if he were unacquainted with such causes (I am describing what is not rare, but may be observed at many concerts). And even I was able to hear the deathless *Cavatina* without evaluation. The power of the impassible musicians was not resented—what a strange thing! for we all had the habit of freedom. (How am I to continue, reader, now the narrative has come to this pause of what may not be described?) A very small child came from the field and started with fright, seeing all asleep or dead. At the turn of the melody,

some of the dead shed tears, in respect for Ludwig Beethoven brought in his fifty-second year to such a turn of the melody. Music looses the soul so flow the tears; soon the breath is formal with the song. Thanks to these tears, to the turn of the melody, it is possible again to describe the scene. We are often, in touching on what is not proper to words, faced with a grave problem of style, namely: how to begin again; unless by luck what is not proper to words, as the music, freely returns, as in these tears, to words.

5.

The last number on the program comprised the rededication of the billboard left standing, in some remarks by Gregory Dido. By this time it was late in the afternoon, the ovoid sun almost dropped behind the hill, tinging all linen. Gregory said: "Why we at all make a point of saving and transforming a portion of this old relic—acceptance of the past! triumph over the past!—is

a philosophic question; maybe one of the boys can write an article about it."
(Laughter.)

"*You do it, Gregory Dido!*" cried Mrs. Troy.

"You would not think," I thought, "that this cheerful man, whose entire vocation seems to be these neighborhood ceremonials, is the poet of Desire and Terror, who questions every one without exception." But I was wrong, for it was only this cheerful man, whose entire vocation was neighborhood ceremonials, could have been that poet.

"Our friend Councillor Morison asked me to decorate the board," said Dido. "I've done so in the simplest way I could. Certainly another could do better, but it doesn't much matter for this country billboard. But in any case, as a more general principle, I should like to suggest the following:

"In the public vehicles we might post an occasional poem, a mathematical theorem, or an account of the reasoning behind a beautiful physical experiment. Anything, I mean to say, embodying a single worthwhile act of thought.

"I am not sure how far this principle can be extended, to billboards and so forth, for we can make too great an effort—who can deny it ?—to occupy our souls, to preoccupy our souls . . ."

I, and the others, leaned forward to give our best attention to a lengthy exposition. But at this moment the sun set and Gregory, whose habit was never to lose sense of the simple and important rhythms, remarked: "You see, my dear friends, the day has ended again."

But having said so, he could not bring himself to break the silence of the pure daylight of the beginning of evening; so he merely made a gesture and a couple of lads climbed up and loosed the yellow curtain overhanging the board. There was disclosed a sentence elegantly printed and a large circle, as follows:

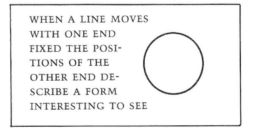

This was all that was hidden behind the lemon-yellow curtain, just as behind the maroon was nothing but a linden-tree.

"The word 'describe' is not well enough chosen," thought Miss Campbell, teacher of English.

6.

High over the hill gleamed the star Venus ("afterthought of the Sun"). The meeting broke up.

I have failed, I fear, to catch the spirit of this first May 9th celebration, which began on that day so casually, and has since become the prototype of every communal "May Ninth." Such was the origin of the maroon and lemon, of the linden-tree, of the customary reading of the poems of Gregory Dido and Harry Walker, and of so many other traditions. But I have failed especially, I know, to imitate the social peace and easy subtlety of the day; perhaps what I have described seems even pedantic!

What is the spirit of May Ninth? Different thinkers emphasize different aspects: Some the radical turning away from the centrifugal culture of pre-revolutionary days; others again emphasize precisely the transforming of that culture. Some call May Ninth the "holiday of the Arts." Others, more philo-sophically, declare it is "dedicated to each thing enjoyed in itself alone."

But to my mind, no explanation is adequate that does not *begin* from the sense of social peace that existed first at that time among such critical and exact minds (even profound and sad minds) as Gregory Dido, Meyer Leibow, Martha Aaron Troy, and Charles Maritimus. Just what is new in May Ninth (it is as old as music and science!) is the unique coupling of fastidiousness and love. And yes! to my mind—as evening fell on the first May Ninth, and the planet Hesperus was in the sky, there was most of love.

Chicago
January 1937

The Commodity Embodied in BREAD

> A commodity is therefore
> a mysterious thing simply because—
> CAPITAL, BOOK I, I, 4

—for Ben

At the Super Market, a certain prospective purchaser was frantic, pale and flushing by turns, and alternately clutching and holding out a two-dollar bill, which everyone knows to be unlucky. It was Mr. Impetigo! the same as once bought the dozen gross of scissors to benefit by the wholesale price, and so always had many scissors lying around. He was thrifty on a lavish scale. But today he wanted only a single metal stew pot.

The trouble was—it was really, we shall see, in Impetigo's bad education, his aggressive sociology—the proximate trouble was that a little sprocket seemed to have been dislocated in the machinery of the Economy. The Aluminum Company of America (*Alcoa*) had just advertised its new kitchenware: "these utensils will wear forever"; "they will shine on the wall"; "no dirt in the curves of an aluminum pot." The advertisement ran a page in aluminum paint in *The Saturday Evening Post*; and it aroused in Impetigo's breast—as in whose not?—a strong desire to purchase such a pot.

On the *same Tuesday*, however, the Company withdrew all this line from production, distribution, and sale. This was because it was equally essential to set this metal aside for the National Defense.

Here, then, was the *zealous* Mr. Impetigo in a moment of frustration—

He cried, "I want the pot with the Titegrip cover—"

The counter girl said, "The Boy Scouts will collect your aluminum on the Fourth of July."

No no! this actual frustration was not what was making Impetigo so frantic, bringing him even to the edge of what is called a "nervous breakdown." After all, he really needed the stewing pot, and such actual impasses lead at worst to physical, not mental, disorders. But it was the horrors of the imagination! Thus, Mr. Impetigo did not drive, but he knew well that the night service at Texaco Gasoline Stations is a refreshing pause for the motorist who, after weary riding through the rain, can *count on* a cheerful greeting. But the fact *also* was that it was forbidden to sell gasoline after sunset and every station was closed and dark. Now imagine—one need not imagine it, it was in a memorable picture—the anxious motorist on the road, his lights glaring in the pelting rain; but he thinks that *round the next turn* (as the ad said) there will be comfort, ha—

Mr. Impetigo was above all an economist. On the one hand he saw with satisfaction that the advertising was becoming keener: the people were responding to it with enthusiasm; there was nothing that everybody did not want and indeed did not absolutely need to have. What a flow of the Commodities this promised! On the other hand, he saw with dismay that the private incomes were inadequate.

The face of the economist went white—

2.

It is a pleasure to turn from this little frenzy to the serene and cheerful confidence of Mr. Tobias Thomas, who was also at the Market on this Tuesday evening.

With a smile of *amusement* Tobias watched the anxiety of Impetigo under his Panama hat.

"Give me a loaf of bread," he said to the girl with easy assurance.

"Here it is, it is eleven cents," said the blonde merchant, producing from the shelf the shining waxen wrapper given form and body by the doughy mass within.

"Is it eleven cents?" asked Tobias, knowing it well, but drawing out even this preliminary with a certain piety. "Eleven cents."

"*Here* is the money" said the man quietly, and laid down a dime and a cent on the counter.

Obviously this act, of Exchange, had a certain sacramental character— But no! for look, instead of resting in the moment, or expressing any emotion whatsoever, Tobias leaned confidently across the counter and said in a low voice: "Now, Miss, supposing wanted to change this bread, eh? Supposing my wife wanted a different brand?"—

This was apparently absurd! The package was Silver-Sup, the same as he bought every day, and that was advertised on the radio by a famous horse. There was no doubt that this was the package.

"You may bring it back if you haven't broken the wrapper," said the businesslike girl.

Ah! Now Toby took up his purchase, whose waxen wrapper, stamped with the name Silver-Sup Silver-Sup and an equine design, was secondarily protected in a manila bag; and he left the Market.

The reader would have thought—is it not so?—that the moment when the man Bought and Paid For the Commodity was the pregnant moment: the moment charged with invisible power to move and keep in motion the two billion human inhabitants of the world and many dumb beasts; to call into being their tools, conveyances, and—in imitation of the First Day itself—their lights. This was indeed a moment! it rested on a mystery. Yet Tobias, though assuming, as we have seen, a decent demeanor in the face of the Exchange, was an orthodox believer and reserved his *unlimited* awe for the consummation of the mystery itself.

There is a form of heresy—perhaps Mr. Impetigo was such a heretic—that rests its faith *in* circulation rather than *by* circulation. Fascinated by the rapid, the accelerating, exchanges—a study which could indeed distract even an acute mind with its intricacy—these persons vainly imagine that such quasi-visible goings-on are the force which keeps us all as we are and which therefore merits our *deepest* meditation. Once I described a hero of this heresy of Exchangism, the Eliphaz, who sought to turn all his property into money and wrote down his abomination in the *Book of Endlessly Accumulating Zeroes Without an Integer*. But in the end, these persons are Money-changers.

The essential mystery is simple. It does not require of us subtility, like that of Mr. Impetigo, nor heroic inventiveness, like the Eliphaz; but it is for ordinary persons.

On the way home, Tobias once opened the mouth of the manila bag and looked inside. This brown bag had absolutely no primary significance; it was even given away gratis to all who participated in the social acts. There was none too poor to be given a paper bag.

And now, leaning in the doorway of the Apartment house and smoking a pipe in the sunset, Toby saw G. A. Jensen, the Scandinavian janitor with his walrus mustaches. The two exchanged a cheerful greeting. "Good evening," they said. Tobias, the tenant, liked Gustavus Adolphus, who serviced the building and analyzed the Garbage.

But if he knew the truth he might have been disturbed, for the fact was that the Swede was a natural philosopher, with little or no belief whatsoever.

The Apartment house—so named because all the units were enclosed apart—was an imposing structure of six stories with four Apartments on each. The stories were designated by numerals, the Apartments on each by the letters A, B, C, D.

Tobias dwelt with his family in Apartment 3 C in the rear.

These Apartments were rented on the Market, and each painted afresh for its new tenants. When the Lease was signed, they moved in; they scratched the paint with a knife, and the Apartment was then considered out of circulation.

Round the table of Tobias Thomas, besides the master and his wife, were the three children it was necessary for each pair to beget, taking account of accidents.

The eldest, John, understood that when the hermetically sealed package is opened, the goods is out of circulation.

The middle child, June, knew that the package was bought for money at the Market.

The youngest was too small to have any understanding, but shouted "bru-le-bullah! bru-le-bullah!" meaning "bread and butter."

Mimi Caffrey Thomas, the wife of Tobias, prepared a shining white platter, with a border of gilt panels containing carmine roses with pale green leaves, to receive decently the whited and rather worthless body of the Commodity after it was taken out of circulation.

Tobias raised aloft the Bread.

—At this reach of inwardness, it is necessary to observe verbal niceties. When I speak of the Bread with a majuscule B, it is the Bread par excellence (*eminenter*) that stood on the counter. There is no doubt that this was the same Bread that Tobias now held in his two hands; for *all* of us may, with our animal hands, *lay hold* on the Commodity in some shape or other. At the same time we must speak, with a b-minuscule, of bread as mere bread. This is to speak physically (*naturaliter*), but there is no help for it, for in the end all language has this natural origin.

Ought we then to refer to the physical bread perhaps as "bread," in quotation marks? No no! this timidity and arrogance (it is both), which *seems* to free our society from material bonds, in reality robs from us the wonder and the glory of our existence, which is just that we, as we are, not "we" in quotation marks, somehow do lay hold of the Bread. It seems innocent to say "bread" in quotation marks: it is Docetism. But follow it through! and it is *Exchangism* and the doctrine of the *Book of Endless Zeroes Without an Integer*. It is frenzy and no peace.

In the end we must keep steadily in mind the words of Marx: "The Commodity is therefore a *mysterious* thing."

Again he says: "When it steps forth—" he is referring to the physical table, the physical bread—"when it steps forth as a Commodity, it is changed into something transcendent."

"The existence of the things *qua* Commodities . . . has absolutely no connection with their physical properties and with the material relations rising therefrom."

Tobias tore the wrapper of the loaf of bread, and the exchange-value departed from the Commodity.

This sacrament—this service—this sacrifice of the real being of the Commodity—*sealed* and *revivified* the identification of Tobias and his family with the unity of the imperial Economy.

So long as every one of us can partake of this death, earning by arduous works the *fact* that the Commodity is destroyed for us, the Economy is secure and will not degenerate into chaos. The exchange-value has vanished! By this ever-renewed *fact* the several billions of the world find occupation for their time and the order of the classes is maintained.

At this same instant, the Exchange-value is potentially given again.

In this simple service the family found peace, having bought and in the relevant sense consumed. How different this is from the torment of the Impetigos and the Eliphazes, raging in the Market and their hearts pounding at the late Figures, as if this were the only service! But they do not put their trust in the ultimate Security.

The Eliphaz, intent on changing all the capital into interest, regarded the ultimate consumption, of which we have just seen an exemplary observance, as the original sin!

It was seven P.M., and over the radio sounded the loud whinny of the famous horse himself, whose name was Silver.

The buzzer of the dumbwaiter rang, for the Garbage; and the mother rose to put on the day's refuse, including the waxen wrapper which was now, of course, an insignificant husk.

"Garbage!" sang up the voice of Gustavus Adolphus through the long shaft. The buzzers were sounding also in 1 C, 2 C, 4 C, 5 C, 6 C.

The small child was greedily stuffing a slice of the white bread into its mouth, and Tobias, with fatherly indulgence, was buttering another slice to follow that.

Perhaps I can say something of this physical bread: It had the potential *virtue* of being quantifiable, in pounds and ounces, for the estimation of the Price. Further, it had the convenience *(convenientia)* of being malleable in lumps or loaves, for the purpose of purchase across the Counter and conveyance. It was destructible, tending to harden, rot, or be devoured, so that it presented no temptation *(scandalum)* to Hoarding. At the same time it was rare, so that unlike the air or earth of which it was composed, it offered an incentive *(fundamentum spei)* to be made the embodiment of the Commodity.

Gustavus Adolphus Jensen was a Garbage Analyst.

This science, sorting out the elements into a battery of cans, he pursued partly for the sake of the Economy, reclaiming the precious foils and metals, and the fats and the bones. But mostly he studied the Garbage just to pry and to know.

This, like all learning, gave him *power* over every single Apartment.

He was a natural philosopher and did not judge the bread in terms of its sociological virtues. But not believing this, he fell into superstitions of his own: for instance, he was a believer in the Vitamins.

A little Swede with walrus mustaches, he stood beneath a feeble light in the basement, cautious, often using a tweezers. Slit the manila bags up their backs, picked a pair of spectacles from among the grounds and eggshells, and drew off the serums in syringes. The midges flew toward the light, and Gustav had a little monkey who, curling her tail round a pipe, delighted in snatching the insects from the air.

These were the revealing remnants of private lives.

Sometimes in the Garbage of 1 C he found her golden wedding ring, which he discreetly placed in the mail box.

Something terrifying! 2 C *never sent down any Garbage* at *all*. But it was only an Exchangist, intent on turning *all* his property into fungible goods and storing it up against the Day.

Every evening Gustav shook his head disapprovingly when he found the wrapper stamped Silver-Sup Silver-Sup. It was his belief that 3 C would be wiser to buy instead the ochre wrapper of Lugan's Gluten, on which was plainly stamped the formula "1200 units vit. B1, USP."

—But the great time was Monday morning when descended bales and bales of the *Sunday Times* and nothing else besides!

The monkey had the face of a malicious old person, alert and lively without any curiosity. Sometimes she stood with her long tail drooped over one arm, like the train of a dress. At other times she arranged her tail in a perfect circle on the floor and squatted in the middle of it.

New York City
October 1941

Terry Fleming, or Are You Planning a Universe?

1.

Mother told Terry that his father was dead. But when he grew old enough to read and to ferret in the trunk, he found newspaper clippings that his father was in jail. He was excited. His father was not dead but alive, not nothing but a person, not nowhere but in a place. He was angry with his mother anyway, now he was angry with her because she tried to hide his living father. She kept secrets from him, he kept his secret from her; but he had the advantage, because he knew.

His father and his father's plight seemed wonderfully interesting to Terry and he bragged to his mates in school. "*My* father is in a tremendous jail. It goes on more'n fifty miles. It's far away." His schoolmates were doubtful how to take this novelty. Those to whom the word *jail* meant something vaguely guilty and frightening were stirred to awe and envy, because what is guilty is forbidden and what is forbidden is delightful without limits. The thought of this ecstasy communicated itself from them to Terry. He radiated privilege.

He bragged to his teacher Miss Agostine that his father was in the great jail. She started and Terry was convinced that there was something unbelievable. So he insisted, to enjoy the reaction again and again. But when she showed signs of pity, he felt contempt and anger and said, "What do you know about jails, you old maid?"

To preserve his little glory he made a devaluating judgment of them all.

His schoolmates, fortified by information from home, conspired to take him down a peg, and at the corner after lunch they greeted him with the outcry, "Your daddy's a jailbird."

But Terry said serenely, "What do *you* know about jails? My daddy's alive. My daddy's alive and in jail. Even my Mom tried to keep it secret from me, but I found it out by reading. It's in the papers. He's not nowhere. Yeow! *My* daddy's alive, he's in jail."

2.

Terry's father, Dick Fleming, was inured. Whether in fear or perverse hope, he could not foresee any extraordinary punishment that they could inflict on him that would not be indifferent, indifferently sad, to him. When he first reached this condition, his attitude was exasperating to the prison authorities; it seemed to be insolent, defiant and provocative, a show of force to be met with new force. But there was no increment of reaction on his part and even a superficial observer could see that his expression was not a judgment of them nor of his relation to them, but of a certain relation to himself. To create such an inward-turning relation was the purpose of their reformatory, and therefore usually they now let him be.

Punished, or let be in his cage, Dick Fleming felt no anger. He had achieved a control of his feelings that prevented the fruitless anger from rising and disturbing the pleasure of surcease from pain. The worst pain would be to repeat the process of bursting with anger and swallowing the anger. Of turning four colors: red, black, white and purple: for there is the red anger of boiling anger, the black anger of settled wrath, the white anger of blazing fury, and the purple anger of suppressed rage.

The expense of soul in repeating this fruitless process was too exhausting to endure. Dick was preoccupied with avoiding the pain of the rising of the instinctive reaction of anger, and he was inured to the hurt, usual or extraordinary, that they inflicted on him. He did not fear anything but the obliterating fury itself, that would obliterate first himself.

But when he slept, he dreamed of the fire. We others dream of the fire with its features and colors and licking its objects: houses burning, explosions, and bolts of electricity. But the fire that Dick dreamed of was more like the dark fire of physics, an invisible mass not even hot because it touches no objects—the fire itself, filling a space, where nothing else can be, except that occasionally there is a white flash and annihilation because of some flaw in the perfect destructiveness.

3.

"My father is a king," thought Terry. "Enemies have locked him in jail. They have cruel guards and use heavy stone and iron to keep him unknown. But his dignity shines.

"They gave me to a gypsy. My real mother is dead."

Terry was too prudent to brag to his schoolmates that his father was this important person. But his knowledge of it enabled him sometimes to withdraw from stupid competitions with a distant smile. But the secret of it isolated him from his friends and he had no other confidants.

Terry did not let on to the woman he housed with that he knew she was a gypsy.

"Also, my father has a daughter, my older sister," thought Terry. "She is beautiful and she has let-down hair. She is not in jail, but she has a way of getting in to see our father. She works on the outside with our party. She is the one I must get in touch with, to know what to do next."

But it was not the case that Terry met his sister on any corner, although he had a suspicion that certain persons, by their dignity, belonged to their party; but he was too prudent to be forward. Instead, what he recognized clearly, by their pretended dignity and their cruelty, were the enemies. He learned to mark how they usurped privileges and were abusing them. The enemies did not aim any special attacks at Terry himself because he kept his secret too well, that it was *his* father who was the king. Terry saw that most of the kids were ignorant sheep who did not know what was going on, and they were the most abused.

Sometimes he was buoyed up by hope. At other times, especially in the anxious dark before sleep, Terry felt that the enemy regime was becoming the accepted order of things: the king was literally rotting away in jail and it was too late to rescue him. The world was closing in and there was no way of making a break-through, even if he met his sister.

Most of the day he was neither elated nor anxious but masturbated with dogged courage.

4.

Are *you* planning a Universe? Are you thinking of creating a *Universe*? Here are some *do's* and *don'ts* to bear in mind. If you follow these simple suggestions you will have a better chance of being content with your Universe.

Don't have any "chosen people." The fancied advantages of such an arrangement are found to be far less than the complications that arise.

Do have a good supply of material on hand, so that at the last moment you don't have to skimp on whole realms of being.

Don't try to settle everything beforehand, but *do* have a reserve for unfore-seen changes, so that you don't end up stuck with an undesirable scheme and hating it.

Do show a little pity.

If you're planning a Universe. If you're thinking of creating a Universe.

Do show a little pity.

Don't hide your face too completely, because you might as well get some satisfaction out of your handiwork.

Do give the souls a little substance along with their necessary flexibility, or they will become complicated to the point of monotony.

Don't have any "chosen people."

If you follow these simple suggestions, you will have a better chance of being content with your Universe.

Do try to keep it clear what is nature and what is violence.

Don't hurry, putting in a week's work and thinking you can have something to be proud of.

But *do* let yourself go, according to your whim. Remember that it's your show from the beginning to the end.

But *don't* have any "chosen people."

And *do* show a little pity.

If you're planning a Universe. If you're thinking of creating a Universe. Here are some *do's* and *don'ts*. Follow these simple suggestions and you will have a better chance of being content with your Universe.

Don't forget?

New York City
June 1, 1947

Eagle's Bridge:
The Death of a Dog

We stopped our car by the bridge and went down to the bank of the river to eat lunch. The rapid stream swept onward, past its dark pool. On the map the place was Eagle's Bridge. The few houses were white and substantial; there was a barn-red general store across the road from our car. Our little black dog gladly leaped out the car window even before we stopped, waited for us, and preceded us down the steep path that was obscured by flowering bushes; and she lapped the river.

Suddenly in the dark pool, near the shore, I saw a great dark bass looking out at us. He must have been thirty inches long. In high excitement I cried out to my boy, and the fish turned and vanished in the depths. "Here is a fish this big!" I exclaimed. "I think it was a bass." Matty came, but there was no longer a fish to be seen. "Why don't you go get your line and fish him?" I said.

My wife, my son, and I were pleasantly wasting a month driving across mountains and lakes of the Northeast, and we might as well loiter an hour here as elsewhere. Eagerly Matty climbed up through the flowering bushes to get his rod from the car, while our little black dog followed him halfway up and ran back to us on the shore, for her business in life was to shepherd us together, hastening nearsightedly to each one and leaping up on us, doubling back to make sure. She was always bewildered. We stopped so often she could not judge if we were going to get into the car again and drive off; but then she had to be in the car first, as if to make sure that she was not left behind.

Matty returned and began to fish for the dark master of the pool under Eagle's Bridge with a red and silver striped spoon. It would have given him immense satisfaction to catch the great fish I had seen, and we would have been immensely proud of him with his fish. "I ought to use a worm," he said judiciously. I thought so, too, and began to scratch with a stick for some worms, but the soil was too wet and sandy.

Sally, however, climbed up the steep path through the flowering bushes and I knew that she, in her practical way, was going to get a tablespoon from the car and dig up above where worms were more likely.

There was a pause of silence on the bank of the river sweeping under Eagle's Bridge, and one could hear the gentle waters, and the breeze in the leaves of the trees. Matty was fishing in the pool, where somewhere in the submerged rocks that great fish was lurking, while the red and silver striped lure flicked on the surface.

Then I heard Sally's voice call out from above, "Paul, come up here a moment." It was the deep and strained voice that she has only when something is very wrong and must be attended to at once. She had used it when the house was on fire. I did not hesitate and climbed up the steep path through the bushes with foreboding. I could not imagine how she could be hurt—her voice did not sound like that. Was it the car?

I emerged, and she was seated on the concrete foundation of the iron bridge holding in her lap our little black dog, Lucy. Blood was slowly dripping out of the dog's mouth onto Sally's white and black print skirt. Sally's face was set in despair. The dog's head did not sit right; her eyes were closed and she was dying. Beyond, through the bridge, I could see the black car that had hit her, stopped at the other end. The man was walking back toward us.

"Her heart is still beating," said Sally.

"What shall we do?" I said.

It was our little Lucy with her beautiful glossy coat that had, on this trip, become more full and glowing every day. I reached out my hand and touched her fur.

"Don't touch her!" said Sally unaccountably.

"Why shouldn't I touch her?" I cried.

"Her heart has stopped beating," said Sally.

The tears welled hot in my eyes, and I began to sob, turning away to look down from the bridge. "Oh, Christ," I said, "how are we going to tell Matty?... She loved me so."

She loved each of us in a different way, as dogs do. She jumped for joy when I came home and bounded from room to room and came back and leaped up on me, yipping, and would not stop, trembling and frantically wagging her tail, until I bent down and let her kiss my face.

Matty was below, happily fishing the pool. She was his first dog.

Sally sat with despair on her face and my heart was bleak. As if peacefully, our little black dog lay in my wife's lap, in her arms. I touched her, she was still warm; her eyes were closed. The blood ceased dripping from her mouth.

"I went across the road to dig," said Sally. "I didn't think she was up here—" We had always been so extremely careful with the dog—just for this—shouting at her, grabbing her by the collar, putting her leash on: for she was always impetuously leaping and bounding.

The man came up to us. He was white-haired, and he had a lined, rather hard face and frightened eyes. "Whose dog is it?" he asked.

"It was our dog," said Sally.

"I stopped right away," said the man. "We have a law in this state—"

"It's all right, mister," I said, "there's nothing to do about it."

"I stopped right away," he said.

"It's all right, mister," I said harshly. "You just go on your way."

He hesitated.

"You just go away," I said.

Yet I did not notice him going away. Probably the dog had leaped out from behind our parked car.

"I heard a thud," said Sally, "I thought the car had hit a bump."

"Let's bury the dog," I said. I hesitated. "All right, I'll go and tell him." And I directly went down the steep path, pushing through the flowering bushes, with the definite steps with which one does a fatherly duty. The car had swiped the dog on the side of the head and she must have felt no pain at all. It was not as if her back had been broken and she had screamed. (So I tortured myself.) The boy was out on a little point of land around a copse of bushes, trying to disengage his line that was caught in the rocks in the depths.

"Matty," I called, "come here at once. I have to tell you something."

She had always been a happy little dog, and she looked so sweet there, dead in Sally's lap. She had really loved only three things: us and food and to sally forth in the world triumphantly barking, holding her feathers high. She had had plenty of that.

"My line is stuck," said Matty.

"Break it off," I said.

He came edging around the copse of bushes with his rod, trying to keep his shoes dry. I told him that Lucy had been hit by a car and was dead.

"Do you want to come up and see her?" I asked.

"No!" he said. "No!" He turned away and sat in the bushes and began to bawl.

"She—she looks all right—" I began to say, but left him. I went back up the path.

"He won't come up," I said to Sally.

I went across to the general store to buy a shovel and they began to look to see if they had one in stock. "My dog just got hit and I want to bury her. Can you *lend* me a shovel?" I said.

"Take the shovel outside by the barrel," said the man.

"Where?" said Sally. "Down by the river," I said. "You'll have to come down with the dog. Can you get down the path carrying the dog?"

I began to have strong flash-memories of the dog—leaping, always leaping, straight and high up in the air to catch her ball. The boy was sobbing, hidden in the bushes, in the sullen and withdrawing way that he has when he feels he has been betrayed. I found it hard to dig in the stony sand. I had picked a spot above the usual flood line, in a little clearing behind the copse of bushes. But of course the spring torrent would flood it out.

When Lucy would get the ball, she trotted off triumphantly with it and tried to keep it away from us, even while she came back, wanting us to get it and bounce it or throw it again. She was bewildered and torn between the twin desires of having the ball as her own possession and playing catch with us. Finally she would come to terms with love and lay the ball at our feet. But sometimes she would trot spiritedly with it in big circles, triumphantly waving her plume, and we thought she was like a circus dog.

"Dig it deep," said Sally. She was there carrying the body of the dog, whose eyelids now had fallen half open. I took off my shirt and cut away into the stony sand and kept digging.

Then there was a gray hole and its heap of stony dirt, and the dog was lying in the hole drawn up in a fetal position, as in those uncovered graves of primitives. The dog's head did not sit quite right; her eyes had the glazed look of a dead dog. But her coat was burnished like black fire, and the auburn was shining through. We had never seen it so beautiful. The fur was still alive. In that gritty hole she lay like a black star. "Shall I make Matty come?" I said. Sally looked at me with a face of despair.

"Matty," I said firmly, "come and bury your dog." To my relief, he let me bring him by the hand. I gave him the shovel.

Meantime I had the thought to get some rocks to pile on the grave. I pulled and tugged at big stones rooted in the sand; I collected a few stones big as a football and big as a fist; and my eyes kept welling with tears. I reasoned it was two things: first, of course, my pathetic mournfulness because this dog had been the only thing in the world that simply loved me and showed her joy when I came. But secondly—and this it was that seemed to bring on the tears—it was that she had such a lovely spirit, whether human or not, leaping and eager, indefatigable, wanting to come along and be included, obviously joyful when the least occasion offered (and there were many): and also bewildered—that was an important part of it—perhaps even a little stupid, for she was only a dog. O our little Lucy! I was caught by grief as I bent over to tug at a stone by the river-bank—who had been so animated and happy and persistent to get close and in-between and be included: whose heart was nothing but love. At first she had not been the kind of dog I prefer; but she had won us by the spirit in her.

It was happening terribly swiftly. Hit and dead and buried by the river, and off to drive away. One did not have a chance to take it in.

Very thoroughly, as if it were a duty that he willingly took on himself, Matty was filling up the hole with the big shovel. And now the two, the boy and his mother, were placing the stones on the little grave.

Was the great dark fish looking at us from his pool? Or was he simply lurking, in his meditation, in the depths among the rocks? I had a flash image of that dark fish, that he was a spirit of death. And if only I had not seen him, and had not had the thought to fish for him when we stopped for a rural lunch! Just so, Sally was thinking her vain regretful thoughts, for she said, "I wasn't thinking about the dog at all when I crossed the road. We were always so extremely careful."

They were standing there. It is a little round grave piled with a few stones. Down under the right of the bridge toward Route 22, until the spring flood washes it away.

"She was always a happy little dog," I said, to say something.

"Yes, because we were always very good to her," said Sally. Especially she.

Matty did not want to talk. "Let's get away from here," he said.

I climbed up to take the shovel back to the store, leaving Sally to collect our gear, while Matty wound up his broken line. We were in bleak silence. Our party was empty of its spirit, and we did not want to do anything except drive the two hundred miles home as quickly as possible. Our car was not going to be crowded any more—it was without its little pest who kept snuggling into the front seat and annoying the driver.

"It was too sudden," said Sally. "One moment she was there, and the next moment she was not." It was too quick, the way she died and we buried her and were driving away in the car without her. We did not have a chance to take it in; and therefore I am telling it again.

For a couple of weeks we had come on a long and somewhat hazardous voyage, over high mountains and some bad roads. It was as if we had to offer some sacrifice, in order to get home safe, and so we stopped at Eagle's Bridge, and I saw that cursed death looking at us from his pool.

"I'll drive," said Sally stolidly, still wearing her face of despair, as if she thought that I, if I drove, would somehow be desperate and reckless. I gave her the keys.

New York City
August 1960

From *The Empire City*
The Politics of Lothario

I have not seen one well-bred man since I came to New York. At their entertainments there is no conversation that is agreeable; no modesty, no attention to one another. They talk very loud, very fast, and all together. If they ask you a question, before you can utter 3 words of your answer they will break out upon you again and talk away.

— John Adams, 1774

1. History of a Campaign Against War

When Lothario Alger was in college, he was a vigorous leader in a fight against war, to expel from the school every vestige of militarism, every uniform, every colonel, every student corps whether compulsory or voluntary. This fight was directed not against the possibility of war (at that time there was no such possibility), but against the idea of the possibility; and it was correlated with mighty international efforts along the same lines, led by governments that had just won the victory in a generally disastrous war, though one not so disastrous to the victors as to the vanquished.

It was the aftermath of a great war (1914–1918), and far from there being a new danger of war, it was above all necessary to remove all traces of that old awful war before it was even possible to think of waging a new war. The student agitators were glad to be of service to help clear the atmosphere, so that everywhere could shine bright peace. Even the professors recanted the lies that they had told in the interest of the old war. Whenever anyone died who had been connected with that war, such as a statesman, a commander or even a garrulous veteran of one's acquaintance, on *all* sides there was discreet satisfaction; but every such death might well have caused a pang of dread, for when they were all dead it would easier to recommence.

Now was the era of peace, quite essential for international trade in the capital, raw materials, weapons, new inventions and the exchange through spies of strategic innovations in order to make possible an equitable new war. And Lothar and his friends, at the cost of being themselves expelled from school, succeeded in eliminating every vestige and idea of the old war.

Their plan was, along with this victory, to fight also against colonial imperialism; but at this time that institution was not popularly connected with the old war as such—it rather belonged to the fruits of victory—so that on this issue there was not the same popular support, and no international support, and here perhaps they did not succeed at all. Yet the enormous success that they did achieve, they summed up in the formula: "Comrades, we have made a dent!" And they felt that *if they carried through the struggle on any real issue, they would destroy the capitalist system.*

Soon new war clouds gathered thick and black, and the well-armed hostile powers were threatening to destroy the generally unprosperous order of civilization. Lothar and his friends, who were—because of their previous success—important youth leaders (though they *were* growing older), now resolved on measures of heroic resistance to the inevitable war. It was necessary, they argued, that at no point in the general peaceful order should a break occur, for if it did the entire order of civilization would at once be destroyed. (A lot of people didn't care much whether it was or not.) The formula of the friends was: "The peace is indivisible." It was true that several breaks had occurred already and indeed it seemed that the entire system was being destroyed.

Yet there were many arrangements and deals still possible under the old co-operative system; this form of commerce was internationally called the Appeasement. So the young people took a great oath: that in no circumstances whatsoever would they ever allow themselves to be drafted for any war whatsoever. That was flat, wasn't it? In the circumstances this resolve was revolutionary and would overturn the entire capitalist system, for since the system was now about to thrive on the carefully prepared breakdown of the system, the effort to carry through the conservation of the system would surely overturn the system itself. But of course, as it proved, there were still many profitable arrangements to be made under the peaceful system, though not exactly, from a certain point of view, according to the plan of those who took the great oath.

Finally, at the time of our history, the storm of war was modestly raging everywhere. In the Empire City preparations were being made, including the registration and draft of all the young men. And the youth leaders—by now they were rather old for youth leaders—seeing the opportunity to work among the masses on this important issue, proposed the following practical program: A raise in the soldiers' pay to $30; adequate furloughs for all draftees; healthful conditions in the cantonments; democratic political representation for privates (through the youth leaders); and several other good and necessary immediate aims. They felt that by pushing through this program, they could eventually overturn the entire capitalist system.

2.

"Wait a minute, not so fast," said Lothar, a little troubled. "Our course of the last ten years is not altogether clear to me. First we pledged in no circumstances to allow ourselves to be drafted; now we are demanding adequate furloughs."

"True. But it is necessary to carry on the struggle on the issues actually confronting the people. If we can assure military democracy, we can easily change the nature of the war and eventually overturn the entire capitalist system."

"What do you mean 'true'?" cried another comrade, trained in the C.P. "What he says is a lie. He has no knowledge of history. He's a wrecker."

For the time being, Lothar disregarded this second fellow, and addressed himself to the reasoning: "You say the issues actually confronting the people, etc. But these issues have actually been presented to us by Eliphaz, haven't they?"

"Of course! If you choose to put it that way. They are presented to us by History, as our comrade says, by the dynamics of society."

"But why is the issue drawn exactly here?" cried Lothar. "Why not urge abstention from the registration and draft altogether, as we agreed?"

"That's illegal. The penalty is three years in jail and ten thousand dollars fine. Is it revolutionary to sit in jail? Who's got ten thousand dollars?"

"Ah! It seems," said Lothar bitterly, "that once we began to operate within the framework of *their* system, our program did not develop exactly according to *our* plan. All this comes originally from the fact that there is a registration of our date and place of birth. Why did I fail to take advantage of the fact that I was expelled from school?"

"You mustn't lose your head, Lothar! Remember that *that* agitation was successful and we made a dent. Your present attitude reminds me of the time when the I.W.W. expelled the lumbermen from the union because they *won* a strike, since winning meant signing a contract! You make me laugh."

"You think that was so absurd?" cried Lothar miserably. "If we hadn't been successful, in a certain sense, all along the line, we shouldn't now be asking for adequate furloughs. You're the ones who make *me* laugh. Ha!"

"What did I tell you?" said the comrade trained in the C.P. "He's an idealist, a wrecker."

3. Trying to Register

Because of the peculiar dynamics of his soul, Lothario tried to register for the draft nevertheless.

To his surprise he found that he could not fill out the registration questionnaire which bristled with personal, economic, political and ethical questions impossible for him to answer unambiguously. Every question, he now discovered, presupposes a theory of the nature of things: exclusive alternatives are proposed, of which you are to choose one, or say Yes or No; or a genus is given with a species to be filled in. But in the first case Lothar most often found that the middle was not excluded; and in the second case, when he found that the genus was nonexistent, he was at a loss for the species. These questions, for the most part, failed to correspond to anything in his experience.

The registrar was a helpful young chap named Cooley, a secretary of the Y.M.C.A.—for it was the Imperial policy to keep the draft entirely out of the hands of the military, whose methods were too crude for sociological accuracy.

Cooley was puzzled by Lothario's replies. "Let's see then," he began briskly: "*Are you married or single?*"

Lothario explained that he was no longer living with his legal wife—in fact she was now married to somebody else, though whether legally or not he didn't know because he didn't know whether the divorce ever went through. He himself still occasionally sent her money for support. He had, however, two children by another woman, who was in a sense his present wife, but this relationship didn't count for the purposes of the registration, he supposed, since she was able to support both herself and the children, and he didn't like her anyway. He resided with his sister and brother.

"I see—I see," said Cooley and wrote down: *Single.* "*Do you have any dependents?*"

Lothario's dependent for the purposes of the Imperial relief was Horatio, who was, however, Laura's dependent also. ("Was this quite honest?") The fact was that Lothar had many dependents for whom he felt responsible and therefore needed the money, since he belonged to a rather large organization many of whose members often had to come to him for assistance, despite the fact that they were on relief. Besides he partly supported his perhaps-wife, though since he was marked "single" this could hardly count.

"Yes, I see—I see," said Cooley and wrote down: *None.* "*Are you employed?*"

"Employed?" asked Lothar unbelievingly.

"That is, are you employed? Do you have your own business? Or are you out of work?"

"Oh. Now I dig you. What is involved here," explained Lothar, "is a theory of vocation and avocation, work and leisure, the ratio between a certain number of hours of labor time, a certain quantity of commodities produced or exchanged, or services rendered, a certain stipend and a quasi-political relationship between the entrepreneur and his aides."

"Precisely!" said Cooley enthusiastically.

"I don't believe in any of that," explained Lothar.

The facts were that he was a member of a fairly large organization run not for profit; a considerable amount of money passed through his hands; sometimes as need arose he appropriated some for his own use; at other times he scrounged from anywhere what he could for his friends: they kept no books.

"Ah, what is the name of this organization?"

"Unfortunately I can't tell you that," explained Lothar.

"But previously you said you were on the Imperial relief?"

"Yes."

"Fine," said Cooley, and wrote down: *Relief.*

"Oh, I must explain to you that I am by vocation a musician."

"A musician! Do you mean you are a professional musician?"

"A vocation is not a profession," said Lothar gravely.

He began to explain that he was the composer of a book of études for the piano, a concerto in no key—

But Cooley interrupted him and asked: "Is this secret organization of yours perhaps a kind of orchestra?"

"An orchestra? No. That is to say, yes . . ." faltered Lothario. For now suddenly he saw the fallacy of this interrogation and he lost heart.

Once again! Once again his earnest effort to co-operate was thwarted

"*What is your education?*" asked Cooley.

"I was expelled from school," said Lothar dully.

Ah, I see——how unfortunate," said Cooley and wrote it down. "*Do you have any serious diseases?*"

" I am sick at heart," explained Lothar.

"That's bad," said Cooley, and wrote: *Heart disease (no document).* "*Do you have any conscientious objections to the war?*"

"Yes! Yes! I have the most serious objections!" cried Lothar so eagerly that Cooley looked up for the first time.

"*According to the tenets of what religious group?*" he dutifully continued.

At this intimate question Lothar became enraged. He snatched the paper from under Cooley's fingers and looked at it trembling.

"In what kind of world does the young man live who made these questions up!" he shouted. "What kind of witty ambiguities must I invent today in order to live a little longer in this Empire City?"

"I beg your pardon—" said Cooley.

"No! How would *you* know? I'll go down to the capital and confront him face to face, and I'll prove that it's he and not I who has perverted our dear English tongue! . . .

"Ah, here is a question of *fact* that I can answer unambiguously!" he said. "*When and where was I born?* I was born in the Empire City on such a day 19—.

I see that this has assigned me a place and time to go astray on all the other points. But how could I go so far astray in a single generation?" And he tore up the questionnaire and rushed out of the room.

Once again! Once again his earnest effort to restore the original social peace of his early childhood—before the birth of Laura, before the coming of Horatio into a gypsy life—when the first child, the mother and father were a serene and regular constellation like those triplet suns which revolve around one another, around their epicenters, little perturbed by the crowds of heaven: it lay there shattered—once again!—his effort to belong. To have had a Golden Age is fatal to all the rest of one's life!

But he had no cause to be amazed that he had gone so far afield in a single generation, for any single alienating principle, such as honor or pleasure or common sense, operating continually, can achieve any degree of peculiarity you want.

4.

He decided, instead, to register under the Alien Registration Act, whereby all aliens must be registered and fingerprinted. Apparently he was not so certain of the "time and place" of which he had just boasted.

"Since you were born in this country," said the officer, a military man, "you must at some time have forsworn your allegiance or you would not be an alien. Precisely when and where did this occur?"

"It was not by any single act," said Lothar. "In a sense there has been a progressive alienation."

"A progressive alienation! I have not heard of this category."

"Maybe the critical moment occurred this morning in my own neighborhood."

"In your own neighborhood! This morning! What kind of garbage are you telling me here? To what flag do you imagine that you swore allegiance this morning?"

"To what flag? To what flag?"

"Yes, you heard me. To what flag do you adhere?"

"I—"

"Have you registered for the draft?" asked the officer bluntly. "You have to register *whether* you are a citizen or an alien."

"I am a citizen of Equity!" cried the young man sententiously. "I can bear arms only when I have a conviction which with regard to your present war I do not feel!"

"Of *Ecuador*?" cried the officer disbelievingly. "Show your passports," he said sternly.

"From a certain point of view I am a citizen of this country," said Lothar proudly, "and a better one than you are!"

And with this remark he stood up and walked out.

This sentiment was sometimes expressed by the slogan: "If Thomas Jefferson were alive today, he'd be a member of the C.P."

The officer promptly phoned the Bureau of Investigation to follow the case of Lothario Alger, presumably a draft dodger (penalty three years and $10,000 fine).

The Social Compact

If a man be held in prison or bonds or is not trusted with the liberty of his body, he cannot be understood to be bound by Covenant to subjection; therefore he may, if he can, make his escape by any means whatsoever.

— Hobbes

1. How Lothair Stood Behind the Bars

When he was first locked behind the bars, where he could not *persist* in being of service (whether we were willing or not), Lothair did not pace like the crazed tiger, nor stare dumbly through the opening, but he grasped with his hands the two end bars and stared at the middle bar. A sympathetic critic would say that the trouble with Lothair was that he had stubbornly wanted to *serve* in his own way. But this is a convenient lie, for one cannot serve in one's own way, but only in someone else's need, to which one gives heart, head and hand. This makes it almost impossible to serve at all (though one can try), because *A*'s need is not amenable to *B*'s heart, etc.; nevertheless, Lothair persisted, not in trying to serve, but in actually serving, until he was jailed.

Now of all the lovely outgoing acts of the soul, it is only service that can be frustrated by bars. For if you jail a lover, will not his love turn first to dreams, then strongly burn for invisible or perhaps divine loves? And if you jail an artist, a thinker, they are still free, to dance with rage and count the bars. A moralist is freer still: he has himself to control. But a man of service can only grasp the bars with both hands and press his head against the middle one, while the courage drains from his heart.

2. How Lothair Tirelessly Committed Himself All the Way

Nettled, our sympathetic critic cries out: "I am suspicious of this man who will not show his face. Why doesn't he serve himself? 'If I am not for myself, who is for me?' Why doesn't he *be* himself? For in the end this is the only way to benefit mankind. But he offered me a hand—good! I rejected it—too bad. Why did he persist in making a nuisance of himself?"

What is this word "rejected"? The man wills to serve you. It is not up to you to accept or reject. You in fact have a society with its conditions. If he chose to serve according to your conditions, what could *you* do about it, except suffer the advantages? Now there is another man who relies on himself and on nature, and he works, as you say, in his own way: *him* you can disregard; in all likelihood he judges that you are quite demented anyway and he is unwilling to waste his strength in your conditions or baffle his wits on your wrong view of the problems. But how could you disregard Lothair? He reserved judgment as to whether society was sane or mad; he took its existence as prima-facie proof of its possibility; he tirelessly committed himself, at need, to every one of the conditions—to the very conditions that were creating the desperate need (but he always thought he saw a way out). Then, in the end, there was Lothair, insistent on being of service—just when all the rest were breathing sighs of relief at the prospect of getting rid of it all, or of some of it, by rushing into destruction; or of letting it just close in, and dying. Lothair refused to let the war solve the problems. At this moment it was necessary to jail him.

3. How Lothair and Eliphaz Were Adversaries

Lothair and Eliphaz were adversaries *point by point.* It was therefore not surprising that both of them execrated the violence of the world-wide total war. By multiplying his enterprises, Eliphaz succeeded in draining the good use from each thing in turn and giving it a value in zeros without an integer. With patient flexibility, Lothair countered him by demonstrating a social possibility nevertheless in each exchange, in each loss—like a tireless swordsman, always on the defense, intent on keeping us all alive, and waiting. (Waiting for what?) But the hearts of the people were not so great as those of their champions; they did not have an *idea,* and without an idea it is impossible to be endlessly patient. Soon therefore they degenerated into violence on each other. Violence is too quick; it is too close; it does not exhaust the soul. It is not objective. It does not nourish (*educare*) the tender strength of the animals into humanity.

4. Why It Is Dangerous to Frustrate a Man of Service

But ah, when you frustrate the efforts of a man who is really intent on serving you, the effect is not what you hope for. He does not withdraw. On the contrary, he says to himself: "These persons need me more desperately than I conceived. I thought it was just a case of so and so, but in fact it is the much deeper need of such and such." Then, in a short time, he comes to offer you a hand—and to your terror it looks like a fist. He used to have a plan according to the conventions you were conscious of; but now it seems almost to be—direct action. And what if the *blow* should surprise in you the knowledge that you did not know you knew?

Do you think, on his part, that it's not a terrible thing for a man like him to have to change his theory?

5. The Social Contract

One day Lothair pressed his forehead against the bar and groaned: "The social compact is abrogated that I used to have with these people." (For the first time in his life he spoke of the people in the third person rather than in the first person, or in moments of towering anger or love in the second person.) "I for my part fulfilled it to the letter, and I am a close reader; but these ignoramuses have alienated themselves from communication."

The tears began to flow from his bland gray eyes when he thought: "It was not by any decision that I entered that compact, nor did I enter it so much as I was nourished by it into my growth. From the very beginning I learned how to warp the language and to aim at ordinary goods by indirection. But it was not asked, it was not agreed, that I take leave completely of my wits and honor. This we would see to step by step. I was willing to take my chances.

"But this compact was for mutual life and service; and when they threaten to take away my life and they deprive me of my liberty, then it is my duty to consider myself again in a state of nature.

"What a hard saying! I was not trained to live by force and fraud without a care, without the counsel and the resistance of my obstructive friends. What! Am I supposed to learn the language anew and try, a late learner, to say simply what is the case? And to aim directly at what it is I want? I have not been like artists and the sages who from the beginning refused to associate with these people (and maybe they were in the right after all!); now they can speak with ease and play even deadly games. But nothing occurs to me except to growl and bare my teeth.

"Alas! *Those* people"—he now came to say *those*—"have alienated themselves from the natural generation. They have lost patience. They have forgotten the continuous association between their hearts and the way they move about the streets. They take gambler's chances. Their architects are crazy. Violent! Violent!

"Ha! If my neighbors have begun to have bad dreams, is it therefore I who am alienated from nature?"

As he said this, the tears were scorched from his eyes, which began to flame. He ungrasped the bars and began to pace to and fro in the cage.

6. How Lothair Enjoyed a Good Sampling of the Creation

> Ten steps from one corner to another is already something. If I
> repeat them one hundred and fifty times I shall have walked one
> verst.
>
> — Kropotkin, *Memoirs of a Revolutionist*

It was lovely in the cell (once one agreed to recognize it as a place in its own right); it was an excellent example of the created space: transparent, and actually alight and bounded by color—a kind of brownish gray. Here four right angles exhausted a plane, and planes cut planes in neat lines. From place to place, motion was continuous, so one could stride from corner to corner without vanishing or necessarily stopping short, until the wall. If one interposed a hand with extended fingers before the window, a shadow fell on the floor.

The food (such as it was) was as it should be: unlike the human organism but potentially like it, so that it was transformed by digestion into Lothair. The air supported slow combustion in the lungs and would have allowed a match to burn if one had a match. The iron rang with its beautiful elasticity: the sound echoed and reechoed so fast that one could not analyze the clang but could only marvel.

There were eighty-three wasps, some of them vainly crawling up the wall and slipping back. Lothair offered his services to them, lifting them to the sunny window. They did no harm, unless one annoyed them. He was pleased to consider himself a friend of the wasps.

Suddenly he was stung, once, twice, in either hand. He restrained the impulse to lash back with reflex rage. Instead, he was sorely puzzled: how could one tell just what it was that annoyed a wasp? This made it difficult to befriend them—according to *their* need—with heart, head and hand.

7. The New Directive

Having entered the state of Nature, Lothair now lived in the world without bars. The others were behind the bars. For bars, the bars that imprison, are in the soul; those other things, the iron obstacles that restrict your movements, are just tough obstacles. As we say, no holds barred.

Behind the bars was the corridor, and trebly behind bars, the office.

It was only in a potential sense that there existed any other natural men and other lovely places, for Lothair was a bad prisoner, incommunicado. Inasmuch as he had been indisposed to co-operate with those people previously, why should they have expected him to co-operate now? Lothair often failed to co-operate.

Behind the bars was the office! Suddenly there came to the office a new directive, direct from military headquarters. At last the conscription had been removed from civilian authority and given to the military. This resulted in a new *policy* of great moment to Lothair. The new policy was to create an army primarily for victory, no longer primarily as a means of organizing society. This meant a quite different standard of soldierly efficiency.

The new directive was that Lothair and his friends were henceforth to be called "stinker cases." They were by no means to be accepted or forced into the Army; on the contrary, they were to be discarded, forgotten, their names lost in the files. If a man was not eager to be a soldier, if he had a second thought about it, if perhaps he had expressed his dubiety by cutting off his fingers, such a man was a "stinker case;" he would not make a soldier.

Previously, as we saw, if a man was absolutely unwilling, then the whole force of the state was brought to bear to weed *him* in. This cost a good deal for education, policing and psychiatry; it was destructive of the *esprit de corps*. But now if a man didn't want to be a soldier, he didn't have to be a soldier. (There were no longer any such men anyway.) Furthermore there was a shortage of labor.

8. How Lothair Cried Out for Victory

Lothair was brought to the office to hear the new directive.

Craftily he observed that the window was open and had no bars.

"Alger," said the administrator, "you are a stinker case."

He looked about: there were two guards, but they were at ease, with their mouths open.

"Out of you we shall never make a soldier. Why should we feed you here?"

A rifle was held in nerveless fingers.

"On the other hand, if you work for your living—it makes no difference what you do, every job is in the cash nexus—then you will contribute to the victory."

He counted out the steps and blows: one, two and *three*.

"We used to draw the line on the kind of service acceptable. Now we have gotten wiser."

A tulip tree brushed against the wall. Though Lothair had never been an acrobat, today he felt he had a subhuman agility.

"Today," said the administrator, "is the fifteenth of the month."

Great God of Cats! Make this leap sure and Lothair will liberate the tigers on 63rd Street.

"On the thirtieth you will be a free man. Ha!" And he offered his hand.

"Hey?" said Lothair, hearing for the first time and staring unbelieving at the hand.

"I said Ha! And I offered my hand. Ha!"

Lothair seized the desk with his paws and in a voice hoarse and gasping, a bellow and a scream, he said: "I am *tired* of fighting a drawn-out *losing* fight. Now I am longing for *Victory*. With joy. I want to fight with *joy*. Great God of Cats, make this leap sure! Where is the joy to be found again of my fifth and sixth years, before I began to be of service to these people? Be free! Be free, tigers on Sixty-third Street! The compact is abrogated that we used to have with these people." He broke the desk in two and held a part in each paw.

In fright the administrator seized the phone to ask for orders in this unusual case, of a stinker who was psychotic even before they inducted him into the Army.

Lothair tore the instrument from his hand and altogether from the wall.

"How dare you try to communicate after you have alienated yourselves?"

He took the guard's rifle and clubbed him on the head, and on the third count he leaped through the window.

There was a belated shot. There was a Chase. There was a Flight and a Chase. The condition of a chase is that while A moves from L to M, B moves from M to N.

9. In the Scroll of the Cornice

He had made his getaway, and had gotten to New York. He spent the afternoon curled up in the giant scroll of a verdigris cornice, at the tiptop corner of a building, one hundred feet above the avenue.

Here the pigeons came in their pastel rainbow, with distended plumes. They implanted their claws on his back and his head, and sat for an hour. Others sat in an innumerable series on the ledge above his head, and serially took wing in a swirling spiral to the street.

In their close course, the cars below were like the crests of the billows. The pigeons beat in mid-air like a cloud. The soldiers were hunting in three dimensions through the houses.

To Beat the Bush is for A to go to L, M, N, and O in the hope that B is at L or M or N or O. To Beat About the Bush is for A to go to L, M, N, and O in the knowledge that B is at K. But a Wild-Goose Chase is for A to go to L, to M, to N, to O when B is not at the end of this series of places.

A rainspout was trickling within reach, and Lothair took the occasion to wash his socks and handkerchief. He spread them to dry on the verdigris. Very convenient. Looking about he saw that there was a square platform where it would be possible to install a kerosene stove. . .

(I am almost not joking. One cannot imagine the courage with which people take root in what places, and make them habitable and decorate the place. Every place has its peculiar advantages.)

Next moment, with his heart in his mouth he slid five thunderous yards down the slope and hung on with his claws. This was not perhaps a domestic note.

A Close Thing is for *A* to come to L when *B* is leaving L. Nip and Tuck is for *A* to come to M, N, O, when *B* is leaving M, N, O.

10. In Full Flight

Later in the day, they started out again.

As the mist thickened and the evening came on and the Chase sped along the river—for Flight and Chase, however scattered, move as one heedless entity—then each of the soldiers and Lothair himself had his own concern and his own thoughts. Nevertheless they were being fused into one by this fatiguing and hypnotic Flight (for to a candid observer, looking at their drawn faces, it would have seemed that they were all in full flight). There were shots, but they could not hit him.

Now Lothair, beside himself with violent joy, stood behind a tree and blew out the brains of the first boy who loomed on the path.

"Is *this* direct action?" he asked himself bitterly. "And is this mortal blow, given or received, precisely the *immortal* blow for which I am longing?" He broke into the woods in full flight.

The comrades of the boy wept with indignation as they carried away the body.

Nevertheless, they were one and all in full flight together, cast under a spell by the rhythm of their limbs and the serial order of the places through which they passed, in the close mist—when suddenly the shock of death, which is too vast for the heart to take in in one impulse, yet there it was, a single thing after all, released the deep feelings common to one and all.

The meaning of this common feeling was as if each one—but in reality it was one feeling of them all—as if each one stopped in his tracks and asked himself: "What am I doing *here*? What am I doing here so far from home?"

This was the meaning of the arrested motion in the full flight that could be seen in the drawn faces expressing indignation and violent joy, while their limbs sped in rhythm through the series of the places, in the close mist.

The storm broke and the night fell.

There was a volley of shots on the line of 189th Street, and Lothair vanished into his hole.

Next moment a splash could be heard in the river; the soldiers fired; and now they were pursuing Horatio.

11. Addio

When Lothair awoke, the confusion of the misty night had dissipated from his mind, as had the gentle modifications of fatigue, and the disciplinary realities of violence. With peace, rest and clarity his restricted mind was fixed on the one stark insane resolve to open the cages of the zoological garden and let free the beasts. This seemed to him feasible, useful and called for.

The place in the rocks he regarded as his den. His mind was invaded by agonizingly sharp and joyous odors, which in fact existed there, though he had not yet learned to distinguish one from another. He did not think of himself as an animal so much as a kind of panic being; not a proper member of the animal generation, which is always a goat or a bear, but as the Friend of Wasps, the Planner for the Pigeons, and the Liberator of large Cats. The inhibition of his olfactories was loosed, that had set in when he so early became cleanly (not helped either by clouds of tobacco, which in jail he had not tasted). The powerful actuality of this fresh sense gave him a different awareness of participation in the environment than one had had in debates.

If his thoughts once deviated for a moment into an orderly sequence of argument, immediately a nausea and disgust of the smells overpowered him. But now he repressed the thoughts instead of the smells, which in fact were vital to him. (Any train of argument led to an impasse in any case.)

He roughly nudged Horatio awake.

"Get up. Go to the zoo and get the keys."

Started awake, the boy stared up at him in human fright. What he saw was not Lothair, but a shadowy figure of dream who had drawn up a chair by his bedside and sat down. It was a woman, but gracelessly dressed in a gray shark-skin suit and skirt with coarse peach stockings. He could see only the lower part of the figure. He was afraid. She was perhaps his mother whom he did not remember. She was like the notorious Miss Estey, the disciplinary principal who tyrannized over that school of imprisonment and torture from which he had cunningly escaped by tearing up the records. He awoke.

"I am afraid they won't give me the keys, Lothar," he said in a thin voice.

The figure rose in wrath. She was wielding, in a paroxysm of stupidity, a knife—and vanished.

"Get up, damn you!" said Lothair bellowing and screaming

It was only a bladeless knife, without a handle, and Horatio, who was not used to be addressed in this fashion, recovered his happy wits.

"Hell to you," he said cheerfully. He had no intention of conforming to insane plans.

Lothair was choking with nausea at the sweetish smell, the rank and sour flowers, of the human being.

"Look, Lothar," said Horace, who soon had the violent smell of powerful coffee flooding from the stove (for at Harry Tyler's was nothing but the blackest), "it is not impossible to let the animals out. I know. This idea is a little crazy—excuse me if I talk to you like a brother—and obviously people cannot guard against *every* unthought-of crazy surprise. But then what? A few people will get hurt and then they'll soon hunt the beasts down, into corners, eh? They'll haul them back into their cages and station extra guards. And that'll be the end of that. Be reasonable, boy."

His brother was not listening at all, but was respiring with intense excitement. "I am going to lead by my hand the tiger burning bright, and the grinning crocodile and the giraffe, to visit the sociological museum, and to *see* how it is that those people exist."

His thought was that the city was a vast sociological museum kept for the edification of sane animals.

Horatio shook the big fellow by the shoulders. "Snap out of it, boy."

Lothar looked at him with mild gray eyes. "Do you think it's not wicked," he said softly, "that little children are brought so early to see the lovely animals in cages? Won't they dream of it? Won't they be afraid for themselves? Won't they think twice and also have thoughts even before the first thoughts? Is this educational? Is it moral?"

They were like Otello and Iago in the opera who swear, while the trumpets vibrate, *Addio.*

"I swear to you, brother," said Horatio Alger, clenching his fists not yet full-grown, "that I will one day appear in force at those schools and bring back the lovely pleasures of human lust."

12. Noblesse Oblige

The invaluable happiness of liberty consists, not in doing what one pleases, but in being able, without hindrance or restraint, to do in the direct way what one regards as right and just.

— Goethe

The curator of the zoo was Mynheer.

When Horatio, who had had no intention of conforming himself to an insane plan, came into the curator's office, he was very thoughtful. He sat and looked thoughtfully at his brother-in-law for a long time.

Finally Mynheer looked up from his bits of paper—for the most part he did not use documents with propositions, but little folded-paper combinatories, "thinking machines" as Patrick Geddes would say, for in the end much of his vast work of administration did not require thought but the application of the same formulas to one field after another.

Horatio said, "Why is it that *you* serve?"

The Dutchman growled and bared his teeth.

Startled, the youth faltered: "I mean—what is the advantage of it? Have *you* made a social compact with these people? This I find hard to believe, because you're always too far ahead of the game."

"Why am I serving them—'these lunatics'?" he said in the deathless tragic phrase of Dr. Freud ("*diese mishugeneh*"), "and meanwhile the centuries are lapsing away—"

And hoarsely, not like the inheritor and sovereign peer, but gasping, like a wounded animal, he said: "*Noblesse oblige: this* is why I serve them. I *can*, they cannot, therefore I must. What? Would it be possible for me to look on at work botched, and plans founded on simple ignorance and omission, when I have only to turn a hand? (Not that anything comes of it, for my heart is not in it.)

"It's hard for me to rally to it again and again.

"Little brother! Clever little brother! I am warning you. Excellence is a *disease*. To be able is a disease. It lays on you an obligation that you can't avoid and can't fulfill. It eats the joy out of your heart—except the one joy serene, of *doing* what your hand shall find."

13. Advantages and Disadvantages of Harry Tyler's Place

Harry Tyler's place was now the strictly private address of the brothers Alger. It had certain domestic advantages. It was the only home in all of the Empire City where one could beach and bathe out of the front door, except that at present they dared not venture forth. There were no neighbors, but the passers-by were superior to the average: adventurous or philosophic persons, or persons haunted. Persons haunted, and they saw shapes in the rocks that were not there, or they failed to see shapes among the rocks that were there. The view was without a peer in Europe or the East.

It was a location worth taking root in, and decorating the place, and, as Harry used, putting out a flag.

Just now the great disadvantage was the approach, the entrance and the exit. One had to crawl, flatten himself against a rock, hide where the rats were. Occasionally a shot rang out and this was not a domestic note.

The State of Nature

If men should ever beasts become
bring only brutes into your room,
and less disgust you'll surely feel.
We all are Adam's children still.

— quoted by Goethe

1.

The zoo was a pleasant square, surrounded on three sides by the cages of the beasts, the yellow wolves frenziedly pacing, the aloof giraffes, the crazed cats. Busy people were content to pause here awhile and enter into conversations without being introduced to one another. The pool of live water where the sea lions swiftly swerved from bumping their snouts was asymmetrically central, and into it the people gazed in absorption, or, staring, made jokes. And round the inner square the architect had thrown a raised terrace which was still in the square, so that being still in the pleasant square one could also gaze upon the square.

Everywhere were such varyingly permanent things of interest—live water and spectators and pacing beasts—that could occupy yet hardly dominate attention, ever the same and endlessly changing, why should not people pause here and eventually be at their ease? The abominable roar of the (caged) lion seemed to have an infinite hollow sounding board in which it became muffled and lost.

It was a cunningly laid out plaza that seemed to have no entrances or exits (for one came in round the cages), so that the people rested in a limitless moment.

On the fourth side, on the raised terrace, were tables and eating. Lothair was having his lunch there, waiting for the salvo of noon. Emilia and her boy were down below, observing and discussing the tiger burning bright. With thin lips, Horace was watching the people watching. I myself was all eyes for the bear on his (barred) hillside. And Harry Tyler—

People moved, singly or in groups, in all six directions. Others were content to stand, distraught. The rapidly pacing or trembling beasts were vibrating in their restricted places. Sometimes, as if new created or vanishing away, people slipped sideways through the invisible exits.

Withdrawing, upward and away from the pleasant plaza (reversing the bomber's angle), at a distance of a few hundred feet one no longer felt that he was in that square, although it still looked like a square of people. At this distance, of this size, the people were like the dolls of childhood—dear, close, lost! Withdrawing! Withdrawing!

Depriving one's self still farther of the plaza of our people—would not the possible return be in the form of a blow?

(Reversing the ballistic parabola), at a distance of several thousand feet one could no longer distinguish that that speck in the vast ugly fly heap was a pleasant square of people in our beautiful Empire City. Here, where the bomb rode at rest under the plane, the bombardier in the deafening silence was not at his ease in any plaza endlessly beguiled.

The fatal clock was ticking fast, and the instruments were vibrating in their cages.

The bombardier is lonely, yet he is not conscious of the absence of the people. (Is it not something immortal, the absence of the people?) He is intensely concerned with what he is about.

From the height of an airplane it is impossible to see the plan of a city square; by the plan I mean the life. A good architect does not take account of such aerial views. Even from a motorcar one can see only landscape and enjoy the pleasures only of banked highways. It is necessary to go on foot to be content to pause awhile and to enter into conversations without introductions.

From the height of an airplane only the Rocky Mountains or the ocean can make an impression. (These one does not destroy with bombs.)

The bomb is at rest in the undercarriage—in a region of ticking machines and the immortal absence of the people.

Now, supposing that (at the bomber's angle) this bomb were released and rapidly approached its target.

At a distance of a few hundred feet would not the pleasant square begin to loom, peopled, clear, close, lost? No longer depriving one's self! But what a thing it is to be returning in the form of a blow!

Here is the square, the environment of society! and one is again a part of it.

2.

With noisy relish Lothair was addressing himself to two pork chops on his dish and meanwhile chattering away to himself. But, no, he was talking not to himself but to the two chops. He cut off a good bite and chewed it and exclaimed:

"First rate! Really, the food here's first rate. Don't you find it so? Big portions, too. This is the first real meal, you know, I've had in four years. Go ahead, take some more o' the Burgundy. Oof, wasn't it a close call this morning when I sneaked out? Shh, not so loud." He looked about. Then, pointing thoughtfully with his knife and fork, ready to attack again, he said, "I suppose the food doesn't seem so good to *you* as it does to *me*. It's a pity."

He silently ruminated this a moment and repeated, "It's a pity. It's a pity. There aren't so many things in the world worth eating as good food. What do you think? Yes, enemies. Plenty of people seem to know about this place already. Nobody tells me anything."

He savagely gnawed the bone.

"Well, old chop, that puts you in your place. Very good, too. Now, what's the matter with your friend? . . . Brother wouldn't eat; he said he wasn't hungry. Me, I'm always hungry. I like the smell, I like the smell. So much the worse for him. *Clean plates*! That's what my mother always used to say. For God's sake!" he cried, shaking the chop furiously and talking to it. "If you people can't appreciate food any more, what in hell is the use? Ha!"—bite—"Next"—chew—"they'll feed one another intravenously. Do you think I'm joking? This they call the high standard of living. I like to bite! I like to chew! I like the smell!"

He glowered at his interlocutors, but they were forever silent.

"My father," said Augustulus to Emilia—the mother and boy were leaning on the railing of the tiger at rest—"my father has cages in which he doesn't keep animals. He's a sergeant soldier an' he has bullets what don't shoot you. Thing is, it's not nice. The man should let the tiger out o' the cage—*isn't* that right, mummee?"

"Yes, Gus. It's mean to keep the animals locked up in cages."

The tigress' gums were black as onyx, and the saliva dripped in slow beads from her furry mouth. Her tongue clicked regularly against her bottom fangs when she inhaled to open wide her throat for the great drafts of oxygen to support the furious combustion of her soul.

"Before he had a uniform, mummee, before he had a uniform how can they tell my father was a sergeant soldier? My father's dead now, but he'll come back after the war's over, isn't that right, mummee? Thing is, when they all go back on the ships an' then the war's over. Some o' the ships get sinked. My father an' I think it's mean to keep the animals in the zoo, don't we, mummee? . . . Mummee! He's getting up! He can't come out, can he, mummee?"

When this crazed tigress went to and fro in her restricted space, she pulled herself by the forelegs but hardly moved her hind legs at all—they seemed almost as if atrophied. But they were powerful. They were for springing.

"God can make my daddy alive, can't he? Why can't God put people together again if they have been killed and send them down from heaven? I know why, because he hasn't got the things together, all the stuff. After the war God will have everything again. We have to wait until after the war, then God can put people together again."[*]

Harry Tyler, who was one of those waiting for the salvo of twelve, kept scowling upward at the planes. "Oh, shut your friggin' trap, who cares?"

"Look at that babe there," he said, "bustin' up her gocart happy as a friggin' lark. Go teach her not to bust it when everywhere she looks there's holes i' the walls."

The lioness kept sending forth her infinitely hollow roar. "Oh, Jesus, hush up, miss," said Harry, "or I'll cram my cock down y'r throat."

The woman standing next to him gave him a startled glance and walked away.

Harry liked to watch the blond seal silently swerving from wall to wall.

Another man was gaping at the giraffe and craning his own skinny neck, popping the Adam's apple. He earnestly stuck his thumbs through his hair for horns.

Everywhere there was an affinity, deep or ridiculously apparent, between the persons who were so earnestly staring and the totems that they were staring at. I knew a little red-haired lady, quick as a fox, who used to watch for hours in front of the quick fox. But why do I, who do not look anything like the brown bear (at least so I think), stand by preference here, watching the bear on his rock? It is because I like to hug tight.

Stretching his little arms over the railing, Augie was chanting, "Tiger, Tiger" and "My Father and I." When his mother saw that he was becoming overexcited and tried to draw him away, he sharply rejected her and rhythmically screamed, "No, No"—a scream when the cat stepped to the right and a scream when she stepped to the left. Emily said firmly, "Come," and seized his hand. He sank his teeth in her hand and, when she cried out, he tore himself free and with great deliberateness persistently knocked his head against the railing.

With tight lips Horace watched them one and all from the terrace and said nothing. He wore a mixed expression.

---

[*] Quoted from Bertie in Anna Freud's *Infants Without Families*.

The expressions on the faces are *simple* or *mixed*. They are simple when there is one feeling (or compatible feelings) and this is a specification of the habitual character, as the choleric man will scowl and bare his teeth, and the lines that are already there merely deepen. In the conditions of society it is rare to see a simple expression; and it is rarely in a work describing society that the writer can accurately declare that his personage wears a simple expression, suffering an original instinctual feeling, or a simple instinctual deprivation.

An expression is mixed when there is a conflict of feelings or when the feeling supervenes on a face already marked by a contrary habit. Wry, sly, quizzical, rueful, lewd, smirking, vacant, haughty: these are expressions rather elaborately mixed. Most often the expressions seen in society are the supervention of a kind of lust, eagerness or curiosity upon timidity; or inattention upon timidity. A "bored look" is the supervention of inattention upon timidity; it is not placid but twitches and tics.

One would have said that the habit of little Horatio, of the boy of eleven that we used to know, had been simple, eager alertness (an expression alternating with, not contrary to, lasciviousness, merriment, fits of tears); but now here was the adolescent leaning on the balustrade with a "look piercing sharp," lips so thin, eyes so very cold—an expression mixed of aversion and judgment overlaying the habit of attentiveness; a look that neither "drank in the scene" nor repelled it, but that "held the scene in its place" (but how long can this steely contest endure?)—then, had that old expression truly been a simple eager smile? Had not the ever-ready smile been a little sharpened at the corners with fright?

He held the scene in its place, waiting for the salvo of twelve, as if, when finally he took it in, it would be at one bite.

3.

The quiet drumbeat was not the salvo of twelve.

It was the approach of a small parade of *evacués* on their way.

Girls and boys, of the ages of five to fifteen, going with their teachers to where, it was hoped, the war would not strike.

Charmed by the far-off sound of fife and drum, the lion forgot to roar, and the people fell back on either side.

The parade entered the square, marking time.

The boys were the better drummers, but the girls knew how to march.

From the balls of the feet, in a rhythmic wave, with a flourish of the calves and an uplift of the knees, and a shake of the hips and a flirt of the shoulders, to the tips of the fingers, to the toss of the smiling head, the dance of the march possessed the girls.

The raised toe curled and the planted toe rolled, syncopating the beat.

They exhibited themselves, and their nascent breasts, as though they had costumes to show.

By comparison the vigorous boys had feet of lead.

But the boys were the better drummers!

The snare drums repeated crescendo the one cumulating rhythm:

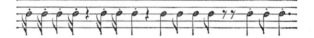

Their pianissimo was a crisp whisper; their piano was a speaking voice; their forte made the heart resolve, their fortissimo knocked you out of bed.

As the bass drum beat they stepped forth, and the fife began the tune.

What a joyous scene it was for me! To see my girls and boys walking out of this place of danger! I say "my" girls and boys, for I saw some among them whom I myself had taught (and they taught me a thing or two). When these caught sight of me, do you think that they did not break ranks and run to me exclaiming? It was a good, undisciplined parade; once they had got the wild music going, halfway across the square they broke step. I looked carefully but I could not see a mixed expression on their faces. I prayed: "May the powers of the heaven and the earth continue to spring alive in every act of these dear girls and boys. May no resentful teacher frown upon their glorious inventions, but all nourish them still with true stories of what is and of the few ancient human days."

Soon they were gone, and the wild music died away.

They left us in the unpleasant plaza among ends of conversations.

The muffled drumbeat was the salvo of twelve.

4.

Next moment the animals were let out of their cages by Lothair and his lieutenants.

At first the people, who were accustomed to looking on at a spectacle and exchanging conversation, looked on also at this, but silently. So for the first fractions of a minute there was no disorder, haste or outcry as the wolves trotted free and the bear ambled forth. It was altogether quiet, for the animals, too, held their peace. In places, where the beast had passed, a rank odor lay on the air. It was during this preliminary pause of surprise that the tigress mounted the pedestal of a statue of a tigress, in a position to spring.

Without transition, without transition this first pause of surprise passed over into silent panic fright. As if there had been no new experience, no new experience, to stun, to stun the mind and create the condition for panic fright. But as if this spectacle were what they had already been experiencing, what they had been experiencing, all along. That on the pedestal there were two tigresses. It was because the people in the closed plaza were unaccountably at ease, each staring at the animal for which he had a deep affinity, that they now went through an experience already experienced. And their reactions were inevitable.

The noise that began to rise in the square was absolutely unnoticed by anyone, although each one was contributing to it, and the beasts reacted with abominable cries. (The beasts were not panicked because they were not a herd.) It rose to a steady roar. Many of the people opened flashing jackknives. Since, as we have said, there were no apparent exits from this companionable plaza, there was no tendency for the people to run wild in panic fright and trample one another; but one or two persons, who had previously been about to leave, proceeded with the suggestion as if under hypnosis and slipped sideways through the invisible doors. Some of the animals ran out.

The giraffe, when his raised head with its ears and horns could be seen over the wall, was puny and ridiculous against the towers of the Empire City.

Grasping her firmly by the ring through her nose, Lothair was leading up the steps the shaggy yak with wide-thrown horns and apparently making an oration to her that could not be heard in the clamor. Clamor, but stationary and not disorderly, for the people were as yet too new in the state of nature, too new in the state of nature to know what to do next. What odors to distinguish, to move by what impulse toward what good, and to reason with natural symbols. It was necessary for those who were more accustomed to this way to take the lead.

The tigress sprang, separating herself from the statue of a tigress.

In one spring she threw the child Augie to the pavement and, recoiling on her haunches, she sank her teeth in his throat and shoulder. His mother, frozen fast, screamed a human cry. Horace leaped to the rescue, but the tigress snapped at him once and flung him away with a sideswipe of her heavy paw; then he lay stunned. The child whimpered and died.

Now when the tigress sprang, the curator, who had been watching startled at his window—startled but not panic-stricken—raced onto the square. Mynheer was not subject to the panic paralysis of the crowd; methodically he seized his revolver, and his instantaneous conscious plan was to get close enough to the tigress to shoot safely. At this moment, however, the well-known voice of Emilia spoke a human cry. *This* had not entered into his calculations, and he stood stunned on the threshold. He was prepared for every crisis and inured by long experience to every blood-curdling shriek. But the cry of Emily was a cry of recognition, it was a human cry, it was a human cry of recognition of a suicidal loss. It was torn from her deeper than any passion. But this was beyond the depth of Mynheer's stoical composure, and he stood as paralyzed as the rest. Now many people were giving blood-curdling shrieks.

When the tigress sprang, Horace was not startled. (He had in part prepared the event.) His eyes, which had been narrowed on the tigress, opened wider, and when the beast sank her teeth in the child they opened wide with horror. Emily's outcry made him terribly sad, but he was not stunned, and he leaped down the steps to seize the child from the animal's jaws.

It was not an heroic deed, for a hero seldom fails. This is not because we call him a hero when he has succeeded but because it is in the nature of a hero to succeed. The action of a hero follows after he has been stunned and every conscious volition and strength have been canceled from his soul; then he acts with preternatural clarity, delicacy and force. He does not inhibit himself. The energy of his senses, his reason, and his muscles is the streaming of life. (You cannot foresee what ordinary person will become such a hero.)

When the tigress snapped at Horatio, he felt a painful stinging in his right hand. The blow of the heavy paw struck him across the hips and he lay near by, unable to move. But he saw that he had lost two joints of the small finger of his right hand and he crammed the stump of the finger in his mouth, so the blood trickled from the corners of his unsmiling lips.

Crouching with her chest on the ground, head sunk between her shoulders, and her tail in an almost rigid wave in the air but sometimes lashing the tip of it from side to side, the cat was devouring the child. She did not look at the prey but glassily across it. (To Horatio it seemed that she was looking at him, as he was looking at her.) Then again she left the food a moment, to prowl and growl in front of it, guarding it, guarding herself against surprise.

The child was dead from the beginning and had a simple expression on its face.

The tigress used her forepaws to push the meat in toward her, worrying it, unsheathing the claws—almost as if the paws were grasping hands; but they were not hands, and there was a pathos in this defect in a being otherwise so beautifully equipped.

Horatio looked on at it, not hypnotized or fascinated (as if perhaps his soul had some other resources kept in abeyance while he feasted his eyes), but his attentiveness was now his only resource and his only possible natural action, so that his face wore an unmixed expression of attentive fright. This attentiveness was the specification of this fright. It did not mark itself by deepening any lines on his boy face but by drawing the flesh still more taut, so that the bony face knuckles shone; and his hair stood on end. Meantime his mouth was clamped on the small finger of his right hand, and the other fingers were bars before his eyes.

It was only a short time that passed this way. (All told, it was not three minutes since the salvo of twelve.) But it seemed very long because the close, simple experience was not set off by anything.

However it was—possibly because his senses began to blur and he was about to faint with shock—half-seeing the blur of animals moving about, young Horace (like Siegfried in the play who also infantilely sucked on his finger), with rapture Horatio imagined that he could understand what the animals were saying to each other. And he would never be frightened again, because this understanding was more original than fright (more original than alertness); it took precedence. He laughed because what they were saying was an old joke. They were talking about the Great War.

"More than twenty million human beings have been killed in it so far," said one of the animals.

"Ha!" said another. "They must be having plenty of good food."

5.

Mounting the steps, Lothair, leading by her nose ring the shaggy buffalo and with his right arm lovingly round the neck of a ewe of the Andes—and all of them flown about by a cloud of pigeons—was exclaiming:

"Dear friends, let me show you a little how those people make it impossible for themselves to live."

He seemed to imagine that the curator's mansion at the top of the steps was the city itself, and he pointed it out as the sociological museum that they were now visiting.

"My sacred cow, and you, mistress of the shepherds that have copper skin," he said to his animals at either hand, "and you birds of Aphrodite, do you see any covert here, to lie down and make love in it? Do you know that in these endless streets if you and I should be spontaneously touched by a charming desire, you will not find a copse of alders or a deep field or a cove of hedges starred with syringa or even a haymow, to withdraw there and lay each other bare. 'Ha,' I see you ask with consternation in your eye, *'what is one supposed to do?'*"

The buffalo had turned on him her enormous liquid brown eye.

"In order to make love *here*," cried their guide, "it is first necessary to pay rent. Yes—yes," he said eagerly—as if no one would believe it—"it is often in hotel rooms that they let their tired youth be thrown. But I think that by the time we have crept off, out of the sunlight, out of the star dust, to such a cribbed and profit-making cave, my organ will have become flabby and useless; we shall no longer be drawing deep breaths; there is no infinity to the housed orgasm, limited also by a clock.

"Come, sniff at this woman. You draw back. What is it? Soap. There is nothing to smell here but soap and flowers, as if she were a vegetable and not descended in the generation of the beasts. This is perhaps something to browse on; would you, if you were a bull, be inspired by it to make a pass of love? . . . See, she is frightened. She does not want to be touched. And yet she is dressed, according to our human tastes (it would be hard to explain them to you), she is dressed to excite me, to attract me. I *am* excited, I rise; I am attracted, I approach. See? Now she is trained to cry out in fright and fly in panic. Tell me, are not these persons demented? But sometimes she does not fly in panic but freezes in panic. This is good. Good for me, not so good for her.

"Are you surprised that the people of this city do not reproduce their kind, and if the countryfolk did not replenish the place from generation to generation, soon it would be void of life except for the pigeons, the rats and the flies?

"What have I to do with such customs?" he said bitterly, and he began shamelessly to make passes of love at the Andean. "Te llama llama?" he asked, smirking at his little joke.

Above the wide-thrown horn of the yak, the liquid brown eye of the sheep, the distended pinions of the pigeon, the face of Lothair wore nothing but mixed expressions, succeeding one another with such extremity that you would have despaired of ever finding nature underneath.

The cow gave forth a long bellow.

"True!" said Lothair (but it was not the case that he could really understand the language of the animals). "Everywhere signs of war. There's even more aggressiveness than is normal, because of the frustrations. Does it promise well? I see you are kicking up your heels and stamping and bellowing, and your eyes are flashing. There is a war. The war is the Law of Tooth and Nail. You say, '*Ha! There is at least this!*' . . . No such thing! The war is long and far and wide, but I have not heard that there is a general use of teeth or of nails. It is rare, rare that they gouge the eyes or tear the lip or break the back or twist the testicles. How does the flurry of rage burst out? (You will laugh when I tell you.) In mechanical *explosives*!

"They go off almost out of sight and hearing. Far off. As in a dream. One pushes a little button.

"Meantime the anger accumulates in the soul. It does not find expression. It is not purged away. After the war is over, will not these overstimulated people be even more frustrated than before?

"Look! Up there! I'll show you what I mean. See—you can hardly see him in the clouds—a man is consulting his dials. Do you think he will be any the more amiable after he has let loose the bomb?

"Small satisfaction! Powerful stimuli and small satisfactions! Not only here but in every department of the museum.

"There's a reason. I'll tell you why. You're a smart creature and you can laugh at a joke. The only way to keep up the profits is to create a wide demand, and the only way to have a wide demand is to provide temptation for some elementary, universal, instinctual want. These clever men and women have devised excruciating crude temptations. Crude! You don't know how crude—I would be ashamed to give examples. But—and here's the joke—the balance of the society, the great social machine, is so—delicate—that the full satisfaction of a single one of those elementary wants would fatally derange everything! Supposing a person were satisfied with love, and he had struck a blow tooth and nail and, having been reduced to hunger, now he was replete, he shat where he stood!—do you suppose that such a person would drag himself from sleep early in the morning, and drag himself to work for money, and be on edge lest tomorrow he fail to be satisfied?

"When suddenly one day one of the brothers or sisters initiates a chain of direct actions—who knows who will be torn limb from limb?

"Excellent! Here is the department of eating and drinking. Shall I tell you something about the food of these curious people, for whatever you may think, they do not eat one another?"

But at this moment he saw Mynheer, the curator, standing in the threshold, the unsmoking revolver still in his hand.

"Ah, it is my brother-in-law!" said Lothair with delight. "Well met, brother-in-law. . . . This is a perfect specimen—there is no better," he whispered to the buffalo. "Allow me to introduce you to one another:

"This is the buffalo from Todanadad, much venerated by the natives of that plateau who have indeed subordinated and atrophied the entire remainder of their social lives to the maintenance of her purity of strain and to milking her for the production of a clarified butter called ghee.

"And this," he said more coyly than affectionately, "is a little friend of mine. Se llama Llama.

"And these—" pointing to his shoulders, for a pigeon had perched on each—"are the pigeons, to provide suitable rookeries for whom the men have built the towers of the Empire City.

"And this, my friends, is my brother-in-law, the Mynheer Colijn. He is the corresponding secretary of two dozen societies and institutes, including the Society for the Preservation of Cultural Relics and the League for the Destruction of Historical Monuments, the Psychoanalytic Institute and the Society for the Propagation of Vice, the Institute for Constructive Bombardment, the Town Planners Association, etc., etc. (But he has been unable, I am told, to maintain marital relations with my sister Laura.)

"Come, brother-in-law," said Lothair, "what are you doing out of your cage?"

And, taking Mynheer by the hand, he led him to an empty cage and pushed him roughly inside.

Mynheer let himself be dumbly conducted. Why did he?

He was paying the penalty for the fact that he had been stunned when he heard the human cry.

Mynheer was responsible for his intellect. He had a scrupulous honor with regard to being refuted. If he came to be refuted, he did not overlook it, nor pass it by, nor act as if this made no difference to him, nor defer it for another time; but he broke into a sweat, his hair stood on end and he could not sleep easy till he knew better. Now the worst refutation was a surprise that could paralyze action, and he had been so surprised and had not acted. Then Mynheer did not feel now that he could judge the other till he had himself sought through and solved that human cry and again made his theory, whole and perfect. Then why should he not allow himself to be conducted—for a quarter of an hour?

(The panic in the square had already, as we shall see, been solved by Emilia.)

"See the man in the cage?" exclaimed Lothair. "I, too, once lived in a cage, before the social compact was abrogated that I had with those people. Do you know what are the bars of this cage? Let me tell you."

And not otherwise than a cartoonist for the political press, Lothair—who fancied that he was living in the state of nature, yet even now was creating a cartoon for the political press—assigned a label to each of the bars of the cage in which Mynheer Duyck Colijn was dumbly standing.

"This bar," he said, "is *Liberty*.

"And this bar is *Education*.

"This bar is the human *Standard of Living*.

"And this bar is *Justice*.

"And the man," said Lothair with a choking voice, "is held in this cage *incommunicado*."

6. The State of Nature

But with quickening breath and lips opening in an anticipatory smile and eyes shining for joy—and no need now to suck his finger for fright—Horatio was listening to what it was that the animals were really saying to each other.

And they were saying, again and again, in a thousand actions and attitudes, the simple paragraph of Johann Goethe:

"I ever repeat it, the world could not exist if it were not so simple. This wretched soil—it has been tilled a thousand years, yet its powers are always the same: a little rain, a little sun, and each spring it grows green and so forth."

"A little rain, a little sun, and so forth," said one.

"They must be having plenty of good food," said another.

"The world could not exist if it were not so simple."

Did Lothair imagine that the society of those people (such as it was) existed because of their demented notions and by means of their contradictory institutions? And that these were the essence of their society? No such thing! In medicine there is a famous maxim:

"*One cannot explain a positive effect by a negative cause.*" Nothing comes from nothing. The society *existed,* in so far as it existed, because of elementary desires and the wonderful virtues of courage, patience, the extraordinary endurance of the people.

"Why should he speak of 'those people'?" thought Horatio. "I, too, have such desires and I think I have such virtues. They and I and the rest of these beasts: we all."

"A little rain, a little sun," they were saying.

"I evermore repeat it!"

"One cannot explain a positive effect by a negative cause."

"Nothing comes from nothing."

One had only to observe a single one of the beasts, the little cat or the burly bison, to see that one could not explain a positive effect by a negative cause. Surely they were saying this very clearly. Yet it was necessary to lie awhile in attentive fright, sucking on a finger, and with a simple expression on one's face, to understand that it was indeed this that they were saying:

That "the world could not exist if it were not so simple."

"They have already killed twenty millions: there must be plenty of good food."

That it *existed,* such as it was, by elementary desires and hardy virtues. That it would be saved, when it would be *saved,* by simple revulsion—what an unsubtle observer might even call simple disgust.

If one lay there quietly to watch the tigress devouring the child, then one could hear what they were saying: "This wretched soil—

"This wretched soil: it has been tilled a thousand years."

"Nevertheless, its powers are always the same!"

"Each spring it grows green."

"I evermore repeat it!"

"A little rain, a little sun, and each spring it grows green and so forth."

7. An Heroic Deed

Before the tigress sprang, Emilia was clinging hard to the hand of her little boy, but he bit her and drew free, and wanted to be free, and wailed, "No, no!"

And when the tigress sprang, it was impossible for the mother to move. For irrevocably, and from bottom to top, the mother child within her, that took the place of her self, was rent into its parts. This had been the "semiperma- nent establishment" for which she had used to long, and for a few years she had enjoyed it; it had been the masculinity of which, as a little girl, she had felt herself deprived. But the ties of it were already strained.

If the tigress had sprung two years before, would not the mother also have sprung, tigress for tigress? But now she was guilty, she had a mixed desire. It is by such causes that one explains the fact that a person is frozen into inaction.

She gave a human cry. It was a cry of recognition of her own dear soul, self. It contained in it the three wailing voices of loss, grief and mourning. And immeasurable, the wail of the newborn. This cry lasted a long time, drawn out for a moment, and nearly every soul in the square was brought to a pause, each in its own way. But the soul that has given such a cry is no longer responsi- ble for the guilty effort to cling to what has now been recognized as irrevo- cably torn away; it is free from the burdens of possession; it is released from the strains of willing different things. Will not such a cry prolong itself to the moment when at last its purity begins to jangle into a peal of victory?

Then the living Emilia became a heroine and she performed a heroic deed which, by its nature, could not fail.

Walking rapidly and almost unseen, she carried the small children, struck silent by her touch, into the restaurant. She wheeled a perambulator. She sta- tioned a guard to open and close the door.

When she gave unhurried orders, they were obeyed. This was partly because her intuition did not fail to select the woman or boy who would obey.

Her mind was clear and conscious; her senses were supernormally alert, so that they penetrated every corner, and her memory did not fail to recall to her what was hidden. But she moved without apparent will. That is to say, she did not feel, as she calculated each thing in turn, that there was an *extra* moment of committing herself to the result of the calculation.

Without alarming the tigress, she lifted Horatio in her arms and bore him to safety. At this time, feeling himself in her arms, he fainted away. She gave the directions to treat him.

Then she returned to where the remains of the body of her child were lying, the tiger pacing short steps in front of it and slowly lashing only the tip of its tail. But the beast did not disturb her, but growled when she took off the black coat of mourning that she was wearing for her husband and her father (disclosing underneath a party dress) and wrapped little August in it and, weeping softly, she carried him away.

By this time the police had converged with their firearms. Most of the people in the square had taken refuge in the cages. Many of the beasts were simply browsing in the park.

The zoo attendants began to wheel up their moving cages.

A shot rang out, restoring (as Horatio had predicted) the conditions of the social peace.

8. The Elephant

The elephant had not offered to budge from his enclosure, but remained immobile in the center of the asphalt yard surrounded by mighty bars. The bars, the elephant, the floor and the sky were gray.

Lothair turned this corner, arrayed with his pigeons, but otherwise alone.

"*Eliphaz!*" he exclaimed, impatiently shaking free of the birds.

"Why don't you come out, old sir?" he pleaded, taking hold of the bars. "I specially directed that you also should be let free. You have been encaged as much as any of us, whatever superficial people may have thought.

"I looked for you, but they told me you were dead. The boy lied to me. Why did he? Why are they afraid to tell me anything? Trying to humor me. Does he think I hate *you*, old friend? Imagine if we hated each other among these— petty bourgeois! But you have had the virtues of a grand bourgeois: invention, abstention and daring. Those other persons do not even know what a virtue is.

"You're offended with me, Eliphaz!" he cried, stepping through the wide-apart bars and approaching. "You don't say anything. I'm surprised that you should be a hard loser. It was always a fair hard fight between us. Dirty and cunning, but never capricious, never *un*reasonable. When I was beat I over-looked it. Why don't you now forgive and forget and be friends?"

Like a cow at the auction—who stands unconcernedly in the center while the auctioneer explains her points and the bids fly back and forth—the elephant lifted his tail and defecated and then, after his fashion, ambled forward to the bars.

"Oh," cried Lothar, "you're pretending that you're still the cashier at the bank, looking through the bars and counting out the currency. But those days are over, old man! They are over. Since the compact is abrogated that we used to have with those people.

"You didn't abrogate it; I am not accusing you of it. We two should have kept the peace, such as it was, but those people were at the end of their resources.

"Now there is a new order of things.

"*Is there a new order of things?*" he asked, staring about uneasily, and half comprehending that it was the elephant pen at the zoo, between the gray pavement and the gray sky. "Is this direct action? And is this the use of words to say what is the case? Is this the elementary desire? And are these the hardy virtues of courage and endurance?

"Where are my friends? Where is Henry Faust to celebrate with me our entry into the state of Nature? Didn't we use to say that this would be the ceremonial of the glorious day: that the trusting brothers and sisters would sit down together and exchange their true thoughts? I cannot associate with birds and beasts as if they were the same as I. If I do not associate with people, with whom shall I associate?"

Suddenly he was seized with wild rage and indignation that he was *still* being held incommunicado. "*Talk* to me, you stupid, unoffending beast. Am I again cut off from all communication? You have become as huge and quiet as an elephant." And he began to beat the side of the animal with his fists.

With a quick step the brute trampled on him and kicked him out of the enclosure.

Mynheer's Valedictory to Man

Piet Duyck Colijn & Duyvendak van der Meer comes from among the dunes. Sand in his hair, in his eyelashes, mixed with the saliva on his chin, as if he had been sleeping there. Not possessed enough of himself to brush himself clean. The tears of sorrow are streaming down his dirty cheeks; his intellectual countenance is opened with grief.

He has seen a vision, or dreamed it; it is no longer sure to him what is a dream and what is waking reality.

The grownup is crying, little Joan hushes herself in awe and curiosity. Her father does not set her down; though astonished he says nothing, but he lays his right arm round Piet Duyck's shoulders. It is new to him to see such sorrow, and he cannot think what could bring this man to this dismay.

Duyck neither rejects the friendly embrace nor smiles wanly acknowledging it, nor again redoubles his grief, nor is comforted any; but his mature tears flow on; still, he is not shaken by orgastic sobs, but as if another thought brings new tears, and there is always another thought.

"I won't ask you what's the matter, friend," says Harry Tyler, "because I know you and I know it is badly the matter if Piet Duyck is crying; worse than I or you can cope with. So you'll have to go on crying till there's no more. No help for it. But please, allow me, let me wipe the sand from your face and brush it out of your hair. Close your eyes."

Mynheer closes his eyes, and the sailor performs this office for him, of wiping his face and brushing off his clothes. The child, still on her father's left arm, looks on solemnly.

His eyes shut, Mynheer sees nothing but the darkness. Owai! But it was from just such total eclipse that the bad vision first rose in view.

Facing eastward over the ocean, the beginning of May, in the first hours after midnight, when the high spirits have sunk to their lowest, he opened his eyes and expected to see again Pegasus bounding from the horizon as he does in that place at that hour of that night. The dunes lurked in their darkness, as usual. The long comber shone in a few points of starshine. At hand the point of a blade of dune grass drew an accurate circle in the sand. In the soft breeze.

The constellation that arose, that began to arise, was not the winged inspiration mounting with his slow bound. It was something new, not seen before.

It was Man. The constellation *Man* appeared on the horizon, and slowly as the hour passed reared to his full height.[*]

Mynheer's jaw hung down and he looked there with startling eyes; and when the stars were all displayed (only a few) he began to weep and could not stop.

For what is raised as a constellation of stars into the macrocosm is something that will not change (such as it is). What is in the stars is no more on earth. It is the immortal death in the soul we project in abstractions that imitate, by their abstractness, the nonexistence of that which is. Then good-by.

Good-by to the race of animals that invented half a dozen ways of making fire; and by flags and flashing mirrors, smoke and radio waves signaled across vast distances. Who accumulated the records of their litigation in volumes of the Common Law. Good-by.

Good-by to the kind that proved again and again that songs of the throat can fall heavy with heart, subtler than swords, breathing also courage and ambiguous with anguish: who would have thought it was possible if Man did not prove it so in act? Good-by to dancers, used to dance, lightly imitating the inward in outward motions of the limbs and recreating the world in double and triple time. Good-by to one certain gloomy beast who carved the unfinished in rocks.

For if it is the valedictory of Man that flows and leaps in his mind, there is matter for Mynheer to weep for a long time, well into the dawn, and after that— as now he thinks of kinds and classes of men and now of this man or that man.

Good-by to those who used to cut and polish little stones for prismatic lights, and measure the rainbows. To those others who by addition combined small pieces of iron and stone into immense bridges and towers. Good-by to the kinds of men characterized by city names, Florentines, Ninevites, New Yorkers. Good-by to the inventors of ingenious machines who in illiberal times still found objects for their busy wits. Good-by to intrepid sailors led on and on when they were afraid: it is not the case that one would have expected this until the Man proved it in act. Good-by to those who suggested to themselves to be disgusted with such and such good meat, and those who used to make boundaries and cower on one side of the boundary they themselves made. Also, good-by to the poet of *Manfred.*

—Do not misunderstand; it is not I who am weeping or pretending to weep, for I am rather filled with hate and resentment of men. But Mynheer, the

---

[*] So Parker saw it

intellect, is weeping at every thought. And he cannot dam such a flood of tears by nice distinctions of good and bad, sensible or senseless—rather that this race of animals was so, this was how it was.

He will not exhaust his mournful thoughts, for almost everything he thinks of is Man, of Man, by Man, etc. Even so the indefinite series can be summed up briefly as a few stars in the macrocosm.

Good-by to the famous pairs and triangles of lovers and the solitary unloved lovers; and to the lovers and loveless nameless, that one used to pass by in parks—these all transforming lust in ways that one would not have counted on. Good-by to those sage or mad in peculiarly human ways. Also to those specifically malevolent and destructive, torturers and self-tortured, as only this race was able: and now afterward the thought of them is shining lovely enough. (But it was not by signal malevolence that Man ceased to exist. Well! Good-by also to the stupid ones characteristically human, who used not to know enough to come in out of the rain.) Good-by to the knightly heroes. Good-by to the Master of the Way, who lay seventy years in the womb in order to show what it was to be full-formed a Man before submitting to the accidents of the world.

This had a nature, like any other animal race; but it was not easy to guess at that human nature till one saw it realized, in history, in its acts: that it could harmonize three or four voices musicianly (the child's voice leading the melos), and grapple ships in a naval war. Good-by to the ignorant armies that clashed by night on the plain. To the human young that used to have for a few years such astonishing curiosity. And to the eccentric ones with punch-drunk eyes, like trumpeters of the Salvation Army. The race that wore a variety of hats.

Good-by to Jean and Franz and Paul Klee: it is not from some other seed of life the like will be produced (improbable enough as it was). Good-by who rode horses as part of their bodies like Centaurs, and drove cars as if they were born shod with metal wheels.

Human reader! It's not I who am pretending to weep (rather I'm hateful and resentful); but it's Mynheer who is mourning the thought of every formative spirit that made him a man, such as it is: if Man ceased to be. Picture it to yourself and tell it over; if man ceased to be.

Good-by! Good-by to gamblers who risked fortune on the turn of a card. Good-by to ballplayers. Good-by to devoted women who tried to make sorrowful men happy, and also to the Philistine who robbed her husband of his strength.

For when such a flood of tears is once let loose, one does not make nice distinctions of good and bad, friendly and hateful, clever and stupid; but it is all one race that is lost; it was so; that was how it was. Good-by.

The thought of this kind and that kind, of this man and that man, occurs to him and makes Mynheer's tears flow; and it seems that he will never be able to stop crying over the lapse and ending of Man (that we others, full of hatred and resentment, think of lightly enough; but do you picture what it means, and tell it over, the End of Man?).

It is Man who is wont to project the immortal death in the soul as an abstraction that imitates, by its abstractness, the nonexistence of that which is. And there he is, rising, a constellation in the Great Cosmos.

A Community of
Human Relations

"You see a guy is going to cut your throat, you keep out of his way.
That's right."
"Naa! You cut his throat before he cuts yours."

— West 38th St. Pier

The intention of the building-sacrifice was to create spirits, to make
a beginning.

— Rank (after Kleinpaul)

1.

Lothair and Emilia were now man and wife, but they were not blessed with
children, whether she was barren or he impotent or that together they could
not generate a child. Together, in the world as it was, they were physically, psy-
chologically, socially and metaphysically incapable.

They were physically incapable because they did not copulate. And inas-
much as they wanted above all things to have a child, a child to endure *for*
them as they staggered toward their deaths in the storm of hours thick and fast,
they were saddened not to apply themselves. Untwining themselves from the
entwined wreath of praise.

But Emily was emotionally barren because of the living horror in her of
the moment when the tiger slew her child and she cried out; this horror indig-
nantly rejected the seed of the maniac who had let the beast out of the cage
(nor would it have accepted any other man's). And Lothair was emotionally
impotent, for he imperially wished to lift by himself the whole city, as we saw,
the table and the floor attached to the table, and the walls, and the house; but
by willing it he could not make the flesh of his own penis rise.

It was not interesting for a child to be born in 1948. One did not observe,
at the birth of a child, any especial enthusiasm or hope, or even fear or sur-
prise, that here was something new, a further possibility in the continuity of
humanity. It was not interesting for a child to be born then because our ways
were well miscalculated to prevent his being a hero. It was possible for quite

serious persons to ask themselves, "What for? Is it convenient or inconvenient to have a child? Is it useful for the child? Does society need another child?" These were not very daring questions; one answer or another, to have a child was not a daring deed; but without daring there is nothing interesting. So they were sociologically incapable.

Emily and Lothair were sad and horrified and holding on too tight and bored. Yet even so we know, as Franz said, that an operation of nature could get them past insoluble dilemmas. But it was metaphysically impossible for them to have a child (this follows simply from the fact that they did not have a child), as if the vital principle were tired, had withdrawn—from our animal species that did not know how to care for itself. Perhaps men had, by secondary evasions and tertiary satisfactions and quaternary elaborations that were neither defensive nor satisfactory but nothing at all, men had so cut themselves off from nature and natural conventions that they could no longer draw on natural energy to recreate themselves—as if to say, "Man ceased to be human around 1870, or some other date." But then a new child would be born strange into a *nonexistent* species; no such child could get itself born. We were metaphysically childless, as if now the energy of our generation were concentrated in the one action of immortality, the imitation of our non-existence, to become (as Parker saw it) a constellation in the sphere. As if to say,

> I hunted it, and I have eaten it
> (now let me sleep). Ach, what I ate
>   was how it lay there dead: *this* virtue
>   has passed into my second-nature.

Beware of these gorgons, because the sight of them turns you to stone, even if they sit there crying tears.

2.

But Mynheer flew there with his bright mirror like Perseus.

He said, "I do not know exactly, though I could make several shrewd guesses, why couples are childless; but at the least we can get some help from the elementary statistics. Since more children are born in the country, you two ought to move to the country. Also you ought to have a human community where you and this child can directly satisfy, to a degree, the various rather few simple wants of human nature. This is obvious."

"There is no such human community," said Lothair.

"No, there is not; but we can invent that," said Mynheer.

"What! *Again?*" cried Lothair unbelievingly, for he himself used to be a greedy inventor of Utopian places in order to divert himself from the fact that his teeth were aching.

"Why not again? Do you have something better to do than to live as sensibly as you can manage? But let's not get complicated. First, do you two have sexual intercourse?"

"No," said Emily.

"Ah, you see? We hit on something right off. It's necessary to fuck if you want to have children."

3.

"Easy to say! I also have heard of this newsy hypothesis!" said Lothair bitterly.

"But her flesh shrinks in horror, and mine is clamped in a death grip, trembling. Trembling and does not loose—you see how it is!" he held out his mighty hand—that was not, however, trembling, so far as one could see. These were fantasies of his.

Then Duyck looked directly in the faces of these two gorgons and his heart turned to heavy stone within him. He faltered.

"What's the matter—are you ill?" they cried solicitously.

"It's nothing. This—" He took out his heart from his breast, a small handful of stone. "A cornerstone for building a good city."

4.

It doesn't exist but we can invent that: so Mynheer used to say readily (I have known such persons). Without despairing, or else despairing, he still used to assign to the intellect the role of knowing reasons and making something by means of the reasons. He did not merely notice with alarm, as we others learned to do in the middle of the twentieth century, writing up these notices for literary magazines. But he went to work. The folk had become demented: this did not paralyze him, though it had to be taken into account.

"Oh, reasons are as plentiful as blackberries," said the poet, meaning excuses, rationalizations. Good reasons are not so plentiful as that, but they are not rare; they are perhaps as plentiful as apples on poor trees (some trees have none, in poor seasons, and the seasons have been poorly).

It was not even the case that all of Mynheer's projects, sprung from simple reasons, were unsuccessful.

And now, turning over in his mind the thought of a Community of Human Relations to provide for the formation of a child's personality and sometimes absently hefting the heavy stone that fitted the palm of the hand, as if he were about to let it fly as a missile—he rapidly jotted down some notes on the back of a marriage-license:

We need, he figured,

> "1 nursing mother: matrix of affection and elementary satisfaction.
> 1 rival bad-mother (aunt type), for the attachment of rage and nausea.
> 1 rival good-mother (big-sister type), desire without tangible satisfaction.
> 1 neutral older woman, to bridge the gap to apathy.
> 3 or 4 fathers (uncle type): manly identification, threats of maiming; gain of security by learning to play off one against another. (Teacher, policeman, mother's mate, mother's lover.)
> 1 older brother: the model to be avoided.
> 1 younger brother, the favorite (Abel type): a convenient object for murder.
> 1 male sexual friend: projection of narcissism.
> 1 male nonsexual friend: the rival.
> 1 other friend, either sex: object of selfless devotion.
> 2 or 3 other males, roughly contemporary: the gang.
> 1 outsider: the scapegoat.
> 1 older girl friend, sexually active, to force him to overcome the Oedipus situation.
> 1 younger girl friend, for fearless exploration, for playing the father role.
> 1 maniac, all is not what seems.
> 1 old person, dying.
> 1 stranger to the society: infinity of mystery.

Total   22 persons

So many! Mynheer whistled with surprise; even so far it came to more than twenty persons to ensure the development of a personality. Besides, there would have to be a few animals, to establish the continuity of the species. And an Angel? Also, the social engineer had to provide a Factor of Safety, for it was unlikely that every person would enter into every needful relation.

At first Mynheer considered a large factor, 5, five persons for each role. But it was enough to have 3, for when confronted with any three, the comparative soul always sees one to favor and one to disfavor and one to seek as an ally. Also, it tended to limit the size of the factor that each person was likely to play several roles: the mate is the interloper, the scapegoat is the object of selfless devotion, etc. Mynheer therefore chose a factor of 3 and he decided that the Community required: $22 \times 3 = 66$ persons.

"It is a suburban community," he concluded, "weighted heavily toward the children and boys and girls."

5.

Our friends (1948) were hungry and thirsty and lonely to live in a community of human relations. They were lost, lonely, and out of touch in the community in which indeed they did live; it was no community, for them or anyone else, because in it one did not flow in the elementary human relations.

Leaving it—with a burst of joy at leaving it!—they carried with them the joyless faculty of being Out of touch with one another in elementary human relations. Nevertheless, there was an advantage in leaving the lonesome community that indeed existed to flock to the invented community that did not exist, in which also they would not flow in the elementary human relations: because in the new community they could reveal their naked hatred.

They chose a pleasant place, provided with the four elements, earth, air, water and fire.*

The air in this place was a flexible medium somewhat infiltrating into their animal bodies and furnishing no strong obstacle to motion through itself. A certain number of the settlers were able to feel the ambience of this air, as in and out it rushed and lay about them as they moved. The earth here was well connected with the center: it gave adequate support to standing and walking and even running, by offering an equal and opposite reaction to the pressure exerted on it. But there were few of the settlers who could feel their legs planted on this bedrock ground. The water in the place they chose had the remarkable virtue of fluidity; it broke into drops and reunited in a flowing body, and as if effortlessly it flattened itself in level pools wherever there was a depression. Yes! There was a high rushing foaming fall of water that fell in an instant still in a flat unrevealing pool reflecting the blue heavens and the clouds. And lastly there was the dark fire that burst into visibility whenever it struck something not transparent, as their faces.

From these kinds of matter, certain vegetation of weeds and flowers found nourishment, and animals too could subsist there. Perhaps a human community could here appoint itself.

Perhaps? Alas, there was no proof! There was no demonstrative proof that a particular commonwealth *must* appoint itself, just here, just itself, namely a human community, a community of human relations, one with mothers and

---

* Since we come again to a physical plan, I must explain how it was that Mynheer's wife Laura was not present and in charge of these arrangements. To put it bluntly, she had gone crazy and would not leave the house. She suffered from a socio-psychological complaint whose salient symptom Kenneth Burke was, I think, the first to identify: she imagined that she was the personality expressed in the pictographs: the ⅓ of a housewife who rides on ¾ of a bicycle wearing 1 ½ shoes, and so forth. This made it difficult for her to collect herself sufficiently to adventure abroad.

brothers and friends and rivals, amid the known and the unknown. Why this particular thing, in a world generally provided with air, earth, water, and fire? Why must it appoint itself into existence; how was it justified to, how would it venture to? Yet if it did not appoint itself, who would appoint it?

Yet it was impossible to live not in some human community in just such a place provided with earth, air, etc. *Either* it was necessary to appoint oneself (one felt no such necessity), or it was impossible to live at all. It was a dilemma.

The prospective settlers stared at one another with fright.

It is of course always difficult to conclude to a particular, to bring it into existence; nevertheless, this always occurs, as if "by an operation of nature," proved from the beginning of time—as it seemed that the human community had also existed. But now we asked in our misery, how is this justified? And *if* one asked, what kind of answer did one expect? Obviously it was impossible.

The prospective settlers would willingly have fled in every direction, back to the human community they had left. But to what community? No such thing any longer existed; they had left it with a burst of joy.

Harry Tyler, who had a collection of jokes for all occasions, told them the joke about the three displaced persons. "Where are you bound?" one asked another. "I think I'll go to London. And you?" "I intend to go to Paris. . . . And where are you going?" they asked the third. "Me? I'm going to South Africa!" "To South Africa! So far?" "So far from—where?"

6.

But Mynheer said—for he was learned and could recall old stories and rites for emergencies, something to tell oneself and to perform in order that life may meantime begin to flow again—he said:

"We must sacrifice a life to the beginning of our community, as Remus was slain by his brother in order that Rome might have a beginning. If a life is given, the city will begin of itself: that is, we shall have a spirit. We shall not need to justify our city—the dead man justifies it; the city lives and what is living justifies itself. The only question is this: which one must be slain and plowed into the field?"

The question was met by silence and no lively enthusiasm. Lothair, Emilia, Harry Tyler and the others measured the speaker with their eyes, and measured one another. Feeling himself the target of so many eyes, Mynheer licked his lips and hefted the black stone that fitted the palm.

He held the stone out to them to see and said, "This is my heart turned to stone: the heart of understanding when it looked full at such and such feelings in the world, instead of looking glancingly, like Perseus, in a mirror. I propose now to hurl this as a missile, and we can bury the crushed skull in the field as the sacrifice for our city. *Whose?*"

He raised his forearm, and they cried out and fell back.

Droyt Duyvendak did not fall back, but he asked his father angrily, "Why are *you* exempted? Ask anyone here whether *you* are not the most likely candidate!" The youth was in an ugly mood that reflected the mood of the crowd, and they advanced a little on Mynheer.

But the tears flooded Horatio's eyes and he said in a choked voice: "Ow! In the days of the Grand Piano they slew my only friend, Raymond, who where'er he walked, etc.; and during the war my chosen father and Arthur died; and now because of this cursed community, that I for one shall be no brother in— for I cannot rid myself of the void roundabout me as I go, the presence of their absence—for *this* am I also to lose Piet Duyck, the subtilest and one of the best? I'm not yet at the point to say, 'Let *me* die rather!' But from this moment on I do not intend to stop wailing." And he began to wail in an eerie way. It was worse than anything.

Craftily and winningly, Minetta Tyler said, "I think you all look at this proposed sacrifice too one-sidedly; you think it's so bad to be the one chosen, and expend your pity and fear on him. I for my part consider that role with equanimity. Bang! I'm dead—and what about afterwards? Ha! Now I'm permanently *under* that city, or built *into* that wall; there I am for keeps, you can't get rid of me now. Won't I haunt that city of yours? Don't worry; I'm not thinking of anything vindictive, obviously we love one another dearly or what are we doing here together? But a spirit has to play little tricks, exert an influence . . .

People laughed, baring their teeth.

7.

"Well, I didn't go to South Africa after all!" This was a large redhead unknown to anybody, who kept circulating and annoying people. Often new faces turned up at our meeting, sometimes they became old faces, sometimes one never saw them again. The oddity of this fellow was that he refused to tell his name or say whose friend he was. He said he was the third displaced person in the joke and had decided not to go to South Africa but to go to a community with human relations. "To a *community*! So far?" "So far from *where*?" He was a humorist; one soon recognized his type and became bored.

He persisted in explaining himself. He had come in order to fill the community role of the Stranger, the one whose presence opens the mind of the growing boy to the fact that the world is infinite. He was practicing the part, he explained; he had ideas for it. "For instance, I have to change costumes; otherwise the kids get used to me and I'm not the same thing. But every couple of days I put on a different mask. See? I'm willing to work hard at being the Stranger; it fits me." In fact he had brought a mask with him and slipped it on; his red hair showed, he was not concealed at all. He was grotesque. "I'm not a Jew!" he protested—he seemed to be an Irishman. "The Jew is the outsider, the Scapegoat, but I'm the Stranger, see?"

He had another routine that was so complicated that one could not resist a wintry smile. "Sixty-six! Sixty-six persons," he said, "you know what that means?" Nobody knew. "Look, twenty-two—" he held up two fingers on each hand and then clasped the two 2's together—"that means a buddy-fuck, two buddies with two girls. Thirty-three—" he held up three fingers on each hand and clasped the 3's together "that's a gang-shag. Fifty-five! There's a lovely number. Body *and* soul. I give you my heart and my hand, that's true marriage." He clasped his hands in an agony of sentiment. "Now if you hold up six fingers on each hand and bring them together, then you have a real community. A community of human relations. Ha, try it sometime."

By evening, however, when the thinner light revealed things more coolly in their places, this same merry-andrew began to seem sinister. He had been drinking a good deal. "You lousy community-seekers!" he hissed, in the otherwise quiet, "you're chicken-shit scared of death. That's why you pile in pell-mell on top of one another. As if you did that in order to live in a community of human relations. . . . Why did *I* come here, among these chicken-shit community-seekers? Do I love you, you particular, you particle, you biped. Ha! They all have two feet—what's that to me?"

"Nobody invited you. Why don't you go away?"

"Hell, I'll go away! Can you make me?" He was a competent Stranger; he had the knack of clinging grimly where he didn't belong.

8.

In the darkness their eyes were narrowed to slits—jaw thrust forward. A man turned a flashlight on another, bathing the object of hatred in light; also the startled eyes of the hated could not quite make out what was looming in the darkness.

A bell tolled. And they said:

"I hate you damned children and mate; you have imprisoned me and I cannot go free where there is a passing hope of transient joy before I shortly die.

"I hate myself for a coward to be so imprisoned.

"I hate you for the sexual demand you make that I force myself to, to live up to an acceptable standard, and I hate you because you do not satisfy my sexual demand.

"I hate you who wake me when I need to sleep; I hate you who do not take care of everything for me.

"I hate you boring friends who do not consult the hour that it suits me to have your company. That hour would never strike!

"I hate you desirable strangers who do not befriend me.

"Because much of this is due to my cowardice and stupidity, I hate myself the more and I hate you the more. I have gotten no satisfaction from being reasonable and just, yet I feel guilty for being unreasonable and unjust; I hate you who make me feel guilty.

"You who shatter the quiet of my meals with clamor and temper, so I do not enjoy the delicious food. And you who make my gorge rise to food I do not like.

"I hate the dog that shits in the street.

"All such I should be content to see blotted from existence."

While the bell was tolling, it was being said:

"You successful one! I should like to turn you upside down and dash your brains on the pavement.

"I hate you sufferers who dampen my joy.

"I hate you who neglect and do not praise me; but I will shine in such glory that you won't dare to open your traps, though you still won't see the point.

"I hate you who do not give me money when I need it, who do not guess that I need it when I am too stiff-necked to ask for it.

"I despise myself for a beggar. I hate my poor clothes and I hate you who are ashamed of my poor clothes, but worst of all I hate you who overlook me because of my poor clothes. You I must rip.

"I hate you pretended friends for not putting me in the way of something to my advantage; I hate you for not seeing in what a state of need and frustration I exist; I hate you for presuming to perceive it.

"I hate you who hurt my feelings by breaking the appointment, and you keep me on edge by treating at leisure something urgent to myself.

"I hate you fool who cross me in argument and keep on going after I have got your drift and am ready to reply. (This deserves grating.)

"I hate you who eat apples loudly."

The bell was fiercely tolling stroke after stroke and it was being said:

"You children, I cannot breathe when you are around and there is no order; no doubt I should like you to die of those illnesses that cause me so much anxiety. But even worse I hate you grownups who are cruel to children and beat them.

"I hate you who have beat me, and all who are strong enough to beat me.

"I hate you who exact punishment from people for past offenses.

"I hate you I fear.

"I hate myself for hating myself, as if I did not need—and merit—a little sweet consolation.

"I hate myself for thinking swarms of thoughts and not breathing the air and taking in the scene. For not giving in easily to such pleasure as is offered.

"I hate you who warped my feelings and ruined my happiness; I hate you whom I see busy about the same with others; and I hate myself for lacking courage to prevent it.

"I hate the order of things that could, it seems, so easily have given me happiness, because my wants are simple."

Many other things were being said in hatred, some peculiarly but most by most. I for my part was also present, in my usual capacity, and I added: "I hate this poetic art, particularly when I consider those works and moments of it that have been my joy and pride, and I see that to be their poet it was necessary for me to have been myself, to lead the wretched life that I have led. That I sacrifice to a happiness hardly mine at all—for those moments pass as in an apathetic dream, and they recur, as still they recur, to me ever more tired and spent. I have sacrificed to the life of the art what might have been a life of mine, not to speak of consequent poverty, public neglect, spite and envy both taken and given. So much for these poems and for my life; yet strike me dead if I mean to say any harm of the Creator Spirit."

The bell tolled the stroke of twelve.

"—The Creator Spirit, in whom we find such sense as we do find in a universe that otherwise does not seriously recommend itself."

A Boyish Game

Meantime, in the cone of light—the circle of a dozen boys closed in on Terry, pounding him; sound of their hitting fists; and he cried out.

They withdrew, as a circle, and the beaten boy staggered a moment and gasped. He braced himself and advanced a step with clenched fists, for it was now his turn to choose who would be beat.

"Pick Albie!" cried a boy (not Albie).

"Hit Droyt, he's got it coming."

"No; Berryman!"

But the boy slowly moved in the circle, narrowing his eyes. Suddenly he hit the largest boy in the face, Droyt.

Like a wave the circle opened back from this victim—Terry slipped into his position—and the circle came forward again, beating Droyt. He was angry and his eyes flashed and he clenched his fists, but he bore the beating without flinching. "Two hands!" he cried outraged—this was unfair, they were supposed to punch with only one hand, "I'll get even with you, brother."

"I'm Lefty," cried Lefty. "Can't I use my best hand?"

They withdrew, and Droyt stood in the center, gasping.

"Pick Albie!"

"No; Berryman!"

There was one boy whose name nobody mentioned, to be beat. He was neither the largest nor the smallest; he was not enviably handsome nor able; or perhaps he might have been enviably so, but he had the vitality to give his attention to each of us. Attentive desire shone quietly from his presence and he was our darling; yet in the melee he threw his punch as hard as any.

"For Chrissake, sock Berryman, he's got it coming to him!"

"Shut up, you bastard," said Berryman; "let him pick who he wants."

Droyt did not move about the circle, but slowly turned his head from side to side, all around to take in all of us narrowing his eyes. It was terrible; each one had the moment to conjure well with the reason that Droyt had to hate him. Narrowing glance and flinching glance.

"Make up your mind."

We were well warned; yet when his body flew toward me and I felt the heavy blow between the eyes, it was as if the abyss had opened without a warning, and I might have fallen down. The interval was long—but not endless. The circle of my comrades fell away.

What did one understand, standing staggering gasping in the Center of the hated—the hated but no longer feared? Bracing oneself. One understood that the game was universal. I do not mean that it was impersonal, that it was not this or that individual that they meant to hurt. On the contrary, how else should the universal cause come into existence except just through personal animosities, given and taken, for reasons peculiar in the history of each individual? But one understood that it was a universal repetition, and one felt supported by the motions of the world, as one stood in the center with whirling head, coming back to myself. Now it was *my* turn to choose.

"Pick Albie!"

"Sock Droyt again; he's got it coming to him."

I looked with narrowing eyes at the faces that were hateful but not fearful. I was inspired by universal thoughts; therefore, I easily, guiltlessly, advanced toward that interloper in my security who knew well who he was and cringed before my glance. I hit him, and slipped into his place. The circle closed in on him in fury and, to my joy, he cried out.

The boys were tired, all staggering—influenced by the jarring motions of the stars. The circle no longer formed itself with neat clarity, the victim was swaying before he was beat. It was a ragged pattern; all were falling, flinging themselves, into the center. Shining with an internal clarity.

Yes! Now it was a simple thing to pick on precisely our favorite—who gave to us his lovely attention. To single him out! Two or three were being pushed into the center at once. The pounders were being pounded. We could not bear to leave our darling behind, solitary, when we fell down. All were punching all.

9.

"Please put out those lights and let's get some sleep," some one suggested mildly.

Mynheer said, "Right! In my opinion there's enough hatred felt here to inaugurate community relations. Nothing to found empires on, no spectacular bloodcurdling curses, parricide and blasphemy—only the conjugal annoyances, maltreatment of children and economic complaints of 1948; but enough, enough to cement the human relations. The community of human relations exists."

It existed, for we were falling asleep together, performing the interesting social act of falling asleep together. Some drop off at once, some toss awhile, a few lie awake a longer time, but in the end heavy sleep subdues them nearly all. (With us, the first to fall asleep was the professional Stranger, snoring in secure confidence.) Also an occasional voice, a last thought, breaks the silence of falling asleep.

Lothair said: "This person who complains against the order of things because it has not granted him a few simple wants: he is suffering an illusion. His wants are speciously simple. Among all unattainable wants he has chosen a few and speciously simplified them and set them up as his program, in order to be angry with more self-righteousness. Hm. Then he says, 'My wants are so simple *why* don't I get what I want?' Hm."

Our community existed fine; no need to prove it. There was not one of us who did not have fair samples of mothers, father types, teachers, seducers, maniacs, scapegoats, etc.—everything necessary for the formation of our personalities. With few exceptions our personalities were perfectly, fully formed. Our community was unsatisfactory in—shall we say?—many ways, but no doubt of it, it was close, tight.

Another last thought broke the silence, a sudden laughter, and the pretty dancer Rosalind said: "This artist! Ha, ha, ha. He speaks of a life sacrificed to the life of the work instead of being lived as *his* life. *What* life, his life? What does he know about what it would be? Isn't it plausible—eh?—that it would have been something more ghastly? It's rich, how people carry on."

"Maybe so," I began to protest, "but *I'd* like to be the arbiter of that; after all—" But she was already asleep. I am one to lie long awake.

10.

Certainly our communal relations were dense enough to allow a man and a woman, Lothair and Emily, to roll together and copulate, and so they did, under their cover. Their rigid grip on their feelings was somewhat loosed by fear of death and the expression of hatred, and they enjoyed themselves, came to a pleasurable orgasm.

They wept. And fell asleep.

And as happens in a fair proportion of copulations, the semen fertilized the egg and it was a beginning to the forming of a child that would likely be born into the community of human relations. Possible also in these days (the possibility is proved by the actuality)—a place of air, earth, water and fire—in the line of the generation of the animals from long ago. From such products, such freeborn heirs of the process of time, we may study the nature of the vital spirit.

Now the offspring who was thus engendered was St. Wayward.

The Trial

1.

We know that when Horatio was a small boy he was registered for school, but he looked sharp and he stole the records. "When there's no record in the whole world," he childishly boasted, "then they don't even *start* to look for you!" A woman there with red hair had written it down, but he waited until she went to the toilet and he stole it, and ran out into freedom.

Indeed, it took more than two decades, almost a generation, up to the day when he was ready to become a father, for them to trace him and track him down.

The method used by the police was a simple but laborious one. They used the Average Statistics refined and corrected to account for the least one. At first the graphs and tables indicated nothing at all. Then there was a certain vague and wandering aberration—like the distracting influence of the unknown planet that proved to be Neptune. Always there was one too many in the world, or one too few on the books, which was more important. And finally it was clear that the unknown was here and now, and it was Horatio. The one who was alive without a registered footprint, learned without a school record, well and fed without a security number, working without papers, natively pious without the oath, scheduled for death not in the army. You can imagine that as the evidence of such a thing accumulated, the authorities passed uneasy hours—

> looked at each other with a wild surmise,
> silent.

But the prosecutor, whose name was Antonicelli, said cuttingly, "And supposing we make the *opposite* assumption, that we have made a mistake, that that *exists,* that the record is incomplete?" And following this hypothesis he said at last, "*There* is the man!"

They came for Horatio in the dead of his night of glory, when he was willing to be in love and his breathing animal was again about to reach out for satisfaction but now with full strength and joy: then the guards came. The truth was known and he was trapped.

Poor brave child! He had so shrewdly and boldly played for it that he won more than we ordinarily live; so that it took them nearly a generation, until he himself was willing to be one of the fathers, to drop on his shoulder the heavy hand of guilt.

2.

It is shameful to tell it, but he was so overcome with confusion that he was resourceless, not even angry. Instead, as they hustled him off to prison he tried to be friendly and reasonable. "Why am I in the wrong?" he protested. "What have I cost you?"

"That's just it!" cried the officer merrily. "I don't catch on much, but in your case, it seems, there's this whole list of accounts you've fucked up. Money set aside for education—no taker! Money set aside for safety—no taker! Money set aside for vocational guidance—no taker! Money set aside for uniform and burial—no taker! How long could that go on? *It even began to show in the graphs.*"

"So I'm here because you owe me money," said Horatio, near to tears.

"That's it!" The officer laughed. "Ha, ha, ha."

Other officers took it up. "Ha, ha, ha, ha, ha."

The iron door clanged shut.

"Ha, ha," sounded through the iron door.

"At least I don't enjoy the joke," thought Horatio. "I'm not so sick that I have an American sense of humor. . . . Real bars.

". . . Rosalind. Rosalind, I love you." He shook the bars.

Love was his true concern—he could not drive it from his mind. With terrible gloom, as the footsteps receded down the corridor and vanished, he sat on the floor and remembered Franz's friend in Prague, who likewise was arrested at the moment of falling in love, of giving in to love. "What?" he groaned. "Am I now going to die like a dog?" He thought of the throat-cutting knife.

"My Empire City isn't Prague!" thought the dear loyal native Son. "And anyway, that's not my style."

3.

Arrested, he was taken, abruptly, back to the age of six—the attitude of the time of being locked up in the closet for being naughty. Therefore, once he had recovered from his confusion—too late to seize practical opportunities—it was natural enough for him to turn his mind to fun and games. In jail, there were several opportunities for childish sport. To cite an amateur of the subject (C. Bennett):

> Most prisons have a vulnerable ventilating systems which opens into
> corridors through panels equipped with Allen-head screws. An Allen-

head screwdriver may, with patience, be shaped from a large nail. The water-supply and waste pipes are usually run in these ducts. This ventilating system is a hollow steel drum, and a proper beating administered in the panels will carry through the entire institution, officers' sleeping-quarters included.

If the cell doors are of the individual-lock type plus a master control operated manually or electrically from a box available only to the officer, the entire cell block may be put out of operation in a few minutes by stuffing paper clips, spring steel, fork tines and similar obstacles in the keyhole.

In the case of concrete construction, there is a procedure known as 'building a battleship' which involves 10 or 15 men locking arms. They count 1, 2, 3, and all jump together. When two or three tons of men land on a small area of floor, most buildings feel it. In steel-tank jails, marching in unison around uprights will shake bolts and rivets loose, and can even effect welded construction.

An inventive genius took a couple of pieces of toilet tissue, smeared them with stale mustard [Why the substitute?—P.G.], wrapped them in another piece of tissue and tossed them out the window. The officer elbowed the crowd out of the way in his dash to pick up the secret message.

[Also] cautious sabotage and the stupidity strike, plus slowdown wherever applicable. The plumbing, lighting and communication systems are vulnerable. Schweikism is the last resort . . .

—There was thus several good opportunities for fun and games, age six. But they were not unlimited.

Horatio, to tell the truth, did not at all find, like Lothar his brother, that a prison cell was a good sample of all the universe there is—even though a straight line there is still the shortest distance between two points, and the light leaps through a transparent medium, and whatever goes up comes down. When he had thought it was a good sample, Lothar was demented; whereas Horatio was on the brink of being sane.

He sat down on the floor, morose.

4.

Was he guilty?

He was guilty. The fright that had arisen in his breast, contrary to reason and nature, remained there, its meaning unknown. And the disgrace of attempting, because fright had him by the throat, to put on a friendly face and talk his way out. He sat trembling with shame.

The past, like a breaker, broke abruptly on him and stunned and stopped him. Something he did not understand and did not take into account, when he was about to be in love, laid an iron grip on his right shoulder and congealed every muscle of his throat and the back of his neck with guilt. He could not turn his head about to face it.

This past was not the remembered history. He could remember stealing the document, the act that estranged him from these people. There was nothing in that image that awakened nameless fright. The characters, the act, the shrewdness, the moment of decision of the small boy watching and seizing the chance: there he recognized himself as he knew himself. Just what he could not remember in the episode was what must have been present in it, the breathless agony of fear of the small boy—that he now felt. In a flash he recalled the other scene from that early time, when he had found himself in the school building; and in a stone court many were clumsily tramping together in a circle, rhythmically chanting:

Oafy bees!
Barley boes!

while a great woman rang on a piano. A bell jangled; the rooms poured out hundreds. He backed into a stairway and fell. . . . Sitting on the floor of the jail, he painfully added to that memory the motive of it, that he had wandered into the stone court by a yearning curiosity, to *be with* those tramping boys and girls, he was so lonely. Good! Now he was (in principle) with them.

A Jacob, a domestic thief; an honest wild shepherd, an Esau! "Naturally a man is both of the opposite brothers," Eliphaz used to say. When he thought of the man he had chosen to be his father, the tears boiled in Horatio's eyes.

And he thought of Daphnis, of Daphnis and Chloe. How the literary convention was not fantastic but precisely realistic, that when the affairs of the lovers reach a tragic impasse, some mysterious memento of the distant past, an amulet, a birth sign, is found and disclosed. But "Horatio and Rosalind," it seemed, belonged to the stories with unhappy endings. Except—

He did not believe it. For before those terrible times he could remember, and that haunted him, stealing the records, fainting in the courtyard, there must have been a time when he was the obvious free-born heir of social nature herself (and her husband, whoever he was). There were plenty of souvenirs of it! He laid his hands on his handsome body and touched his beautiful penis; humming,

Nor you nor I
nor any one knows
how oafy bees
and barley boes.

And with this delicious comforting idea he fell asleep, still humming

> Waiting for a partner
> waiting for a partner

5.

More than willing to make love to Rosalind and be in love with her, Horatio had delayed simply because he did not at the moment have an animal urgency to it; and now, as he relaxed into slumber singing, she at once appeared to him in a dream little altered from her appearance to him awake, and his animal interest in her was lively.

She was quite orange, with flashing white teeth, and they were already on an island in the South Seas surrounded by the breathing deep blue ocean.

The water, when they swam underwater, was soft and transparent, and they wondered at the life in the depths: Sea horses, starfish and medusae, and tropical fish and sea dragons; an octopus. The sea horses stood still suspended in mid-space; the tropical fish lightly undulated their fins. Everything was near to waking actuality, like a colored cinema travelogue. There was a faint savor of strangeness, for they named the beasts in French. "*Hippocampe—Méduse—Pégase—Actinies—Eponge—Pieuvre. Etoile de Mer—*

"*Etoile de Mer. Hippocampe.*"

With nothing but this faint taste of strangeness, that also was not improbable in French Tahiti, Horatio swam body to body with the orange girl and enjoyed an orgasm of sweet satisfaction and power. The ejaculation hung in the water like still another curious beast of the creation. He did not awake.

They came ashore, buffeted somewhat by the breakers and scratched by the coral. The landscape was a bit wilder, more fantastic, less cinematic. The color of it was tawny and rupose. The air was a little chill, and laughing they chased each other to be warm; not clear which was chasing which—in an ovate circle—but both were willing to be caught. And once again the dreamer experienced a pleasurable orgasm, somewhat violent, a little torn from him—but with only such superficial pain as a strong swimmer feels dragged scratched on the coral, or a child feels when his mother laughs at him with pointed teeth, but he knows she is teasing. He did not awake.

These islands were subject to volcanic earthquakes. One took that for granted, no enigma, exploring in the interior heights. The burnt-out volcanic craters; the sign, as Barth used to say, that a fire was once here, the Bible stories the history of the dealings of the unknown God with mankind. . .

Horatio awoke, without fright, very satisfied with his pleasant love-making. Stretched out on the hard floor, he could perceive fairly clearly how the parts of his body were the space and world of the scenes of the dreams he had been dreaming. Whenever he could perceive this: that the space of the dream was his relaxed body, as well as that the actions of the dream were his wishes, he believed that he understood the dream well enough—he was dreaming awake. He was not one to need to explore the little dark corners; he was Daphnis, destined to be pleased.

But Rosalind lay all night in icy immobility, like the Sleeping Beauty waiting to be wakened with a kiss.

6.

Next morning, evident to all was that Horatio was a man in love, breathing ability. The guards saw it and did not fear for him. His power was well-nigh irresistible; it was with difficulty that one set up against it defenses of spite and resentment.

They conducted him to the courtroom: it was as if the guards were his entourage of the happy and brave.

Horatio was five feet ten inches tall, well set-up, well hung. His hair was chestnut with a streak of fair. He was not one of the tall dark lovers haunted of romance; nor a golden adolescent. He was twenty-seven years old. His face was frank, but not more ingenuous than fitted his age. His like was to be seen frequently, every way remarkable—

He had round him a blue field, shot with sparks and flashes of orange. His voice had in it the memory of songs. An orphan, he was not yet a father. It did not present itself to him as a question, whether or not he was justified. His eyes were seeing.

When they entered the court, he saw with a start of delight that the judge at the far end of the room was Judge Halloran, the same that he had resuscitated from the asphyxiation. (But it was not, of course, by accident that good chance befell Horatio.)

Also that the judge, underneath his handsome black judicial robe, was wearing a soft collar and a flowing green tie, as though every day were St. Patrick's Day. His hair was shining white and his cheeks were pink—indeed, he looked like a Jesuit I once studied under, who had spent a year of penance in Kansas and now, back in the university of our Empire City, was relishing the life created by God and man.

A trial was in progress.

7.

This was a celebrated but rather banal case of a great and successful entertainer, a kind of comic musician, sued by a girl for breach of promise, unacknowledged paternity and support. He was very rich and she was suing, hopefully, for a large sum.

The comedian—who was a marvelous comedian, the delight of millions, and this was why the case was celebrated—was gloomily trying to establish that he hardly knew the girl, that, anyway, she was a whore, that the baby was not his, and that the suit had begun in blackmail: to make him pay to save his reputation, but he wouldn't do it.

The girl—who was a very ordinary girl—succeeded in establishing that he was a lascivious person, and she claimed that he had promised her fame and fortune in the theater.

Judge Halloran stood up and asked, "Does anyone have anything further to say, before I charge the jury?"

"May I speak, your Honor?" called out Horatio from the back.

"Ah, it's you!" cried the judge, recognizing him with a start of surprise and mixed feelings. "What are you doing here?"

"I am guilty of what they charge me of!" said Horatio, not with the voice of a man who regards himself as guilty of any damned thing whatever. "But may I say something to the point of this trial in progress?"

His presence was in fact irresistible, and the judge said, "Speak up!" muttering to his clerk, "You see there a man in love. Look, it is rare. Shall I call this natural phenomenon to the attention of the public?"

"How can they help but see it?" said the clerk.

Horatio spoke out in anger:

"You wretched ungrateful people! It is the same story again and again. This great artist gives you delight that you greedily take, rightly, for we sorely need it. But then he proves to be lascivious, pleasure-starved perhaps beyond the average, and also bold enough to snatch something for himself, driven to boldness, for he is depleted by art, courageous for he is an artist. Suddenly you are resentful, censorious: why should *he* have this? What! Do you think something comes from nothing? Can he delight you without hungering for pleasure himself? You are superstitious, you think everything is done with mirrors, but in natural magic you refuse to believe. The artist himself is ignorant of the divinity working in him; he makes the music by inspiration and lives his life a pathetic blunderer; you take in the music greedily and turn on him in fury. You are disgusting; I bother to say it because I need your love and aid, you are the only society that there is.

"But now you, you stingy comedian!" cried Horatio, addressing the defendant. "What do you think you are, amassing this wealth for yourself and not generously giving it out to these girls whom you need? For heaven's sake, be generous, light-handed, lighthearted. I don't doubt that you started in poverty, that deep down you are fearful of returning to poverty; you try to erect bulwarks against the fear. No use, you can never have money enough to make you feel safe. Please, you are gifted by luck, rich by luck, not your own doing; you know this as well as I. (Is this what makes you fearful? You think your fortune is not deserved? Rest assured: nothing is deserved by us, and everything is due us.) If I were you I should, as guiltlessly as possible, deal generously with that pretty girl and all the rest."

The judge said, "This man has spoken exactly to the point of the case. I should myself have seen it, given time. I advise the jury: adjudge him innocent with costs; and I'll give her the costs. What is the next case?"

The next case was: *The Sociolatry vs. Horatio Alger*, for persistent treason.

8.

The theory of the indictment for treason was as follows: that by living in alienation among the citizens of the Sociolatry, the Alien destroyed the status. One would have expected an indictment of *Laesa Majestas*, attack on the dignity of the status; but the Sociolators obviously felt that a war was being fought; the status was being not merely insulted but threatened with ruin.

(Our friends, conversely, claimed that the institutions were a treason against Natural Society. So theoretically there was indeed a war: opposing loyalties, opposing treasons. But the legal issue was inextricably complicated because, in our friends' view, so long as the sociolators were living persons they could not help being loyal members of natural society. Only the living dead were treasonable persons, and this class had no interesting members. The dead were valued friends, useful by the presence of their absence.

(I am writing this history according to the conceptions of our friends, which seem to me to explain more of what occurs.)

9.

Antonicelli, the prosecutor, was a lean, dark, handsome flashing-eyed person, haunted in spirit: a typical figure of Romance, loved (but not married) by every housewife-reader.

Horatio took an immediate liking to him; he felt that the judge, the prosecutor, no doubt the jury—everything was favorable to him; and meantime, ceaselessly, moment by moment, he kept radiating the power of being in love.

"When I look at that handsome human face," said Horatio, "the pity of it—that he should end up as a barrister." (After Oscar.)

Nevertheless, Antonicelli was no friend but a formidable opponent.

"I was pleased," he began, "to have opportunity to hear you just now. Let me applaud not only your legal acumen, praised by Judge Halloran, but also your forensic skill, considering that you spoke extempore and no doubt a little overwrought with feeling. I salute a young master. I am not so old myself," he added modestly. "But I was especially interested by the depth at which you attacked the matter; I presume this is your habit. I take it you mean business."

Horatio stared at him blankly. "Yes, I mean business," he said. He narrowed his eyes, "Don't you always mean business?"

"You like to get right to the point," said Antonicelli admiringly. "For instance, you said that this comedian had a certain power—hm, a divine power, shall we say?—this gave him certain rights, etc. That is, power makes right. No? I agree. We need not then waste our time here on legal equities. Perhaps you would insist on 'divine power'?"

"Just power," conceded Horace. "Might makes right; that has been my experience. But please remember I don't try to be consistent. I like to take each case on its material merits. I don't know what to think in general."

"Fine! Fine!" Antonicelli rubbed his long fingers together like a villain, and succeeded in exciting amorous and sadistic sparks from them. "Now let us look at your case from the point of view of your friends."

"Please!" cried Horatio. "I should prefer you to look at it from your own point of view and let my friends be."

"I beg your pardon; this is how I always proceed. It is a safeguard against prejudice. I assume my opponent's point of view and end up with my conclusion."

"I listen with pleasure," said Horatio sincerely.

"Now what is it your friends claim? They claim that our policy is a bad policy, that our justice is bad justice, that our war is a bad war. By bad they mean, I trust, simply that it does not work for happiness but creates unhappiness. Right?"

"Right."

"Believing this, what is their natural obligation as persons trying to be happy? They must disobey our rules that lead to unhappiness."

"Right!" said Horatio. "We do disobey."

"More power to you!" cried Antonicelli enthusiastically. "Everywhere in jail we find that your people are just the finest types, educated, ethical, brave, concerned for the social good.[*] Everybody in society is roused by their example, made thoughtful by their trials, admiring of their martyrdom. In heaven's name, what more could you ask?"

"I *beg* your pardon?" said Horatio in astonishment.

"Certainly. This gives you power; and power makes right. For people—

---

[*] This sentence is quoted from a private remark of the Warden of Danbury Penitentiary (1945).

your friends are the first to claim it—are essentially reasonable and ethical; they can be taught; they are taught by example, by making an intransigent stand for what is demonstrably right, and getting publicity for it. Thus it is, say your friends, that power, the power of the truth and the power of essential humanity, wins its way."

"You wonderfully state the position of some of my friends," said Horace dryly. "May I ask what you are driving at?"

"What am I driving at?" said the other. "I am driving at you. Look, here is your dossier." He held up a fat portfolio.

Horatio did not falter, although it is a formidable thing to be confronted with one's dossier.

"I *look* in this dossier," said Antonicelli, "and what do I find? Do I find an exemplary stand and plenty of publicity? No, I find everywhere nothing. No registration, but no refusal to register. No oath, but no refusal to take the oath. No taxes, but no refusal to pay taxes. Nothing. But nothing! Oooh! I came to this dossier with my heart aflame with potential admiration. 'Here,' said I to myself, 'is a man, a man who can take a dangerous and unpopular stand. So young, so handsome, and a lover. Perhaps, who knows, he will open the eyes of Antonicelli and make a convert.' For I am not too old to learn. . . . No stand. Nothing. But nothing. Instead? Theft. Evasion. Living in a hole in the wall. Silence. Where is the power? Where then is the right? Will this influence people and create a natural society? Could it influence me? Believe me, I was bitterly disappointed. What can I say? Selfish. A common criminal. A thief. A coward."

His argument created a certain effect. Unfortunately for him, however, Horatio kept radiating, moment by moment, the power that belongs to a man in love.

"I understand you," said Horatio. "You would want me to be a more conscientious objector. Then you would be more proud of me."

"You have hit it."

"But my friends who are conscientious objectors and refuse to enlist in the army," said Horatio, "are now in jail."

"Certainly, because they refuse to enlist in the army."

"Ow! I have the strongest objection to enlisting in jail!" exclaimed Horatio. "Institution for institution, it is worse than the army," he said earnestly. "You know, I dislike to discuss these matters on an ethical or sentimental basis, but I think you misunderstand the ethics here. You have a misconception about the ethical rights of young men. My friends, the conscientious objectors, are wrong. I do not have the right to dispose of my body as I see fit, namely, to put it in a jail as a striking public witness of the truth. The youthful body is destined for exercise and to make love, not to languish in a jail; and the youthful soul is destined to be happy and find out a career, but I have seen at a glance that the opportunities for this are quite limited in jail, at least for me. All good is the realization of power, but if the power doesn't flow to us from body and soul, from where shall we draw power?

"No doubt it's true, what you say about the essential rationality of people and the use of strong examples. But I'm not an actor by disposition, and I think it's sinful not to make love. Ha! And here I am talking in public when I'm in love and should go and talk to Rosalind."

"Her name is Rosalind," said Judge Halloran to the clerk. "Please proceed more quickly," he said sharply to the prosecutor. "Can't you see that this boy has hot nuts?"

It was unfair to the prosecutor. Horatio stood there like a prig and not only attracted by his presence but probably had the better arguments, and the judge was predisposed in his favor. Yet so it was.

"Also," said Horatio, "since my friends are the finest citizens, educated, brave and so forth, why don't you let them out of jail?"

"I didn't say the finest citizens," said Antonicelli dryly, "I said the finest types of people in jails. This brings me to my next point."

10.

"*Horatio Alger!*" thundered the prosecutor in a stern voice; and it was evident that the case was going to take a new turn. Up to now he had not meant business, but now he was going to propose the fatal argument, the one of his own existence, the calculated risk that he himself lived by.

"Nearly a generation ago, you formally dissociated yourself from these people. This is in the record.

"Since then you have tried to live as if our society, the society of almost all of the people, did not exist. A hard way to live! But I don't give you any credit for it, for it is nothing but stupidity.

"In the first place, our society is the only society that there is—in what society can you move if not in our society? If you do not associate with these people, with whom will you associate? Therefore, it was not hypocritically, whatever you may think, that I spoke with admiration just now of your friends, the conscientious objectors. For they recognize the fact that we are the society. They take part in our social life by opposing it; they destroy their lives in this loving opposition. This is a necessary, though troublesome, role in our society. We appreciate their heroism.

"But you, Horatio Alger, shut your eyes to us; you are a stupid liar. I cannot say whether you are more of a fool or a rogue. I come to my main point. *You refuse to recognize the existence of the Dilemma—*"

When he said it, Horatio blanched and tightened his fists till the knuckles shone. For he had heard of the Dilemma; well he knew the horned Dilemma. He was moved; but he was not afraid.

"What is the Dilemma? If one conforms to our society, he becomes sick in certain ways. (I grant it, who can deny it?). But if he does *not* conform, he becomes demented, because ours is the only society that there is. *That* is the Dilemma. You are demented. Then how are you justified in your actions? What right do you have to assert, not your excellence, but your dementia against our security making our complicated lives inextricably confused? Don't we have sorrows enough without being distraught by your demented fantasies? But you do it to undermine our morale. You are destructive, distorted and full of hate. It is *in principle* impossible for you to be otherwise. Do I make myself clear?"

Antonicelli spoke soberly and connectedly, but his face was purple with rage.

But Horatio, as he stood, was flaming with a deep blue field. He prayed, "Aphrodite, mother of love, help me now." And he said:

"The Dilemma is a powerful argument. In principle it is irrefutable. And I have nothing to offer against it except—a fact. It is impossible in theory, but in fact the human animal has regenerated itself from its wound. The blood clots; protected by the clot, the flesh grows under; and the wound is healed. There is a scar or not a scar. The broken bones also knit together.

"*Natura sanat*, Nature heals. What is needed from us is to stand out of the way, to allow a little freedom for the regenerative forces (no forces of ours), and in heaven's name, an abeyance, an abeyance of the pathological pressure.

"It is true that I was very young when I made the rupture with the sociolatry that I have not seen reason to bridge. To start so young was my misfortune—for a hard way hardens. But also, as it turns out, it was my good luck. For it has given me a long time to gather a little force of my own, to learn viable habits to make a little freedom around me, and to win an abeyance, an abeyance.

"Prosecutor, you present to this court a powerful, an irrefragable proof that I am demented, distorted and destructive. But I present a wonderful fact that makes your argument wither away. Here I am, scarred with such and such scars, but by ordinary grace, no doing of mine, I am in love."

It was the fact, inexplicable but obvious.

Antonicelli shrieked with fury and clutched at his collar. "*Gaaaa!* I bring public evidence and arguments, and he dares to stand up with an unconfirmable putative fact! A private sentiment, hedged round with hints of miracles! So *he* says, so *he* says! But I look in *my* heart and I do not find that it is possible for *any*one to be in love. Then what?"

This he ought not have said. For no sooner had he looked in his heart and asked the question, he emitted a wheezy gasp and, ceasing to clutch at his collar, threw up his hands and fell down with the asphyxiation. This was simply the fact.

"Hilarious Archer, save him, for you can!" shouted the judge, leaping to his feet.

But Horatio had already leaped the fence and had set to work.

"This man already saved me from asphyxiation another day," said the judge. "He has this power. I came back from the dead, and I am sure that the fact that he alleges is so. And now in open court, positively and negatively, positively by what he is and negatively by the fate of Antonicelli, the fact establishes itself. The court is adjourned. Nolle prosse. Free the prisoner."

The prosecutor began to revive very soon.

"It is a mild attack," said Horatio. "So handsome and romantic a man, with such dark fiery power, is not seriously ailing, he is strong; but therefore with all the more savagery he is killing himself. He must by no means continue this lying career."

12.

"Horatio," said the judge, as they left the place—the judge, as was his custom, putting an arm a little tenderly around the young man's shoulders—"I know you despise me for continuing in this official position. But I confess, I like the salary, the dignity, the perquisites and the salary. Frankly, I don't feel an inner impulse to change."

"You make me ashamed," said Horatio. "I am too much of a prig as it is. Why should I despise you? I'm not doctrinaire. You'd be wrong to change if you don't want to change. Let be."

"I couldn't do much harm there, I think?" said the judge hopefully.

"No, you couldn't! It's not my experience," said Horatio Alger judiciously, "that neat merry lascivious pink-cheeked bibulous skeptical old gentlemen do much harm at all. They are the school of Anacreon. *Somebody* has got to expound the accumulated ancient lore of the people, embodied in the common law, and it couldn't be better than Judge Halloran! My friends don't disapprove of the law and the judges, only the jails."

Poems

The Lordly Hudson

"Driver, what stream is it?" I asked, well knowing
 it was our lordly Hudson hardly flowing,
"It is our lordly Hudson hardly flowing,"
 he said, "under the green-grown cliffs."

Be still, heart! no one needs your passionate
 suffrage to select this glory,
 this is our lordly Hudson hardly flowing
 under the green-grown cliffs.

"Driver! has this a peer in Europe or the East?"
"No no!" he said. Home! home!
 be quiet, heart! this is our lordly Hudson
 and has no peer in Europe or the East,

 this is our lordly Hudson hardly flowing
 under the green-grown cliffs
 and has no peer in Europe or the East.
 Be quiet, heart! home! home!

Birthday Cake

Now isn't it time
when the candles on the icing
are one two too many
too many to blow out
too many to count too many
isn't it time to give up this ritual?

although the fiery crown
fluttering on the chocolate
and through the darkened room advancing
is still the most loveliest sight
among our savage folk
that have few festivals.

But the thicket is too hot and thick
and isn't it time, isn't it time
when the fires are too many
to eat the fire and not the cake
and drip the fires from my teeth
as once I had my hot hot youth.

Fever and Health

Fever is beautiful the twinkling
campfires of the resistance
the scorched earth and the strait pass,
though it is terrible to watch
the history of the disease
and the wrong banner flying.

But the loveliest thing the violent stars
roll as they rush is animal health!
the three gaits of locomotion
and the fourfold gamut of song
and practical syllogism
and hammering and careless love.

Such beauty as hurts to behold
and so gentle as salves the wound:
I am shivering though it is not cold
and it is dark though it is noon.

My ears are ringing, a vital fire
has stunned my hands and feet.
I am without desire
and at peace as on a height.

This lust that blooms like red the rose
is none of mine, but as a song
is given to its author knows
not the next verse yet sings along.

You ask what I am muttering
stupefied, it is a prayer
of thanks that there is such a thing
as you in the world there.

For Henry Hudson

I like to think because my Captain proved
there was no Passage, mind and body lost
in ice and darkness, *therefore* all the rest
directed South their prows and richly thrived
on the possible, rewarded for they braved
the possible with pineapples and rust-
colored wives. I envy. Yet I must
continue as my great Captain believed:
There is a shorter Passage!
                          I have learned
nothing. I have steered into ludicrous
inlets and explored them to the marsh.
I have sat bawling studying the charts.
The fog no longer lifts where I cruise
and flecks of snow shine on my chest and beard.

One thing, thank God, I learned, the grisly face
of Hope to abhor, her eyes bloodshot with dreams,
her hair unkempt with fury. Lying streams
out of her mouth and men drink it. Alas,
if you look ever in a looking-glass
and see an ugly Hope in hungry flames
devouring you—so the unreal seems
real and the impossible to come to pass
possible—see, when you look again,
Disappointment! But *this* face of pain
is mine, which I and all my family have,
my mother wears it in her southern grave,
my sister grown old woman has it, and
my brother building buildings rich and grand.

From *Little Prayers*

The flashing shadow of the sun
in the bloody window made me turn
    and face his face, and I saw
    over his shoulder You.

Everywhere I look about
are there outlines of truth and art
    breeding in the dark of this
    moment at the edge of the abyss.

Father, guide and lead me stray
for I stumble forward straight my way
    undeviating, I do not
      notice the pleasant bypaths that

make us this world surprising nor
the precipice that sinks before.
    O give me ground for next a step
    to stagger walking in my sleep.

By trials too hard for me beset
with awkward courage toward my death
   I stagger; every usual
   task I perform and, as I fail,

fashion the art-works to me given;
but lust is mercifully riven
   from me with hope, for ever our
   task is measured to our power.

Jail and blows, being a coward,
I dread, but I am inured
 to be misunderstood,
  because the common reason, God,

commures with me. Let them refute
the propositions I have put
 with nail and hammer on the door
  where people pass, upon the square.

My anger has become
a settled rage. I am calm
    but I no longer wish to touch
    human flesh with tender lust.

Lord, give me back my lust to touch
human flesh, or else teach
    me some otherwise to make sense
    of my experience.

Creator of the worlds, O joy
of speed! and when the powers that lie
   latent into being break
    I shall confront the onward wreck

because I am in love with
the nature of things unto death
    and as they loom, say, "Lo!"
    Lord rescue me, this road I go.

All men are mad some way: O Lord
Thou takest it not hard
    but when the rage is in me most
    by healing death deliverest.

I shall not fear, my strongest will
cannot deliver me to hell
    forever, for an Angel with
    a lamp appears in my death.

If I undertake to say
the conscience of my country,
   I only do my duty.
   But, Lord, it was not I

who chose it, but the hungry heart
and level look that you allotted
   to me when you did burden
   with different gifts different men.

I am willing, God, to say
just how it is with me,
    the prayer best I can.
    But look, again and again

to say that we are dying
—this message is boring.
    "No, you do not need
    to write that down," He said.

I have no further grief in me.
I can imagine, no, foresee
   the losses I will suffer yet,
    but my eyes do not get wet.

When once the brass is burnished, Sire,
there is no use of further fire,
   it is a mirror. But it can be melted,
    Sire, and destroyed.

My Bible text, when I grew
old enough to be a Jew,
    was God to Abraham did say
    Lech lcha, "Go away."

I was thrilled, being a boy,
at this portentous destiny,
    but to me You did not give
    a hundred fifty years to live.

Hush. Where shall I go,
Tour-Guide? Show, show
    me the map and circle
    the place with Your pencil.

Some happy folk their faith
and some their calling doth
    justify, but Lord,
    I am justified

by the beauty of
the world and my love
    of your animals, though I
    haven't been happy thereby.

Sometimes I said I was marooned
sometimes that I was imprisoned
   or was in exile from my land
   or I was born on the wrong planet.

But my daily fact, Lord,
is that awake I am a coward
   and in my dreams that say the cause
  I have lost the address, I'm confused.

I ask the Lord, "Who are You?"
though I know His name is "Spoken to."
    Hoping but I am not sure
    His name might be "I am who answer."

With certain faith let me continue
my dialogue with Spoken-To.
    Hope has always been my curse,
    it never yet came to pass.

The crazy man that you meet
talking to himself on the street
    is I, please gently lead him home.
    Creator Spirit come.

From *North Percy*

Pagan Rites

Creator Spirit come
by whom
    I'll say what is real
    and so away I'll steal.

When my only son
fell down and died on Percy mountain
    I began
    to practice magic like a pagan.

Around the open grave we ate
the blueberries that he brought
    from the cloud, and then we
    buried his bag with his body.

Upon the covered grave
I laid the hawkweed that I love
    that withered fast
    where the mowers passed.

I brought also a tiny yellow
flower whose name I do not know
    to share my ignorance
    with my son. (But since

then I find in the book
it is a kind of shamrock
    Oxalis corniculata,
    Matty, sorrel of the lady.)

Blue-eyed grass with its gold hexagon
beautiful as the gold and blue
    double in Albireo
    that we used to gaze on

when Matty was alive
I laid on Matty's grave
    where two robins were
    hopping here and there;

and gold and bluer than that blue
or the double in Albireo
    bittersweet nightshade
    the deadly alkaloid
      I brought for no other reason
      than because it was poison.

Mostly, though, I brought some weed
beautiful but disesteemed,
    plantain or milkweed,
    because we die by the wayside.

(And if spring comes again
I will bring a dandelion,
    because he was a common weed
    and also he was splendid.)

But when I laid my own forehead
on the withering sod
    to go the journey deep,
    I could not fall asleep.

I cannot dream, I cannot quit
the one scene in the twilight
    that is no longer new yet does
    not pass into what was.

Last night the Pastoral Symphony
of Handel in the key of C
   I played on our piano
   out of tune shrill and slow

because the shepherds were at night
in the field in the starlight
   when music loud and clear
   sang from nowhere.

Will magic and the weeks placate
the soul that in tumbling fright
   fled on August eighth?
   The first flock is flying south

and a black-eyed susan
is livid in the autumn rain
   dripping without haste or strain
   on the oblong larger than a man.

Creator Spirit come
by whom
   I say that which is real
   and softly away I steal.

Going mad with melancholy
I write down words that make me cry
   —yet let me speak no ill of the
   Creator Spirit who does not forsake me.

We do not choose the real, she
whispers and I obediently
   write it down, often in horror
   of the things that are.

The beauty of the world
—I still am hungry for it—
to me was always poignant
being in exile,
I see it through a gleam of tears
—it does not nourish much.

Sally and I are living on
—I see it in her eyes—
it is a kind of bond between us
sure, where much is false.
And what a thing it is
to be living on.

I picked a sprig of dogwood
blossoms from the grove
to bring to my pretty home
where we have many flowers,
they are a kind of bond between us
—I pick them where I wander—

and then we hold each other close
sometimes for an hour
that has no words,
looking at the withering
dogwood from the grove
in our pretty home.

The Russians Resume Bomb-Testing, October 1961

My poisoned one, my world! we stubborn few
physicians work with worried brows and speak
in low voices; in the epidemic
our quiet will is only what to do.
The time is Indian summer and the blue
heaven is cloudless, but the rains will reek
with poison and the coming spring be sick,
if fire has not blasted us in the snow.

The virtue of physicians is compassion:
we do deny that you are as you are
and will to make you otherwise. Creator
spirit come, and join our consultation;
we do not have the leisure to despair,
but we cannot without new inspiration.

The Americans Resume Bomb-Testing, April 1962

My countrymen have now become too base,
I give them up. I cannot speak with men
not my equals, I was an American.
Where now to drag my days out and erase
this awful memory of the United States?
how can I work? I hired out my pen
to make my country practical, but I can
no longer serve these people, they are worthless.

"*Resign! resign!*" the word rings in my soul
—is it for me? or shall I make a sign
and picket the White House blindly in the rain,
or hold it up on Madison Avenue
a silent vigil, or trudge to and fro
gloomily in front of the public school?

Kent State, May 4, 1970

Ran out of teargas and became panicky,
inept kids, and therefore they poured lead
into the other kids and shot them dead,
and now myself and the whole country
are weeping. It's not a matter of degree,
not less not more than the Indo-Chinese slaughtered,
it is the same. But folk are shattered
by home truths—as I know who lost my boy.

I am not willing to go on this week
with business as usual, this month this year
let cars slow down and stop and builders break
off building and close up the theater.
See, the children that we massacre
are our own children. Call the soldiers back.

1945–1970

Men are under a curse, it is cause and effect,
I am not speaking superstitiously,
since they exploded in the mushroom cloud
the bomb in Japan.
Having put so much mind in it,
they cannot now turn mind away from it,
and they have contaminated to the spell
the mind of the world. It is no longer willed.

Surely some of the scientists foresaw this future,
some of them were wise men as men go,
yet right on busy in the dark they worked.
In the myth, as we tell it to ourselves,
it was Hitler who rent the veil
and let insanity begin to leak
into history. But our sanity
has been precarious for centuries.

Those people never knew what hit them.
Simply, a hundred thousand were atomized
and later the survivors' hair fell out
and then their skin fell off and then they died.
But lo the big surprise
Jack-in-the-Box remains
to preside over the diplomacy
of a new heavens and a new earth.

When my life-time ago I swore
—I've kept the pledge and I am sixty—
that I would never stay in the same room
with persons who mention war as a reasonable policy,
I didn't think that I would one day walk
the alleys of a lunatic asylum
named Deterrence, and my little daughter
will probably be the last generation.

"Whom the gods would destroy, they first make mad"
—yes, but what am I to do
with this fatal proposition
that is not political?

Creator Spirit, of whom I say no ill
and no dismay and you are still my fact,
yet I do not believe that you will spring
wet like the fountain in the waste for Hagar
among these men, for they are mesmerized.
Oh maybe the Messiah will come somewhere
and sound his horn Sleepers Awake,
but I have never had *this* crazy hope.

I do my duty therefore for *no* reason,
as Kant said, just to make sense.
It is easier in great things than in small
that crave joy-food just to live on awhile.

Go tell Aunt Rhody, go tell Aunt Rhody,
go tell Aunt Rhody the old gray goose is dead.
I drove my wheel too far when I was a boy
and I jerked off a couple of times too many
I once had an awful scare
and I have been to San Diego.
Oh the number of the speeches I have made
is like the witch-grass in the garden
and the press-conferences for peace
have been almost as many as the wars.
But now my stare is fixed, my blood congeals:
he asks me for another essay on the schools,
his letter flutters from my nerveless fingers.
She died in the mill pond, she died in the mill pond,
she died in the mill pond standing on her head.

Where is the little old woman in tennis shoes
    who knew all the annoying facts and figures
and stirred up trouble at the planning-board?
    They humorlessly shot her dead in Georgia.

Up here we used to laugh at her a little
    though she was generally in the right,
she certainly had no head for politics
    being only a little old woman in tennis shoes.

Today we smile at the thought of her.
    Isn't it strange how we are almost pleased
as we affectionately bring these daisies
    to her daughter and her grandchildren?

It must be because she was so old
    and soldierly, and in her way quite perfect,
quite perfect, she was in her way quite perfect,
    and therefore she is in her way quite perfect.

Darius, says Herodotus, invaded Greece
because he had a sprained ankle;
these wars are anyway so senseless
it might as well be this,
or that he had ants in his pants.

Karl Marx explains it by business profits
—that hardly ever eventuate.
Maybe it's a lust for suicide
guiltless because they go en masse.
Tolstoy was frankly puzzled.

But that erudite historians
and common folk who should know better
seem to take war for granted,
this I will never understand,
I'm queer. Yes! it must be that.

So as I grow old I philosophically compare
the various bleak conditions of mankind,
the refugees of Bengal mother and infant,
the son dead young as mine is dead.
But I cannot, cannot yet, combine in one
vision the universal panorama
all flesh is as the grass and very good
with the ever unique woes that people suffer.

Let me praise rapid speech
that says how a thing is
in my dear English tongue
that I learned from a child;
forty years and more
carefully I have copied
the meters of my breathing
and pruned out words not mine.

Proverbs of a Small Farm

If the raccoon gnaws ten percent of the corn,
don't set a trap, plant another row.

If spinach goes to seed too soon,
try it twice, then plant chard.

Don't fight the cabbage worms
if store-bought is good and cheap.

Do very little "on principle,"
life is hard enough as it is.

Honor the weeds that love your land
and call them flowers, they seed themselves.

When phoebes nest in the barn, you have no choice
but to leave the big door open also to thieves.

Many things will grow in the North Country
that they don't grow,
but then it's hard to give away your surplus
that they won't eat.

Nature is profligate, usury is natural,
but *you* must not pocket the increase.

One spring when the snow melts, my asparagus
will finally be big enough for someone else to eat.

In the Jury Room, in Pain

Waiting to whimper or for Messiah
it doesn't matter much
if I wait in the jury room
of the Criminal Courts Building
until the prosecutor
challenges me again
because I don't believe
in *their* penal system

or if like yesterday I hover
eight miles high until
the iron roc descends
it doesn't matter where.
In between is better
than whence I came or where I go
to be with my headache
alone in purgatory.

Here watchfully I wend
and wander through the wonderful
landscape of Pains
where unexpectedly
the ache-trees in the grove
blossom into flowers
and small birds murmuring
hop from twinge to twinge.

Oh the days have vanished quickly by
during which I made a library
of useful thoughts for the Americans
and became a famous man;
but the one empty night of torment
in which I do not fall asleep
is when I write the poem
that says how my life was.

My poor one! Ocean.
Poisoned by mercury.
You who were so vast
you were our boundary.
The big fishes are sick
with mercury and lead
where the waves pound down
and leap in spray off Makapuu.

Before I die
I shall go to Scotland
and hear like Felix Mendelssohn
the horns of Fingal's Cave
where the waves pound down
where they leap in spray
where the waves pound down
and where they leap in spray.

Unexpected Sunflowers

O radiant you sunflowers abound
on Thirtieth Street and Tenth Avenue
spectacular where no one would expect you,
but *I* know, my birthday comes around,
to look there for you lush on barren ground
with hairy leaves. The buds are cut like beau-
tiful emeralds.
             Let me pick a few
of these wildflowers native among abandoned
trucks and empty freightcars and warehouses
and bring them home and put them in a vase.

I cannot look away. Their symmetry
is Mediterranean and their energy
Northern, and each has the majesty
of the sun alone in the blue sky.

Out of every wave lapping over the ledge
of lava flames a streak of emerald.
The flat sea is turquoise
—a streak of emerald—
transparent to the coral floor
—a streak of emerald—
a man o'war like a drop of blue ink floats
—a streak of emerald.

Sources of Selections

"Preface" from *Utopian Essays and Practical Proposals* (NY: Random House, 1962, xi–xvii).

"The Anarchist Principle" first published as "Reflections on the Anarchist Principle," *Anarchy 62* (April 1966, 15–16).

"Freedom and Autonomy" first published as "Just An Old Fashioned Love Song," *WIN* 8 (February 1972, 20–21). Extracts from *Little Prayers and Finite Experience* (NY: Harper and Row, 1972) along with new material.

"Reflections on Drawing the Line" and "What Must Be the Revolutionary Program?" from *The May Pamphlet* [second version], in *Drawing the Line* (NY: Random House, 1962, 10–18, 34–37).

"The Missing Community" is from chapter xi of *Growing Up Absurd* (NY: Random House, 1960, 216–230).

"Civil Disobedience" first published as "Reflections on Civil Disobedience," *Liberation* 13:3 (July/August 1968, 11–15). Originally prepared for a conference on civil disobedience at Kenyon College, this essay is an early version of material in *New Reformation* (NY: Random House, 1970).

"Crisis of Belief" is from "Anarchism and Revolution" in *The Great Ideas of Today*, ed. Robert Hutchins and Mortimer Adler (Chicago: Encyclopaedia Britannica, 1970, 61–65).

"Getting Into Power" is edited from the essay published in *Liberation* 7:8 (October 1962, 4–8).

"Social Criticism" [1963] first appeared in *Decentralizing Power: Paul Goodman's Social Criticism,* ed. Taylor Stoehr (Montreal: Black Rose Books, 1994, 1–10).

"Politics Within Limits" from *Little Prayers and Finite Experience* (NY: Harper & Row, 1972, 35–77).

"Introduction" to *Communitas* [1947] is taken from the paperback edition, Percival and Paul Goodman, *Communitas* (NY: Random House, 1960, 3–22).

"Two Points of Philosophy and an Example" was first delivered as a paper at the Smithsonian Institution Annual Symposium in February 1967, and then printed as the lead essay in *The Fitness of Man's Environment* (Washington, DC: Smithsonian Institute Press, 1968, 27–38).

"The Human Uses of Science" was first published in *Commentary* 30 (December 1960, 461–472); the version printed here was published in *Utopian Essays and Practical Proposals* (23–48) as "'Applied Science' and Superstition."

"The Present Moment in Education" was first published in the *New York Review of Books* 12 (April 10, 1969, 14ff). The version printed here was published in *Summerhill: For and Against* (New York: Hart Publishing, 1970, 205–222).

"The Universe of Discourse in Which They Grow Up" was first published in *Channels* (Fall 1963, 5–15), later revised as chapter 5 of *Compulsory Mis-education* (NY: Horizon, 1964).

"The Unteachables" was first published in *Orientation/1964* (July 1964, 20–24), later revised as part of *Compulsory Mis-education* (1964).

"Youth Work Camps" was first published in *Dissent* 9:1 (Winter 1962, 64).

"The Present Plight of a Man of Letters" was Goodman's address to the Midwest Modern Language Association's meetings. Published in *Criticism and Culture,* ed. Sherman Paul (Iowa City: Midwest Modern Language Association, 1972, 1–9).

"Format and Communications," chapter xi of *Speaking and Language* (NY: Random House, 1971, 200–223).

"The Shape of the Screen and the Darkness of the Theatre" was first published in *Partisan Review* 9:2 (March–April, 1942, 141–152); the version published here is from *Art and Social Nature* (NY: Vinco Publishing Co., 1946, 72–85).

"Designing Pacifist Films" was first published in *Liberation* 6:2 (April 1961, 4–7). The version published here is from *Utopian Essays and Practical Proposals* (1962).

"Literature as a Minor Art" from *Dissent* 5:3 (Summer 1958, 291–293).

"Popular Culture" from *Poetry* 74:3 (June 1949, 157–165).

"Western Tradition and World Concern" from *Art and Social Nature* (NY: Vinco Publishing Co., 1946, pp.50–58).

"Literary Method and Author-Attitude" from *Art and Social Nature* (NY: Vinco Publishing Co., 1946, 86–98).

"Wordsworth's Poems" from *New York Times Book Review* (January 12, 1969, 2, 20).

"Notes for a Defense of Poetry" sections 1 and 2 only, from *Speaking and Language* (NY: Random House, 1971, pp, 224–234).

"Anthropology of Neurosis" from *Gestalt Therapy* (NY: Julian Press, 1951, 307–319).

"The Tree of Knowledge and the Tree of Life" from *Kafka's Prayer* (NY: Vanguard, 1947, 5–55).

"Post-Christian Man" first published in *WMFT Prospective* 10:11 (November 1961, 8) as "We are Post-Christian Men"; version here is from *Utopian Essays and Practical Proposals* (1962).

"Beyond My Horizon" from *Little Prayers and Finite Experience* (NY: Harper and Row, 1972, 79–123).

"Iddings Clark" [1933] first published in *Horizon* 9 (February 1944, 107–115).

"A Cross-Country Runner at Sixty-Five" [1936] first published in *New Directions in Prose and Poetry 5,* ed. James Laughlin (Norfolk, CT: New Directions, 1940, 39–52).

"A Ceremonial" [1937] first published in *New Directions in Prose and Poetry 5,* ed. James Laughlin (Norfolk, CT: New Directions, 1940, 3–18).

"The Commodity Embodied in BREAD" [1941] from *The Facts of Life* (NY: Vanguard, 1945, 90–98).

"Terry Fleming, or Are You Planning a Universe?" [1947] first published in *New Directions in Prose and Poetry 10,* ed. James Laughlin (Norfolk, CT: New Directions, 1948, 373–377).

"Eagle's Bridge: The Death of a Dog" [1960] first published in *Mademoiselle* 54 (April 1962, 190–192), later used as chapter 7 of *Making Do* (NY: Macmillan, 1963).

Selections from *The Empire City* (NY: Bobbs-Merrill, 1959, 43–49, 203–212, 227–243, 298–301, 305–317, 376–389).

Poems are, with a few exceptions, from the earliest book publications – in *The Lordly Hudson* (NY: Macmillan, 1962); *North Percy* (Los Angeles: Black Sparrow Press, 1968); *Little Prayers and Finite Experience* (NY: Harper and Row, 1972); *Collected Poems* (NY: Random House, 1973).

ABOUT PM PRESS

PM Press was founded at the end of 2007 by a small
collection of folks with decades of publishing, media, and
organizing experience. PM Press co-conspirators have
published and distributed hundreds of books, pamphlets,
CDs, and DVDs. Members of PM have founded enduring
book fairs, spearheaded victorious tenant organizing
campaigns, and worked closely with bookstores, academic conferences,
and even rock bands to deliver political and challenging ideas to all walks of
life. We're old enough to know what we're doing and young enough to know
what's at stake.

We seek to create radical and stimulating fiction and non-fiction books,
pamphlets, t-shirts, visual and audio materials to entertain, educate and
inspire you. We aim to distribute these through every available channel with
every available technology—whether that means you are seeing anarchist
classics at our bookfair stalls; reading our latest vegan cookbook at the café;
downloading geeky fiction e-books; or digging new music and timely videos
from our website.

PM Press is always on the lookout for talented and skilled volunteers, artists,
activists and writers to work with. If you have a great idea for a project or can
contribute in some way, please get in touch.

PM Press
PO Box 23912
Oakland, CA 94623
www.pmpress.org

FRIENDS OF PM PRESS

These are indisputably momentous times—the financial system is melting down globally and the Empire is stumbling. Now more than ever there is a vital need for radical ideas.

In the three years since its founding—and on a mere shoestring—PM Press has risen to the formidable challenge of publishing and distributing knowledge and entertainment for the struggles ahead. With over 100 releases to date, we have published an impressive and stimulating array of literature, art, music, politics, and culture. Using every available medium, we've succeeded in connecting those hungry for ideas and information to those putting them into practice.

Friends of PM allows you to directly help impact, amplify, and revitalize the discourse and actions of radical writers, filmmakers, and artists. It provides us with a stable foundation from which we can build upon our early successes and provides a much-needed subsidy for the materials that can't necessarily pay their own way. You can help make that happen—and receive every new title automatically delivered to your door once a month—by joining as a Friend of PM Press. And, we'll throw in a free T-Shirt when you sign up.

Here are your options:

- **$25 a month** Get all books and pamphlets plus 50% discount on all webstore purchases
- **$25 a month** Get all CDs and DVDs plus 50% discount on all webstore purchases
- **$40 a month** Get all PM Press releases plus 50% discount on all webstore purchases
- **$100 a month** Superstar—Everything plus PM merchandise, free downloads, and 50% discount on all webstore purchases

For those who can't afford $25 or more a month, we're introducing **Sustainer Rates** at $15, $10 and $5. Sustainers get a free PM Press t-shirt and a 50% discount on all purchases from our website.

Your Visa or Mastercard will be billed once a month, until you tell us to stop. Or until our efforts succeed in bringing the revolution around. Or the financial meltdown of Capital makes plastic redundant. Whichever comes first.

Drawing The Line Once Again
Paul Goodman's Anarchist Writings

Edited by Taylor Stoehr

ISBN: 978-1-60486-057-3
$14.95   128 pages

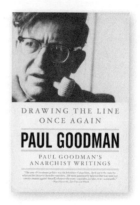

Five years after his death in 1972, Paul Goodman was characterized by anarchist historian George Woodcock as "the only truly seminal libertarian thinker in our generation." In this new PM Press initiative, Goodman's literary executor Taylor Stoehr has gathered together nine core texts from his anarchist legacy to future generations.

Here will be found the "utopian essays and practical proposals" that inspired the dissident youth of the Sixties, influencing movement theory and practice so profoundly that they have become underlying assumptions of today's radicalism. Goodman's analyses of citizenship and civil disobedience, decentralism and the organized system, show him Drawing the Line Once Again, mindful of the long anarchist tradition, and especially of the Jeffersonian democracy that resonated strongly in his own political thought. This is a deeply American book, a potent antidote to US global imperialism and domestic anomie.

"Paul Goodman has been one of the few integrated and hence liberated people of our age... He may well have been the only truly seminal libertarian thinker in our generation."
—George Woodcock, historian of anarchism

"Paul Goodman brought a new invigorating stream into American anarchism, simply through his insistence that in all the problems of daily life we are faced with the possibility of choice between authoritarian and libertarian solutions. Taylor Stoehr's sympathetic editing introduces Goodman's social criticism to a new generation."
—Colin Ward, community planner and public intellectual

"When I get confused about what is happening and what to do about it, I miss Paul's eager and perceptive counsel... The important thing about Paul is that he raises the right questions. The fact that most of his answers are brilliant gives the reader an extra bonus."
—Dave Dellinger, peace activist and founder of *Liberation* magazine

"The core of Goodman's politics was his definition of anarchism... look not to the state for solutions but discover them for yourselves... He most passionately believed that man must not commit treason against himself, whatever the state—capitalist, socialist, et al—commands."
—Nat Hentoff, *The Village Voice*

New Reformation
Notes of a Neolithic Conservative

Paul Goodman
with an Introduction by Michael C. Fischer

ISBN: 978-1-60486-056-6
$20.00   200 pages

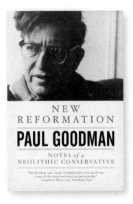

New Reformation was Paul Goodman's last book of social criticism. The man who set the agenda for the Youth Movement of the Sixties with his best-selling *Growing Up Absurd*, and who wrote a book a year to keep his "crazy young allies" focused on the issues as he saw them, stepped back in 1970 to re-assess the results of what he considered a moral and spiritual upheaval comparable to the Protestant Reformation—"the breakdown of belief, and the emergence of new belief, in sciences and professions, education, and civil legitimacy."

Michael Fisher's introduction situates Goodman in his era and traces the development of his characteristic insights, now the common wisdom of every radical critique of American society. A poet and novelist famous in his day for books on decentralization, community planning, psychotherapy, education, linguistics, and media, nowhere is Goodman's voice more prescient and still relevant than in *New Reformation*.

"As this decade in America careens, recoils, and shrieks along, Paul Goodman appears increasingly as our most exemplary intellectual, that is, the most deeply representative and the most worthy one."
—Theodore Solatoroff in *The Washington Post*

"Goodman's frightening brilliance and integrity scared people, for his was the honesty of the moral man who saw things and connections with clarity that others did not even know were there. Writers and thinkers have a vogue. They are in fashion or forgotten. If Goodman is forgotten, if his work is found only in ash heaps, it is where humanity will end up."
—Marcus Raskin, co-founder, Institute for Policy Studies

"His pleading, sane, frank, troubled and by now tired voice is one of the truest and wisest in American life."
—Kenneth Keniston, *New York Times*

From Here To There:
The Staughton Lynd Reader

Edited with an Introduction
by Andrej Grubačić

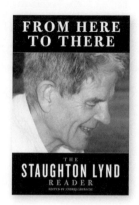

ISBN: 978-1-60486-215-7
$22.00   320 pages

From Here To There collects unpublished talks and
hard-to-find essays from legendary activist historian
Staughton Lynd.

The first section of the Reader collects reminiscences and analyses of the 1960s.
A second section offers a vision of how historians might immerse themselves in
popular movements while maintaining their obligation to tell the truth. In the last
section Lynd explores what nonviolence, resistance to empire as a way of life, and
working class self-activity might mean in the 21st century. Together, they provide
a sweeping overview of the life, and work—to date—of Staughton Lynd.

Both a definitive introduction and further exploration, it is bound to educate,
enlighten, and inspire those new to his work and those who have been following
it for decades. In a wide-ranging Introduction, anarchist scholar Andrej Grubačić
considers how Lynd's persistent concerns relate to traditional anarchism.

*"I met Staughton and Alice Lynd nearly fifty years ago in Atlanta. Staughton's reflective
and restless life has never ceased in its exploring. This book is his great gift to the next
generations."*
—Tom Hayden

*"Staughton Lynd's work is essential reading for anyone dedicated to implementing
social justice. The essays collected in this book provide unique wisdom and insights
into United States history and possibilities for change, summed up in two tenets:
Leading from below and Solidarity."*
—Roxanne Dunbar-Ortiz

*"This remarkable collection demonstrates the compassion and intelligence of one of
America's greatest public intellectuals. To his explorations of everything from Freedom
Schools to the Battle of Seattle, Staughton Lynd brings lyricism, rigour, a historian's
eye for irony, and an unshakable commitment to social transformation. In this time of
economic crisis, when the air is filled with ideas of 'hope' and 'change,' Lynd guides us
to understanding what, very concretely, those words might mean and how we might
get there. These essays are as vital and relevant now as the day they were written, and
a source of inspiration for activists young and old."*
—Raj Patel

Demanding The Impossible

Peter Marshall

ISBN: 978-1-60486-064-1
$28.95   840 pages

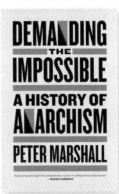

Navigating the broad 'river of anarchy', from Taoism
to Situationism, from Ranters to Punk rockers, from
individualists to communists, from anarcho-syndicalists
to anarcha-feminists, *Demanding the Impossible* is an
authoritative and lively study of a widely misunderstood
subject. It explores the key anarchist concepts of society
and the state, freedom and equality, authority and power and investigates the
successes and failure of the anarchist movements throughout the world. While
remaining sympathetic to anarchism, it presents a balanced and critical account.
It covers not only the classic anarchist thinkers, such as Godwin, Proudhon,
Bakunin, Kropotkin, Reclus and Emma Goldman, but also other libertarian figures,
such as Nietzsche, Camus, Gandhi, Foucault and Chomsky. No other book on
anarchism covers so much so incisively.

In this updated edition, a new epilogue examines the most recent developments,
including 'post-anarchism' and 'anarcho-primitivism' as well as the anarchist
contribution to the peace, green and 'Global Justice' movements.

Demanding the Impossible is essential reading for anyone wishing to understand
what anarchists stand for and what they have achieved. It will also appeal to those
who want to discover how anarchism offers an inspiring and original body of ideas
and practices which is more relevant than ever in the twenty-first century.

"Demanding the Impossible *is the book I always recommend when asked—as I often
am—for something on the history and ideas of anarchism.*"
— Noam Chomsky

"*Attractively written and fully referenced... bound to be the standard history.*"
— Colin Ward, *Times Educational Supplement*

"*Large, labyrinthine, tentative: for me these are all adjectives of praise when applied to
works of history, and* Demanding the Impossible *meets all of them.*"
— George Woodcock, *Independent*

Damned Fools In Utopia: And Other Writings on Anarchism and War Resistance

By Nicolas Walter
edited by David Goodway

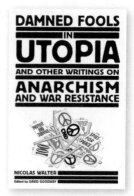

ISBN: 978-1-60486-222-5
$22.95   304 pages

Nicolas Walter was the son of the neurologist, W. Grey Walter, and both his grandfathers had known Peter Kropotkin and Edward Carpenter. However, it was the twin jolts of Suez and the Hungarian Revolution while still a student, followed by participation in the resulting New Left and nuclear disarmament movement, that led him to anarchism himself. His personal history is recounted in two autobiographical pieces in this collection as well as the editor's introduction.

During the 1960s he was a militant in the British nuclear disarmament movement—especially its direct-action wing, the Committee of 100—he was one of the Spies of Peace (who revealed the State's preparations for the governance of Britain after a nuclear war), he was close to the innovative Solidarity Group and was a participant in the homelessness agitation. Concurrently with his impressive activism he was analyzing acutely and lucidly the history, practice and theory of these intertwined movements; and it is such writings—including 'Non-violent Resistance' and 'The Spies for Peace and After'—that form the core of this book. But there are also memorable pieces on various libertarians, including the writers George Orwell, Herbert Read and Alan Sillitoe, the publisher C.W. Daniel and the maverick Guy A. Aldred. 'The Right to be Wrong' is a notable polemic against laws limiting the freedom of expression. Other than anarchism, the passion of Walter's intellectual life was the dual cause of atheism and rationalism; and the selection concludes appropriately with a fine essay on 'Anarchism and Religion' and his moving reflections, 'Facing Death'.

Nicolas Walter scorned the pomp and frequent ignorance of the powerful and detested the obfuscatory prose and intellectual limitations of academia. He himself wrote straightforwardly and always accessibly, almost exclusively for the anarchist and freethought movements. The items collected in this volume display him at his considerable best.

"[Nicolas Walter was] one of the most interesting left intellectuals of the second half of the twentieth century in Britain."
—Professor Richard Taylor, University of Cambridge

"David Goodway has done his usual excellent job of selecting an interesting and varied collection [and] contributed a most useful and informative introduction..."
—Richard Alexander, *Freedom* on *The Anarchist Past*

SPECTRE CLASSICS **from PM Press**

William Morris: Romantic to Revolutionary

E. P. Thompson

ISBN: 978-1-60486-243-0
$32.95   880 pages

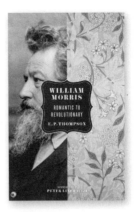

William Morris—the great 19th-century craftsman, architect, designer, poet and writer—remains a monumental figure whose influence resonates powerfully today. As an intellectual (and author of the seminal utopian *News From Nowhere*), his concern with artistic and human values led him to cross what he called the "river of fire" and become a committed socialist—committed not to some theoretical formula but to the day-by-day struggle of working women and men in Britain and to the evolution of his ideas about art, about work and about how life should be lived. Many of his ideas accorded none too well with the reforming tendencies dominant in the Labour movement, nor with those of "orthodox" Marxism, which has looked elsewhere for inspiration. Both sides have been inclined to venerate Morris rather than to pay attention to what he said. Originally written less than a decade before his groundbreaking *The Making of the English Working Class*, E. P. Thompson brought to this biography his now trademark historical mastery, passion, wit, and essential sympathy. It remains unsurpassed as the definitive work on this remarkable figure, by the major British historian of the 20th century.

"*Two impressive figures, William Morris as subject and E. P. Thompson as author, are conjoined in this immense biographical-historical-critical study, and both of them have gained in stature since the first edition of the book was published... The book that was ignored in 1955 has meanwhile become something of an underground classic—almost impossible to locate in second-hand bookstores, pored over in libraries, required reading for anyone interested in Morris and, increasingly, for anyone interested in one of the most important of contemporary British historians... Thompson has the distinguishing characteristic of a great historian: he has transformed the nature of the past, it will never look the same again; and whoever works in the area of his concerns in the future must come to terms with what Thompson has written. So too with his study of William Morris.*"
—Peter Stansky, *The New York Times Book Review*

"*An absorbing biographical study... A glittering quarry of marvelous quotes from Morris and others, many taken from heretofore inaccessible or unpublished sources.*"
—Walter Arnold, *Saturday Review*

Anarchism and Education: A Philosophical Perspective

Judith Suissa

ISBN: 978-1-60486-114-3
$19.95   184 pages

While there have been historical accounts of the anarchist school movement, there has been no systematic work on the philosophical underpinnings of anarchist educational ideas—until now.

Anarchism and Education offers a philosophical account of the neglected tradition of anarchist thought on education. Although few anarchist thinkers wrote systematically on education, this analysis is based largely on a reconstruction of the educational thought of anarchist thinkers gleaned from their various ethical, philosophical, and popular writings. Primarily drawing on the work of the nineteenth-century anarchist theorists such as Bakunin, Kropotkin, and Proudhon, the book also covers twentieth-century anarchist thinkers such as Noam Chomsky, Paul Goodman, Daniel Guerin, and Colin Ward.

This original work will interest philosophers of education and educationalist thinkers as well as those with a general interest in anarchism.

"This is an excellent book that deals with important issues through the lens of anarchist theories and practices of education... The book tackles a number of issues that are relevant to anybody who is trying to come to terms with the philosophy of education."
—*Higher Education Review*